Encyclopedia
of the Incas

Encyclopedia of the Incas

EDITED BY
GARY URTON AND
ADRIANA VON HAGEN

ROWMAN & LITTLEFIELD
Lanham • Boulder • New York • London

Published by Rowman & Littlefield
A wholly owned subsidiary of The Rowman & Littlefield Publishing Group, Inc.
4501 Forbes Boulevard, Suite 200, Lanham, Maryland 20706
www.rowman.com

Unit A, Whitacre Mews, 26-34 Stannary Street, London SE11 4AB

British Library Cataloguing in Publication Information Available

Library of Congress Cataloging-in-Publication Data

Encyclopedia of the Incas / edited by Gary Urton and Adriana von Hagen.
   pages cm
 Includes bibliographical references and index.
 ISBN 978-0-7591-2362-5 (cloth : alk. paper) — ISBN 978-0-7591-2363-2 (electronic)
 1. Incas—Encyclopedias. 2. Incas—Civilization—Encyclopedias. I. Urton, Gary, 1946–, editor.
 II. Von Hagen, Adriana, editor.
  F3429.E495 2015
  909'.0498323—dc23

                                                                           2015006444

∞™ The paper used in this publication meets the minimum requirements of
American National Standard for Information Sciences—Permanence of
Paper for Printed Library Materials, ANSI/NISO Z39.48-1992.

Printed in the United States of America

CONTENTS

THEMATIC CONTENTS

**Warfare, Expansion, and Relations
with the Provinces**

Spanish Invasion and Conquest

INTRODUCTION

The Inca Empire was the largest state of the Pre-Columbian New World, greater by far in extent and number of subjects than either Mesoamerica's Aztec Triple Alliance or the Maya city-states. The territorial boundaries of the Inca Empire at its height extended almost 5,000 kilometers (3,000 miles) from just north of the present-day border between Colombia and Ecuador; southward along the spine of the Andes through Peru, Bolivia, and northwest Argentina; and down to the Maule River, about 100 kilometers south of Santiago, Chile. The Pacific Ocean formed the western boundary along this vast stretch of territory, while to the east, the frontier generally coincided with the Andean foothills that formed the upper watershed of the Amazon River (in the northern half of the empire) and the Paraná River (in the southern half). Within this extensive and ecologically highly diverse territory—from the flat, desert, coastal plain eastward, rising to soaring mountains and then dropping sharply down to dense tropical forests—the Incas exercised an unstable, contested suzerainty over myriad ethnic groups speaking a host of different languages and dialects.

How did a single ethnic group, even one that claimed divine ancestry, subdue the many different peoples who occupied this vast territory and maintain some degree of control over them, even for the empire's short life span, ca. AD 1450–1532? This is the challenge that we take up in the *Encyclopedia of the Incas*, the first encyclopedia ever produced on this great autochthonous American empire. To meet this challenge, the editors have drawn on 35 highly knowledgeable Inca specialists, each of whom has contributed one or more entries dealing with a topic on which they have special knowledge and expertise. We will have more to say later about the selection of authors and the general rationale for the organization of the encyclopedia.

The purpose of this introduction is two-fold: to provide readers with an understanding of the principal challenges faced by scholars who study Inca civilization and to introduce the Incas to nonspecialists by providing a broad overview of the Incas and their empire through which the specific entries in this encyclopedia may be understood in their larger context.

SOURCES: THE CHALLENGES OF STUDYING
A NONLITERATE CIVILIZATION

Unlike other pristine states of the ancient world (i.e., Mesopotamia, Egypt, China, and the Maya of Mesoamerica), the Incas did not invent a system of writing. They did, however, develop a unique and extraordinarily complex record-keeping system based on *quipus*—knotted-string devices made of spun and plied threads of cotton or camelid (llama and alpaca) fibers. Most of the information these devices retain remains opaque to us today. While we know from postconquest Spanish accounts that *quipus* were used to register all manner of administrative information for the Inca state (e.g., census and tribute records), and while we are able to interpret the quantities of items knotted into the cords, researchers have not succeeded in determining how the names and identities of the various categories of information were registered. Therefore, unlike researchers investigating any of the other great ancient civilizations, who can read what those people said about themselves, scholars cannot draw on firsthand accounts written by the Incas; rather, Inca specialists are forced to rely on two other sources of information: archaeology and the accounts written by Spaniards following their invasion of *Tahuantinsuyu*, as the Incas called their land, beginning in 1532.

These sources have advantages as well as problems. Though the archaeological record (e.g., the built environment, such as the remains of houses and roads, and material remains, such as ceramics, metal works, textiles, etc.) bears witness to Inca activities and achievements, they do not "speak for themselves." While these empirical resources provide a base of materials for analysis, nonetheless, artifacts must be interpreted, and the analysis of the archaeological record is fraught with uncertainty and ambiguity. What is the absolute age of an object? Why was it produced, how was it used, and when and why was it discarded? These questions and many others open up the past to different viewpoints and interpretations.

Documents about the Incas and their past written by Spaniards in the years following the conquest often have the ring of authority. Caution, however, must always be exercised when reading such accounts. First, since they were usually based on the testimony of informants about events that took place before the conquest, we will never know what really occurred or how the events, forces, and consequences of the conquest may have affected Native testimony in early Colonial times. Second, not only Native Andean informants, but also Spanish authors of Colonial documents may have had reason to skew an account, depending on the interests and motives of the new, European overlords of the Andean world.

For the many reasons cited above, constructing an accurate and reliable picture of life in the Andes before the Spanish conquest is a challenging business. Nonetheless, we believe that the information offered in this encyclopedia provides as knowledgeable, detailed, authoritative, and fair an accounting of Inca realities as can be constructed with the resources available to scholars today.

The overview of Inca civilization that follows draws on both archaeological and documentary (i.e., Colonial era) sources of information. Our purpose in sketching the general outlines of who the Incas were, how they rose to power, and how they established and maintained control within the territory they knew as Tahuantinsuyu ("the four parts bound together") is to provide a general framework of the institutions and practices of Inca rule that may facilitate the reader's investigation and appreciation of the entries that make up the *Encyclopedia of the Incas*.

WHO WERE THE INCAS AND HOW DID THEY RISE TO POWER?

Spanish accounts of what the Incas said about their own origins and nature claim that the Incas' ancestors were brought into being by a creator-deity, Viracocha, on the shores of Lake Titicaca. From there the ancestors traveled underground northward from Lake Titicaca and reemerged —following the path of the sun and thus establishing their divine connection to Inti, the Sun—at a place called *Pacariqtambo*. Later, the ancestors trekked to a nearby valley where they founded the city of Cuzco, which would become their capital. The ancestor-king, Manco Capac, founded a dynasty of some 11 kings (the number varies in different accounts) who ruled in succession from the founding of Cuzco until the coming of the Spaniards in 1532.

The history of the first eight Inca kings is lost in the mists of time. It is with the ninth king, Pachacuti, that some Inca specialists believe we enter discernible historical time. Pachacuti is characterized in the chronicles as an Andean version of Alexander the Great, expanding the boundaries of what would become the imperial domain far beyond the region of Cuzco. Pachacuti was credited with founding many of the institutions of governance from his time (perhaps around the 1470s) forward. Subsequent kings further expanded the imperial boundaries north and south along the spine of the Andes, until the empire reached its greatest extent. This coincided with the arrival in 1532 of the Spanish invaders under Francisco Pizarro, who found Tahuantinsuyu embroiled in a war of succession between two brothers, Huascar and Atahualpa. In under a year, Atahualpa had killed Huascar, Pizarro had executed Atahualpa, and the Inca Empire had begun its rapid and inexorable collapse.

Archaeology tells a different and more complicated story about the rise and expansion of the Inca Empire. This story begins before the appearance of what later became the identifiable markers of Inca material culture in Cuzco, including fine ceramics in a variety of standardized forms decorated with geometric designs; settlements built around large plazas with low platforms with a hole for ceremonial offerings to the earth (*ushnus*); and architecture of the finest stone masonry often displaying trapezoidal windows, niches, and doorways. In pre-Inca times, the Cuzco valley had been occupied by colonists, administrators, and possibly warriors from a complex, probably state-level society, known as Huari, from the region of Ayacucho, to the west of Cuzco. These Huari peoples exploited the Cuzco valley and neighboring regions for a variety of purposes, not all of which are entirely clear. In the Cuzco valley, they probably set up some of the institutions—such as tribute from subordinate peoples in the form of corvée labor; the production and offering of luxury goods as a mode of forming alliances; and other practices—that would be adopted by the immediate ancestors of the Incas.

The early Incas seem to have descended from local inhabitants, possibly a few ethnic groups (e.g., the Pinahua and Ayarmaca) represented by cultural remains, notably a ceramic style known as *Killke*. Scholars believe that the Killke culture evolved over time into early Inca culture, influenced by interactions with other ethnic groups in the general Cuzco region. Around the early fifteenth century AD, the peoples of the Cuzco valley had achieved a degree of political, economic, and ritual evolution and development sufficient to identify the nascent Inca state. These early Incas initiated a course of rapid expansion, either conquering or forming alliances with peoples ever farther from the Inca heartland, until, with the conquest of other existing regional states, the empire had taken on the dimensions and institutions of governance that are described in the Spanish accounts written in the first half century or so following the Spanish invasion.

HOW DID THE INCAS ESTABLISH AND MAINTAIN CONTROL OVER SUBJECT PEOPLES?

States and empires, whether ancient or modern, can exercise power in two ways. One option is force; that is, by establishing sufficient police and military forces not only to conquer opponents, but also to establish control over subject populations and to maintain the peace. This is a very expensive and costly form of power, requiring extensive surveillance and a highly efficient system of moving forces around the land. While the Incas certainly had the infrastructure to move forces around the empire using their famous road system, it is clear from the revolts and outright rebellions that plagued the Incas and that the Spaniards recorded in their chronicles, that in many parts of the empire state control was tenuous and there was considerable underlying discontent with the demands made by Inca rulers.

The second form of state power depends on the cooperation of the governed with state institutions. In order to achieve this so-called hegemony, the state institutes policies that accord closely (or, at least, that are perceived to accord closely) with the values and practices of the governed. The state must design administrative units and procedures to garner a high level of conformity by local populations with state plans and expectations. Hegemonic power aims at achieving the legitimacy of rule by virtue of cooperation, not force. It appears from archaeology and the Colonial historical record that the Incas made use of both of these forms of power, although they clearly preferred cooperation over force.

The Inca use of force is clear in the archaeological and historical records. At numerous strategic sites around the empire, the Incas built military installations from which they could conquer and oversee potentially rebellious populations. While the arsenal of Inca weapons, comprising slings, clubs, and lances, was not extensive by fifteenth- and sixteenth-century European standards, it appears nonetheless to have been adequate to subdue even the most recalcitrant of Andean opponents. It was not until the Incas faced the Spanish conquistadors, with their steel swords and guns, that their weapons proved woefully inadequate.

Beyond acts of conquest and the waging of war against resistant and rebellious populations, the Incas have long been recognized for their highly efficient system of administration. It was this administration, built around a number of highly effective institutions, that appears to have had the greatest influence in the establishment and maintenance of Inca power across the empire. We can, however, only cover some of the principles and institutions of Inca governance. Some of these are highlighted below, and many more are detailed in the various encyclopedia entries.

Principal among Inca institutions and practices of governance were dualism, hierarchy, ancestor worship, reverence for the divinity of the Inca lineage, the recognition of kin groups known as *ayllus*, and the worship of weather and creator gods, as well as *huacas*, sacred places, that united related groups of people spread out over the Andean landscape. All of these institutions and principles were incorporated into the grand, synthetic organization of political, social, and religious practices that regulated life in the Inca capital. This complementarity of institutions and practices, from the capital down to the smallest villages in the hinterlands, formed the basis for the convergence of values and practices between the Inca state and its subject populations. This helped forge a collective identity that was the bedrock of Inca power in Tahuantinsuyu.

More specifically, there appears to have been a fundamental complementarity of social structure and organization between Cuzco, the capital, and settlements in the hinterland. For instance, when we look at the documentary evidence, we find that communities throughout the Andes in early Colonial times were commonly organized in a dualistic manner—that is, villages were usually divided into two parts. This division could be based on some physical feature, such as a river or an irrigation canal. These dual divisions, commonly referred to as *moieties* (halves), often represented the highest level of social organization in Andean villages. The two halves, which are commonly called *hanan* (upper, superior) and *hurin* (lower, inferior/secondary), were often composed of multiple kin groups known as *ayllus*. Further, the *ayllus* were commonly ranked hierarchically within their respective moieties (first, second, third, etc.).

Early Spanish accounts of the organization of the capital, Cuzco, state that the city was divided into Hanan Cuzco and Hurin Cuzco. Hanan Cuzco was in fact higher in elevation than Hurin Cuzco. More important than topography, however, was the fact that Hanan Cuzco had ritual priority over Hurin Cuzco. In addition, the social groups—royal *ayllus*—descended from the first five Inca kings were located in Hurin Cuzco, while the royal *ayllus* descended from the last six kings were located in Hanan Cuzco. Therefore, both in the capital and in the smallest settlements far from Cuzco, there was a complementarity in the dualistic, hierarchical—upper vs. lower—categories that organized social, political, and ritual relations within communities across the empire. This social structural similarity represented a deep level of convergence between the Incas and their subject populations.

Nevertheless, not every organizational scheme of the Inca state aligned with the interests and traditions of their subjects. This was the case, for instance, with decimal administration. In their system of tribute labor (*mit'a*), the Incas organized state workers into decimal groupings—from small, local groups of 10 laborers, to five such groups totaling 50 laborers, to two groups of 50 composing groups of 100 (*pachaca*) workers, and on up, through units of 500; 1,000; 5,000; and so forth, to the largest unit of state labor organization, that of 10,000 workers, referred to as a *hunu*. The decimal system seems to have been in place in the region around Cuzco, as well as in the large quarter of the empire northwest of Cuzco, known as Chinchaysuyu.

To the southeast, however, in the large quarter known as Collasuyu, (including present-day Bolivia), the decimal system appears to have met considerable resistance, especially among Aymara-speaking populations around Lake Titicaca. The large confederations of different ethnic groups in central Bolivia were among the empire's most rebellious populations, and one form of resistance to Inca control was persistent attempts on the part of these peoples to disregard decimal organization. (An analogy to this reaction against attempts at change and standardization in fundamental values might be the way North Americans have consistently evaded efforts to impose the metric system!)

People in the capital and those throughout the hinterlands also shared a reverence for the ancestors. In the case of the Incas in Cuzco, this took the form of ritual celebration and worship of the mummified bodies of the dead Inca kings. Unlike ancient Egyptian mummies, which were hidden away in deep royal tombs, the mummies of Inca kings were kept in the temple of Coricancha ("enclosure of gold") in Cuzco, and were frequently carried on litters to the main plaza of the city where they participated in ceremonies and festivals with their living descendants. In the countryside, the *ayllu* kin groups also mummified and worshipped their ancestors. *Ayllu* ancestral mummies were commonly kept in *machays* ("caves"), or in *chullpas* ("burial houses"), located near the settlements occupied by their descendants, who regularly visited the ancestors, changed their ancestors' clothing, and offered them food and drink. Ancestor worship was organized hierarchically across the empire, with the mummies of the Incas receiving the highest ritual priority, followed by the mummies of high-ranking *ayllus*, and the mummies of lower-ranking commoner *ayllus* at the bottom and worshipped only by people in local settlements. Ancestor worship represented an important focus of religious practice shared by the Incas and their subjects.

The Incas grafted onto ancestor worship another level of state religion, overseen by a hierarchy of priests, that focused on a pantheon of deities, including the creator-deity (Viracocha) and the Sun (Inti) at the top, accompanied by a host of deities linked to powerful natural phenomena, such as Lightning, the Rainbow, and Thunder. The commemoration and worship of these deities in state-sponsored festivals attended by local officials and the general populace were important features of the Inca exercise of power and control over subject populations.

Finally, we note another feature of Inca imperial organization that brought state interests directly into contact with local communities throughout the empire. All land—and, according to some reports, camelid herds—was divided into three parts. While Colonial sources on this matter have never been adequate to allow us to map out this division of lands into thirds in any given region, it is clear that the "thirds" were not equal in size; rather, they were portions, the precise dimensions of each of which would have been worked out, on the ground, between Inca and local officials. In this division, one-third of the land belonged to the Inca and was used locally to produce crops and raise herds in support of state projects. Another third was assigned to the gods of the empire and was used to support religious rituals and ceremonies, as well as the priestly hierarchy that attended to those events. The final third of all land (and herds) was set aside for the use of the commoners. These latter lands, which were designated for the support of the *ayllu* kin groups, were managed by the local lords (*curacas*) who were also responsible for recruiting their fellow *ayllu* members, in decimal groupings, to work the lands of the Incas and the gods.

On the occasion of large work parties, Inca state administrators sponsored elaborate feasts of food and drink, drawn from the goods stored in state storehouses. This largesse was understood by everyone as reciprocity by the state toward local populations for the labor they provided in caring for the lands and herds of the Incas and the gods.

This overview gives only the barest of outlines of what is known about the Incas, their mode of living, and the institutions and practices by which they governed the peoples of the central Andes within the land they knew as Tahuantinsuyu. All of the topics discussed above and many others are discussed in entries in the *Encyclopedia of the Incas*. The reader may find it beneficial, in searching for entries on certain issues, to consult the thematic table of contents, which follows the regular, alphabetical table of contents at the beginning of the volume.

RATIONALE AND OBJECTIVES FOR WRITING AND COMPILING AN ENCYCLOPEDIA OF THE INCAS

The idea for this encyclopedia came by way of an invitation from a former editor at AltaMira Press (now Rowman & Littlefield), Wendi Schnaufer. As we are two Inca specialists who have both worked for years studying and writing on various aspects of this ancient South American civilization, we were intrigued by the notion of producing an encyclopedia on the Incas. For one thing, we felt that the existence of such a venerable scholarly instrument as an encyclopedia would represent a validation of sorts, a marker of the maturity and increased importance of Inca civilization and Inca studies in the eyes of the wider world.

It should be said that Inca studies have long taken a backseat to the far more developed and expansive fields of study of the Maya and Aztec societies of pre-Columbian Mesoamerica (modern-day Mexico and Central America). Those two ancient American civilizations, both located reasonably close to the United States, and therefore accessible to North American scholars, have attracted an enormous amount of attention from Western scholars since the end of the nineteenth century. In addition, both the Aztecs and the Maya possessed writing, which means that we have statements and commentaries from people within these societies about themselves and the world(s) they occupied. The Incas, on the other hand, who occupied a region of the Americas located much farther away from the economic and political (not to mention academic) centers of North America, and who did not invent a system of writing, have long been something of a step-child to their Mesoamerican counterparts. Despite these circumstances, Inca studies have flourished over the past half century or so. It may be of interest to the reader to consider how, when, and why this "florescence" took place, and how it helped shape the contents of this encyclopedia.

The mid-twentieth century witnessed tremendous growth in the number of scholars studying the Incas as well as a broadening of the range of their national origins, including (in addition to Latin America) North America, Europe, Australia, and Japan. Some of the major scholarly figures of the past half century, each of whom is represented by an entry in this encyclopedia, include Franklin Pease and María Rostworowski in Peru, and John Murra, John Rowe, and Tom Zuidema in the United States. Other researchers have certainly made significant contributions to Inca studies during this period, but we believe that one can argue that, based on the publications authored by the handful of scholars mentioned above, as well as by the large number of PhD students produced by several of them, these particular individuals have played critical roles in stimulating a broadening and intensifying of Inca studies from the 1940s through to the present day.

Each of the scholars noted above was instrumental in advancing the field of studies known as ethnohistory, the anthropologically informed study of the chronicles and documents produced by Spanish administrators, soldiers, and priests who produced written accounts of the Andean world in the decades following the Spanish invasion of the Inca Empire in 1532. The anthropological slant to these scholars' historical studies came from ethnographic research they conducted in Andean communities as well as from their involvement—either personally or via their students—in archaeological research. Through these scholars' publications, and those of other Inca scholars, many of whose works are referenced in the bibliographies in this encyclopedia, we are vastly better informed about the Inca world today than we were in the mid-twentieth century. This wealth of knowledge, built on archaeological and ethnographic fieldwork in Andean communities and ethnohistorical research in archives and libraries in Latin America, the United States, and Europe, is the foundation on which the *Encyclopedia of the Incas* is built.

How did we decide which topics to include as entries and whom to invite to write the entries? We began by reviewing the tables of contents and indices of several recently published textbooks and monographs on the Incas. Next, we drew up a list of basic topics, individuals, and issues that we felt should be covered in the encyclopedia. We aimed at a middle ground in drawing up the final list of entries represented in the table of contents. Had we included entries on all people, places, events, and so forth, named in the Spanish chronicles, this work would have come to resemble a dictionary more than an encyclopedia. Our task was to produce the latter type of work; that is, we aimed not simply to define terms and identify individuals, but rather to provide knowledgeable, extended commentary on what we have judged to be the most important, central items concerning the civilization of the Incas.

As for the Spanish chroniclers whom we have selected for inclusion, we have generally limited these to the earliest and most deeply informed observers of the Inca world who arrived in the Andes from the time of the conquest through the early decades of the establishment of the Spanish colony. This generally takes us through the major chroniclers who wrote up through the middle of the seventeenth century (e.g., Bernabé Cobo, 1653). In addition, we felt that it was important to focus on the principal Spanish sources that have been translated into English and that therefore will be readily accessible to the readers of the *Encyclopedia of the Incas*. This edition of the encyclopedia is aimed primarily at an English-speaking audience. We hope to provide a Spanish translation, for which other sources may be added, in the not-too-distant future.

At the other end of the spectrum of inclusiveness, we have tried to avoid identifying topics for entries that are so broad that one would need to write an entire book about a selected topic in order to do it justice. The exceptions to this guideline are certain wide-ranging topics—that is, religion, architecture, farming—that indeed have been treated in many book-length studies, but which must be included in any encyclopedia that would pretend to have adequate coverage of the major features of a civilization. These latter topics are covered in entries written by experts who have provided comprehensive, yet concise, overviews. Thus, in drawing up a list of topics for entries, we have aimed generally at a middle ground, by selecting topics for entries that have considerable substance and which can be reasonably covered in one, two, or in some cases, several pages of text.

In order to make this encyclopedia not only comprehensive, but also a manageable tool for gaining deeper knowledge about the Incas and their civilization, we have provided readers with four resources for navigating the entries; these include: (1) a thematic table of contents, (2) cross-referencing within entries, (3) suggestions for further reading at the end of each entry, and (4) a comprehensive index. The thematic table of contents, which follows the general, alphabetical table of contents at the beginning of this work, is intended to aid the reader in identifying both the broad topics covered in this work, as well as the individual entries that fall under those general headings or "themes."

As for cross-references, these take two forms in this encyclopedia. If an item mentioned in an entry is covered in its own entry, we have highlighted the latter entry identification in bold print (e.g., "The chronicler **Bernabé Cobo** discusses this matter extensively"). On the other hand, if cross-referencing to a second entry is appropriate, but the topic of that entry is not mentioned, we supply a callout to the relevant entry "(see **Cobo, Bernabé**)." We hope that the frequent use of these two modes of cross-referencing entries will provide readers with effective means for navigating the encyclopedia, following up the reading of one entry by reference to other relevant entries.

The "further reading" list at the end of each entry indicates the basic texts and other resources—printed or digital—that readers may wish to pursue in order to deepen their knowledge and understanding of the subject matter of that entry. Recognizing that the majority of our readers will be English-speakers, we have restricted most (though not all) of the references to English-language resources. As mentioned earlier, we anticipate that this encyclopedia will be translated into Spanish in the future, at which time we will work with the authors to provide additional (or alternative) Spanish-language references. We have also provided website addresses for relevant online resources.

Finally, readers will find a comprehensive index at the end of the encyclopedia. The index lists not only entries in the encyclopedia, but also names or terms relating to other items of possible interest mentioned and discussed in one or another of the entries, but that may not themselves be subjects of an entry. In the index, we have also provided the range of different spellings that one may encounter for a given term in the two major orthographic systems found in source materials (see the section "A Note on Orthography," below). In addition, when the subject matter of the name or term for an item in the index is not immediately understandable (e.g., *mit'a*), we provide an English term or phrase in the appropriate place in the index that will guide the reader to that entry (e.g., "corvée labor").

The authors of the entries that make up this encyclopedia are scholars and other specialists from a wide range of specializations and disciplinary perspectives, each of whom has conducted years of research on the topic(s) on which they have contributed. Our authors—35 in all, including the coeditors—comprise anthropologists, archaeologists, geographers, ethnohistorians, and other specialists from a wide assortment of academic institutions, or independent scholars, primarily from Latin America and North America. A list of the contributors to this work and their affiliations appears at the end of the book.

Our objective in assembling the *Encyclopedia of the Incas* has been to provide readers with as comprehensive, detailed, and authoritative an encyclopedia as can be reasonably constructed on the fascinating civilization of the Incas and the major contributions made to its study by leading scholars. By incorporating a wide range of information authored by scholars working in a range of disciplines today, we hope that we have been successful in synthesizing what is known about Inca civilization and that we will have thereby set a standard for referencing and commenting on scholarship on the Incas that can be built on and expanded by future generations of scholars.

A NOTE ON ORTHOGRAPHY

Quechua, the lingua franca of the Inca Empire, was not a written language. The first Spaniards to describe what they saw in a strange and foreign land transcribed what they heard, or thought they heard, in often different ways; for instance, *huaca* (sacred place/object) may be spelled in different sources as *guaca* or *waka*. In this work, we have chosen to use the spellings that readers will most commonly encounter in the Colonial sources; these are primarily Hispanicized spellings of Quechua and Aymara words, the two principal source languages of Inca studies. Spellings of terms found herein may occasionally differ from those found in some recently published sources, particularly those that have followed recent efforts to standardize spellings using a newer, more linguistically and phonologically grounded orthography. We believe, however, that the reader should be able to move between the different orthographies without too much effort or confusion. In addition, the index provides alternative spellings for many of the terms that one may encounter in different sources.

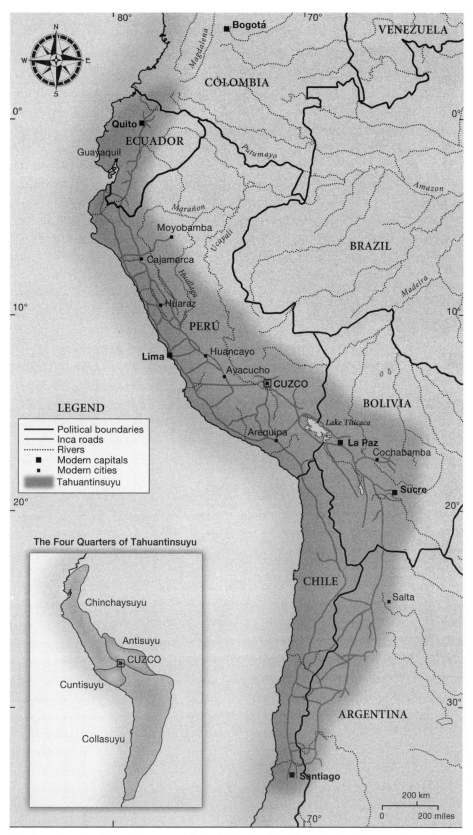

The Inca Empire, Tahuantinsuyu, at its height, showing the extent of the empire and the road system that linked Cuzco, the capital, to its distant provinces. Inset: the *suyu* divisions of the empire. Julia L. Meyerson (after Morris and von Hagen 2011).

A

ACLLACUNA

No group of women received more attention in the written accounts of the Inca Empire than the *acllacuna* (*-cuna* is the plural suffix in Quechua), the Inca's "chosen women" (from **Quechua,** to choose). Chroniclers were fascinated by the *aclla*, likening them to Rome's "vestal virgins," to nuns of the Catholic Church, and even to the many wives in a sultan's harem. Reports describe how the *aclla* were selected and allocated, their internal organization, and their duties. Most agree that *aclla* were "chosen" by male representatives of the Inca Empire during periodic visits to conquered territories. Ranked according to beauty, family standing, and provenance, these young girls and adolescents were sent to the *acllahuasi* (aclla house or center) in Cuzco and the empire's provincial capitals. There, aclla were taught "female tasks"—spinning, weaving, and the preparation of special foods and beverages, such as **chicha** (maize beer), integral to Andean religious traditions. Aclla held positions of honor in Inca ceremonies and their weavings were treasured as ritual objects and as imperial gifts. Chroniclers were intrigued by their life trajectories: some remained in their provincial capitals, others were sent to far-flung Inca centers, while still others became prized secondary wives of Cuzco noblemen or of the **ayllu** elite. The most esteemed—often daughters of high-ranking, provincial families—entered the royal entourage itself, as wives of the Inca or wives of the Sun. Some would be ritually sacrificed in formal ceremonies and consecrated to Inca rule (see **Capac Hucha**).

Aclla emerged in the context of the "conquest hierarchy" (see **Women**), a symbolic, classificatory structure, transformed by imperial dictates into an institution of cultural politics. According to this cultural frame, non-Inca populations were classed as "conquered women"; and the Inca, as the conqueror and spouse of them all, had the right to determine their placement as secondary wives, religious officiants, or sacred beings. No longer regarded as members of their natal *ayllus*, the *aclla* lived as crown subjects, embodiments of the Inca state and directly under the Inca's domain.

The *aclla* institution was both a symbol and a manifestation of Cuzco's dominance. Responses to Inca demands for "chosen, conquered" women were equivocal and of two minds. We know little about how *aclla* experienced their changed status; but male voices have entered the record. Some provincial authorities called the forced resettlement of women a detested form of tribute, the personification of their loss of political autonomy. For others, however, giving an *aclla*-daughter to the Inca was a means to

Felipe Guaman Poma de Ayala's drawing of an *acllahuasi*, house of the *acllacuna*, or chosen women. The *aclla* spun yarn, wove fine cloth, and brewed maize beer for the rulers and the state religion. Guaman Poma de Ayala, Felipe. *El primer nueva corónica y buen gobierno*. Edited by John V. Murra and Rolena Adorno, 273/298. Mexico City: Siglo Veintiuno, 1980 [1615].

ensure favor and privilege. And those provincial leaders who welcomed Inca rule and willingly entered into an alliance with Cuzco also readily gave daughters to the Inca regime, believing it an honor.

How did the beneficiaries of these Inca gifts assess their new fortunes? Having multiple wives worked to the recipient's advantage in several ways. Not only did *aclla* represent a bond with reigning power holders, but they also, through their labor, became economic boons for political ends (see **Labor Service**; **Weaving and Textiles**). In the Andes, largesse cemented political ties and both Inca and provincial authorities needed textiles to distribute to their constituencies and superiors as a sign of generosity and obligation. Who wove these textiles? Wives. So *aclla* were not only alienable objects that Inca rulers could distribute to meet needs of government, but their labor, crucial for cloth production, was desired to keep the wheels of the Andean political economy running smoothly. As befitted their standing, secondary wives were also beneficiaries of Inca largesse, receiving material rewards in the form of land grants and labor. These grants also supported their children who formed lineages of high imperial standing.

The most renowned *aclla* never became living wives, but were sacrificed and put to death in the service of imperial rites of power (see **Capac Hucha**). The chilling history of Tanta Carhua gives us a window into these gendered ceremonies of conquest. Tanta Carhua, the young daughter of a local *curaca* (headman), was "chosen" by the Inca to represent her province in the yearly commemorations of the Sun. This momentous, holy day was a celebration of Inca rule, as *aclla* throughout the empire, accompanied by their **huacas** (titular deities) and local headmen (*curacas*), performed rituals of public obeisance to the Sun and the Inca king in Cuzco. After the Inca himself, with great ceremony, paid them homage, some *aclla* were deified in Cuzco; others, like Tanta Carhua, led processions home. Tanta Carhua, feted for a second time in her conquered province, was buried alive in the "lands of the Inca," which bordered on the lands of her *ayllu*. By imperial rite and decree, Tanta Carhua was made holy. Tanta Carhua, who once belonged to an *ayllu*, was transformed into an Inca divinity. And, like other imperial gods, Tanta Carhua received lands and labor to maintain the religious organization established in her honor. Tanta Carhua's death also marked her father's—and his lineage's—ascendancy in Inca politics; her father became the region's principal authority and its representative to Cuzco.

The *aclla* were sacred and they were chaste. As wives of the conquering Sun or of the Inca, their standing as imperial subjects was couched in religious and sexual terms. Chastity was a proscription unique to the *aclla* and it was tied to the design of the "conquest hierarchy," the designation of *aclla* as "conquered" wives, and the novel dictates of sexual purity and control. The *aclla's* sacred standing in imperial organizations belied, perhaps, the empire's most extraordinary intrusion into the lives of "the conquered." The *aclla*, as an institution, deprived "conquered" *ayllus* control over their own continuity, their autonomous creation and existence. The *aclla's* significance in the Andes was tied to the particular way in which gender symbolism, sexuality, and relations of conquest were fused to structure—and consecrate—Inca preeminence. Through imperial transformations of the conquest hierarchy, Cuzco's political rule was gendered and sexualized (see **Women**). The *aclla* were called "sainted" women, but they were "chosen" by Inca men, bestowed by Inca men, and granted to highly ranked men, as gender and sexual regulation gave form—and sanctity—to the Inca Empire's dominion over other Andean peoples.

Further Reading

Gose, Peter. "The State as a Chosen Woman: Brideservice and the Feeding of Tributaries in the Inka Empire." *American Anthropologist* 102, no. 1: 84–97, 2000.

Silverblatt, Irene. *Moon, Sun, and Witches: Gender Ideologies and Class in Inca and Colonial Peru.* Princeton, NJ: Princeton University Press, 1987.

■ IRENE SILVERBLATT

ADMINISTRATION

The Spaniards who toppled the Inca Empire found it convenient to view the Inca ruler as an absolute monarch who could be engaged as an ally or deposed and replaced with a more pliable substitute. The failure to achieve a lasting partnership with an Inca ruler raised questions of what kind of Colonial administration Spain might develop in the Andes, which led to a fierce debate over the "good government" of the Inca Empire. As the Spanish crown centralized its administrative authority and frustrated the feudalistic ambitions of the early *conquistadors*, Spanish monarchs desired to know how Atahualpa, the Inca ruler murdered by the Spaniards, and his ancestors had ruled (see **Invasion, Spanish**). Early descriptions of Inca imperial hierarchy focused on administrative practices before the conquest as a means of identifying legitimate ways that the Crown could lay claim to indigenous labor and productive resources. The diverse ideological aims of

ACOSTA, JOSÉ DE

José de Acosta was born in Medina del Campo, Castilla la Vieja, Spain, in 1540, and trained at the Jesuit college of Alcalá de Henares, where he taught theology before coming to Peru in 1572. He lectured in theology at Lima's University of San Marcos and later traveled to Cuzco, Arequipa, La Paz, Potosí, and Chuquisaca (Sucre), learning some Quechua and collecting material for his book. In 1576, Acosta was named head of the Jesuit order in Peru, and in 1579 he founded a parish in Juli, on the shores of Lake Titicaca. In 1586, he returned to Spain via Mexico, where he lived for a while. He died in Salamanca in 1600.

Although Acosta wrote a treatise on evangelization, he is best known for his *Historia Natural y Moral de las Indias* (Natural and Moral History of the Indies), published in 1590. The first part of his chronicle deals with the natural history of the New World and the place of the Americas in global history, while other chapters cover the history of the Incas and the Aztecs. In the final section, the curate-chronicler tried to demonstrate that the natural proclivity of the Native peoples of Peru and Mexico to accept Christianity reflected the role of divine providence rather than the arrival, before Columbus, of an evangelizing apostle.

Further Reading

Acosta, José de. *Natural and Moral History of the Indies*. Edited by Jane E. Managan. Translated by Frances López-Morillas. Durham, NC: Duke University Press, 2002.

Marzal, Manuel M. "Acosta, José de (1540–1600)." In *Guide to Documentary Sources for Andean Studies, 1530–1900*, edited by Joanne Pillsbury, vol. 2, 11–15. Norman: University of Oklahoma Press, 2008.

■ ADRIANA VON HAGEN

Colonial writers and their Andean informants contribute to contradictions in narratives of sovereignty and administrative hierarchy, although there is general agreement about many elements of imperial statecraft.

To rule over a diverse and far-flung realm, the Incas employed a range of administrative strategies that varied in intensity and adapted to local conditions. Research in recent years has revealed that Inca rule was either "direct" or "indirect." In cases of indirect rule, the Incas governed through local allies—coastal rulers and highland headmen—who remained in power but gave limited tribute to the Inca ruler and allowed state officials to develop resources not in use at the time of annexation. Several chronicles indicate that the Incas attempted indirect rule as an initial strategy during their early period of territorial expansion, but they also note that local leaders frequently rebelled against their new lord once the Inca army had moved on to another part of the Andes. The suppression of rebellions typically brought the implementation of direct rule, including the establishment of the imperial administrative hierarchy and the introduction of key state institutions, such as the Sun cult and the *acllahuasi,* house of the chosen women (see **Acllacuna**).

A provincial administrator displaying *quipus*. These knotted accounting devices were crucial to administering the far-flung provinces of the Inca Empire. Guaman Poma de Ayala, Felipe. *El primer nueva corónica y buen gobierno*. Edited by John V. Murra and Rolena Adorno, 320/348. Mexico City: Siglo Veintiuno, 1980 [1615].

Direct and indirect rule represented two distinct sources of power held by Inca rulers. As founding ancestors of a royal house, the Inca ruler and his principal wife wielded the power of a lord and lady of vassals—and they could hold dominion over other rulers and leaders who submitted to their authority and law. This sort of power was not absolute or unchallenged. The male ruler (**Sapa** **Inca** [sole or unique Inca]) delegated some of his power to close relatives who acted as his lieutenants, but he also had to address attempts by noble Inca factions and provincial rulers to stymie his wishes. There are also accounts of the *Sapa Coya* (sole or unique queen) fulfilling administrative functions, in one case intervening to bring a resistant female ruler into line. Many Inca client rulers were also marriage allies, bringing them into generations-long relationships with the Incas, and adding complexity to the political factions at the capital. At a conceptual level, the Inca capital functioned as the house of the Inca and his wife, and the Inca ruler oversaw civic ceremonies, provided households with food and gifts, and dispensed legal and moral justice to the inhabitants of the city. Over time, the power of ruling households extended to include resources beyond the Cuzco region, and rulers reassigned some individuals in rebellious provinces to permanent service as *yanacuna*, or retainers (see **Labor Service**). Royal lineages dominated the resources and populations of the capital region, and they also occupied the highest administrative positions in provincial regions.

Direct rule combined elements of the kin-based power of the Inca ruler and a more regular and bureaucratic administrative hierarchy called *decimal administration* (see

Administration, Decimal). This form of rule relied on an office, called *curaca*, or local lord, who oversaw administrative units that ideally ranged from units of 10 households to province-level units of 10,000 households. Decimal units could be joined together under a single *curaca*, and the larger ones often combined households from different kin groups, communities, and ethnic identities. Inca nobles maintained the administrative link between the *Sapa* Inca and the highest *curaca* offices. Uncles or brothers of the ruler served as provincial governors, who established administrative units, monitored population change, presided over ceremonial activities, and ensured that tribute demands were fulfilled annually. These officials, often referred to as *apu* (great lord), conducted regular inspections with the assistance of **quipu** specialists who maintained records necessary for the process. Annual inspections tallied people and herd animals, assigned households to tributary service, and confirmed that service assignments had been completed. Other high officials were charged with the maintenance of the **road** and **bridge** system that bound the far-flung Inca provinces to the capital, as well as the management of royal holdings and ritual installations found across the empire.

Decimal administration imposed a more regular administrative hierarchy across the empire, in a way that distributed power unequally. Ideally, all *curaca* appointments came from the Inca ruler, and appointees had to travel to Cuzco to receive their office and the privileges that came with it (such as the right to sit on a stool, or *tiyana*). The Inca ruler and a few other nobles made the most important policy decisions, passing their commands on to high-ranking *curacas*, many of whom enjoyed power and privileges beyond their status before the Inca conquest. Administrators in charge of several hundred or thousand households often oversaw people belonging to other kin networks or ethnic groups, and they appear to have had some latitude in determining which households would carry out tributary labor tasks, some of which were dangerous and required extensive travel. Whereas upper-level *curacas* enjoyed some power in the implementation of Inca demands, low-ranking *curacas* were expected to carry out their assignments, and were held accountable for households that did not do as ordered. The power to resolve disputes and punish wrongdoers had a correspondingly unequal distribution—local *curacas* could mete out corporal punishment, but only Inca officials could deliberate on serious offenses, and the Inca ruler took sole responsibility for overseeing the moral and legal order of the imperial capital and its noble occupants (see **Crime and Punishment**).

At the time of the Spanish conquest, the Inca Empire was governed by a diverse set of administrative strategies. Royal Inca lineages dominated the administration of the Cuzco region in a manner that was distinct from most imperial provinces, using a series of palaces and rural estates to rule over retainers, production specialists, and labor colonists drawn from the periphery (see **Estates, Royal**; **Labor Service**). The central highlands between Quito and La Paz display consistent evidence of direct rule, and documents from several provinces provide proof of decimal administration.

The Incas built enclaves and way stations in the southern periphery of the empire, but large administrative centers and key state institutions appear to be absent across much of what is today northern Chile, northwest Argentina, and the Bolivian *altiplano*. Parts of the Atacama Desert and the southern coast of Peru have very little evidence of Inca administration. To the north, the Incas occupied a frontier in the Quito area that appears to have combined aspects of Inca royal domestic power and military occupation. The ruler Huayna Capac moved his family to the frontier, where the nobility established family estates and took large numbers of rebellious Cañari and Chachapoya as *yanacuna* (see **Labor Service**).

On the Pacific coast, Inca rule remained indirect in many places where local states and empires had flourished previously, although the empire invested in constructing roads, minor centers, and agricultural resources in the middle and upper valleys connecting the coast with the highlands. Archaeology and ethnohistory are challenging the top-down descriptions of Inca direct rule, but helping to explain how the empire governed such a large and diverse population.

Further Reading

Burger, Richard L., Craig Morris, and Ramiro Matos Mendieta, eds. *Variations in the Expression of Inka Power.* Washington, DC: Dumbarton Oaks, 2007.

Covey, R. Alan. "Chronology, Succession, and Sovereignty: The Politics of Inka Historiography and Its Modern Interpretation." *Comparative Studies in Society and History* 48, no. 1: 166–99, 2006.

D'Altroy, Terence N. *Provincial Power in the Inka Empire.* Washington, DC: Smithsonian Institution Press, 1992.

Julien, Catherine J. "How Inca Decimal Administration Worked." *Ethnohistory* 35, no. 3: 257–79, 1988.

Malpass, Michael A., and Sonia Alconini, eds. *Distant Provinces of the Inka Empire.* Iowa City: University of Iowa Press, 2010.

Morris, Craig, and R. Alan Covey. "The Management of Scale or the Creation of Scale: Administrative Processes in Two Inka Provinces." In *Intermediate Elites in Pre-Columbian States and Empires,* edited by Christina M. Elson and R. Alan Covey, 136–53. Tucson: University of Arizona Press, 2006.

Murra, John V. "Social Structural and Economic Themes in Andean Ethnohistory." *Anthropological Quarterly* 34, no. 2: 47–59, 1961.

Niles, Susan A. "The Nature of Inca Royal Estates." In *Machu Picchu: Unveiling the Mystery of the Incas,* edited by Richard L. Burger and Lucy C. Salazar, 49–70. New Haven, CT: Yale University Press, 2004.

Salomon, Frank. *Native Lords of Quito in the Age of the Incas.* New York: Cambridge University Press, 1986.

Zuidema, R. Tom. *Inca Civilization in Cuzco.* Austin: University of Texas Press, 1990.

■ R. ALAN COVEY

ADMINISTRATION, DECIMAL

The administration of Tahuantinsuyu, the Inca Empire, involved the management by local, provincial, and Cuzco officials of all affairs pertaining to the wealth of resources owned and controlled by the Inca state. The administrative records themselves, which took the form of the knotted-string *quipus*, included **census** and tribute records, as well as information pertaining to the production, storage, and disposition of goods stored in state warehouses located around the empire (see **Storage**). To understand how the administration functioned, it is important to note the peculiar nature of tribute in the Inca Empire, which demanded labor, rather than goods, from subject peoples. Sources differ as to whether this labor demand was required only of men, or if women were included as well. Tributaries were able-bodied men (and some sources say women) between the ages of 18 and 50.

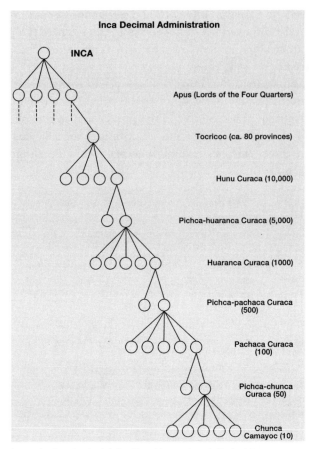

Inca decimal administration hierarchy. Julia L. Meyerson.

In the state labor draft, known as *mit'a*, subjects were required to work a certain number of days each month on state projects, including the construction and maintenance of state facilities such as buildings, **roads**, **bridges**, storehouses, and so on. This system of labor, known as corvée, was organized, at least ideally, in a decimal manner. At the local level, groups of 10 workers (*chunca*) worked together under the leadership of one of their members (the *curaca*). Five groups of 10 workers formed a larger group of 50 workers; two groups of 50 formed a group of 100 (*pachaca*) workers, and on up—combining the organizational principles of 5 × 2—to larger groups of 1,000 (*huaranga*), 10,000 (*hunu*), and 40,000, a grouping that did not have a name but that was the largest unit of administration and labor organization in the empire. What is termed the Inca system of "decimal administration" was the entire apparatus of producing and maintaining census counts, assessing tribute levels for population centers, and the monitoring by state officials of compliance with the demands of the labor tribute.

The administrators who oversaw this decimal hierarchical administration were similarly organized in a hierarchical fashion. Each quarter of the empire (*suyu*; see respective *suyu* entries: **Antisuyu**, **Chinchaysuyu**, **Collasuyu**, and **Cuntisuyu**) had a head administrator (*apu*) who served the Inca in Cuzco. The four quarters of the empire—Tahuantinsuyu—were divided into some 80 provinces, each governed by a *tocricoc* (overseer), who was responsible for all administrative matters within his province. The *tocricocs* were each attended by a hierarchically arrayed cadre of knot keepers, the *quipucamayocs* (knot makers/organizers). The knot keepers were responsible for maintaining local, on-the-ground records and for sending that information on to the higher-level knot keepers at provincial accounting centers. The accountants in the provincial accounting centers apparently reported their information directly to the head knot keepers of their respective *suyu*, in Cuzco. Archives of knot records were reportedly maintained in the various provincial accounting centers, as well as in the capital.

It is important to note that, while the decimal administration appears to have been more or less well developed in **Chinchaysuyu**, the large quadrant of the empire located to the northwest of Cuzco, the same cannot be said for the region of **Collasuyu**. In this vast quarter of the empire, located southeast of Cuzco and including the Lake Titicaca region and other Aymara-speaking areas of present-day Bolivia and northern Chile, there appears to have been active resistance to Inca attempts to impose the decimal organization.

Further Reading

Covey, R. A. "Inka Administration of the Far South Coast of Peru." *Latin American Antiquity* 11, no. 2: 119–38, 2000.

Julien, C. J. "How Inca Decimal Administration Worked." *Ethnohistory* 35, no. 3: 257–79, 1988.

LeVine, T. Y. "Inka Labor Service at the Regional Level: The Functional Reality." *Ethnohistory* 34, no. 1: 14–46, 1987.

Morris, C. "Inka Strategies of Incorporation and Governance." In *Archaic States*, edited by G. Feinman and J. Marcus. Santa Fe, NM: Schools of American Research, 1998.

Murra, J. V. "The Mit'a Obligations of Ethnic Groups to the Inca State." In *The Inca and Aztec States, 1400–1800: Anthropology and History*, edited by George A. Collier, Renato I. Rosaldo, and John D. Wirth, 237–62. New York: Academic Press, 1982.

Pärssinen, Martti. *Tawantinsuyu: The Inca State and Its Political Organization*. Studia Historica 43. Helsinki: Finnish Historical Society, 1992.

Rowe, J. H. "Inca Policies and Institutions Relating to the Cultural Unification of the Empire." In *The Inca and Aztec States, 1400–1800: Anthropology and History*, edited by George A. Collier, Renato I. Rosaldo, and John D. Wirth, 93–118. New York: Academic Press, 1982.

Urton, G. "La administración del estado inca por medio de los quipus." In *Señores de los Imperios del Sol*, edited by K. Makowski, 93–110. Lima: Banco de Crédito, 2010.

Urton, G., and C. J. Brezine. "Information Control in the Palace of Puruchuco: An Accounting Hierarchy in a Khipu Archive from Coastal Peru." In *Variations in the Expression of Inka Power*, edited by Richard Burger, Craig Morris, and Ramiro Matos, 357–84. Washington, DC: Dumbarton Oaks, 2007.

Zuidema, R. T. "Bureaucracy and Systematic Knowledge in Andean Civilization." In *The Inca and Aztec States, 1400–1800: Anthropology and History*, edited by George A. Collier, Renato I. Rosaldo, and John D. Wirth, 419–58. New York: Academic Press, 1982.

■ GARY URTON

ANDES, CENTRAL

The Incas arose and expanded in the highlands of western South America, which have been known as the Andes only since the late Colonial period. Previously, *Andes*—a

Famed for his efforts at investigating and attempting to stamp out native "idolatries" in Cuzco, Arequipa, and Ayacucho, Albornoz was born in Andalusia, Spain, around 1529. We do not know much about his early life, although it is clear that he was ordained as a secular priest before traveling to the New World. Within a year of his arrival in Peru in 1567, he became involved in an ecclesiastical *visita*, inspecting parishes and investigating native religious practices in Arequipa. He attended and probably testified at two great provincial church councils—the Third Lima Council, in 1583, and the Fourth Lima Council, in 1591. During his long career, he was accused of taking goods from Indians on his anti-idolatry inspection tours. He was cleared of all charges, and subsequently sought recognition for his work by the award of a bishopric or archbishopric, to no avail. He is thought to have died around 1610.

The principal work by Albornoz that pertains to the study of the Incas is a document entitled *Instrucción para descubrir todas las guacas del Pirú y sus camayos y haziendas* (Instruction for the Discovery of all the Huacas of Peru and Their Keepers/Officials and Property"), which was probably written between 1581 and 1585. This document describes different types of Andean cults, the properties endowed to them, as well as the names of a great many *huacas*, or sacred places, in and around Cuzco and southern Peru including Arequipa and Ayacucho, as well as a few in northern Peru and as far north as modern Ecuador. In its detailing of *huacas*, aside from those that pertained to Cuzco's **Ceque** system, as recorded in the chronicle of **Bernabé Cobo**, Albornoz's account provides us with insights into Andean concepts of the "sacred" linked to places in the landscape beyond the Cuzco heartland.

Albornoz was also instrumental in persecuting native peoples involved in the *Taqui Oncoy* (dancing sickness), an indigenous messianic movement that swept through the southern highlands of Peru in the 1560s and early 1570s. Adherents of the Taqui Oncoy sought to revive lagging respect and worship of the *huacas*, calling for the expulsion of the Spaniards and a return to the state of affairs under the Incas. The illustrated chronicle of **Felipe Guaman Poma de Ayala** includes a drawing of Albornoz in the guise of an ecclesiastical inspector, directing the capture of an adherent of Taqui Oncoy. In ferreting out and documenting native religious practices of the early Colonial period, Albornoz brings to our attention much of what are presumed to be long-standing, preconquest religious beliefs and practices of common people outside Cuzco.

Further Reading

Duviols, Pierre, ed. "Un inédit de Cristóbal de Albornoz: La instrucción para descubrir todas las guacas del Pirú y sus camayos y haziendas." *Journal de la Société des Américanistes* (Paris) 56, no. 1: 7–39, 1967.

Millones, Luis. "Albornoz, Cristóbal de (ca. 1529–ca. 1610)." In *Guide to Documentary Sources for Andean Studies, 1530–1900*, edited by Joanne Pillsbury, vol. 2, 21–25. Norman: University of Oklahoma Press, 2008.

■ GARY URTON

The Cordillera Blanca in Ancash dominates Peru's central Andes. Adriana von Hagen.

Spanish deformation of the **Quechua** word *Anti*—referred to the eastern forests in the direction of the rising sun. A shift in meaning gradually took hold as the name *Andes* became attached to the mountains in general and then to the entire highland arc from Venezuela to Tierra del Fuego. That 7,000-kilometer-long (4,350-mile-long) complex of mountain chains, plateaus, and valleys was raised by mountain-building collisions as the lighter Nazca tectonic plate off the western shore of the continent slid under the heavier South American plate. From the Paleozoic to the Pleistocene, folding and faulting of sedimentary rocks, igneous intrusions, volcanic outpourings, glaciation, and erosion by water molded the diverse character of these mountains and their borderlands.

The midsection of this South American arc from northern Ecuador to northwestern Argentina is known as the Central Andes. The expression "Central Andes" now in common usage refers to not just the highlands, but also to the coastal region and the eastern slope. In broadest outline, this heart of the Andes consists of two main parallel-trending *cordilleras*, or ranges, that merge in a high-altitude tableland known as a "knot." Beginning at the Pasto Knot (1°30'N) in southern Colombia, Ecuador's two major mountain chains enclose between them a series of 10 basins. The cordillera to the west has 19 volcanoes; that to the east has 20 volcanoes, of which the highest is Chimborazo (6,310 meters [20,701 feet]), once considered to be the world's highest mountain. These two chains converge southward in the Loja Knot (3°50'S), out of which extend three chains covering northern highland Peru. An emblematic mountain landscape in this zone is the Callejón de Huaylas, which forms the upper Santa valley that separates the Cordillera Negra (to the west) from the higher, snow-capped Cordillera Blanca in the central chain. Huascarán (6,768 meters [22,205 feet]) is the highest and most climbed peak there. The rain and melting snow from westward-draining mountains were unequivocally vital to the development of all the coastal civilizations.

Southward the chains converge in a knot around Cerro de Pasco (10°45'S), out of which two main cordilleras align in a north-south direction. Volcanic landscapes dominate the western chain with lava 2,500 meters (8,202 feet) thick, and featuring the iconic peaks of Coropuna (6,425 meters [21,079 feet]) and Misti (5,822 meters [19,101 feet]). The eastern cordilleras have glaciers on many peaks above 5,200 meters (17,060 feet) whose meltwaters feed streams tapped for irrigation. Southeast of Cuzco, the Cordillera de Vilcanota holds the fabled peak of Ausangate (6,384 meters [20,945 feet]) and, beyond that, Quelccaya (5,470 meters [17,946 feet]), which is covered by the largest expanse of glacial ice in the Central Andes.

Two major rivers, the Urubamba and the Apurimac, flow northward more or less parallel until they join in the eastern forest to become the Ucayali River. Whereas the Urubamba valley contained an Inca road and was an important zone of food surplus, the even deeper Apurimac is narrow, dry, sparsely endowed with flat alluvial spaces, and has no easy route for human movement through it.

The western and eastern cordilleras converge in the Nudo de Vilcanota (14°30'S) and southward from it two mountain chains again follow parallel but more distant paths. The western chain, studded with volcanic cones, forms the border between Bolivia and Chile. About 400 kilometers to the east is the eastern chain, where at 16°38'S in northern Bolivia, the glaciers begin at 5,486 meters (17,999 feet). In comparison, on Huascarán, 1,350 kilometers (839 miles) to the north in Peru at latitude 9°07'S, the permanent snowline starts at 3,962 meters (12,999 feet), a difference explained by shorter days and thus lower rates of snowmelt on Huascarán. Covering the 400 kilometers between the two cordilleras is the *Altiplano*, a plateau 3,700–4,000 meters (12,139–13,123 feet) above sea level, whose northern portion is dominated by Lake Titicaca, the largest body of fresh water in the Andes. High evaporation and low rainfall in the southern portion of the *Altiplano* have created not just desert, but also a stark landscape of salt pans and salt lakes.

Differences in exposure explain many of the rainfall patterns in the Central Andes. On the coast of Peru and northern Chile, low cloud banks hang over the west side of the western cordillera. Air cooled at its base by the cold, northward-flowing Humboldt (or Peru) Current keeps the daily high temperatures below 25°C (77°F) for most of the year and generates frequent mist but virtually no rain. In this 2,200-kilometer-long (1,367-mile-long) desert strip, the natural vegetation response varies from a thorn tree woodland and shrubby plant formation known as *lomas*, to the sheer absence in southern Peru and northern Chile of any plant life. The physical geography on the east side of the eastern cordillera is completely different. There, moist air from the Amazon rising along the mountain front releases high amounts of rain that supports a low but dense forest with tree ferns and epiphytes. Away from influences emanating from the east or the west, highland precipitation is heavily seasonal with frequent thunderstorms from November to April. Clear skies and cold nights dominate the period from May to October.

Central Andean ecology is exceptionally diverse. Referring here only to Peru and the standard classification of the so-called Javier Pulgar Vidal model, 84 possible ecological distinctions can be collapsed into eight zones. Two of them are at low elevations, the dry coast (*chala*) and the forested plains (*omagua*) of the Amazon Basin to the east. From east to west, six are arranged attitudinally, beginning with the *rupa rupa* (high jungle), *yunga* (semitropical), *quechua* (temperate), *suni* (cold temperate), *puna* (microthermal), and *janca* (perennial snow). How the Incas characterized their diverse ecology cannot be known for certain, but the practice of moving colonists to similar environments from which they came suggests a nuanced view of their multilayered habitat.

Extreme environmental heterogeneity and an array of domesticated plants as well as some animals (see **Animals, Domesticated**; **Foodstuffs, Domesticated**) gave rise to certain practices that survived the Spanish invasion. In one form of vertical land use, farmers grew crops and kept llamas and alpacas at different elevations to reduce subsistence risk. Alternatively, different social groups, such as *puna* herders and valley agriculturalists, set up an exchange system based on resource complementarity. The great staple of the high Andes above 3,300 meters (10,827 feet) has been the potato, a crop that falls into several different species and many cultivars. In the southern half of the Central Andes, Andean people learned to preserve potatoes in the form of *chuño* by exposing them to daytime sun and nightly freezes that broke down the cell walls of the tubers thereby extracting the moisture. Camelid meat was also salted and dried. Dehydrated food was storable and light in weight, which facilitated the food needs of the Inca armies. It is perhaps significant that Inca expansion began in southern highland Peru where, unlike in northern Peru, the climate permitted the manufacture of *chuño*.

Maize became a staple in temperate Andean valleys hundreds of years before the Incas arose. By fertilizing and irrigating, the Inca achieved maize surpluses. By constructing stone-faced **terraces** and **irrigation** canals, they created more arable land, much of it devoted to maize. Other indigenous adaptations assured or improved agricultural productivity. Among them were raised fields (to prevent crops from rotting in poorly drained ground); lagoons (to store water for irrigation); and sunken fields on the desert coast (dug down to the groundwater table). Large engineering projects not only aided agriculture, but also modified the habitat. In the Urubamba valley near Cuzco, the Inca straightened the river's meander plain, reconfiguring the valley floor to create more agricultural land and control flooding.

A complement of hardy crops and domesticated camelids made it possible for more people to live above 3,000 meters (9,843 feet) in the Andes than anywhere else in the world. That was true in the Inca period and remains so today. The Incas did not avoid even extremely high elevations; they mined gold from quartz veins above 5,000 meters (16,404 feet) on the flanks of Ananea and Illimani, two snowcapped mountains in the eastern cordillera.

The Inca incorporated the arid coastal region into their imperial design and yet, for all their manifold accomplishments, they did not effectively colonize the hot jungle valleys to the east. The cultivation of **coca**—the mildly narcotic leaf over which the Incas held a quasi monopoly—emerged only in the fifteenth century, under a controlled regime in which most workers were brought in on temporary work stints. Poor soils, vector-borne infectious disease, and an unwillingness to adapt to local exigencies discouraged Inca settlement in that region.

Through the millennia and starting well before the Incas, inhabitants of the Andean highlands ingeniously dealt with the drought, frost, soil erosion, landslides, and earthquakes that made life so unpredictable. Overcoming an unusually difficult terrain, the Incas put into place a **road** network of ca. 40,000 kilometers (25,000 miles).

In short, the Incas welded together a vast, sophisticated polity in spite of manifold disadvantages of human life in a fractious and disaster-prone mountain domain. At the same time, however, the mountains provided enough of a buffer from most outside influences for the Incas to have created a civilization that, by any world standard, was truly unique.

Further Reading

Gade, Daniel W. *Nature and Culture in the Andes.* Madison: University of Wisconsin Press, 1999.
Pulgar Vidal, Javier. *Geografía del Perú. Las ocho regiones naturales.* 9th ed. Lima: Peisa, 1987.

■ DANIEL W. GADE

ANIMALS, DOMESTICATED

The Incas were familiar with all the native South American animal domesticates: Muscovy duck, guinea pig, llama, and alpaca, as well as the introduced domesticated dog.

The Muscovy duck (*Cairina moschata*) is a large duck commonly found throughout the neotropics, where it is often referred to as *pato casero* (house duck), *pato criollo* (native duck), or *pato real* (royal duck). Little is known of its early domestication, although wild flocks range throughout wetlands and crop fields from coastal Mexico to the Gran Chaco of Argentina. The bones of the Muscovy duck are occasionally identified in archaeological sites. It was also frequently depicted in Moche and Chimú pottery, and its plumes incorporated into Chimú and Inca featherwork. To the Inca, it was known as *ñuñuma*, a name that the chronicler **Garcilaso de la Vega** mentions is derived from the **Quechua** word "to suck" (*ñuñu*) because of the sound it made while eating. Early Spanish accounts describe its captivity in neotropical house yards, much like today. Although it is assumed they were used principally for meat and possibly eggs, the chronicler Francisco de Xerez's early account of the fateful meeting between Atahualpa and Pizarro describes gifts offered by an Inca messenger that included two loads of dried and skinned ducks that were to be prepared into powdered fumigants used by the nobility (see **Invasion, Spanish**).

The guinea pig (*Cavia porcellus*), or *cuy* (Quechua), is a medium-sized caviomorph (infraorder of South American rodents grouped according to shared cranial morphology) whose suspected wild ancestors (*C. aperea* or *C. tschudii*) inhabit the Andes from Peru southward into the lower elevation grasslands of Argentina. Although caviid skeletal specimens are frequently recovered in archaeological sites, some of great antiquity, *cuy* is believed to have been domesticated by at least 3600 BC in the central Andes. Archaeological evidence includes occasional associations of mummified *cuy* with human burials, and accurate depictions on Moche pots. As access to camelid herds and hunting of wild animals was controlled by the Inca state, domestically raised *cuy* and ducks were conceivably the few regular meat options available to commoners. *Cuy* flourish on food scraps provided in the darkened settings of domestic dwellings. Although the chronicles mention that *cuys* were common and abundant, their consumption may have been restricted primarily to special occasions. According to the Jesuit scholar **Bernabé Cobo**, *cuys* were consumed with their skin, like a piglet, or prepared with hot peppers and river pebbles in their belly to create a highly appreciated stew called *carapulcra*. Frequent sacrifice of

This chronicler of Inca history, commonly referred to as Padre Oliva, was born in Naples, Italy, in 1574, and entered the Jesuit order there in 1593. Anello Oliva traveled to Peru in 1597, where, upon arrival, he was ordained into the priesthood and soon began evangelization among Native peoples, especially south of Cuzco, in Juli, Oruro, La Paz, Potosí, Sucre, Cochabamba, and Arequipa.

Anello Oliva is known primarily from his work, *Historia del reino y provincias del Perú y vidas de los varones insignes de la Compañía de Jesús* (History of the Kingdom and Provinces of Peru and the Lives of Notable Men of the Jesuit Order), which he began around 1608 and completed in 1631. This work was composed of four books, only the first of which, his *History of the Incas*, survives. Arriving in Peru relatively late, as compared to other generally better-known chroniclers, Anello Oliva made use of several of the earlier chronicles, most notably those of **Garcilaso de la Vega**, **José de Acosta**, and **Pedro de Cieza de León**. He also drew heavily from information provided by a native lord (*curaca*) of Cochabamba, a man named Catari, who claimed to be descended from Illa, supposed inventor of the *quipus*, or knotted-cord records. In addition, Anello Oliva's text drew on a famous lost work by **Blas Valera**, a *mestizo* (mixed indigenous/Spanish) Jesuit from Chachapoyas, in northern Peru. Valera's text is described as a "vocabulary," numerous entries of which are incorporated into Anello Oliva's *Historia*. It has also been suggested that Anello Oliva had access to some portions of **Felipe Guaman Poma de Ayala's** then-unpublished *Nueva corónica y buen gobierno*.

Anello Oliva's own history of the Incas contains much information not attested to in any other surviving chronicles, such as the inventor of the *quipus* and the name of the Inca lord who discovered the solstices (Capac Raymi Amauta), as well as the names of several Inca kings (mentioned only in a work by Fernando de Montesinos), who supposedly ruled Peru before the short list of a dozen or so kings commonly recognized by most chroniclers (see **King List**). Recent studies have argued that much of Anello Oliva's text was expunged by order of his Jesuit superiors in Peru, especially his condemnations of Spanish policy in Peru. Despite the elimination of this material, the Jesuit General in Rome refused to permit the publication of Anello Oliva's work. His text was not published until 1895, by which time all but the first of the four books were lost.

Anello Oliva's name is also implicated in the complicated history of a set of documents, often referred to colloquially as "the Naples documents," which are said to contain certain texts written by Anello Oliva himself. One of these, which supposedly dates to 1637, pertains to the life of Blas Valera, and claims that Valera had been persecuted by the Jesuit hierarchy and that he recorded history using the knotted-cord *quipus*. A document by Anello Oliva dated 1638 makes even more extraordinary allegations about Valera, saying that the *mestizo* chronicler had not died, as claimed, in the English sacking of the Spanish port of Cádiz, but that he had survived, surreptitiously returned to Peru, and there wrote the work, *Nueva corónica y buen gobierno*, which most scholars believe was written and illustrated by Felipe Guaman Poma de Ayala. Controversy continues today over the legitimacy of the Naples documents, with some scholars insisting on their veracity and others claiming that they are fraudulent—perhaps even modern fakes.

Further Reading

Anello Oliva, Giovanni. *Historia del reino y provincias del Perú y vidas de los varones insignes de la Compañía de Jesús*. Edition, prologue, and notes by Carlos M. Gálvez Peña. Colección Clásicos Peruanos. Lima: Pontificia Universidad Católica del Perú, Fondo Editorial, 1998.

Hyland, Sabine. *The Jesuit and the Incas: The Extraordinary Life of Padre Blas Valera, S.J.* Ann Arbor: University of Michigan Press, 2004.

———. "Anello Oliva, Giovanni (1574–1642)." In *Guide to Documentary Sources for Andean Studies, 1530–1900*, edited by Joanne Pillsbury, vol. 2, 34–36. Norman: University of Oklahoma Press, 2008.

■ GARY URTON

cuys featured in Inca notions of complimentarily, interdependence, and reciprocity. They could be beheaded, burned, or cut open for propitiation, placation, thanks, and requests. *Cuys* were used in Inca times, as they are today, in **divination** and curing; their bodies were eviscerated, entrails were examined for omens, and the afflicted could be rubbed or wiped with meat, fat, or viscera.

The camelids, llamas (*Lama glama*) and alpacas (*Vicugna pacos*), were the only large mammals to have been domesticated in the western hemisphere. Llamas may have been domesticated from a northern variant of wild guanacos (*L. guanicoe*) whose populations were widely distributed on both sides of the Andes from Peru to Tierra del Fuego. Descendant llamas are currently found in South America from Ecuador south to northern Argentina and central Chile. Imperial Inca expansion amplified their distribution. Alpacas may have been domesticated from a northern form of wild vicuñas (*V. vicugna*) whose populations have a restricted geographical distribution in the high Andes above 3,000 meters (9,843 feet) above sea level. Descendant alpacas in South America are today found in high-altitude pastures (*bofedales*) from central Peru to northern Chile, and in coastal areas of Peru. Although it is unknown when camelids were first domesticated, growing evidence suggests they had assumed importance to highland peoples by at least 8,500 years ago. Although four species of potentially interbreeding hybridizing camelids are scientifically recognized, indigenous classification includes many variants based upon elaborate hierarchies of color and fiber characters. Pre-Hispanic management likely involved strict herd control.

The importance of domesticated llamas and alpacas to the Incas is demonstrated by their comparable mythical origins from lakes and springs. They first appeared with Inca ancestors who emerged from a cave at Pacariqtambo (see **Myths, Origin**), enjoyed a mythical and ritual life, which paralleled that of humans, and were associated with events surrounding the end of the world. Llamas could also be mummified, or burned and placed

Alpacas, valued for their silky fiber, in their corrals in the southern Andes of Peru.
Daniel Huillca. TAFOS Photographic Archive/PUCP, Lima, Peru.

in tombs of deceased nobility. Camelids provided the Incas with meat and fiber and
were used as beasts of burden. Their skin, sinew, tallow, and bones were made into usable
products, their dung fertilized fields and was burned as fuel, and they played major roles
in ceremonial life. Although the early Spanish chronicles emphasized the large numbers
of camelids in state-controlled herds, **John V. Murra** indicates that community flocks,
usually tended by younger villagers, were also present.

A family and their small herd of llamas in Canas, Cuzco, Peru. Nieves Callasi.
TAFOS Photographic Archive/PUCP, Lima, Peru.

Camelids were consumed both as fresh meat and as dried and salted *charqui* (meat), although their regular consumption was likely restricted to elites and to the Inca armies. Otherwise, camelid meat was somewhat of a luxury for commoners, only available during ceremonial occasions or through widespread distribution after sacrifices. In addition to its use as a lubricant, camelid fat was used in marriage rituals, offerings, sacrifice, and burned with coca leaves for divination. Camelid bones were fashioned into tools for working leather and weaving textiles. Sandal soles were created from llama hides softened with fat, skins were used as water containers, and slings were made from tendons. Dung was used for fuel and fertilizer. Young llama bucks, packed with loads of up to 29 kilograms (65 pounds), were driven in dry season caravans that traveled an average of 17.7 kilometers (11 miles) from daybreak to noon when they stopped for water and pasture. Crown herds were primarily used in army campaigns to carry supplies and tribute goods, and were eaten or offered as tribute. Camelid fiber, a state prerogative, was deposited in storehouses and issued to subject peoples who, as a function of their labor obligation, reciprocated with woven cloth. Alpacas provided the major source of Inca fiber, while llama fiber was used for making ropes and coarser cloth.

Llamas were preferred for ritual use and served as multipurpose sacrificial offerings. Garcilaso mentions that young llamas were the most esteemed solar sacrifices. Male llamas and barren ewes followed in order of preference, while the magistrate **Juan Polo Ondegardo** mentioned that fertile females were never sacrificed. Llamas were the most important animals in the Inca religious cycle. They were roasted and consumed in feasts during elite funerals. Llamas were sacrificed during eclipses, full moon ceremonies, investitures, before and after wars, and to ensure good harvests. Llama viscera, in particular, were important for prognostication.

Domesticated dogs (*Canis lupus familiaris*) were early introductions into the western hemisphere from Asia and may have descended from ancestral Eurasian gray wolves (*C. lupus*). Illustrations such as those accompanying the chronicle of **Felipe Guaman Poma de Ayala** often depict Inca dogs with a medium-sized body, short legs, pointed snout and ears, long curly tail, and short hair. Early attempts to classify Native American dog breeds recognized this Inca dog along with long-haired and pug-nosed varieties. Dogs in the Inca world were likely little more than omnipresent companions and scavengers, despite the chronicler Garcilaso's assertion that they held religious importance among many pre-Inca people. The *Huarochirí Manuscript* (see **Avila, Francisco de**) relates how the Huanca people of the central highlands were transformed into "dog eaters" upon the defeat of their deity *Huallallo Carhuincho* whom they propitiated with dogs. Dogs also figured in Inca history and cosmology. An early document by Agustín de Zárate recounts the story of provisioned caves used by the Inca to escape a universal flood, from which they sent dogs to test whether the waters had receded. Garcilaso maintains that during lunar eclipses the howling of tied and beaten dogs awakened the moon from her sickness. In the afterlife, dogs were occasionally encountered by, or associated with, humans in their journeys after death.

Further Reading

Cobo, Bernabé. *History of the Inca Empire: An Account of the Indians' Customs and Their Origin, Together with a Treatise on Inca Legends, History and Social Institutions.* Translated and edited by Roland Hamilton. Austin: University of Texas Press, 1979 [1653].

Donkin, R. A. *The Muscovy Duck,* Cairina moschata domestica*: Origins, Dispersal, and Associated Aspects of the Geography of Domestication.* Rotterdam: A. A. Balkema, 1989.

Gade, Daniel W. "The Guinea Pig in Andean Folk Culture." *Geographical Review* 57, no. 2: 213–24, 1967.

Garcilaso de la Vega, El Inca. *Royal Commentaries of the Incas and General History of Peru.* Translated by Harold V. Livermore. Austin: University of Texas Press, 1966 [1609].

Gilmore, Raymond M. "Fauna and Ethnozoology of South America." In *Handbook of South American Indians,* edited by Julian H. Steward, Vol. 6, 345–464. *Bureau of American Ethnology Bulletin* 143. Washington, DC: Smithsonian Institution, 1950.

González, Carlos, Hugo Rosati, and Francisco Sánchez. *Guaman Poma. Testigo del Mundo Andino.* Santiago: Centro de Investigaciones Diego Barros Arana, 2002.

Murra, John V. *The Economic Organization of the Inka State.* Greenwich, CT: JAI Press, 1980.

Polo Ondegardo, Juan. "Of the Lineage of the Yncas, and How They Extended Their Conquests." In *Narratives of the Rites and Laws of the Yncas,* translated and edited by Clements R. Markham. Works issued by the Hakluyt Society, No. 48. London: Hakluyt Society, 1873.

Salomon, Frank, and George L. Urioste, eds. and trans. *The Huarochirí Manuscript.* Austin: University of Texas Press, 1991.

Steele, Paul R. *Handbook of Inca Mythology.* Santa Barbara, CA: ABC-CLIO, 2004.

Wheeler, Jane C. "South American Camelids—Past, Present and Future." *Journal of Camelid Science* 5: 1–24, 2012.

Xerez, Francisco de. *Verdadera Relación de la Conquista del Peru y la Provincia de Cuzco.* Colección de Libros Raros y Curiósos que Tratan de América, vol. 1. Madrid: J. C. García, 1891.

Zárate, Agustín de. *The Discovery and Conquest of Peru.* Translated by Thomas Nicholas. London: Penguin Press, 1933.

■ PETER W. STAHL

ANTISUYU

The Inca *suyu* or quadrant of Antisuyu embraced the forested slopes of the Andes to just west of north and just south of east of **Cuzco**. At the same time, Antisuyu was one of the quadrants of the capital, whose plaza served as the axis of the empire's territorial divisions and, by extension, the roads to the four *suyus*. Along with **Chinchaysuyu**, it formed the upper, or *hanan,* half of Tahuantinsuyu, the "four parts bound together" that comprised the Inca Empire. Some scholars believe that Antisuyu included the entire eastern slope and adjoining tropical lowlands along the length of Tahuantinsuyu rather than the wedge-shaped area north and east of Cuzco, but the evidence weighs in favor of the smaller quadrant. The Inca province of Chachapoyas, for example, which straddled the eastern slopes of the Andes in what is today northern Peru, was considered to have formed part of Chinchaysuyu. The Incas often defined regions geographically, according to their proximity to main roads, and in the case of Chachapoyas, it lay off the "Quito road," that is, the Chinchaysuyu road.

In the early years of imperial expansion, the four *suyus* that encompassed Tahuantinsuyu (Chinchaysuyu, Antisuyu, **Collasuyu**, and **Cuntisuyu**) may have been roughly equivalent in size. While Chinchaysuyu and Collasuyu expanded far to the north and south, respectively, to become the largest *suyus,* geographical factors constrained the growth of the smaller *suyus,* Antisuyu and Cuntisuyu (the Pacific Ocean to the west and the tropical Amazonian lowlands to the east, respectively), the latter a region often beyond the reach of imperial control.

The cloud forest settlement of Choquequirao perches high above the Apurimac River west of Cuzco, in the province of Vilcabamba. Adriana von Hagen.

Most importantly, Antisuyu furnished the empire with tropical resources. The cloud forest provinces, settled by colonist coca farmers, supplied much of Cuzco's **coca**, the mildly narcotic leaf on which the Incas held a quasi monopoly. These tropical areas, including the adjacent lowland forest, provided other highly sought-after resources, such as cotton and hot peppers, as well as honey, resin, beeswax, dyestuffs, hardwood, medicinal and hallucinogenic plants, animal pelts, live animals, and especially, the **feathers** of brightly colored tropical birds to dress the nobles, the soldiers, and the *huacas*.

Ensuring access to tropical resources and trade networks along the Amazonian tributaries, perhaps by allying with local chiefs, was crucial to Inca success in the region. In some cases, key alliances may have allowed the Incas to exploit some exchange networks, a policy that may have served as a model for Inca strategies in "managing" the tropical lowlands, from the forested Andean slopes bordering northernmost Chinchaysuyu (modern Ecuador) to the Chaco plains flanking Collasuyu in the south (modern Bolivia, bordering on Paraguay).

■ ADRIANA VON HAGEN

ARCHAEOLOGY, CUZCO

As the Incas grew to be a regional political power, they dramatically transformed Cuzco, their capital. These changes are reflected in the archaeological record, making it possible to reconstruct how the Incas developed from, as pioneering Inca scholar **John H. Rowe** put it, a "straggling collection of poorly built houses" in the Cuzco basin to the core of the largest native empire in the Americas. Although Rowe argued that Cuzco became a metropolitan center after Pachacuti Inca Yupanqui defeated the Chancas of Andahuaylas around the mid-fifteenth century AD, recent surveys and systematic excavations have

Chokepuquio in the Cuzco valley, Peru, flourished after the fall of Huari ca. AD 1000 and before the rise of the Incas, around AD 1400. The structure seen here heralds the large halls that flanked Inca plazas. Adriana von Hagen.

revealed that Cuzco developed as an urban center and imperial heartland gradually over several centuries. With radiocarbon dating, scholars today find that sites historically associated with rapid expansion under Pachacuti were already in the process of abandonment during his reign, which pushes back initial growth through the heartland to around the twelfth century (the beginning of the Killke period [see **Chronology, Inca**]). During the approximately three centuries of sociopolitical consolidation in the Cuzco region, the Incas faced resistance from some neighbors and successfully established alliances with others (the latter would become known as **Incas by Privilege** and were provided special status and rights not held by other neighbors). They created a mosaic of semiautonomous remaining allies who were left in their ancestral villages and a series of repurposed **royal estate** lands in places where groups were particularly rebellious.

By the fourteenth to fifteenth centuries, the Incas transformed the area of **Cuzco** between the Huatanay and Tullumayu Rivers into a centrally planned urban core that became the cosmological center of a nascent empire. Much of Inca Cuzco was destroyed in the 1536–1537 siege when rebellious Inca forces tried to retake the city from the occupying Spaniards, and during the ensuing centuries of urbanization. These processes make it difficult for archaeologists to study the city systematically. Although dozens of archaeological excavations have been carried out in urban Cuzco, many are not published and thus, archaeologists often rely upon eyewitness accounts from the early Colonial period to describe the city.

The greater Cuzco region—the Inca heartland—was composed, however, of not just the planned urban core but also the suburbs and rural areas, where Inca and migrant residents settled near improved farmlands. The city and its hinterland covered some 11 kilometers (7 miles) of the Cuzco basin toward the south. In the rural regions beyond the hinterland, stone-lined agricultural terracing and royal estates dominated, with provincial laborers reset-tled amid local ethnic groups. The ethnic and ritual boundaries of the Inca heartland were located some 50–80 kilometers (30–50 miles) from the urban core. Archaeological surveys and excavations have revealed that the Inca transitioned from just one of many competing groups to the most politically powerful entity in the central Andean highlands.

As the Inca state developed, dramatic changes occurred between the eleventh and six-teenth centuries. Archaeologists use Killke pottery, a pre-imperial ceramic type, to identify early Inca sites and to reconstruct the relationships the Cuzco Incas had with their Incas by Privilege neighbors. While Killke pottery was probably produced within Cuzco, early Inca rivals created contemporaneous types, including the Lucre ceramic style of the Pina-hua and Mohina ethnic groups to the east and the Colcha style of the Chillque group to the south. Where Killke pottery is recovered, archaeologists argue that the early Incas had extended their territorial control or created alliances with neighboring groups. Another indicator of the transition to Inca rule is **architecture**, as pre-Inca sites are marked by a preponderance of small, circular domestic structures. The Inca constructed well-planned, rectangular buildings and enclosures to administer these sites in the later periods, while Inca households resided mostly in rectangular configurations as well.

During the Killke period, Inca rivals developed several nucleated, large villages around the Cuzco region. South of Cuzco in Paruro, however, a different pattern dominated. Several ethnic groups lived in undefended, scattered, small agricultural villages that did not change significantly with Inca incorporation. In Lucre and Huaro to the southeast, however, the Huari of Ayacucho had previously established a highly visible colony at Pikillacta and other sites around the sixth century, though it declined by AD 1000 (see **Chronology, Pre-Inca**). After that time, nearby Chokepuquio—occupied since the Huari era—grew nearly as large as the early settlement of Cuzco. As the head of a complex political group, possibly the Pinahua ethnic group, Chokepuquio competed with Cuzco. After AD 1000, Cuzco felt so threatened by these neighbors that it made the Oropesa basin a buffer zone between Cuzco and Lucre. A void was left between Inca-controlled and Pinahua-controlled territo-ries, with the exception of the fortified site of Pucara Tipón. When Lucre finally fell under Inca dominion, the ruler Viracocha Inca, Pachakuti's father, developed Tipón into a royal estate and populated the zone with laborers to support newly improved agricultural lands.

North of Cuzco, the Incas allied with some groups, while those settled across the Vilcanota River were incorporated later. The Anta ethnic group northwest of Cuzco, for example, was a large group consolidated as Incas by Privilege. Their possible center, Ak'awillay, continued to be occupied in the imperial period. In contrast, the Ayarmaca polity of Maras and Chinchero and their possible capital at the large site of Yunkaray ex-perienced a different relationship with rival Cuzco. They abandoned their territory after generations of struggle with the Incas and were resettled into several villages around the heartland, while their homeland was largely converted into royal estates.

In the Urubamba valley, the Cuyo ethnic group and others lived at higher eleva-tions prior to Inca incorporation. The Cuyo slowly abandoned their principal site of Muyuch'urqu for the new site of Pucara Pantillijlla in the Chongo basin and gradually moved down in elevation toward the valley bottom under the Incas, perhaps to be nearer to farmlands to fulfill tribute obligations. In the Chit'apampa basin, political groups that were capable of coordinating labor lived on defensible ridges and hilltops prior to the Incas. Upon incorporation in the late Killke period, the Incas built administrative structures at some of these settlements before a longer-lasting transition to lower elevations and more dispersed, valley-bottom settlements was carried out. Around the Urubamba valley, state and noble construction projects fueled by tribute labor transformed the landscape, parts of the river were canalized to create imposing terracing projects, and populations shifted toward a large royal estate at Pisac.

During the Killke and early Inca period, settlements in the Cuzco basin increased in number and size and began to form a metropolitan capital. As some groups resisted Inca rule in rural Cuzco, conflict increased, a trend that is corroborated by skeletal trauma evidence. The growing Inca polity found advantages over its neighbors and emerged as the most powerful player in the Cuzco region. By AD 1400, the Inca produced standardized, imperial style architecture and **ceramics**. The Cuzco basin filled up with new villages, hamlets, royal estates, and an influx of migrant laborers attached to the state and the nobility. **Sacsahuaman**, a large fortified site also used for major ritual events, was constructed around a Killke complex northwest of the city.

At the height of Inca rule, Cuzco was a wealthy city that was planned and built to highlight its profane and sacred connections to the heartland and beyond. Royal **roads** emanating from a large plaza near its center led to four administrative regions (*suyu*). This dual plaza was a multifunctional space where the activities of the Aucaypata side could be observed by provincial elites and non-Incas from the Cusipata side. Archaeological excavations in the plaza have recovered wall foundations, platforms and subterranean canals, as well as decorated Inca-style feasting ceramics and figurines made of gold, silver, and Spondylus shell buried beneath a layer of Pacific coast sand. A line of four miniature llamas was found oriented toward Huanacauri, a prominent mountaintop in Inca origin stories.

The Huari site of Pikillacta in the Cuzco valley, Peru, predated the rise of the Incas by several centuries. Adriana von Hagen.

Other important imperial monuments within urban Cuzco included the **Corican-cha**, the house of the *acllacuna*, and palaces for rulers, their wives, and some siblings. The Coricancha was the central temple dedicated to the sun and other deities, with a series of small temples within an enclosure built over Killke remains. Urban palaces included internal domestic spaces for royal residents, as well as water features and large halls (*callanca*) for public interactions with the nobility. The fine masonry of these Inca buildings was constructed from stone provided by Cuzco valley quarries such as Wacoto and Rumicollca (see **Quarrying and Stonecutting**). Around these quarries, archae-ologists find unplanned settlements, possibly representing housing for quarry specialists. In contrast, other towns within the heartland are well planned and orthogonal (built along perpendicular axes), such as the elite settlements of Calca and the Qosqo Ayllu sector of Ollantaytambo.

As regional populations increased, changes were made to the political economy of Cuzco. Early Inca growth coincided with regional climatic conditions that favored in-tensive irrigation agriculture. This agricultural strategy allowed the Incas to transform the Cuzco landscape into terraced and irrigated lands and to build storage complexes for the subsequent surplus crops (see **Storage**). Storehouses in the heartland were different from those of the provinces: they stored multiple types of products in a single structure, unlike the specialized architecture of provincial *collca*, and some Cuzco storehouses were adapted structures from pre-Inca groups, such as the Ayarmaca. The Inca also invested in expanding the **roads** coming into and leaving from Cuzco and built way stations (*tambos*) such as Tambo Real on the Anta plain that linked the heartland to Chinchaysuyu, the northwestern quadrant of the empire.

In order to construct and maintain these intensified resources and monumental ar-chitectural projects, the Inca brought in new populations. Labor specialists and retainers were resettled throughout the region, which created a multiethnic heartland that is only recently being studied through domestic excavations. Bioarchaeological studies point to increased frequencies of cranial vault modification (a trait associated with group affilia-tion) among human remains from rural Cuzco, while analysis of dental enamel (strontium isotope evidence) indicates where migrant individuals spent their early lives. Many of these migrants were brought to Cuzco to labor on the royal estates, which served as cen-ters of wealth production for noble families. Underused tracts were improved upon and uncooperative local groups lost their lands in favor of estate development. Royal estates such as Pisac and Chinchero included elite residences as well as temples, baths, ornamental canals, and terraces, and were surrounded by storehouses, gardens, camelid corrals and pastures, hunting preserves, and other resources.

The inclusion of temples at royal-estate palaces is symptomatic of the importance the Incas placed on the sacred. Cuzco was surrounded by natural and human-built fea-tures imbued with symbolism. The anchor of this sacred landscape was the *ceque* system, a series of 42 imagined lines that emanated from the Coricancha and connected at least 328 shrines (*huacas*). *Ceque* surveys found that named sacred places corresponded to hills, palaces, temples, fields, tombs, ravines, caves, quarries, worked stones, and more. Offerings were made to these shrines as important locales for Inca origins and relevant sites for particular lineages. The dedicated fields and herds that were needed to provision the ritual practitioners who maintained the *ceque* system fomented the transformation of Cuzco's countryside.

As the Incas developed their state and expanded to form Tahuantinsuyu, the heartland changed dramatically. New styles of pottery and architecture helped to create a visible imperial identity that was exported to the provinces, while provincial migrants were resettled into the imperial core to support the growing economic demands of a thriving heartland. Archaeological studies help to identify the timing and nature of these transitions and to pinpoint the differences among urban, suburban, and rural areas of Cuzco. The Incas faced a diversity of local responses to their expansion, which produced a heterogeneous heartland marked by increasingly dense populations, agricultural intensification, an obvious accumulation of surplus, investment in royal estates, and a complex and integrated sacred landscape tied to imperial origins.

Further Reading

Andrushko, Valerie A., Michele R. Buzon, Antonio Simonetti, and Robert A. Creaser. "Strontium Isotope Evidence for Prehistoric Migration at Chokepukio, Valley of Cuzco, Peru." *Latin American Antiquity* 20, no. 1: 57–75, 2009.

Bauer, Brian S. *Ancient Cuzco: Heartland of the Inca.* Austin: University of Texas Press, 2004.

Covey, R. Alan. *How the Incas Built Their Heartland: State Formation and the Innovation of Imperial Strategies in the Sacred Valley, Peru.* Ann Arbor: University of Michigan Press, 2006.

Farrington, Ian S. *Cusco: Urbanism and Archaeology in the Inka World.* Gainesville: University Press of Florida, 2013.

Rowe, John H. "An Introduction to the Archaeology of Cuzco." In *Papers of the Peabody Museum of Anthropology and Ethnology* 27, no. 2. Cambridge, MA: Harvard University Press, 1944.

■ KYLIE E. QUAVE

ARCHITECTURE

From masterfully fitted stone masonry to dramatic mountaintop settings, Inca architecture has captivated popular and scholarly imaginations for centuries. Its ability to impress is not an accident but a result of imperial intentions. The state carefully controlled the design, construction, and use of architecture so that the built environment could serve as a critical tool in Inca conquest strategies. The Incas created a unified vision of their empire by spreading their distinctive architecture (and artifacts) throughout the lands they had conquered. This architecture was designed to manifest the Incas' integration with the sacred landscape and validate their rule, serving as a visual reminder to conquered populations of Inca might. Because of the importance of the Inca built environment, they paid considerable attention to how structures were seen, approached, and experienced.

The distinctiveness of Inca architecture was largely achieved through the employment of a stable and legible repertoire of seven core elements: (1) single room, free-standing rectangular structures; (2) gabled or hipped roofs; (3) trapezoidal doors, niches, and windows; (4) battered (sloping) walls; and (5) distinctive bonded masonry styles (ashlar and polygonal) (see **Quarrying and Stonecutting**). Inca architecture was carefully laid out, so that it often (6) incorporated natural stone outcrops, and (7) controlled the ap-

A double-jamb, exterior niche at the temple of Huaytará, one of several settlements with fine architecture found along the road that connected Cuzco with the Pacific coast. Adriana von Hagen.

proach to (and directed the experience through) Inca settlements. While not every location presented all the features described above (new forms, elements, and materials could be incorporated), builders made sure to include enough of the core elements to mark the site as unmistakably Inca.

One of the reasons Inca architecture is so readily recognizable is that it was designed by specialists who produced state-approved designs. Architects who came from the elite of Inca society and skilled contractors oversaw construction. Before ground could be broken, landscape and architectural models were made to visualize the new areas that were to be developed and new complexes that were to be built (see **Planning, Settlement**). These models were brought to authorities, including the Inca ruler himself, for approval, ensuring that the final project properly represented state directives. The architects and contractors then implemented the designs with the large labor force available to the state (see **Labor Service**). The simplified repertoire of buildings, materials, construction, and motifs enabled the largely unskilled labor force to erect a multitude of imperial Inca sites as rapidly as Tahuantinsuyu, the Inca Empire, expanded. The result was a unified vision of the Inca presence that pervaded the Andean landscape.

The basic Inca building type, a freestanding rectangular structure, made up the vast majority of buildings and allowed for a great diversity of functions to occur in Inca settlements. The Inca combined these rectangular structures in a variety of ways, differentiating them with meaningful openings, such as single- and double-jamb doorways, windows, and niches. These buildings ranged across a wide, but continuous, spectrum in size and were used to create a variety of settlement types, such as administrative centers, way stations, royal estates, and temple complexes.

The Incas included a diversity of functions into their standard rectangular structures. Therefore, it is not surprising that the Incas saw function as the most important factor in defining a building type. There were, for example, buildings that stored food, drink, and other goods, such as the *akahuasi* (house of *aka*, or maize beer; *chicha*), *churaconahuasi* (warehouse), and *llaxtahuasi* (store house for captured goods). They also had houses de-

Finely built stone walls with trapezoidal niches and doorways are hallmarks of the Inca architectural style, shown here at Pisac above Cuzco's Urubamba valley. Adriana von Hagen.

voted to special services, such as the *masanahuasi* (house for drying clothes), and for special people, such as the *acllahuasi* (house for chosen women), *huatayhuasi* (house for prisoners), *sankahuasi* (house for prisoners who committed grave offenses), *ayahuasi* (house for the dead), and the *uacchahuasi* (house for "orphaned" children, specifically those of the ruler and a low status wife). The Inca designed other *huasi* for intimate bodily needs, such as the *punonahuasi* (house of sleep and sex) and the *acahuasi* (house of *aca*, or feces).

Less often, the Incas developed building types according to facture, or the manner in which it was made. Examples include the *callancahuasi* (house made of *callanca*, or ashlar foundation stones), or according to form, such as the *muyuhuasi* (circular house), the *quencohuasi* (turned or zigzag house), and the *marcahuasi* (house with lofts). Occasionally, the Incas designed building types that involved both form and function, such as the *cuyusmanco* and *carpahuasi* (two imperial buildings with distinctive doorways associated with the Inca ruler and governance), as well as the *sunturhuasi* (a tall structure that had the appearance of a mountain or pyramid, used by a ruler for viewing activities on the plaza).

The simple building kit and system of design and construction allowed Inca architecture to be highly adaptable and very site specific, addressing the local landscape, both physical and cultural. Thus architecture could underscore the Incas' negotiated relationship with a local group, such as the people of Chincha, who lived on Peru's south coast, by inserting their distinctive architecture within a Chincha-style complex. When necessary, the Incas incorporated local building practices, materials, and forms into their provincial architecture. The complex reasoning behind these localized designs is just now coming to light by scholars. Thus, there is much left to learn about the great variability in Inca architecture across the vast expanse of Tahuantinsuyu, the Inca Empire.

On the coast the Incas built with adobe and occasionally in stone; here the site of Paramonga on Peru's north-central coast. Adriana von Hagen.

Inca architecture also varied through time. The average size of buildings, for instance, increased across time in royal landscapes; there was a slight increase in building size at Topa Inca Yupanqui's estate in Chinchero and building dimensions grew conspicuously at Huayna Capac's estate in the Urubamba valley (see **Estates, Royal**). In the latter, the size of openings (windows, doorways, and niches) and ceiling heights also increased dramatically. In addition, new building types, such as the *cuyusmanco*, were introduced into the architectural canon, while others, such as the *carpahuasi*, may have evolved (and thus changed considerably) over time. Like the study of architectural change through space, the study of how Inca architecture changed across time is only in its infancy. What is remarkable, however, is that despite this variation across time and space, Inca settlements across Tahuantinsuyu still retain enough of the standardized practices that they read as distinctly Inca. In doing so, the Incas succeeded in making their ever-expanding presence in the Andean landscape visible to all.

Further Reading

Dean, Carolyn. "The Inka Married the Earth: Integrated Outcrops and the Making of Place." *Art Bulletin* 89, no. 3: 502–18, 2007.
———. *A Culture of Stone: Inka Perspectives on Rock.* Durham, NC: Duke University Press, 2010.
Farrington, Ian S. *Cusco: Urbanism and Archaeology in the Inka World.* Gainesville: University Press of Florida, 2013.
Gasparini, G., and L. Margolies. *Inca Architecture.* Translated by P. J. Lyon. Bloomington: Indiana University Press, 1980.
Kendall, A. *Aspects of Inca Architecture.* Part 1, *Description, Function, and Chronology.* Part 2, *Description, Function and Chronology.* Oxford: B.A.R. International Series, 1984.

Malpass, M. A., ed. *Provincial Inca: Archaeological and Ethnohistorical Assessment of the Impact of the Inca State.* Iowa City: University of Iowa Press, 1993.

Moorehead, E. L. "Highland Inca Architecture in Adobe." *Ñawpa Pacha*, no. 16: 65–94, 1978.

Morris, C. "Enclosures of Power: The Multiple Spaces of Inka Adminstrative Palaces." In *Palaces of the Ancient New World*, edited by S. T. Evans and J. Pillsbury, 299–324. Washington, DC: Dumbarton Oaks Research Library and Collection, 2004.

Morris, C., and D. E. Thompson, *Huánuco Pampa: An Inca City and Its Hinterland.* London: Thames and Hudson, 1985.

Nair, S. *Of Remembrance and Forgetting: The Architecture of Chinchero, Peru from Thupa Inka to the Spanish Occupation.* Doctoral Dissertation, Architecture, University of California at Berkeley, 2003.

———. "Inca Architecture and the Conquest of the Countryside." In *Architecture—Design Methods—Inca Structures*, edited by J. Dehlinger and H. Dehlinger, 114–25. Kassel: Kassel University Press, 2009.

———. *At Home with the Sapa Inca: Architecture, Space, and Legacy at Chinchero.* Austin: University of Texas Press, 2015.

Niles, S. "Architectural Form and Social Function in Inca Towns near Cuzco." In *Current Archaeological Projects in the Central Andes: Some Approaches and Results.* Vol. 210, edited by A. Kendall, 205–33. Oxford: B.A.R. International Series, 1984.

———. *Callachaca: Style and Status in an Inca Community.* Iowa City: University of Iowa Press, 1987.

———. "Inca Architecture and the Sacred Landscape." In *The Ancient Americas: Art from Sacred Landscapes*, edited by R. F. Townsend, 346–57. Chicago: Art Institute of Chicago, 1992.

———. "The Provinces in the Heartland: Stylistic Innovation and Architectural Variation near Cuzco." In *Provincial Inca: Archaeological and Ethnohistorical Assessment of the Impact of the Inca State*, edited by M. Malpass, 145–76. Iowa City: University of Iowa Press, 1993.

Protzen, J.-P. *Inca Architecture and Construction at Ollantaytambo.* New York: Oxford University Press, 1993.

———. "Inca Architecture." In *The Inca world: The Development of Pre-Columbian Peru, A.D. 1000–1534*, edited by C. Bákula, L. Laurencich Minelli, and M. Vautier, 193–217. Norman: University of Oklahoma Press, 2000.

■ STELLA NAIR

ARITHMETIC

Most of what is known about Inca arithmetic results either from modern study of the Inca accounting device, known as the *quipu,* or from the analysis of mathematical principles incorporated into Inca buildings and other structures. *Quipus* were designed to permit the recording of numerical values in the base-10, place-value numeration system that was characteristic of **Quechua**, the *lingua franca* of state administration in the Inca Empire. Studies of *quipu* records show that the Incas employed a wide range of arithmetical operations, including addition, subtraction, multiplication, and division, as well as the calculation of fractions and ratios. Inca accountants and mathematicians knew the concept of zero and used it in their calculations and recording of statistical data.

While numerical data were recorded on the *quipu,* this device was not used for performing calculations. Rather, colonial era chroniclers' accounts and administrative documents attest that calculations were performed by means of a variety of counting devices, such as stones, maize kernels, or other small objects. Calculations with these devices were carried out on stone, ceramic, or wooden objects called *yupana,* square- or rectangular-shaped slabs containing numerous depressions or compartments within which the

A *yupana*, a device used to tally sums with kernels of maize or small stones, can be seen in the lower left-hand corner in this illustration of a *quipucamayoc* (quipu reader/maker) displaying his *quipu*, or knotted accounting device. Guaman Poma de Ayala, Felipe. *El primer nueva corónica y buen gobierno*. Edited by John V. Murra and Rolena Adorno, 332/360. Mexico City: Siglo Veintiuno, 1980 [1615].

counting devices were moved in the process of calculating. Once the calculations were completed, the resulting values would be knotted into *quipus* for display and transport.

Further Reading

Ascher, M., and R. Ascher. *Mathematics of the Incas: Code of the Quipu*. Mineola, NY: Dover Publications, 1997.

Lee, V. *Design by Numbers: Architectural Order among the Incas*. Wilson, WY: Sixpack Manco Publications, 1996.

Urton, G. *The Social Life of Numbers: A Quechua Ontology of Numbers and Philosophy of Arithmetic*. Austin: University of Texas Press, 1997.

■ GARY URTON

ASTRONOMY

The overwhelming majority of information pertaining to Inca astronomy comes from accounts written by Spaniards in the first few decades following the conquest of the Inca Empire. Due to the almost complete extermination of coastal populations soon after the Spanish conquest, most of our information on this topic pertains to highland beliefs and practices, although scattered data are available for the coast. While some of the accounts from the Inca capital of **Cuzco** report on pillars or other constructions built to incor-

A carved rock surrounded by a curved wall at the Torreón temple, Machu Picchu, Peru. The structure may have served as a celestial observatory. Adriana von Hagen.

porate alignments to, or permitting the sighting of, astronomical phenomena, very little evidence of any such constructions has ever been identified or studied systematically by archaeologists. Therefore, we are left primarily with the Spaniards' accounts, as well as what has been recovered from present-day Quechua-speaking populations, who in a few ethnographic studies retain information pertaining to the sun, moon, and stars that accords strikingly with testimony on astronomical phenomena provided in the early Colonial-era, written testimony.

Inca worship of the Sun (*Inti*) was a central feature of Inca state religion, as the Inca himself was considered to be the Son of the Sun, while his wife, the *Coya* (queen) was considered to be descended from the Moon (*Quilla*) (see **Deities**; **Religion**). While solar and lunar worship were central elements in Inca religion, ritual, and politics, the celestial bodies of the sun and moon themselves were observed closely, especially for calendrical purposes. Chroniclers inform us that a series of pillars for viewing the annual (apparent) north/south movement of the sun was constructed on the hilltops around Cuzco. The accounts of the arrangement and spacing between the sun pillars vary considerably in the various sources, and there have been many attempts to reconstruct the system of solar observations in the capital. Pillars would certainly have marked the two solar extremes, the solstices, but it is unclear from the testimony exactly how the additional pillars were arrayed, or precisely what they were intended to mark. Inca astronomers also closely observed the moon. The two periods of the synodic lunar cycle (the 29.5 days of the lunar phases) and the sidereal lunar cycle (the 27.3 days of the moon's monthly north/south movement) appear to have been integrated with the period of the sun's annual movement into the Inca **calendar**. The calendar regulated ritual activities in the city and around the empire, and it was also important in the timing of the agricultural and herding cycles and activities on which the imperial economy depended.

With the exception of Venus, there is little solid evidence in the chronicles that Inca astronomers closely observed planetary motions. The Incas observed Venus of the morning and the evening and both were referred to as *chaska* (shaggy hair). Given the richness and complexity of Inca astronomical observations, it remains a mystery as to why so little attention was apparently paid to the planets. Perhaps evidence for additional planetary observations will be identified in sources in the future.

There are rich sources of information on Inca observations of the stars and constellations. Two factors affecting stellar observations must be taken into account. First, the Inca Empire lay almost entirely within the southern hemisphere (Cuzco, the capital, lies at a latitude of 13°30'S latitude). In fact, one of our sources, the chronicler **Garcilaso de la Vega**, informs us that the Incas were actually intent on carrying their conquests northward from Cuzco to the place "where the sun sat most comfortably between its extremes." The latter would have defined the equinox, the point equidistant between the extremes of the north and south solstice rise and set points. Because of the southern hemisphere location of the empire, the Incas had a view of the stars in the southern celestial hemisphere, including the south celestial pole, although they would not have been familiar with the north celestial pole, or many of the stars and constellations of far northern latitudes in the northern celestial hemisphere. It is important to note that the south celestial pole is not marked by a pole star, such as the star Polaris, which stands at the north celestial pole. It is perhaps partially because of the absence of a persistent view to a fixed pole star that the Incas appear to have had little interest in the cardinal directions.

The second point to take into account concerning Inca stellar observations is that the identities that they assigned to the stars and constellations were ones that were meaningful to them, in terms of their religious beliefs, mythological traditions, economy, and so forth. That is, we should not expect, nor do we find, that the Incas recognized the constellations that are familiar to northern hemisphere stargazers, which mostly come down to modern Euro–North American populations from Greek and Roman traditions (e.g., Gemini, Sagittarius, Cancer, etc.). Instead, the Inca projected into the heavens the identities of the animals, birds, and other objects of nature and culture that made up their own world. Thus, for instance, they recognized in the cluster of stars known to us as the Pleiades a "storehouse" (*collca*), "pile" (*qotu*), or a sign of "sickness" (*onqoy*). This star group was observed closely for making agricultural prognostications. The V-shaped group of stars we call the Hyades was also referred to as "storehouse." Both the Southern Cross and the Belt of Orion were identified as bridges, or upright stakes (*chacana*). As bridges, these two star groupings were considered to span the Milky Way, which was known as *mayu* (river).

In addition to the star constellations noted above, the Incas also recognized what have been referred to as *yana phuyu* (dark clouds). These are dark spots and streaks composed of clouds of interstellar dust that cut through the bright line of the Milky Way, or Galaxy— that is, the "river" in Inca astronomy. As for the dark cloud constellations, one zigzag, or wavy streak was known as *mach'acuay* (snake); close by was a small dark spot called *hanp'atu* (toad); and near that was another dark spot, at the foot of the Southern Cross, called *yuthu* (partridge, or tinamou). A large series of dark streaks west of the *yuthu* was identified as a llama with its suckling baby stretched out beneath it. The mother llama has a long neck with its eyes in its neck (there is no head). The eyes—Alpha and Beta Centauri—were known as *llamacñawin* (eyes of the llama).

These stars and constellations were observed by astronomers, described in myths recorded during the Colonial era, and were passed down through subsequent generations where many are still recognized by people throughout the Andes today.

Further Reading

Bauer, B. S., and D. S. P. Dearborn. *Astronomy and Empire in the Ancient Andes: The Cultural Origins of Inca Sky Watching.* Austin: University of Texas Press, 1995.

Salomon, F., and J. Urioste. *The Huarochirí Manuscript: A Testament of Ancient and Colonial Andean Religion.* Austin: University of Texas Press, 1991.

Urton, G. *At the Crossroads of the Earth and the Sky: An Andean Cosmology.* Latin American Monographs, no. 55. Austin: University of Texas Press, 1981.

———. "Astronomy and Calendrics on the Coast of Peru." In *Ethnoastronomy and Archaeoastronomy in the American Tropics,* edited by A. F. Aveni and G. Urton, vol. 385, 231–48. New York: Annals of the New York Academy of Sciences, 1982.

Zuidema, R. T. "Catachillay: The Role of the Pleiades and of the Southern Cross and α and β Centauri in the Calendar of the Incas." In *Ethnoastronomy and Archaeoastronomy in the American Tropics,* edited by A. F. Aveni and G. Urton, vol. 385. New York: Annals of the New York Academy of Sciences, 1982.

———. "The Sidereal Lunar Calendar of the Incas." In *Archaeoastronomy in the New World,* edited by A. F. Aveni. Cambridge: Cambridge University Press, 1982.

Zuidema, R. T., and G. Urton. "La constelación de la llama en los Andes peruanos." *Allpanchis Phuturinqa* 9: 59–120, 1976.

■ GARY URTON

AYLLU

This term refers to the basic kinship, social, and ritual groupings in Andean communities from the time of the Incas—if not earlier—down to the present day. The term was used as a general classifier, or label, for groups of people formed in any number of ways. In this sense, *ayllu* can be thought of as a general term for classes or categories of things, such as with the terms *genus*, *species*, and *type*. Thus, the term refers to what we understand as an ethnic group, a kindred, a group of people sharing a common ancestor or an irrigation canal, or groups formed to celebrate festivals or to undertake work projects. *Ayllu* is defined in various historical sources and colonial dictionaries as *band, faction,* or *lineage.* From Colonial records, it appears that *ayllus* took at least two different forms in the Inca Empire.

One form of *ayllu*, typical among commoners, was related to what is termed "vertical archipelagos." While there is some controversy over the makeup of such *ayllus* in pre-Hispanic times, it is generally thought that the members of any given commoner *ayllu* were dispersed across the landscape in multiple scattered settlements—termed *archipelagos*—each one of which gave that segment of the *ayllu* access to resources within its particular ecological zone. As a result of the dispersal of its members, an *ayllu* as a whole would have had access to the wealth of resources across many different ecological zones. Colonial censuses and other administrative documents provide some support for this view,

Although reputedly born in Cuzco to unknown parents, Avila claimed to be of noble Spanish ancestry. Not much is known of his early years, other than that he attended a Jesuit school in Cuzco. In 1592, he entered the University of San Marcos, in Lima, where he earned a doctorate. Shortly thereafter, in 1596, he was ordained, and in 1597 he was assigned as curate in the town of San Damián de Checa, located near the town of Huarochirí, in the central highlands east of Lima.

It was largely Avila's complicated association with a document produced in Huarochirí early in the seventeenth century that distinguishes him as an individual of exceptional importance for Inca studies. He was instrumental in the production of the so-called *Huarochirí Manuscript*, a unique document in the corpus of early Colonial literature known for its graphic, lively, and detailed account of the religious beliefs, practices, and mythology of early Colonial era populations in the highlands east of Lima. Researchers studying this document conclude that the collaboration among indigenous, **Quechua**-speaking informants, at least one of whom was literate, produced the narrative, which was augmented by notes written by Avila. The text is the major Quechua-language document that contains an account of the mythology and religious beliefs of peoples outside the imperial heartland around Cuzco. Additional comments on Avila's activities leading up to, during, and shortly after his involvement in the production of the *Huarochirí Manuscript* will put his motives in their larger context.

Like many curates of the time, Avila seems to have used his post to benefit personally from Native labor, animals, and crops. While one inspection in 1598 praised Avila's pastoral work, a secret inspection carried out in 1600 accused him of abusing his position for personal gain. In 1607, some members of his parish brought a lawsuit against him, accusing him of running illegal businesses, sexually exploiting parishioners, and confiscating their farm animals. Avila spent time in a church prison but before long managed to gain his release. About this time, apparently, he began assembling the *Huarochirí Manuscript*. His knowledge of indigenous religious matters reflected his earlier investigations in San Damián de Checa and surrounding settlements of the continued observance by parishioners of indigenous religious practices and their worship of "evil" and "idolatrous" objects. Aside from rich information on indigenous religious beliefs and practices, the document relates the origin myths of the region's various ethnic groups and *ayllu*s, as well as the epic struggles between ancestral mountain deities and encounters between gods and men in the ancient, pre-Inca past.

Given his subsequent efforts in mounting campaigns to destroy indigenous "idols" in the central highlands, there is every reason to suppose that Avila's motives in participating in the writing of this work were aimed at exposing idolatrous objects and practices that, once brought into the open, could then be rooted out and destroyed. As one commentator has noted:

It [the *Huarochirí Manuscript*] remained his secret weapon in hunting down the three-thousand–plus sacred objects, or huacas, and the mummified ancestors he and his followers destroyed. In his wanderings, **Felipe Guaman Poma de Ayala** met some of Avila's victims and, notwithstanding his own dislike of Andean deities, cursed Avila's mercilessness and his greed: "Oh what a fine doctor, where is your soul? What serpent is eating you?" (Salomon 2008)

Avila not only directed such anti-idolatry campaigns himself, but he also produced a number of other texts intended for others who were involved in the relentless Colonial-era struggles by the Catholic priesthood to combat indigenous religious beliefs and practices.

Further Reading

Durston, Alan. *Pastoral Quechua: The History of Christian Translation in Colonial Peru, 1550–1650*. Notre Dame, IN: University of Notre Dame Press, 2007.

Duviols, Pierre. "Estudio bibliográfico." In *Dioses y hombres de Huarochirí, narración quechua recogida por Francisco de Avila*. Edited by José María Arguedas and Pierre Duviols, 218–66. Lima: Museo Nacional de Historia, Instituto de Estudios Peruanos, 1966 [1598?].

Hampe Martínez, Teodoro. *Cultura barroca y extirpación de idolatrías: La biblioteca de Francisco de Avila, 1648*. Cuadernos para la Historia de la Evangelización en América Latina, no. 18. Cuzco: Centro de Estudios Regionales Andinos "Bartolomé de las Casas," 1996.

Salomon, Frank. "Avila, Francisco de (ca. 1573–1647)." In *Guide to Documentary Sources for Andean Studies, 1530–1900*, edited by Joanne Pillsbury, vol. 2, 58–64. Norman: University of Oklahoma Press, 2008.

Salomon, Frank, and George L. Urioste, eds. and trans. *The Huarochirí Manuscript: A Testament of Ancient and Colonial Andean Religion*. Austin: University of Texas Press, 1991 [1598–1608].

Spalding, Karen. *Huarochirí: An Andean Society under Inca and Spanish Rule*. Stanford, CA: Stanford University Press, 1984.

■ GARY URTON

suggesting that in many cases, the members of any one *ayllu* were distributed in settlements from the Pacific coastal lowlands up to the high Andes and down into the tropical forest. This mode of distributing *ayllu* members across different ecological zones and of sharing all the varied resources available to the members of the *ayllu* is often given as the explanation for why markets did not exist in the Andes before Spanish contact—that is, goods were shared among all the members of each *ayllu*, rather than depending on the institution of the market to distribute goods.

While Colonial documentation is not sufficient to allow us to produce an inventory of all such commoner *ayllus* that existed in Inca times, there were probably hundreds, if not several thousand, *ayllus* spread across the Andes, within the territory of Tahuantinsuyu. This pattern of *ayllu* formation among the vast body of commoners in the empire had political implications as well. That is, as a consequence of the dispersal of different *ayllus* across the countryside, there were often members belonging to many different

Members of an *ayllu*, or kinship group, work together to thatch a roof in Ayaviri, Puno, southern Peru. Gabino Quispecondori. TAFOS Photographic Archive/PUCP, Lima, Peru.

ayllus within any given locale. These local groupings of multiple *ayllus* were commonly organized in dual moiety arrangements, with several *ayllus* in each moiety. The headmen (*curacas*) of the several *ayllus* within a given locale were related to each other in a hierarchical manner, with certain *ayllus* and their *curacas* being superior to others.

Ayllu also appears in a different form, particularly as it related to the social and political organization of the city of Cuzco. That is, 10 of the social groups that made up the population of the capital city were referred to as *ayllus*. These groups were understood by some Colonial informants to have been made up of the descendants of several different groups of people who lived in or near Pacariqtambo, the mythical place of origin of the first Inca king, Manco Capac (see **Myths, Origin**). These groups of people accompanied the Inca ancestors to Cuzco at the beginning of time. Within the fully evolved political system in the Inca capital, the *ayllus* of Cuzco were attached to certain of the **ceques** of the city; as such, the members of the *ayllus* of Cuzco were related but subordinate to the 10 groups in the city who were descended from Inca royalty. The latter, descendants of Inca nobility, made up the 10 *panacas* of Cuzco's *ceque* system. It should be noted, however, in what is a particularly confusing feature of our Colonial accounts of the *ceque* system, that a few of the "royal ayllus" (that is, the **panacas**) were actually referred to as *ayllus*. The confusion in nomenclature is probably a consequence of the meager range and quantity of information that has come down to us concerning this important institution in the life of the capital city.

Ayllus continued to be one of the principal units of social organization in Andean communities through the Colonial period, and in some cases villages today are still organized into *ayllus*. Today, the purpose of these groups is realized in terms of local landholding patterns, communal labor organization, and the sponsorship of festivals and other ritual activities.

Further Reading

Murra, John V. "El control vertical de un máximo de pisos ecológicos en la economía de las sociedades andinas." In *Formaciones económicas y políticas del mundo andino*, 59–116. Lima: Instituto de Estudios Peruanos, 1975.

Rowe, John H. "Inca Culture at the Time of Spanish Conquest." In *Handbook of South American Indians*, edited by Julian Steward, vol. 2, *The Andean Civilizations*, 183–330. Washington, DC: Smithsonian Institution, Bureau of American Ethnology, 1946.

Salomon, Frank. "Introductory Essay: The Huarochirí Manuscript." In *The Huarochirí Manuscript*. Translation, annotations, and transcription by Frank Salomon and George L. Urioste, 1–38. Austin: University of Texas Press, 1991.

Urton, Gary. *The History of a Myth: Pacariqtambo and the Origin of the Inkas*. Austin: University of Texas Press, 1990.

Zuidema, R. Tom. *The Ceque System of Cuzco: The Social Organization of the Capital of the Inca*. Leiden, Netherlands: E. J. Brill, 1964.

■ GARY URTON

AYMARA

Aymara is a linguistic family (also called *jaqi* or *aru*) that now consists of only two languages: central Aymara, which survives in the highlands of Lima, and *altiplano* Aymara, which is spoken in Peru, Bolivia, and Chile. Other forms of Aymara that joined those two extremes throughout the southern Peruvian highlands were displaced by **Quechua** even before the time of the Inca Empire. Recent studies indicate that one form, which was spoken around Cuzco, may have been the principal language of the Incas in the mythical period. Like Quechua, Aymara is an agglutinative language, in which words are formed using a very elaborate system of suffixes. As noted in the entry on Quechua, the historical relationship between Aymara and Quechua is not genetic, but one of contact and convergence, in which the former reshaped the latter.

As with Quechua, the Aymara language does not have a name of its own. The Spaniards coined the term in the second half of the sixteenth century, and like Quechua, although more indirectly, it preserves the name of an ethnic group—the Aymaray—from one of the provinces west of Cuzco, which was subjugated by the Incas after their victory over the Chancas. Etymologically, the name comes from *ayma-ra-wi,* meaning a "place with many communally owned farms." As with Quechua, however, there are many similar place names in Peru, and this one refers to the historical *aymarays* at the time of the origin of the Inca Empire. In Spanish Colonial times, the name given to the language was *haqi-aru* (language of the people, i.e., the "Indians"). That term persists, in a contracted form, in *Jacaru,* the local name of one of the surviving forms of central Aymara.

According to historiographic tradition, the language may have originated in what is now the Peruvian and Bolivian *altiplano*, spreading outside that area as a result of the Inca colonization policy, especially their system of *mitmacuna* (see **Labor Service**). That would mean, for example, that the central Aymara dialects might be the surviving traces of the language of *altiplano* colonists who were relocated in the region. Academic experts from fields other than linguistics have traditionally held not only that Aymara originated in the *altiplano*, but that it was spoken by the people who founded the Tiahuanaco civilization near Lake Titicaca. Historical linguistics and a reexamination of some of the earliest Colonial sources from the region, which began in the Andean area in the second half of the twentieth century, however, have discredited that view (see **Puquina**). Experts now agree that Aymara arose outside the *altiplano*, which explains not only the survival of central Aymara, but also the rich tapestry of place names that underlies Quechua and that points to the ancient omnipresence of the Aymara language in the central Andes.

It is precisely the legacy of Aymara place names in Cuzco (in names such as Cuzco itself or Ollantaytambo) that casts doubt on Quechua's Cuzco origins, indicating not only that Aymara existed in that area, but also that it could have been the Incas' mother tongue. That argument became more decisive in the last decades of the twentieth century, when Andean historians found the missing chapters (more than half) of the chronicle of **Juan de Betanzos**. As noted in the entry on Quechua, the first of the newly discovered chapters of that account (chapter 19) included a short text, later known as the "song of Pachacuti Inca Yupanqui," which, according to tradition, was composed on that Inca leader's orders, and which is written not in Quechua, as would be expected, but in Aymara. This indicates that Aymara was both the mother tongue and the principal language of the conquering Inca and his forebears in what became the Inca Empire.

The birthplace of the Aymara language, as well as the way in which it spread throughout the *altiplano*, remains the subject of debate. The most widely accepted hypothesis is that it arose on the central and southern coast of Peru (south of Lima) and expanded, in various stages, toward the southeast, arriving first in Cuzco and later in the *altiplano* before the time of the Inca Empire. Experts disagree, however, about who spread the language and over what time frame.

Further Reading

Adelaar, Willem, and Pieter Muysken. "The Aymaran Language Family." In *The Languages of the Andes*, Willem Adelaar with Pieter Muysken, 259–319. Cambridge: Cambridge University Press, 2004.

Briggs, Lucy. *El idioma aymara: Variantes regionales y sociales*. La Paz: ILCA, 1993.

Cerrón-Palomino, Rodolfo. *Lingüística aimara*. Cuzco: Bartolomé de Las Casas, 2000.

———. "Aimara." In *Voces del Ande*, edited by Rodolfo Cerrón-Palomino, 19–32. Lima: Fondo Editorial de la Pontificia Universidad Católica del Perú, 2008.

———. *Quechumara: Estructuras paralelas del quechua y del aimara*. La Paz: Plural Ediciones, 2008.

Hardman, Martha, et al. *Aymara: Compendio de estructura fonológica y gramatical*. La Paz: Gramma Impresión, 1988.

■ RODOLFO CERRÓN-PALOMINO
(TRANSLATED BY BARBARA FRASER)

BATTLES, RITUAL

While all-out **warfare** seems to have been a fact of life in pre-Inca and Inca times through-out the Andes, there were also occasions when it was deemed appropriate for groups to engage in what are commonly referred to as ritual battles. The term used for such affairs in Colonial sources is *tinkuy*, which may be glossed as "coming together," such as the con-fluences of rivers, although it usually connotes unions that occur in the form of clashes or violent encounters. *Tinkuys* are normally thought to lead to a synthesis—the integration, or mixing of substances or essences of the converging entities. Such encounters might include, for example, two armies meeting in battle (and thereby mixing their blood), two rivers meeting and joining their waters, or a man and a woman coming together in intimate, sexual contact, leading to the mixing of the essences of the two individuals in reproduction. Thus, *tinkuy* referred not only to two entities coming together but, in the act of doing so, of creating a unity of the beings or essences of the two parties so joined.

A man prepares to hurl his sling during a ritual battle in the province of Canas, Cuzco, Peru. Daniel Huillca. TAFOS Photographic Archive/PUCP, Lima, Peru.

Ritual battles occurred on various occasions in Cuzco. For instance, during the month following the initiation of noble youths, which took place at the time of the December solstice, the newly initiated young men met on the plaza in the center of Cuzco. There, dividing themselves into the two social-political groups of *hanan* (upper) and *hurin* (lower) Cuzco, they set about pelting each other with a hard cactus fruit, called *tunas*, or *pitahayas*. The conflict often intensified, and the boys commonly came to blows, testing their strength against their opponents. These formalized clashes of recent initiates, noted the chronicler **Bernabé Cobo**, served to demonstrate who was the strongest and bravest. It is also reported in the chronicles that sham battles were staged to prepare the young men for warfare.

Another chronicler, Fernando de Montesinos, described a most unusual form of what could be described as a "ritual battle." He stated that, if the king wanted to learn the outcome of some battle that was going on at a distance, a priest placed maize kernels in a ceramic container. The grains of corn were named after the captains engaged in the distant battle. The chronicler continues: "The grains themselves then had a great fight, some against others, until the conquered were driven out of the vessel, and then the wizard [priest] told the outcome [of the actual battle] as if he had seen it" (Montesinos 1920 [ca. 1644], see **Divination**).

As for the antiquity of ritual battles, the practice may go back into the pre-Inca past, perhaps as early as the Initial Period (see **Chronology, Pre-Inca**). *Tinkuys* continued through the Colonial period, and in some communities they still occur today. These contemporary battles primarily pit the men of one community against those of a neighboring community, although cases have been reported of ritual battles between *hanan* and *hurin* segments of communities. Present-day participants assert that the objective is at least to draw blood (if not to kill an opponent, which does occur occasionally). The spilled blood is said to fertilize the earth and to be a good omen for the fertility of crops and herds.

Further Reading

Cobo, Bernabé. *Inca Religion and Customs.* Translated and edited by Roland Hamilton. Austin: University of Texas Press, 1990 [1653].

D'Altroy, Terence N. *The Incas.* 2nd ed. New York: John Wiley & Sons, 2014.

Montesinos, Fernando de. *Memorias antiguas historiales del Perú.* Translated and edited by Philip Ainsworth Means. London: Hakluyt Society, 1920 [ca. 1644].

Platt, Tristan. "Mirrors and Maize: The Concept of *yanantin* among the Macha of Bolivia." In *Anthropological History of Andean Polities*, edited by John V. Murra, Nathan Wachtel, and Jacques Revel, 228–59. Cambridge: Cambridge University Press, 1986.

Urton, Gary. "Moieties and Ceremonialism in the Andes: The Ritual Battles of the Carnival Season in Southern Peru." In *El Mundo Ceremonial Andino*, edited by Luis Millones and Yoshio Onuki. Senri Ethnological Studies, no. 37, 117–42. Lima: Editorial Horizonte, 1993.

Zuidema, R. Tom. "Batallas rituals en el Cuzco colonial." In *Cultures et sociétés. Andes et Meso-Amérique: Mélanges en hommage à Pierre Duviols*, vol. 2, 811–33. Aix-en-Provence: L'Université de Provence, 1991.

■ GARY URTON

Born in Marca di Ancona, Italy, in 1557, Bertonio entered the Jesuit order in 1574 and was ordained as a priest upon his arrival in Lima, in 1581. Bertonio was soon assigned to a parish in Juli, on the south shore of Lake Titicaca, where he lived for some 30 years, from 1585 to 1619. During that period, he also spent some time (1599–1603) in the great mining center of Potosí, in present-day central Bolivia. Juli was in the heart of Lupaca territory, one of the great confederations of Aymara-speaking peoples of the Lake Titicaca region. Bertonio learned the Lupaca dialect of **Aymara** in Juli, which was at that time the principal Jesuit center for the study of indigenous languages. He also learned other dialects of Aymara during his time in Potosí, where he served as priest and confessor to indigenous *mit'a* laborers sent from southern Peru and Bolivia to work in the mines as a part of their tribute obligation. Suffering from poor health, Bertonio moved from Juli down to Arequipa in 1619, and finally to Lima, where he died, in 1625.

Bertonio was the author of several works on the Aymara language. An understanding of Aymara grammar and vocabulary is important to students of Inca civilization and culture because most linguists today accept that Aymara was the principal language spoken by the Incas when they settled in the Cuzco region. Bertonio wrote his works on the Aymara language with the assistance of a young Aymara speaker from Juli, Martín de Santa Cruz. Bertonio's first publication was a pair of grammars, one short, the other longer; both are dated to 1603. In 1612, Bertonio published an Aymara translation of the life of Christ, a book of sermons (in Aymara), and what is considered today his most important contribution to Aymara studies, the *Vocabulario de la lengua Aymara* (Vocabulary of the Aymara Language). The manuscript of this great Aymara dictionary is divided into two parts: 474 pages of Spanish-Aymara, and 399 pages of Aymara-Spanish. The *Vocabulario* is a rich mine of linguistic and ethnographic information, giving us insights into the cultural and religious beliefs and practices of Aymara-speaking peoples of the southern Andes at the beginning of the seventeenth century. The work therefore has profound implications for the study of the Incas, who were the ancestors of those Colonial populations.

Further Reading

Albó, Xavier, "Ludovico Bertonio (1557–1619): Fuente única al mundo aymara temprano." *Revista Andina* (Cuzco) 2, no. 1: 223–64. Republication of the introduction to the 1984 edition of the *Vocabulario*.

———. "Bertonio, Ludovico (1557–1625)." In *Guide to Documentary Sources for Andean Studies, 1530–1900*, edited by Joanne Pillsbury, vol. 2, 81–83. Norman: University of Oklahoma Press, 2008.

Bertonio, Ludovico. *Vocabulario de la lengua aymara*. Documentos Históricos, no. 1. Serie Fuentes Primarias, no. 2. Travaux de l'Institut Français d'Études Andines, no. 26. Cochabamba, Bolivia: Centro de Estudios de la Realidad Económica y Social, Ediciones Ceres, 1984 [1612].

———. *Transcripción del vocabulario de la lengua aymara*. Instituto de Lenguas y Literaturas Andinas-Amazónicas (ILLA-A). 2011. http://www.illa-a.org/cd/diccionarios/LudovicoBertonioMuchosCambios.pdf.

■ GARY URTON

It is not known when or where in Spain Juan de Betanzos (also known as Juan Diez de Betanzos) was born, but by the 1540s he was in Peru fighting with Pizarro loyalists in the civil war sparked by Gonzalo Pizarro's rebellion of 1544–1548. After his capture by Royalist troops, he joined their side and shortly after that received an *encomienda* (the grant of oversight of a group of Native peoples to a Spaniard responsible for their welfare and religious conversion in exchange for the right to collect tribute from them) in the northern Titicaca basin. He later became a *vecino*, or citizen of **Cuzco**, where, well regarded as a translator and interpreter of **Quechua**, he wrote a catechism, since lost. In 1544, three years after the murder of Francisco Pizarro in Lima, Betanzos married Pizarro's mistress, a Cuzco noblewoman, Cusirimay Ocllo, known by her baptismal name of Angelina Yupanqui. She had been married to the Inca ruler Atahualpa before becoming Francisco Pizarro's mistress and bearing him two children.

In 1551 the Viceroy Antonio de Mendoza commissioned Betanzos to write *Suma y Narración de los Incas*, or "Narrative of the Incas," a treatise on the Incas. In 1557, the year Betanzos's account ends rather abruptly, he was appointed by Mendoza's successor, the Viceroy Andrés Hurtado de Mendoza, Marquis of Cañete, to act as an interpreter in negotiations with the neo-Inca ruler Sayri Túpac to settle in the Urubamba valley and leave Vilcabamba, where his father, Manco Inca, had created a rump state (see **Vilcabamba**). Betanzos spent the rest of his life in Cuzco, where he died in 1576.

Betanzos's narrative remained unpublished until the nineteenth century, but it was used by **Antonio de la Calancha** and cited by William Prescott in his history of the conquest of Peru, published in 1847. An incomplete manuscript dated 1574 is found in the library of the Real Monasterio de San Lorenzo in El Escorial, Spain, while a more complete version, possibly a sixteenth-century copy, was acquired by the Fundación Bartolomé March in Palma de Mallorca from the library of the Duke of Medinaceli. This so-called Palma manuscript is the basis for a Spanish edition published in 1987 and an English version published in 1996.

The first 18 chapters are devoted to Inca origins and biographies of Inca rulers spanning 12 generations, with an emphasis on Pachacuti. It ends with the reign of Huayna Capac, the last independent Inca ruler. The second part covers the civil war between the brothers Atahualpa and Huascar; the encounter between Atahualpa and Francisco Pizarro in **Cajamarca**; covers the relations between Manco Inca (Huayna Capac's son who was crowned puppet ruler by the Spaniards) and Pizarro in Cuzco, as well as Manco Inca's uprising; and briefly touches on Vilcabamba and negotiations with Sayri Túpac, in which Betanzos took part.

Several scholars have commented on the colloquial style of Betanzos's chronicle, suggesting that many passages are literal translations from the accounts of his Quechua-speaking informants, especially his wife Cusirimay Ocllo and her kin, members of Capac Ayllu, the **panaca**, or royal lineage, of Topa Inca, Pachacuti's son. Betanzos is especially laudatory about Pachacuti, attributing many innovations in Inca statecraft, as well as the rebuilding of Cuzco, to this legendary ruler.

The style of Betanzos's chronicle evokes Inca oral tradition and even emulates, in some passages, the rhythms of Quechua oral narrative. Unlike other works penned by Spaniards, *Narrative of the Incas* often portrays an Inca point of view and has an eyewitness tenor to it, with firsthand reports of Atahualpa's earlier exploits and later imprisonment by the Spaniards in Cajamarca—no doubt the voice of Cusirimay Ocllo—and Manco Inca's siege of Cuzco in 1536.

Further Reading

Betanzos, Juan de. *Suma y Narración de los Incas*. Edited by María del Carmen Martín Rubio. Madrid: Ediciones Atlas, 1987.

———. *Narrative of the Incas*. Translated and edited by Roland Hamilton and Dana Buchanan. Austin: University of Texas Press, 1996 [1551–1557].

Mannheim, Bruce. "Diez de Betanzos, Juan (?–1576)." In *Guide to Documentary Sources for Andean Studies, 1530–1900*. Edited by Joanne Pillsbury, vol. 2, 186–90. Norman: University of Oklahoma Press, 2008.

■ ADRIANA VON HAGEN

BRIDGES

Bridges formed a vital part of the Inca **road** system, playing a strategic role in Inca expansion and control of territories once isolated by natural barriers. Although the Incas never invented the arch, this did not prevent them from constructing sophisticated bridges, including suspension bridges made of spun and braided grass rope that rank among the ancient world's greatest technological feats. Some of these spanned gorges as wide as 45 meters (148 feet) that terrified even the most hardened travelers, because they sagged in the middle and bounced and swayed during the crossing, "looking wonderfully frail and gossamer like," in the words of a nineteenth-century traveler.

In Inca times, *chacacamayocs*, or bridge masters, oversaw key bridges that served as control points, where they charged tolls on the goods being carried. Work groups in *mit'a* or corvée labor, usually formed by villagers living nearby, maintained the bridges, especially the suspension bridges whose rope cables had to be replaced at least once a year.

Less awe-inspiring methods of crossing rivers included bridges that used natural boulders in the river as supports for shorter-span suspension bridges, such as the one that crossed the Urubamba River near the town of Ollantaytambo in the department of Cuzco, as well as cantilevered bridges of stone such as the one still in use in the city of Cuzco in the nineteenth century and illustrated by the travel writer E. George Squier. These bridges had stone abutments and cantilevered stone or wooden superstructures of logs that could span up to 15 meters (about 50 feet). *Oroyas*—still in use today—were composed of baskets suspended from a rope cable (modern ones use steel cables) attached to either bank along which people hauled themselves across the river. On wide rivers with low banks, people were ferried across in boats or rafts, while on slow-moving rivers

As the offspring of Protestant missionaries in Hawaii, Hiram Bingham defied family expectations by becoming one of the pioneers of Inca archaeology. His education at Yale and Harvard focused on nineteenth-century Latin American political and economic conditions, and he was appointed as Yale's first professor specializing in Latin American history. He achieved lasting fame, however, through his early archaeological investigations of three major Inca sites: **Machu Picchu**, Vitcos, and Espiritu Pampa (see **Vilcabamba**).

Inspired by a 1909 visit to Choquequirau, an Inca settlement perched high above the Apurimac River west of Cuzco, Bingham organized an expedition to the forested region of Cuzco in search of the last capital of the rebellious neo-Inca state, in Vilcabamba. In July 1911, Bingham and his team descended the Urubamba River following leads from informants in Cuzco. Although local farmers were aware of Machu Picchu and the other Inca sites encountered by Bingham, it was the publication—especially an entire issue of *National Geographic* devoted to Machu Picchu—that made Machu Picchu famous. In 1912, Bingham returned to follow up on his "scientific discovery" by clearing and mapping the well-preserved **royal estate**, and excavating many of its buildings and burials. Bingham returned to the area again in 1914–1915 to study the road system and other neighboring settlements, but an adequate explanation of Machu Picchu's function continued to elude him.

Bingham achieved fame as a result of his publications in *Harper's* and *National Geographic*, and he used this renown to begin a political career that eventually led to his election as Connecticut's governor and senator. While his archaeological career lasted under a decade, Bingham published several influential works on the Incas, including one of the first studies of Inca ceramics and a monograph on the 1912 Machu Picchu excavations. His pioneering work at Machu Picchu dramatically demonstrated the need to complement historical research with archaeological fieldwork.

Further Reading

Bingham, Alfred. *Portrait of an Explorer: Hiram Bingham, Discoverer of Machu Picchu*. Ames: Iowa State University Press, 1989.

Bingham, Hiram. "The Discovery of Machu Picchu." *Harper's Monthly Magazine* 127:709–19, 1913.

———. "In the Wonderland of Peru." *National Geographic Magazine* 24, no. 4: 387–573, 1913.

———. "Types of Machu Picchu Pottery." *American Anthropologist* 17:257–71, 1915.

———. *Inca Land: Explorations in the Highlands of Peru*. 2nd ed. Boston: Houghton Mifflin, 1922.

———. *Machu Picchu, a Citadel of the Incas*. New Haven, CT: Yale University Press, 1930.

■ RICHARD L. BURGER

The suspension bridge of Queshuachaca near Quehue, south of Cuzco, is made of braided grass rope and spans a 36-meter-wide (120-foot-wide) gorge over the Apurimac River. It is rebuilt every year, using ancient bridge-building technology. Adriana von Hagen.

with low embankments, such as the one that drains Lake Titicaca, people crossed on a pontoon or floating bridge, made of bundles of reeds lashed together and tied to ropes connected to either bank.

The most famed bridge of all, however, was the suspension bridge spanning the gorge of the Apurimac River, west of Cuzco on the **Chinchaysuyu** road. Located near the **oracle** and shrine of Marcahuasi, it achieved fame and literary renown in Thornton Wilder's novel, *The Bridge of San Luis Rey* (later made into a movie), for the beauty of its setting and the fear it struck in the hearts of travelers. The approach is an extremely steep, zigzagging trail, while on the opposite bank the trail passed through a tunnel carved into the living rock and pierced by light shafts. The bridge had stone platforms on either side of the river, where the cables were attached, and stone towers to support the side cables. When Squier crossed the bridge in 1865 (it was abandoned two decades later), he noted that it measured 45 meters (148 feet) in length and at its lowest point loomed 35 meters (115 feet) above the thundering river (Apurimac means "the lord who speaks," alluding to the roar of the river). He observed five, 10-centimeter-thick (4-inch-thick), braided cables of *cabuya* (a natural fiber derived from the leaves of the fique plant, *Furcraea andina*) and a floor made of small sticks and canes fastened with rawhide. The five braided cables were attached to abutments on either side of the gorge.

An earlier eyewitness, **Garcilaso de la Vega**, writing in the late sixteenth century, noted that the materials used in the braided cables depended on local availability—*cabuya*, as in the case of the Apurimac bridge, or *queshua*, a species of grass that grows in the *puna* (above 3,500 meters). Other fibers were also employed. (In fact, a bridge on the upper Apurimac known as Queshuachaca, or bridge of *queshua*, is still rebuilt every year by villagers using technology and principles of labor organization similar to those of their Inca forebears). The single strands of rope, remarked Garcilaso, were braided into a rope and three of these larger ropes, in turn, braided in an even larger rope, and so on, "in this way they increase and thicken the ropes until they are as thick as a man's body or thicker." They swam the cables across the river or hauled them across on rafts. Then the ropes were heaved by a "great crowd of Indians." Once all five ropes were across the chasm, they mounted two large cables—which supported the walkway—over the tops of the stone towers, and attached them through holes carved into the natural rock behind the platform, or around stone beams or anchors.

Further Reading

Bauer, Brian S. "Suspension Bridges of the Inca Empire." In *Andean Archaeology III: North and South*, edited by William H. Isbell and Helaine Silverman, 468–93. New York: Springer, 2006.
Hyslop, John. *The Inka Road System*. New York: Academic Press, 1984.
Squier, E. George. *Peru: Incidents of Travel and Exploration in the Land of the Incas*. New York: Harper, 1877.

■ ADRIANA VON HAGEN

C

CAJAMARCA

In 1532, Cajamarca, a major ceremonial center in the northern Andes, was chosen by Atahualpa and his advisors as the site to meet the invading band of Christians led by Francisco Pizarro. Here, the drama of the initial encounter between Pizarro, the representative of the Spanish crown, and Atahualpa, the de facto leader of the Andean peoples, unfolded (see **Invasion, Spanish**).

The ceremonial complex centered on a large quadrilateral plaza that measured approximately 400 by 200 meters. Stone buildings surrounded the plaza on three sides. One of these contained an image of a snake (*kassa*), known to have been a god to the pre-Inca people of the area. On the fourth side of the plaza was a wall. On one side of the plaza was a square, stepped, and truncated pyramid, variously described in the primary sources as a castle (*castillo*), fortress (*fortaleza, fuerte, usno* [**ushnu**]), or temple with a staircase up to the top. This was the authority's stage from which the Inca officiated, addressed his followers, and sacrificed to his gods. Spanish chroniclers recount how the Inca ruler prohibited the Spanish leader from using this mount lest he be ascribed the spiritual and administrative authority and role that the native populace would attribute to a person who ascended to its summit.

The Temple of the Sun, dedicated to the paramount god of the Incas, and a large structure (the *acllahuasi*) that housed the "chosen women" devoted to weaving fine textiles and brewing abundant quantities of maize beer (**chicha**) were nearby (see **Acllacuna**). Chroniclers also describe *collcas* or **storehouses** filled with clothing, arms, and foodstuffs. A short distance away were the hot springs or baths of Cónoj, where Pizarro's emissaries first located Atahualpa and his attendants.

Further Reading

Polo, José Toribio. "Un convento franciscano." *Revista histórica* (Lima) 1:466–85, 1906.
Silva Santisteban, Fernando, et al. *Historia de Cajamarca*. Cajamarca: Instituto Nacional de Cultura, 1985.
Urteaga, Horacio. *Cajamarca: Apuntes para su historia*. Cuzco: Edit. Garcilaso, 1975.
Urteaga, Horacio. *El fin de un imperio*. Lima: Librería e Imprenta Gil, S. A., 1933.

■ SUSAN ELIZABETH RAMÍREZ

CABELLO VALBOA, MIGUEL

Born in Archidona, Málaga, Spain, sometime between 1530 and 1535, Cabello Valboa (also spelled Balboa or Cabello de Balboa), fought in France and Flanders before making his way to the New World in 1566, settling first in Bogota and later in Quito, where he was ordained a priest, in 1571. He remained in Ecuador for several years before traveling south to Peru in 1580, where he received a parish in Ica, on the south coast of Peru. He later journeyed to Bolivia where, in 1594–1595, he took part in an expedition to the land of the Chunchos, peoples who lived on the forested eastern slopes of the Andes. Cabello Valboa wrote an account of that venture in 1602–1603. Details of his later life are rather sketchy, and it is not known if he died in Lima in 1606, or in Bolivia at a parish near La Paz about that same time.

Cabello Valboa began writing his chronicle, *Miscélanea Antártica*, in Quito in 1576 and finished it in Ica in 1586. This work is essentially a history of the Native peoples of the Andes from biblical times to the arrival of the Spaniards, peppered with erudite references to classical authors. What set Cabello Valboa apart from his contemporary chroniclers, however, is his knowledge of Quito and the lives of the Incas in the northernmost reaches of Tahuantinsuyu. He also used local informants to gather the myths and traditions of the north coast of Peru, in particular an origin myth of the Chimú people (see **Chronology, Pre-Inca**). His account of the Inca rulers and the spans of their reigns, which he claimed were based on *quipu* accounts, begins in AD 945 and assigns incredibly long reigns to rulers before the time of the king Pachacuti. His suggested dates for the reigns of Pachacuti's successors, Topa Inca Yupanqui, Huayna Capac, and Atahualpa, however, are more plausible, and these dates form the basis for one of the more widely accepted chronologies of the Inca kings, that proposed by the noted Inca scholar, **John H. Rowe** (see **Chronology, Inca**).

Further Reading

Cabello Valboa, Miguel. *Miscelánea Antártica. Una historia del Perú antiguo*. Lima: Universidad Nacional Mayor de San Marcos, Facultad de Letras, Instituto de Etnología, 1951 [1586].

Ñúnez-Carvallo, Sandro Patrucco. "Cabello Valboa, Miguel (ca. 1530–1606)." In *Guide to Documentary Sources for Andean Studies, 1530–1900*, edited by Joanne Pillsbury, vol. 1, 91–94. Norman: University of Oklahoma Press, 2008.

■ ADRIANA VON HAGEN

CALENDAR, RITUAL

Inca culture was best described by the early Spanish chroniclers who were able to consult the pre-Spanish memories of local experts from **Cuzco**, the capital of the Inca Empire. Although they provided essential information for reconstructing the Inca calendar system, they limited themselves to reporting a yearly calendar of months similar to the Western calendar. Detailed studies, however, have shown that the Incas developed different ways to register solar, lunar, and stellar movements and their calendrical applications. Most

CALANCHA, ANTONIO DE LA

Born in Chuquisaca (Sucre), Bolivia, in 1584, Calancha entered the order of St. Augustine in Chuquisaca before moving to Lima, where he studied at the Augustinian college of San Ildefonso, and later read theology at the University of San Marcos. He played an important role in the Augustinian hierarchy in Peru, serving as rector of the college of San Ildefonso and prior of Augustinian convents in Trujillo and Lima, where he died in 1654.

Calancha's most important work, the *Córonica moralizada del Orden de S. Agustín en el Perú* (The Moralized Chronicle of the Order of St. Augustine in Peru), the first volume of which appeared in 1638 and the second in 1653, is a history of the Augustinians in Peru. Calancha believed that his order had been preordained to convert the Incas to Christianity. Written in an erudite yet ponderous style, Calancha interweaves information on the Incas, as well as the religion and myths of the Native peoples of Peru and Bolivia, with the evangelizing efforts of Augustinian friars, many of whom were dedicated to stamping out native religion and destroying the **huacas**. For his account of the peoples of Copacabana and the nearby Inca sanctuary of the **Island of the Sun**, he relied, in part, on the writings of fellow Augustinian Alonso Ramos Gavilán.

Calancha's chronicle is unusual for its descriptions of the Augustinian parish at the pilgrimage center of **Pachacamac**, on the central coast of Peru, and the role of the Augustinians in early attempts at evangelizing the exiled Inca court, and its ruler, **Titu Cusi**, in the tropical forest refuge of **Vilcabamba**. He also provides us with one of our most detailed accounts of the techniques of recording information in the **quipus**, the Inca knotted-string recording devices.

Further Reading

Calancha, Antonio de la. *Crónica Moralizada*. Transcription by Ignacio Prado Pastor. 6 volumes. Crónicas del Perú, nos. 4–9. Lima: Universidad Nacional Mayor de San Marcos, 1974–1982 [1653].

MacCormack, Sabine. "Calancha, Antonio de la (1584–1654)." In *Guide to Documentary Sources for Andean Studies, 1530–1900*, edited by Joanne Pillsbury, vol. 2, 95–101. Norman: University of Oklahoma Press, 2008.

■ ADRIANA VON HAGEN

importantly, the Incas integrated the calendar with their social, political, and ritual systems, as well as with seasonal changes, weather observations, and practices in agriculture, irrigation, herding, and stone quarrying. There have also been studies of Inca **quipus**, demonstrating the incorporation of calendar counts in the knotted-cord records.

Of central importance in shaping the Inca calendar were a number of astronomical observations (see **Astronomy**). These included: sunrise during the December solstice; sunset during the June solstice; the sunrises of the two passages of the sun through the zenith at noon; and the two sunsets of the anti-zenith passages of the sun (in the opposite direction from the zenith sunrise point). Inca astronomers were also concerned with observing the yearly movements of the Pleiades constellation, which they termed the "mother" of all the stars. In addition to watching this constellation for weather predictions, they observed the constellation from its heliacal rising at dawn in early June through its heliacal setting at dusk in early April. This pair of observations stood behind the 328-day count of what will be described below as the *ceque* calendar. The Incas also observed the Southern Cross and adjacent stars for calendrical purposes.

Politically, Cuzco was divided into four parts. In descending hierarchical order, the four sectors were known as: **Chinchaysuyu** (I) to the northwest, **Collasuyu** (II) to the southeast, **Antisuyu** (III) to the northeast, and **Cuntisuyu** (IV) to the southwest. *Suyus* I and III belonged to the upper, northern (*hanan*) half of Cuzco and the empire; *suyus* II and IV belonged to the lower, southern (*hurin*) half. The **ceque** system, which was organized within the four *suyus*, can be said to have constituted the framework for the ritual calendar in Cuzco. Within each *suyu*, there were nine *ceques*, or imaginary alignments of sacred places (**huacas**), organized in three groups of three (1 a b c – 2 a b c – 3 a b c). The sets of nine *ceques* were ranked in descending hierarchical order, from west to east. In quadrant IV, however, the *ceques* in two groups were subdivided into six *ceques* while the last two *ceques* were counted as one. Thus the four *suyus* had a total of 41 (9 + 9 + 9 + 14) *ceques*. For calendrical reconstruction here, we assume that the number and arrangement of *ceques* in *suyu* IV was ideally like that of the other quadrants.

The *ceque* system arrangement outlined above was the framework for the "ceque calendar" in Cuzco. Located along the 41 *ceque* alignments were 328 sacred places, or *huacas*. The *ceque* calendar followed a count of days (one day/*huaca*) through the sequence of huacas from one *ceque* to the next; the count of days/*huaca*s in the *hurin* half of the system proceeded in an ascending order; those in *hanan* were counted in descending order. To the total of 328 *huacas*/days was added an additional period of 37 days that was not formally counted in the ritual calendar (328 + 37 = 365). The 37-day period began after the day marking the end of the harvest in Cuzco (at the end of April, in the Gregorian calendar) and ended with the first preparations for the next agricultural season, in June. While the Spanish chroniclers all state that there were 12 months in the Inca calendar, they left uncounted the extra (37-day) period. Ten ranked groups of Inca high nobility, the **panacas**, were responsible for one or another of the months of the *ceque* calendar. The *panacas* were in charge of the tasks, rituals, and myths associated with their respective period in the calendar. The *ceque* calendar documented an annual sequence of events that took into account a variety of solar, lunar, and stellar events, otherwise described in their own regular calendars.

One medium of calendar records was in textiles, as seen particularly clearly in those of the Chuquibamba style, which were produced in the southern Inca quarter of Cuntisuyu, in the Pacific coastal highlands. The organization of elements in the Chuquibamba textiles displays clear principles of Inca calendrical organization and appears to document integrated periods of the *ceque* calendar. Calendrical periods are registered in the Chuquibamba textiles by means of rows and columns of small worked squares in groups of days organized in "weekly," "monthly," and "yearly" periods. While the *ceque* calendar in Cuzco at first sight may seem irregular, it combined and integrated periods that are, in fact, convincingly documented by the textile calendars.

One of the Chuquibamba textile calendars contains a solar year calendar count with months of 30 or 31 days woven into a male tunic with squares laid out in vertical rows. In addition, three different kinds of lunar and stellar calendars were woven into female mantles, using horizontal rows. One mantle appears to derive from observing the 27.3-day movement of the moon from a star or constellation through the night sky and back to that star or constellation, a period known as the sidereal lunar cycle. In order to represent the sequence of months based on the sidereal lunar cycle, the calendar specialists appear to have registered units of 82 days organized in rows of $27 + 27 + 28$ (= 82) days. As the textile calendar could register only alternate rows of 27 and 28 days, this annual sidereal lunar calendar organized the rows of squares as follows: 28 27 28 27 28 27 28 27 27 27 27 27 = 328 (= 4×82). A fragment of another female mantle shows part of a calendar that, in its reconstruction, probably included 13 rows of 28 squares each giving a total of 364 (= 13×28) squares, one unit short of the number of days in the solar (or stellar) year. As all rows in this textile calendar round off the number 27.3 to 28, this appears to have been a sidereal calendar. It is interesting to note that there is little evidence in the Inca calendar of the use of the synodic lunar cycle (29.5 days), the base for monthly periods in European calendars.

Further Reading

Urton, Gary. "A Calendrical and Demographic Tomb Text from Northern Peru." *Latin American Antiquity* 12, no. 2: 127–47, 2001.

Zuidema, R. Tom. "The Inca Calendar." In *Native American Astronomy*, edited by Anthony F. Aveni, 219–59. Austin: University of Texas Press, 1977.

———. "A Quipu Calendar from Ica, Peru, with a Comparison to the Ceque Calendar from Cuzco." In *World Archaeoastronomy*, edited by Anthony F. Aveni, 341–51. Cambridge: Cambridge University Press, 1989.

———. *El calendario inca: Tiempo y espacio en la organización ritual del Cuzco: La idea del pasado.* Lima: Fondo Editorial del Congreso del Perú and Fondo Editorial de la Pontificia Universidad Católica del Perú, 2010.

———. "Chuquibamba Textiles and Their Interacting Systems of Notation: The Case of Multiple Exact Calendars." In *Their Way of Writing. Scripts, Signs, and Pictographies in Pre-Columbian America*, edited by Elizabeth Hill Boone and Gary Urton, 251–75. Washington, DC: Dumbarton Oaks Research Library and Collection, 2011.

■ R. TOM ZUIDEMA

CAPAC HUCHA

Glossed as "royal or sacred obligation" and also spelled *capac cocha* or *capacocha*, the ritual event of a *Capac Hucha* was a gift-bearing procession composed of young boys and girls, as well as young women, destined for sacrifice at select shrines, often located on high mountaintops. Before the processions departed **Cuzco**, the participants took part in an elaborate ritual and "blessing" by the ruler, the deities, and the mummies of the deceased

An array of offerings that accompanied one of the *Capac Hucha*
sacrifices on the summit of Llullaillaico in Argentina, including a
necklace fashioned of Spondylus shell, ceramic plates, richly attired
silver and Spondylus male figurines, and Spondylus and silver llama
figurines. Johan Reinhard.

Incas. *Capac Hucha* sacrifices linked Cuzco, the center, with the outermost confines of
the empire, from the snow-clad volcanoes of **Collasuyu** and **Cuntisuyu**, to islands off
the coast of **Chinchaysuyu**.

While there is some confusion in the various chroniclers' accounts as to when, or on
what occasions, *Capac Huchas* took place, there is general consensus that they were used
to mark cyclical and extraordinary events, as well as special occasions that were of great
regional and imperial import. Annual *Capac Huchas* were dedicated to the health, long
life, and prosperity of the ruler and his principal wife, the *Coya*. Unscheduled *Capac Huchas*, on the other hand, marked times of upheaval, such as illness, war, or the death of a
sovereign as well as natural disasters, such as droughts, earthquakes, or volcanic eruptions.
The *Capac Huchas* performed for such extraordinary events were intended to supplicate
and seek the support of the supernatural powers that controlled these circumstances, with
the hope of returning the world to a state of normalcy and balance.

One example of a scheduled *Capac Hucha* coincided with the yearly oracular congress in
Cuzco, when regional ***huacas*** and their mediums came to the capital to foretell the future.
When the Incas conquered a province, they took a portable version of its leading *huaca*
to Cuzco, where they kept it as an honored hostage. Although the *huacas* were eventually
returned to their places of origin after the provinces had accepted Inca rule, once a year the
foremost *huacas* from around Tahuantinsuyu were required to return to Cuzco, accompanied
by their *curacas* (headmen) and priests, to participate in the oracular congresses.

Officials kept track of the oracles' predictions and awarded those whose prophecies
came true with gold and silver, fine cloth, and llamas. Especially "honest" or accurate
oracle-*huacas* and heads of provinces and lineages, such as **Pachacamac** and **Cate-**

quil, received *Capac Huchas*. All the items destined for sacrifice in a *Capac Hucha* were brought into Cuzco's main square; these included: 200 children aged four to ten, gold and silver figurines, fine cloth, seashells, feathers, and llamas of all colors. These persons and objects were processed twice around the square, in front of the Inca ruler, the images of the main deities, and the embalmed mummies of deceased rulers and their priests. The *huacas,* via their priest-mediums*,* were consulted and asked to make predictions on such matters as whether the Inca would have a long life, if enemies would invade Tahuantinsuyu, or if there would be rebellions. Once the predictions had been made, the offerings were distributed to the *huacas* of the city. Then, the provincial priests received their allotted children and offerings for the *Capac Huchas*, and the processions departed for their designated sanctuaries.

Chroniclers' descriptions of the processions noted that they walked in a straight line, over hills and through ravines until they reached their destination. The processions of children, priests, and sometimes even the children's parents, passed through various regions making offerings to sacred places along the route. While the sacrifice itself was undoubtedly the critical moment of the rite, the elaborate processions and multiple ceremonies that preceded it were of greater religious and political significance. Local peoples often joined the processions as they passed. The accompanying local participants from one region were replaced by those at the border with a neighboring region. In this way, the *Capac Huchas* were critical processes in defining political boundaries across the empire.

Capac Huchas are one of the few Inca rituals described by the chroniclers that have been borne out by archaeology. This has occurred most spectacularly at discoveries made in recent years on the mountaintops of Ampato, in Arequipa, Peru, and Llullaillaco, which straddles the border between Chile and Argentina. The sanctuaries on the summits of these towering volcanoes—for example, in the case of Llullaillaco, rising over 6,000 meters (22,000 feet)—are among the highest archaeological sites ever recorded by professional archaeologists anywhere in the world. Archaeologists have learned remarkable details of the rites performed during the *Capac Huchas* on the basis of these discoveries. Unlike the cyclical *Capac Huchas* described above, these human offerings to sacred peaks may have marked unscheduled events, commemorating a critical episode in the life of a ruler. The boys, girls, and young women who were sacrificed on the mountaintop sanctuaries were sumptuously dressed and accompanied by rich offerings, such as human figurines made of gold, silver, and Spondylus shell, as well as figurines of camelids, Spondylus shell, fine cloth, coca, feathers, and miniature sets of ceramics.

For the populations from which the sacrificial victims—children (aged four to ten) and young women (often selected from among the **acllas**, who were around fifteen years old)—were chosen, these young people may have been regarded as messengers to the sacred mountains, which controlled the forces of nature and were often viewed as ancestors. The chronicler **Juan de Betanzos** remarked that the children were often the sons and daughters of *curacas*, local lords, who considered it an honor for their children to be chosen. Apparently, though, not all parents considered it an honor. For instance, the chronicler **Bernabé Cobo** remarked that some parents were pleased to see their daughters seduced at an early age, because virginity was a prerequisite for selection as a *Capac Hucha*.

Further Reading

Besom, Thomas. *Of Summits and Sacrifice: An Ethnohistoric Study of Inka Religious Practices*. Austin: University of Texas Press, 2009.

McEwan, Colin, and Maarten van de Guchte. "Ancestral Time and Sacred Space in Inca State Ritual." In *The Ancient Americas: Art from Sacred Landscapes*, edited by Richard Townsend, 358–71. Chicago: Art Institute of Chicago, 1992.

Reinhard, Johan, and María Constanza Cerutti. *Inca Rituals and Sacred Mountains: A Study of the World's Highest Archaeological Sites*. Los Angeles: Cotsen Institute of Archaeology, 2011.

■ ADRIANA VON HAGEN

CATEQUIL

The temple of Catequil, which served as the seat of an important oracle and shrine associated with a weather god, local origin myths, water, and fertility, lies southwest of the modern town of Huamachuco, in northern Peru. The ruler Huayna Capac was especially fond of Catequil and its prophecies, which probably favored him, and he spread his cult as far as Ecuador. This not only underscores the power of Catequil's oracle and its acceptance by the Incas, but also demonstrates the sanctuary's rise from the status of a regional oracular shrine to one of empire-wide importance. For not only was it said that Catequil could speak, but also that it had the power to make other oracles speak (see **Oracles**).

Excavations at the site have uncovered Catequil's main temple compound at a place called Namanchugo, at the foot of Mt. Icchal, a mountain with three cliffs that people believed represented Catequil, his mother Mama Catequil, and a brother, Piguerao. The

The oracle of Catequil in the province of Huamachuco, northern Peru, showing the outer and inner patios of the oracle's sanctuary and the canal used in divination rituals to announce the oracle's predictions. Courtesy John Topic, Catequil Archaeological Project.

complex at the site comprised three compounds on top of a low mound with two lateral extensions, resulting in a U-shaped mound with a plaza in front and two wings extending from the sides. The shrine itself, situated on the central mound, measures 3 × 3 meters (10 × 10 feet) on the exterior and contained three libation basins, two in the inner patio and one inside the shrine. Within the shrine, archaeologists found the remains of two canal systems: one carried libations away from the basins, and the other served as a conduit for the pronouncement of oracular prophecies. The shrine's patio is paved with sling-stone-sized river cobbles—perhaps an allusion to Catequil, a weather god who was believed to punish offenders by hurling bolts of lightning with his sling.

The Incas punished shrines whose predictions did not bode well, and shortly before the Spanish invasion, Catequil's prophecies did not favor the ruler Atahualpa. Catequil foretold that Atahualpa would have an unfortunate end in the war of succession with his brother Huascar, accusing Atahualpa of killing too many people (see **Wars, Dynastic**). An enraged Atahualpa spent three months at the sanctuary, directing its destruction. He climbed up to the sanctuary and cut off the head of Catequil's "idol" with a battle ax and then beheaded the old man who served as Catequil's oracular medium.

Further Reading

Topic, John R. "El santuario de Catequil: Estructura y agencia. Hacia una comprensión de los oráculos andinos." In *Adivinación y Óraculos en el Mundo Andino Antiguo,* edited by Marco Curatola Petrocchi and Mariusz S. Ziółkowski, 71–96. Lima: Pontificia Universidad Católica del Peru, 2008.

Topic, John R., Theresa Lange Topic, and Alfredo Melly. "Catequil: The Archaeology, Ethnohistory and Ethnography of a Major Provincial Huaca." In *Andean Archaeology I: Variations in Sociopolitical Organization*, edited by William H. Isbell and Helaine Silverman, 303–36. New York: Kluwer Academic Press/Plenum, 2002.

■ ADRIANA VON HAGEN

CENSUS

The census was the principal instrument of population accounting, surveillance, and control carried out by the Inca state. Spanish sources inform us that the census was the responsibility of the governor, *tocricoc* (seer/watcher), of each province, who kept the figures up to date with the aid of *quipu* accountants. Census figures were reviewed regularly at the provincial level and were reported to the Inca ruler in **Cuzco** annually at the great festival of Raymi, which took place at the time of the December solstice. Provincial census counts were reviewed by inspectors, called *tukuy-rikoq* (the similarity to the title of governor has caused much confusion), who were sent out from the central government on inspection tours every three or five years (sources differ on the period).

The census formed the foundation on which tribute levels in the provinces were assessed and assigned. As tribute was collected in the form of a labor draft, the *mit'a*, which was reportedly, or ideally, organized in a decimal manner, decimal accounting may have been employed in the census (see **Administration, Decimal**; **Labor Service**). While we understand how decimal accounting was applied in the organization of the labor draft, our sources do not clarify exactly how the decimal principle may have been applied in census records. In fact, we are also told that census figures were collected and recorded according to age-grades.

According to the age-grade system, the population was divided into 10 (some sources say 12) age-grades—10 for men, 10 for women. The age-grades organized the population into categories according to stages of life and status (e.g., child, married, warrior, old man/woman), not by years. The Incas appear not to have kept track of their age in years. **John H. Rowe** provides an excellent summary overview on the various, conflicting accounts pertaining to the Inca age-grades.

Further Reading

Julien, C. J. "How Inca Decimal Administration Worked." *Ethnohistory* 35, no. 3: 257–79, 1988.

Rowe, J. H. "The Age-Grades of the Inca Census." In *Miscellanea Paul Rivet Octogenario dicata: XXXI Congreso Internacional de Americanistas*, vol. 2, 499–522. Mexico City: Universidad Nacional Autónoma de México, 1958.

Urton, G. "Censos registrados en cordeles con 'Amarres': Padrones poblacionales pre-Hispánicos y coloniales tempranos en los Khipus Inka." *Revista Andina* no. 42: 153–96, 2006.

■ GARY URTON

CEQUES

Ceques (also spelled *ziqi* [line]) were imaginary or conceptual lines that went out from the **Coricancha**, the Temple of the Sun, in Cuzco to the horizon. The specific direction and conformation of any given *ceque* was defined by a set of between three and fifteen *huacas* (roughly "sacred places") located within the city and the Cuzco valley in a particular direction, as viewed from the Coricancha. Sources tell us there were 41 or 42 *ceques* (one *ceque* was divided into two parts) arrayed in a radial-like system of orientations around the Coricancha. The basic framework of the *ceque* organization was the division of the city (and the empire) into four quadrants, or "parts," designated as *suyus* (see **Antisuyu, Chinchaysuyu, Collasuyu,** and **Cuntisuyu**). Three of the *suyus* (quadrants) of the city had nine *ceques* each; the fourth *suyu* (Cuntisuyu), had 14 *ceques*. What is referred to as the "*ceque* system" was the total system of lines and sacred places in the valley, organized by the four *suyus*, and their collective roles in organizing space, time, social and political groups, and ritual activities across the four *suyus* within the Inca capital.

Information on the *ceques* and the *ceque* system is contained in a relatively late, mid-seventeenth-century Colonial chronicle by the Jesuit **Bernabé Cobo**. The information in Cobo was apparently copied from an earlier, sixteenth-century document by Cuzco's chief magistrate, **Polo Ondegardo**; this document is now lost. The original source of information on the *ceque* system was a *quipu* (knotted-string accounting device), presumably now lost as well, on which the identities of the *ceques* and *huacas* were recorded in the knot record. The account in the Cobo chronicle contains the names and ranks—in a three-tiered hierarchical arrangement (*collana*—high, *payan*—middle, and *cayao*—low)—of the *ceques* as well as the names and usually some information about each of the 328 or 350 *huacas,* the sacred places that made up the *ceque* system. Much of the information on the *huacas* pertains to the sacrifices that were offered at each one of these sites in a round of ceremonies and rituals that constituted the annual **ritual calendar** in the Inca capital.

There is some question about the nature of the *ceque* lines—whether they were straight or crooked, with some lines even crossing over others. Statements from some of the Spanish chroniclers who were familiar with the uses of the system especially for ritual purposes suggest that the lines were perfectly straight, a circumstance that would accord well with data suggesting that Inca astronomers may have viewed the rise or set of astronomical bodies along certain of the *ceques*. Nevertheless, from his exhaustive ethnohistorical and on-the-ground research, archaeologist Brian Bauer concluded that virtually none of the *ceques* ran straight through the valley. The difference between these two interpretations may, however, be a false problem. For just as a map of a subway system may show the routes to be a network of straight lines while travel on the cars through the twisting tunnels follows anything but straight lines, so the *ceque* system may have been conceived of and talked about as a system of straight lines, whereas tracing any given line through the valley would produce a crooked line.

The different social and political groups that occupied one or another of the four *suyus* within the city and valley of Cuzco were related to particular *ceques*. These associations were critical features in defining the ritual and political organization of the Inca capital. Much research has been devoted to analyzing the various Colonial accounts detailing, often in contradictory ways, how the total system of spatial coordinates, temporal periodicities, and sociopolitical groupings was organized.

Beyond its manifestation in Cuzco, one Spanish chronicler states that there were more than 100 towns in the empire that were organized by *ceque* system–like arrangements of lines. Archaeologists have on occasion attempted to identify *ceque* system organizations in Inca archaeological sites, such as at Huánuco Pampa in the north-central highlands of Peru and Incahuasi, on Peru's south-central coast. Finally, we have evidence of *ceque* lines that went for great distances across the Andean countryside, such as one that extended from Cuzco to Lake Titicaca and the site of Tiahuanaco. This very long *ceque* line was important in directing the movement of priests going in procession from Cuzco on pilgrimage to the **Island of the Sun**, in Lake Titicaca, at the time of the June solstice.

Further Reading

Aveni, A. F. "Horizon Astronomy in Incaic Cuzco." In *Archaeoastronomy in the Americas*, edited by R. A. Williamson, 305–18. Los Altos, CA: Ballena Press, 1981.

Bauer, B. S. "The Original Ceque Manuscript." In *Structure, Knowledge, and Representation in the Andes. Studies Presented to Reiner Tom Zuidema on the Occasion of His 70th Birthday. Journal of the Steward Anthropological Society*, vol. 2, 277–98. Urbana: Department of Anthropology, University of Illinois, Urbana-Champaign, 1996.

———. *The Sacred Landscape of the Inca: The Cusco Ceque System*. Austin: University of Texas Press, 1998.

Cobo, Bernabé. *Inca Religion and Customs*. Translated and edited by Roland Hamilton. Austin: University of Texas Press, 1990 [1653].

Hyslop, J. *Inkawasi, the New Cuzco: Cañete, Lunahuaná, Peru*. B.A.R. International Series 234. Oxford: B.A.R., 1985.

Rowe, J. H. "An Account of the Shrines of Ancient Cuzco." *Ñawpa Pacha*, no. 17: 2–80, 1979.

———. "Una relación de los adoratorios del antiguo Cuzco." *Histórica* 5, no. 2: 209–61, 1981.

Zuidema, R. Tom. *The Ceque System of Cuzco: The Social Organization of the Capital of the Inca.* Leiden, Netherlands: E. J Brill, 1964.

———. "Bureaucracy and Systematic Knowledge in Andean Civilization." In *The Inca and Aztec States, 1400–1800: Anthropology and History*, edited by George A. Collier, Renato I. Rosaldo, and John D. Wirth, 419–58. New York: Academic Press, 1982.

■ GARY URTON

CERAMICS

Scattered throughout the territory that once comprised the Inca Empire are fragments of the richly decorated polychrome pottery that distinguish Inca ceramics from earlier styles and point to their manufacture during the Late Horizon time period (see **Chronology, Pre-Inca; Chronology, Inca**). The degree of standardization in the forms and decoration of these wares, as well as their widespread distribution, hint at the importance of this category of material culture to the larger imperial project. The study of Inca pottery offers insights into many different aspects of Inca society and state policy, including the organization of production, consumption and culinary practices, the ways in which status and identity were negotiated, and imperial ideology.

The history of Inca pottery studies begins with **Hiram Bingham**'s detailed analysis of the ceramic materials recovered from the site of **Machu Picchu** in the early 1900s. His 1915 publication offered the first comprehensive classification scheme for the imperial assemblage, identifying 17 different types of Inca vessels. Several decades later, **John H. Rowe**, working with Inca collections from Cuzco and its vicinity, developed another clas-

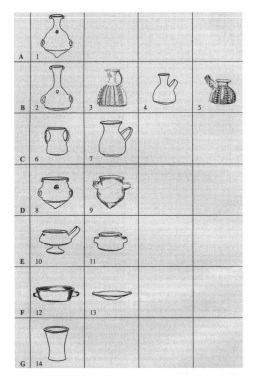

Inca ceramics are divided into seven types, based on their shapes: (1) *aríbalos* (tall-necked jars); (2) other narrow-necked jars; (3) wide-mouthed jars; (4) wide-mouthed pots (*ollas*); (5) vessels with or without feet; (6) plates; and (7) cups. Bray, Tamara. *Latin American Antiquity* 14, no. 1: 12 (fig. 1), 2003, adapted from Meyers 1975.

sificatory scheme for Inca pottery using the type-variety system that accorded primacy to surface treatment and decorative style. A generation later, Albert Meyers devised a new typology for the imperial Inca ceramic assemblage based on morphology, or vessel shape, to facilitate comparative research with Inca materials from the provinces. In Meyers's system, Inca ceramics are divided into seven formal classes: (1) *aríbalos* (tall-necked jars); (2) other narrow-necked jars; (3) wide-mouthed jars; (4) wide-mouthed pots (*ollas*); (5) vessels with or without feet; (6) plates; and (7) cups. Each category contains from one to several forms, with 14 principal morphological types recognized in total.

In general, the Inca state ceramic assemblage comprises a limited number of highly standardized vessel forms. The emphasis on standardization extended beyond basic vessel morphology to encompass vessel proportion and decorative treatment, as well. Statistical analyses have demonstrated a remarkably high degree of adherence to the maintenance of correct proportional relationships between such elements as rim diameter, vessel height, and maximal body diameter, as well as the existence of distinctive size classes for each vessel category. Similarly, it is clear that the unique polychrome style of the Inca state was based on a specific repertoire of geometric motifs typically executed on well-slipped and polished vessel surfaces. In contrast to most other earlier ceramic styles in the Andes, the Incas favored abstract rather than representational or figurative design and decorative elements. Archaeological and ethnohistoric evidence indicates that the Incas relied on enclaves of pottery-making specialists (see **Labor Service**) for the production of imperial state wares, though it is also clear from the archaeological record that local potters engaged in the (probably unauthorized) replication of imperial forms and styles.

The quintessential and most common vessel form within the Inca ceramic assemblage is the tall-necked jar with a wide flaring rim and oval-shaped body commonly known as the *aríbalo* (Meyers's Form 1). This vessel type is readily recognizable on the basis of both formal and decorative attributes. Its diagnostic morphological features include the horizontally flared rim, the pierced lugs on the underside of the rim, the modeled protuberance on the center front, the vertical side strap handles, and the conical base. While the *aríbalo* varies considerably in terms of size—from miniatures under 10 centimeters tall (4 inches tall) to oversized jars more than 1 meter (3 feet) in height—these five morphological features are invariably present.

Similarly, there appears to have been fairly strict rules governing the type and placement of ornamentation found on *aríbalos*. The primary zones of decoration were the neck, the upper shoulder of the back side, and the front half of the vessel body. A large percentage of *aríbalos* utilize one of three design formats on the front panel: the first consists of two central, vertical bands filled with a cross and bar motif, flanked on either side by the genealogical tree motif (formerly described as the fern pattern) (Rowe's Cuzco Polychrome A). The second and third formats involve the use of a single row of rhombuses centered on the front of the vessel, although these differ in terms of the orientation of the motif (both were classified by Rowe as "Cuzco Polychrome B"). When depicted horizontally, the band of rhombuses comprises a stand-alone panel; in the vertical position, the design element is flanked by horizontal registers of pendant triangles or the tree motif. The functional attributes of the *aríbalo*, together with ethnohistoric and ethnographic evidence, indicate that it was likely used for the storage and serving of **chicha** (maize beer; see **Cuisine**).

The second category in Meyers's typology, consisting of narrow-necked, flat-bottomed jars, includes four different vessel forms. As a group, they are distinguished from the *arríbalo* by their flat (as opposed to conical) bases and their generally smaller sizes. The morphological features of the vessels in this category suggest that they likely served as containers for liquids, though given their relative dearth outside the imperial heartland, it may be that access to or use of these was more restricted.

The next category of wide-necked jars with one or two strap handles is also relatively rare. The larger sizes and morphological attributes of the two pitcher-like forms in this category suggest possible decanting or serving functions. The two vessel types included in Meyers's fourth category of wide-mouthed, conical-based pots (Forms 8 and 9) are also primarily known from the heartland. The Form 8 vessel, sometimes referred to as an *urpu*, often exhibits the same type of design formats and motifs found on the *arríbalo*. Both of the wide-mouthed vessel forms are thought to be associated with food processing activities, including fermentation and boiling.

The next two vessels in the typology are the pedestal-base pot (Form 10) and the straight-sided bowl (Form 11). These constitute the third and fourth most common forms in the Inca assemblage, respectively. The pedestal-base pot, which often has a fitted lid, is the only common vessel type in the imperial repertoire that lacks polychrome decoration. This form is found in significantly higher frequencies in the provinces and is generally considered to have served as a portable cooking vessel. The two-handled, flat-bottom bowl (Form 11) commonly exhibits polychrome decoration and comes in a variety of sizes. The attributes of this vessel suggest a likely serving function.

The two vessels included in Meyers's sixth category are plate forms. While the deep (Form 12) plate is known principally from the Cuzco area, the shallow (Form 13) plate constitutes the second most common vessel category in the imperial assemblage and is widespread throughout the Empire. The shallow plate exhibits the greatest freedom of stylistic expression of any Inca vessel form. The morphology and decorative treatment of these plates, which are often found in identical pairs, suggest their use as individually sized serving platters for solid foods.

The last vessel in the state ceramic typology is a tall cup form known as a **kero**. This vessel type was not limited to the ceramic medium and was probably more commonly produced in wood, gold, or silver. Though it may appear a natural form for drinking, its relative rarity and restriction to specific contexts suggest that it may have had a more specialized or limited function within Inca society.

The iconography associated with the imperial state ceramic assemblage has generally been characterized as abstract, geometric, and nonrepresentational. While it has been suggested that Inca iconography held little ideological content, this seems unlikely given its ubiquity and the obvious emphasis on conformity. Recent interpretive analyses of the imperial style have focused on design structure, multiple meanings, and metaphor to gain insight into its potential significance and how it may have functioned as a visual charter for rulership. The elaborate and uniform set of cooking and serving wares comprising the Inca state ceramic assemblage has no precedent in earlier Andean empires. The creation of such a distinctive state pottery ensemble suggests that there existed a close relationship among food, politics, and statecraft in the Inca Empire (see **Cuisine**; **Feasts, State-Sponsored**).

Further Reading

Bingham, Hiram. "Types of Machu Picchu Pottery." *American Anthropologist* 17, no. 2: 257–71, 1915.

Bray, Tamara L. "Imperial Inca Iconography: The Art of Empire in the Andes." *RES Anthropology and Aesthetics* 38:168–78, 2000.

———. "Inca Pottery as Culinary Equipment: Food, Feasting, and Gender in Imperial State Design." *Latin American Antiquity* 14, no. 1: 1–23, 2003.

———. "La alfarería imperial Inca: Una comparación entre la cerámica estatal del área de Cuzco y la cerámica de las provincias." *Chungara* 36, no. 2: 64–79, 2004.

———. "The Role of Chicha in Inca State Expansion: A Distributional Study of Inca Aríbalos." In *Drink, Power, and Society in the Andes*, edited by Justin Jennings and Brenda Bowser, 108–32. Gainesville: University of Florida Press, 2009.

Hayashida, Frances. "Style, Technology, and State Production: Inka Pottery Manufacture in the Leche Valley, Peru." *Latin American Antiquity* 10, no. 4: 337–52, 1999.

Meyers, Albert. "Algunos Problemas en la Clasificación del Estilo Incaico." *Pumapunku* 8:7–25, 1975.

Rowe, John H. *An Introduction to the Archaeology of Cuzco.* Papers of the Peabody Museum of American Archaeology and Ethnology, vol. 27, no. 2. Cambridge, MA: Harvard University, 1944.

■ TAMARA L. BRAY

CHICHA

This term, which today refers to maize beer or other fermented beverages consumed in communities throughout the Andes and Amazonia, was adopted by sixteenth-century Spaniards from Arawak-speaking peoples of the Caribbean or from the Kuna of Panama. The term quickly replaced the **Quechua** name for the drink, *aja,* or *ajsa,* as well as the **Aymara** term *kusa.* Virtually every chronicler who wrote about the Incas noted the enormous amounts of *chicha* consumed at every occasion, ranging from the great festivals in Cuzco's main plaza, where ritual drunkenness prevailed (so much so that one chronicler noted that the plaza's drains ran with urine throughout the day "as abundantly as a flowing spring") to drinking by small groups of laborers tilling a field or building an irrigation canal. The state was required to provide work parties engaged in state **labor service** with food and drink, as part of the Incas' reciprocal labor obligation to their subjects. "They never celebrate an event, whether joyful or sad, in any way other than by dancing and drinking to excess," noted the chronicler **Bernabé Cobo** (1979 [1653]). When a conquered *curaca,* or headman, submitted to Inca rule, the two parties sealed the pact with a toast of *chicha,* consumed in gold, silver, wooden, or ceramic tumblers (the material reflected the status of the drinkers), known as **keros.** *Chicha* was the principal offering made to sacred objects or places, the **huacas.**

Although virtually every ancient civilization consumed some sort of fermented beverage, the enormous investment by the Inca state in increasing maize production, largely for *chicha* production, through conquest is unprecedented in the ancient world. *Chicha* production and state hospitality were crucial to provincial administration. The state's ability to increase *chicha* production was key to political and economic expansion. The maize fields of Cochabamba, in present-day central Bolivia, provide perhaps the most dramatic example of this: there the ruler Huayna Capac transferred the local population to other regions and replaced them with 14,000 *mitmacuna* and *mit'a* laborers who cultivated the maize fields for the state (see **Labor Service**).

The tall-necked jar with a conical bottom, known as an *aríbalo*, was used to store and serve *chicha*, maize beer. Johan Reinhard.

Chicha was brewed on a large scale, often under the direct management of the state. The work was usually undertaken by young women, the **acllacuna**, who lived and worked in state production facilities, known as *acllahuasis* (houses of the chosen women). State involvement in *chicha* production is supported by archaeological evidence from sites such as Huánuco Pampa, an administrative settlement in the central highlands, where archaeologists uncovered remains of the large jars used in the various stages of *chicha* production in a building believed to have served as the local *acllahuasi*. Evidence for *chicha* consumption was uncovered in a royal compound at Huánuco Pampa, where excavators dug up enormous quantities of *chicha* jars. *Chicha* consumption is intimately linked to the narrow-necked jar, ubiquitous around the empire, known as the *aríbalo* (see **Ceramics**; **Feasts, State-Sponsored**).

Chicha was produced in two ways. In the first method, dried, ground corn was placed in the mouth and worked with the tongue until it absorbed saliva. These "salivated" balls of maize were spat into large ceramic jars where they fermented, forming *chicha*. The other method involved soaking fresh maize kernels overnight in ceramic jars and then placing the kernels in layers of leaves until they germinated. The sprouted corn was then dried in the sun and later ground to make *chicha*, by soaking, boiling, and fermenting. Although *chicha* can be produced from other fruits or vegetables (potatoes, peanuts, manioc, the fruit of the *molle* or pepper tree), and its effects can be enhanced by the addition of psychotropic powders such as **vilca** (*Anadenanthera colubrina*) or espingo (*Nectandra* sp.), for the Incas and their subjects, *chicha* made from maize was considered the best, and most prestigious, of all beverages.

Further Reading

Jennings, Justin, and Brenda J. Bowser, eds. *Drink, Power, and Society in the Andes.* Gainesville: University Press of Florida, 2009.

Morris, Craig. "Maize Beer in the Economics, Politics, and Religion of the Inca Empire." In *Fermented Food Beverages in Nutrition*, edited by Clifford F. Gastineau, William J. Darby, and Thomas B. Turner, 21–34. New York: Academic Press, 1979.

■ ADRIANA VON HAGEN

CHINCHAYSUYU

The Inca quadrant of Chinchaysuyu extended west and north-northwest from Cuzco to encompass lands teeming with human and natural resources, making it by far the most prosperous of all the *suyus*. Although smaller than **Collasuyu** in the south, Chinchaysuyu's wealth and population exceeded all the other three *suyus* combined. Along with **Antisuyu**, the tropical forest quadrant, Chinchaysuyu formed the *hanan*, or upper half of the empire. At the same time, Chinchaysuyu formed a quadrant of the capital, Cuzco, whose plaza functioned as the axis of the territorial divisions as well as the nexus of the four main roads leading to the *suyus*. The Cuzco valley's **ceque** system was also divided into four *suyus* and the **huacas**, or shrines, located along the 328 or so imaginary *ceques*, or lines, were ranked accordingly.

Chinchaysuyu included important religious sanctuaries and oracles, as well as several of the largest societies to contest Inca expansion and, along the spine of the Andes, some of the most elaborate stretches of paved road featuring more Inca centers than any other stretch of road in the empire. In northernmost Chinchaysuyu lay Ecuador, the focus of late Inca conquests and source of the sacred Spondylus shell. Harvested from deep coastal

The Inca quadrant of Chinchaysuyu northwest of Cuzco featured the most elaborate stretches of road anywhere in the empire. Here, a section of road near Huánuco Pampa in northern Peru. Ricardo Espinosa/Guías del Caminante.

waters, Andean peoples imbued the shell with prestige and status and regarded it as the single most valuable commodity derived from nature. The Incas and their forebears believed that this coral-colored, spiny oyster was the favorite food of the gods, and that it brought rain, and thus fertility.

As it left the outskirts of Cuzco, the Chinchaysuyu road headed west and at the important junction of Vilcashuaman connected the capital with the principal highland road leading north to Quito, in Ecuador, and a lateral road heading west to the coast (see **Roads**). Scholars believe that many of the sites on or near this westward route marked shrines on a long-distance *ceque* some 400 kilometers (250 miles) long that mirrored the path of the setting sun. The Incas incorporated scores of natural and carved rocks as well as **ushnu** platforms into the cities, shrines, and way stations of this westward route. Settlements located along this road feature some of the most elaborate architecture in the empire; highlights include: Tambocancha on the Pampa de Anta, perhaps a **royal estate** of Topa Inca; the shrine and **oracle** of Marcahuasi (see **Bridges**); Sayhuite and its famed sculpted boulder; and Vilcashuaman and its impressive, terraced *ushnu*, to name just a few.

West of Vilcashuaman the road descended to the coast through the Pisco valley, reaching the temple of Huaytará and, farther along, the adobe settlement of Tambo Colorado, one of the best preserved Inca coastal installations, painted in vivid hues of red and yellow ochre, and white. Just below Tambo Colorado, the highland road connected with the coastal road, leading north to La Centinela in the Chincha valley, seat of an important oracle and capital of the Chincha people. Surrounded by lush fields watered by irrigation canals and flanked by a bountiful sea, Chincha's productive farmland and access to coastal guano islands, used by coastal and highland farmers to fertilize fields, made it one of the richest valleys in the empire. Indeed, Chinchaysuyu may have been named after the Chincha polity.

Chinchaysuyu's coastal road also connected to **Pachacamac**, on the central coast, just south of modern-day Lima, one of the empire's most powerful, influential, and feared Andean oracles. Farther north lay the kingdom of Chimú or Chimor, one of the largest and most sophisticated coastal societies to contest Inca expansion (see **Chronology, Pre-Inca**). After the Inca conquest many skilled Chimú metalsmiths were dispatched to Inca centers to create works in metal for their new masters.

■ ADRIANA VON HAGEN

CHRONOLOGY, INCA

Noble Inca lineages (*panacas*) preserved life histories of their founding ancestors, and they recounted these narratives with specific reference to spans of time that could range from a few months to many years. A *panaca* used knotted **quipu** cords to record key moments in royal biographies that were regularly performed as praise songs (see **Music**) and **dances**. An "official" king list was assembled from these family stories, an abridged compilation of life histories that multiple rulers reassembled, sometimes executing memory specialists and rearranging the order and constitution of the royal line. Inca chronologies focused on the duration of royal activities rather than the passage of years—chronology could be built backward from the present, but it did not flow forward in a linear fashion where

A handful of soldiers entered Tahuantinsuyu with Francisco Pizarro in 1532, and later wrote accounts of their experiences, a genre referred to as "soldier's chronicles." These men were eyewitnesses to the capture of Atahualpa in Cajamarca in 1533 and the events leading up to the encounter between the Spaniards and the Inca forces. Among them are Miguel de Estete, Cristóbal de Mena, Diego de Trujillo, and Francisco López de Xerez.

Cristóbal de Mena was born in Spain and reached the Americas by 1519. He joined Francisco Pizarro in 1531, commanding one of his ships. He has been identified as the possible author of an anonymous account titled *La Conquista del Peru llamada la Nueva Castilla* (The Conquest of Peru known as New Castille). This important source, published in 1534, is the earliest report on the events in Cajamarca and the months leading up to the encounter (see **Invasion, Spanish**). Six months before Pizarro and his men reached Cajamarca in November 1532, a small group reconnoitered the highlands of Piura, in far northern Peru, where they first saw the impressive highland **road** that linked Cuzco and Quito, marveling that it could easily accommodate six horsemen riding abreast. They also explored settlements strung along the royal road, which provided the first view of the empire's sophisticated **storage** system. They admired the buildings and the skill of its stoneworkers, but most of all they were enthralled by the **acllas**, the cloistered, so-called chosen women who wove fine cloth and brewed maize beer, **chicha**.

Francisco de Xerez served as Francisco Pizarro's secretary. Born in Seville in 1497, he spent a decade in Central America and took part in all three of Pizarro's expeditions. On the third expedition, in 1532, he was a horseman as well as a scribe. Xerez was the only Spaniard injured during the capture of Atahualpa, breaking a leg, an event with which he began his account. Because he was Pizarro's secretary, his version of the events in Cajamarca is regarded as the official one, and it is quite detailed. Once he had been awarded his share of Atahualpa's ransom, Xerez returned to Spain a wealthy man, publishing *La Verdadera Relación de la Conquista del Peru y Provincia del Cuzco, llamada la Nueva Castilla* (True Account of the Conquest of Peru and Province of Cuzco, Known as New Castille) in 1534, shortly after Mena's account was completed.

Most published editions of Xerez's *Verdadera Relación* include a report by Miguel de Estete concerning Hernando Pizarro's expedition to **Pachacamac**, a pilgrimage center on Peru's central coast. Estete was born in Spain around 1507 in Santo Domingo de la Calzada. His *Relación del viaje que hizó el Señor Capitán Hernando Pizarro* (Account of the Trip Made by the Captain Hernando Pizarro) chronicles an expedition from Cajamarca to Pachacamac in January 1533, and the return to Cajamarca via Jauja in May 1533. The expedition's mission was to find more booty for Atahualpa's ransom. Estete served as inspector on the expedition; as such, he was charged with accounting for the gold and silver collected on the expedition. Dated

1534, Estete's account is rich in details about the people and geography encountered along the way, and especially about the oracle of Pachacamac.

As his name indicates, Diego de Trujillo was from Trujillo, Extremadura, Spain, where he was born in 1502. He joined Pizarro in 1529 and took part in the capture of Atahualpa in Cajamarca. He later left for Spain but returned to Peru where he was commissioned by the Viceroy Francisco de Toledo in the early 1570s to write an account of the events in Cajamarca. His account, titled *Relación del descubrimiento del reyno del Perú* (Account of the Discovery of the Kingdom of Peru), was completed in 1571. While Trujillo's account was written some forty years after the events recounted, and though the author is excessively boastful about his own role at Cajamarca, in which he in fact played only a minor part, it is valuable nonetheless for its detailed depictions.

Further Reading

Graubart, Karen. "Estete, Miguel de (ca. 1507–ca.1550)." In *Guide to Documentary Sources for Andean Studies, 1530–1900*, edited by Joanne Pillsbury, vol. 2, 206–10. Norman: University of Oklahoma Press, 2008.

Pease, Franklin. "Mena, Cristóbal de (sixteenth century)." In *Guide to Documentary Sources for Andean Studies, 1530–1900*, edited by Joanne Pillsbury, vol. 3, 407–10. Norman: University of Oklahoma Press, 2008.

———. "Xerez, Francisco de (1497–?)." In *Guide to Documentary Sources for Andean Studies, 1530–1900*, edited by Joanne Pillsbury, vol. 3, 752–56. Norman: University of Oklahoma Press, 2008.

Regalado de Hurtado, Liliana. "Trujillo, Diego de (1502–1576)." In *Guide to Documentary Sources for Andean Studies, 1530–1900*, edited by Joanne Pillsbury, vol. 3, 672–73. Norman: University of Oklahoma Press, 2008.

■ ADRIANA VON HAGEN

calendar dates provided a standard marker of time. The **king list** connected the imperial present to the mythical past, defining who was Inca, and helping to explain why some **Cuzco** groups were Inca subjects.

The first Spaniards had little use for Inca history as they plundered the empire, and eyewitness accounts from the 1530s rarely probe more than a decade into the past. The European interest in Inca chronology emerged around 1550 as part of a debate over the legitimacy of Spanish conquests in the Andes. Over time, Spanish writers began to contextualize the Inca dynastic narrative by linking it to the biblical creation story and situating it in emerging universal histories. Several authors, including **Juan Polo Ondegardo**, **José de Acosta**, and **Blas Valera**, estimated the total duration of the Inca dynasty at 350–450 years, whereas a handful of other sources attempt to establish chronology on a ruler-by-ruler basis.

The earliest surviving Inca chronology may come from testimony given by *quipu* specialists in 1542, although this account only survives in an early-seventeenth-century manuscript. This source states that the Inca dynasty endured for 473 years from the time of the founding ancestor to the execution of the last legitimate ruler. It offers no calendar dates, just a ruler's approximate age at death or length of reign.

In 1572, **Pedro Sarmiento de Gamboa** composed a dynastic chronology in consultation with representatives of the royal Inca lineages, linking each ruler with specific calendar dates, as well as to the tenures of Spanish rulers and Catholic popes. Most Inca scholars ignore these dates—not because of the computational errors found in several places, but rather because the lengths of early reigns are too long to be credible. Sarmiento de Gamboa's Inca dynasty begins in AD 665 and includes several reigns that purportedly lasted a century or longer.

Most modern scholarly chronologies derive from the sequence found in **Miguel Cabello Valboa**'s 1586 *Miscelánea Antártica*. The author insists that his dates for the Inca dynasty were based on *quipu* evidence, but does not specify the sources of his information. Cabello Valboa's chronology suffers from the same weaknesses as that of Sarmiento de Gamboa: it begins in AD 945, contains several impossibly long reigns, and is riddled with numerical inaccuracies. Its appeal lies in the apparent plausibility of the dates for the final preconquest rulers: Pachacuti Inca Yupanqui, Topa Inca Yupanqui, Huayna Capac, and Atahualpa.

Writing around 1615, **Felipe Guaman Poma de Ayala** produced an indigenous account of the Inca dynasty that spans more than 1,500 years. He records the age of each Inca ruler at death, as well as a cumulative duration of the dynasty, which is essentially the running sum of the lifespans of rulers. Although many scholars find this chronicle invaluable for developing native Andean perspectives on the Incas, no one takes seriously a span of reigns that averages well over a century. The royal chronology written by Antonio Vázquez de Espinosa in his 1628 *Compendio y descripción de las Indias occidentales* (Compendium and Description of the West Indies) has also been largely ignored in recent scholarship. This sequence is just over 500 years long (AD 1031–1532) and presents the shortest average length of reign, partly because the author includes two rulers—Pachacuti and Inca Yupanqui—who are normally treated as the same individual in other king lists.

None of the sequences described above was published during the Colonial period. The lack of an established chronology throughout the Colonial period made it possible to write new histories that lacked chronology, such as Vasco de Contreras y Valverde's 1649 history of Cuzco, or to propose new estimates for the dynasty and for individual reigns, as Juan Mogrovejo de la Cerda did in 1690. New chronologies continued to appear until the final days of Spanish rule; late sequences included those by Juan de Velasco (1789) and Hipólito Unánue (1793). During the nineteenth century, the emergence of a scholarly tradition of archival research led to the gradual publication of sources such as Cabello Valboa (1840), the *quipu* testimony (1892), Sarmiento de Gamboa (1906), Guaman Poma de Ayala (1936), and Vázquez de Espinosa (1942).

The availability of Colonial chronologies raised the question of which sequence, if any, could be treated as historically reliable. In his monumental *History of the Conquest of Peru*, William Prescott concluded that the number of Inca rulers in the recorded king lists could not account for the timespan presented in sequences by Cabello Valboa or Velasco, and he raised doubts about the interpretive value of many of the chronicle accounts—"so imperfect were the records employed by the Peruvians, and so confused and contradictory their traditions, that the historian finds no firm footing on which to stand till within a century of the Spanish conquest" (Prescott 1847). Prescott's history remained influential well into the twentieth century, when the spread of archaeological research introduced new chronological concerns.

In 1931, Philip Ainsworth Means published *Ancient Civilizations of the Andes*, in which he sought to place Inca and pre-Inca cultures into a general chronological framework derived from the seventeenth-century chronicle of **Garcilaso de la Vega**. The pioneering Inca scholar **John H. Rowe** challenged this approach on grounds that it promoted an early date for Inca expansion that did not conform to the most reliable chronicles, or the archaeological evidence of Inca provincial rule. Rowe advocated an approach to Inca chronology that echoes Prescott: using dates from Cabello Valboa, but only for the rulers from the final century before the conquest. Rowe corrected the calculation errors for rulers from Pachacuti Inca Yupanqui forward, treating them as historical and describing earlier rulers as "legendary" and "mythical."

Rowe's short chronology has been influential as the source of most recent Inca date sequences. Some historicist treatments of the Inca imperial century have attempted to refine the chronology of the last three emperors using details from life histories of individual rulers, as Susan Niles does for the reign of Huayna Capac. Many Inca scholars take a more skeptical approach, identifying the political aspects of the Colonial construction of Inca histories. Given the existence of multiple sequences that allege to have Inca *quipus* and noble testimony as their sources, many scholars worry that the chronicle dates do not represent an accurate or relevant way for representing the Inca past. **Tom Zuidema** has suggested that myth and Colonial-era factionalism influenced the production of the entire Inca dynastic narrative.

Rowe advocated a new Inca chronology just before the advent of radiocarbon dating, which offers new potential for reconstructing aspects of Inca chronology. Radiocarbon "dates" are not calendar dates, but instead calibrated ranges, usually several decades long, of the probable age of organic materials. Archaeology does not date events well, but radiocarbon dating has provided valuable perspectives on the timing of early Inca state expansion and the first imperial campaigns. Archaeological dates have been useful for placing the Incas in a broader prehistoric cultural sequence, but their degree of precision has yet to offer a strong challenge to Rowe's short chronology.

Further Reading

Cabello Valboa, Miguel. *Miscelánea antártica, una historia del Perú antiguo.* Edited by Luis E. Valcárcel. Lima: Universidad Nacional Mayor de San Marcos, Instituto de Etnología, 1951 [1586].

Covey, R. Alan. "Chronology, Succession, and Sovereignty: The Politics of Inka Historiography and Its Modern Interpretation." *Comparative Studies in Society and History* 48, no. 1: 166–99, 2006.

———. *How the Incas Built Their Heartland: State Formation and the Innovation of Imperial Strategies in the Sacred Valley, Peru.* Ann Arbor: University of Michigan Press, 2006.

Guaman Poma de Ayala, Felipe. *The First New Chronicle and Good Government.* Translated by Roland Hamilton. Austin: University of Texas Press, 2009 [1615].

Julien, Catherine J. *Reading Inca History.* Iowa City: University of Iowa Press, 2000.

Means, Philip Ainsworth. *Ancient Civilizations of the Andes.* New York: Charles Scribner's Sons, 1931.

Niles, Susan A. *The Shape of Inca History. Narrative and Architecture in an Andean Empire.* Iowa City: University of Iowa Press, 1999.

Prescott, William H. *History of the Conquest of Peru.* New York: Harper and Brothers, 1847.

Rowe, John H. "Absolute Chronology in the Andean Area." *American Antiquity* 10, no. 3: 265–84, 1945.

Sarmiento de Gamboa, Pedro. *The History of the Incas.* Translated by Brian S. Bauer and Vania Smith. Austin: University of Texas Press, 2007 [1572].

Urton, Gary. "Discurso sobre la descendencia y gobierno de los Incas (sixteenth–early seventeenth century)." In *Guide to Documentary Sources for Andean Studies 1530–1900,* edited by Joanne Pillsbury, vol. 2, 191–92. Norman: University of Oklahoma Press, 2008.

Vázquez de Espinosa, Antonio. *Compendium and Description of the West Indies.* Translated by Charles Upson Clark. Washington, DC: Smithsonian Institution, 1942 [1528].

Zuidema, R. Tom. *Inca Civilization in Cuzco.* Austin: University of Texas Press, 1990.

■ R. ALAN COVEY

CHRONOLOGY, PRE-INCA

Before the Incas, a multitude of cultures rose and fell in the ancient **central Andes**, each one contributing in its own unique way to the cultural legacy inherited by the Incas. Only a few of these are well known and have been studied in any detail. Most archaeologists organize this great mass of data using the chronological scheme developed by **John H. Rowe.** The approximate date ranges for each of his periods and horizons are as follows:

- Late Horizon: AD 1476–1532
- Late Intermediate Period: AD 900–1476
- Middle Horizon: AD 540–900
- Early Intermediate Period: 400 BC–AD 540
- Early Horizon: 1300–400 BC
- Initial Period: 2100–1300 BC

The Initial Period in Rowe's chronology has been divided by some scholars into the lithic and preceramic periods (before pottery), and the Ceramic period following the introduction of pottery (after 1800 BC). Remarkably, ancient Peruvians had already developed civilizations capable of building very large-scale architectural monuments such as the temples of Caral in the Supe valley on Peru's north-central coast by 2600 BC, well before pottery was introduced.

The earliest very widespread cultural unity is manifested in the cult called Chavín by archaeologists. By 1400 BC a religious movement began to spread across northern Peru, incorporating elements from older Peruvian coastal religions and combining them with religious iconography from the tropical forests of the Amazon. Although named for the site of Chavín de Huántar in the north-central highlands, this movement seems to represent a synthesis of cults found throughout a broad area of northern Peru. By 1000 BC Chavín influence had appeared as far south as near modern Lima, and by 500 BC Chavín influence extended from the modern cities of Cajamarca in the north to Ayacucho in the south.

Following the heyday of the Chavín cult—the Early Horizon time period of Rowe's chronology—archaeologists believe that there was a florescence of numerous powerful but less widespread regional cultures. The best known of these are the Moche of the Peruvian north coast and the coastal Nazca. During the Early Intermediate Period of Rowe's chronology, the Moche and the Nazca cultures developed into complex civilizations with their ideology evolving out of the Chavín religious tradition. These societies show increasing complexity and the Moche may have developed into a centrally governed state.

In the southern Andes, in what is today Bolivia, a large ceremonial center developed on the shores of Lake Titicaca. This magnificent city, called Tiahuanaco, was built at an elevation of 3,850 meters (12,631 feet) above sea level on the cold, treeless *altiplano*. The exact dimensions of the city are not yet known, but preliminary studies indicate an urban center of nearly four square kilometers (2.5 square miles). Although this severe environment seems hostile, in prehistoric times it supported one of the densest population concentrations in the ancient New World. Population estimates for the city of Tiahuanaco and its sustaining area range between 570,000 and 1,111,500 people.

First settled around 1000 BC, the site of Tiahuanaco was occupied for nearly two thousand years. It began as a small farming village, but around AD 100 people began to construct monumental architecture, and the site grew to be the capital city of an empire that dominated the southern Andes from AD 500 to 1000, corresponding to the Middle Horizon period of Rowe's chronology. It is believed that the Tiahuanaco Empire established administrative centers and economic colonies throughout the *altiplano* of Bolivia and Peru and along the coasts of southern Peru and northern Chile.

The city of Tiahuanaco is dominated by platform mounds and temples. The largest structure is the platform mound called the Akapana, which measures about 200 meters (656 feet) at its base and was more than 15 meters (29.2 feet) high. In addition to platform mounds, other monumental structures at Tiahuanaco include large, rectangular, stone-walled enclosures and semisubterranean temples, all of finely cut stone.

Entrance to these elaborate buildings and ceremonial precincts was through monumental gateways, the most famous being the so-called Gate of the Sun. The gateways were often monolithic, with the uprights and lintels all carved from a single piece of stone. The lintels were frequently decorated with complex relief carvings that are believed to depict deities of the Tiahuanaco pantheon. The most important of these is thought to be the figure on the Gate of the Sun, the Tiahuanaco interpretation of the old Chavín staff god.

Agriculture and herding of camelids, in addition to conquest and tribute, contributed to the vast wealth that permitted the construction of the great ceremonial monuments of the city of Tiahuanaco and its major administrative centers. Some time between AD 1000 and 1200, however, the Tiahuanaco Empire disintegrated and the great city and its satellite centers were abandoned. The causes of the collapse are poorly understood, but it seems probable that a climatic fluctuation contributed substantially to the demise of Tiahuanaco. The legacy of Tiahuanaco was profoundly influential. Even in Inca times, the site was revered as a holy place. The Incas invented an official history to claim their place of origin as an island in Lake Titicaca and themselves as the inheritors of the prestigious Tiahuanaco tradition (see **Myths, Origin**).

The other great culture of the Middle Horizon was that of the Huari. About 965 kilometers (600 miles) to the north of Tiahuanaco, the Huari capital was located in the Ayacucho valley of the central Peruvian Andes, at an elevation of 2,743 meters (9,000 feet) above sea level. The Huari Empire is represented archaeologically by large architectural complexes found throughout the Peruvian highlands. Huari and Tiahuanaco shared some of the same religious iconography, but they seem to have been separate entities. There is no evidence that one ever dominated the other, although the exact nature of their relationship remains unknown.

The site of Huari was first occupied around 200 BC and, like Tiahuanaco, was only a small settlement until around AD 500. From AD 500 to 900, however, the site grew rapidly to become one of the largest urban centers in South America. Ultimately a city of 500 hectares (1,235 acres), it was occupied by a population ranging from 35,000 to 70,000 people. Unlike Tiahuanaco, the city of Huari has little finely cut stonework. Although monumental in scale, most of its buildings were constructed of fieldstone set in mud mortar and were then covered with smooth coats of clay and gypsum plaster.

A new religion is presumed to have been introduced to the Huari through contact with Tiahuanaco at the beginning of the Middle Horizon. Little, however, is yet understood about this religion. As with most agricultural societies, religion was undoubtedly much concerned with insuring fertility, water supply, and preventing natural disasters. The most prominent deity represented in Huari art was the staff god derived from the Chavín staff god and shared with Tiahuanaco.

Following the introduction of the new religion, the site of Huari soon emerged as the center of an expansionist empire and it embarked on a series of conquests. Although the motive for this expansion is unclear, environmental deterioration may have caused the Huari to conquer their neighbors in an attempt to gain a greater variety of ecological zones in order to insure against crop failure. Whatever the cause, the Huari appear to have organized one of the first conquest empires in the Andes, expanding rapidly to encompass most of what is today highland and coastal Peru.

Like other early Peruvian societies, the Huari imperial economy was based on agriculture and herding. A great variety of foodstuffs, probably stored in state-sponsored storehouses, were produced in numerous ecological zones. In drier environments the state built canals and irrigated fields. Terracing opened new lands, which also increased production. In addition, long-distance exchange supplied scarce luxury goods such as Spondylus shell from Ecuador and **feathers** from the Amazon jungle. To what extent trading affected the economy is unknown. It may have been an upper-class monopoly designed solely to provide the ruling elite with luxury goods.

Huari imperial power lasted for more than four centuries, until sometime between AD 1000 and 1100, when it rapidly disintegrated. The exact reasons are unknown, but the Huari state seems to have suffered from severe over-centralization. These problems were no doubt aggravated by highly variable and unpredictable weather patterns that could severely affect agricultural productivity and state wealth. Like the Tiahuanaco, the

Huari were very vulnerable to major climatic fluctuations. The capital at Huari continued to grow throughout the life of the empire, eventually becoming the largest city ever to appear in pre-Columbian South America. The rulers were thus faced with the twin problems of administering the empire and trying to cope with managing a gigantic urban center that no doubt consumed more and more of the agricultural production. Whatever the cause, by AD 1100 all of the major Huari centers were abandoned and were never reoccupied; the empire had collapsed.

In the culture of the Inca we can see many legacies of their Huari inheritance. The famous Inca **road** system was founded, in part, on the Huari road network. The woven tunics of the Inca nobility are descended from the Huari tapestry tunics. Polychrome ceramics and certain vessel forms were introduced by the Huari. Most importantly, a body of statecraft—invaluable information on state administration and organization—was the legacy of the Huari that enabled the formation of the Late Intermediate Period states and ultimately the rise of the Inca. Indeed, the knotted-string recording devices known as **quipus**, so fundamental to Inca statecraft, were first used by Huari peoples.

Following the collapse of both the Huari and Tiahuanaco empires, there followed a time of great political fragmentation throughout Peru—the Late Intermediate Period of Rowe's chronology. The two great imperial states of the Middle Horizon dissolved into numerous competing kingdoms and chiefdoms. On the north coast of Peru, the great empire of the Chimú developed beginning around AD 900 in the territory that was formerly home to the Moche kingdoms. From their capital city of Chan Chan, the Chimú set out to conquer much of the Peruvian coast and ultimately controlled several valleys north and south of the capital. This great empire would ultimately become the principal rival to the Incas.

In the highlands the situation remained fragmented for a much longer period of time. In Cuzco, the Inca heartland, numerous small kingdoms competed for supremacy. By the mid-fifteenth century AD, the Inca emerged supreme among these warring kingdoms and were able to launch their empire by making use of the knowledge of statecraft and a physical infrastructure they inherited from their predecessors, especially the Huari, Tiahuanaco, and Chimú empires. The Late Horizon of Rowe's chronology corresponds to the dominion of the great Inca Empire.

Further Reading

Bergh, Susan E., et al. *Wari: Lords of the Ancient Andes*. London: Cleveland Museum of Art/Thames and Hudson, 2012.

Burger, Richard L. *Chavin and the Origins of Andean Civilization*. London: Thames and Hudson, 1992.

Kolata, Alan L. *The Tiwanaku: Portrait of an Andean Civilization*. Oxford: Blackwell Publishers, 1993.

Moseley, Michael. *The Incas and Their Ancestors*. Rev. 2nd ed. London: Thames and Hudson, 2001.

Rowe, John H. "An Interpretation of Radiocarbon Measurements on Archaeological Samples from Peru." In *Peruvian Archaeology: Selected Readings*, edited by John H. Rowe and Dorothy Menzel, 16–30. Palo Alto, CA: Peek Publications, 1967.

■ GORDON F. MCEWAN

Born in Llerena, Extremadura, Spain, around 1518, Cieza came to the New World as a young soldier in 1535 where he lived in New Granada (a Spanish Colonial jurisdiction in northern South America) engaged, as he put it, "in conquests and discoveries." Even before he arrived in Peru he felt compelled to write about "the strange and wonderful things that exist in this New World of the Indies." He reached Peru in 1547 to fight on the side of the Spanish Crown during the rebellion of Gonzalo Pizarro, one of Francisco Pizarro's brothers. In 1549, after the rebellion, he cast his weapons aside and "put his quill to the great things that are to be recounted of Peru," traveling down the spine of the Andes and the coast of Peru, to Cuzco, the Lake Titicaca region, and into highland Bolivia.

His masterpiece, the *Crónica del Peru* (Chronicle of Peru), is divided into four parts: the first, referred to as "Part I of the Chronicle of Peru" and the only one published before his death in Seville, in 1554, deals with the geography of the Andes, from New Granada to Argentina. It also describes the cities founded by the Spaniards and the ancient rites and customs of the indigenous peoples he encountered as he made his way south; many of his sources were Native informants. He was one of the first chroniclers to describe Inca **roads**, comparing these "splendid highways" to the ones built by Alexander the Great and other "mighty kings who ruled the world." Although he never reached Chile and Argentina, the southernmost extent of Tahuantinsuyu, the Inca Empire, he based his account of regions he had not visited on information gathered from other sources.

The second part of the *Crónica del Perú*, entitled the *Señorío de los Incas* (Kingdom of the Incas), is a history of the Incas and of "their great deeds and government." Cieza's narrative of the Incas is considered by many to be one of the most readable and reliable chronicles; indeed, many of his astute observations have been borne out by archaeology. In Jauja, in the central highlands, and in Cuzco he interviewed the keepers of the knotted-string records, the *quipucamayocs* (see **Quipu**), admitting that at first he was dubious that information could be recorded on *quipus*, but once the system had been explained to him he was "amazed" at its accuracy. The influence of his contemporary, the chronicler **Juan de Betanzos**, whom he met in Cuzco, is discernable, especially in accounts of Inca myths and rituals, although the sway of other writers is also apparent. Unlike the chronicles written after the 1570s that sought to discredit the Incas as the legitimate sovereigns of Tahuantinsuyu, Cieza demonstrated that they were in fact the rightful rulers (see **Expansion**). The third part of Cieza's chronicle covers the Spanish discovery and conquest of the Inca Empire, while the fourth part, *The Civil Wars of Peru*, tells of the civil wars, among various factions of Spaniards, that undermined Peru's Spanish colonial administration for decades in the mid-sixteenth century.

Further Reading

Cieza de León, Pedro de. *Parte primera de la cronica del Peru* [in Spanish]. 1553. http://www.brown
.edu/Facilities/John_Carter_Brown_Library/peru/peru/spa_deleon.php.

————. *The Travels of Pedro de Cieza de León, A.D. 1532–50, Contained in the First Part of His Chron-
icle of Peru.* Translated and edited by Clements R. Markham. Works Issued by the Hakluyt
Society, no. 33. London: Printed for the Hakluyt Society, 1864. Reissued, New York: Burt
Franklin, 1964 [1553].

————. *The Incas.* Translated by Harriet de Onis. Edited by Victor W. von Hagen. Norman: University of Oklahoma Press, 1959 [1553].

————. *The Discovery and Conquest of Peru: Chronicles of the New World Encounter.* Edited and translated by Alexandra Parma Cook and Noble David Cook. Durham, NC: Duke University
Press, 1998 [1554].

Pease, Franklin. "Cieza de León, Pedro de (ca. 1518–1554)." In *Guide to Documentary Sources for
Andean Studies, 1530–1900,* edited by Joanne Pillsbury, vol. 2, 34–36. Norman: University of
Oklahoma Press, 2008.

■ ADRIANA VON HAGEN

COCA

In 1555 the Spanish chronicler Agustín de Zárate wrote of the rigors of the high Andean environment. To live in these mountains, he said, was to endure rain, hail, snow, and
intense cold. Yet, he added, there were warm valleys where one could cultivate a plant
called *coca,* the leaves of which alleviated pain and hunger and which the Incas prized
more highly than gold or silver.

Chewed with potash or lime, coca leaves mitigate the effects of living and working
in the harsh Andean environment. The cultivation of this hardy bush (genus *Erythroxylum;* family Erythroxylaceae) has a long history in Andean South America; there is
archaeological evidence for its use in Ecuador and the north coast of Peru by 3000 BC
(thus predating Inca civilization by over four thousand years). The Incas considered coca
essential to social and religious life; sharing coca was a gesture of hospitality and regard.
The host of a work party or feast was expected to make liberal distributions of coca to
those in attendance. Since generous feast-giving was a prerequisite for high status and the
ability to mobilize labor, access to coca held political as well as economic significance
(see **Feasts, State-Sponsored**).

The Incas cultivated two varieties of coca. Small-leaved *tupa coca* (Trujillo coca;
Erythroxylum novogranatense var. *truxillense*) grows in the mid to high river valleys of
northern Peru and parts of Ecuador, thriving in arid, rocky soil, 300–1,800 meters
(1,000–6,000 feet) in altitude. Larger-leaved *mamas coca* (Huánuco or Bolivian coca;
Erythroxylum coca var. *coca*) was cultivated along the eastern Andean slopes in high forests,
500–2,000 meters (1,600–6,500 feet) in altitude. Both varieties of coca contain under
one percent by weight of the alkaloid cocaine. Although *mamas coca* tends to have a
higher cocaine content, Inca nobility preferred the taste of *tupa coca,* which contains
methyl salicylate (wintergreen). When masticated with calcium carbonate (ashes or
powdered lime) to form a quid, the leaves are stimulating and temporarily suppress
fatigue, hunger, and thirst. Medicinal uses include the treatment of gastrointestinal prob-

Born in Lopera, Spain, in 1580, Cobo arrived in Lima in 1599. He studied at the Jesuit colleges of Lima and later in Cuzco, where he graduated in theology. He lived in the Titicaca region in 1610 and in 1613, working at the native parish of Juli run by the Jesuit order. Cobo later taught Latin at the Jesuit college in Arequipa before moving to Pisco, on Peru's south coast, to direct the Jesuit college there. He returned to Lima in 1620 and soon embarked for Mexico, where he lived from 1629 to 1642. Cobo then returned to Lima, where he spent the rest of his life until his death, in 1657. He began writing his *Historia del Nuevo Mundo* (History of the New World) in Lima, completing the first part in 1639 and putting the finishing touches on the second and final part in 1653. The manuscript subsequently made its way to Seville, Spain. The first complete edition of Cobo's chronicle was not published until 1890–1893.

Cobo's plan for his work was quite ambitious. He initially proposed to write a total of 43 books divided into three parts, which would deal with Pre-Columbian America, the discovery and conquest of the Caribbean and South America, and New Spain. Only sections of the first and second parts are known to have been completed. These two parts cover the Incas and their land and the founding of Lima by the Spaniards. Cobo's chronicle not only discusses the history and customs of the Incas and the people they conquered, but also touches on such topics as astronomy, religion, botany, and zoology. He conducted interviews with descendants of the Incas in Cuzco, lending an air of immediacy to his account, even if it was written 100 years after the onset of the Spanish invasion.

Like so many authors of his day, Cobo borrowed liberally from other chroniclers, including **José de Acosta**, **Pedro Pizarro**, **Garcilaso de la Vega**, **Cristóbal de Molina**, and Alonso Ramos Gavilán, whose manuscript he relied on, in part, for descriptions of Copacabana and the Inca sanctuaries on the **Islands of the Sun and the Moon** on Lake Titicaca. Cobo's chronicle is especially valued for its account of Cuzco's *ceque* system, which is based on a lost manuscript, probably one authored by **Polo Ondegardo**, in 1559.

Further Reading

Cobo, Bernabé. "Historia del Nuevo Mundo." In *Obras del P. Bernabé Cobo.* Vols. 1–2. Biblioteca de Autores Españoles, nos. 91–92. Madrid: Editorial Atlas, 1964 [1653].

———. *History of the Inca Empire: An Account of the Indians' Customs and Their Origin, Together with a Treatise on Inca Legends, History, and Social Institutions by Father Bernabé Cobo.* Translated and edited by Roland Hamilton. Austin: University of Texas Press, 1979 [1653].

———. *Inca Religion and Customs.* Translated and edited by Roland Hamilton. Austin: University of Texas Press, 1990 [1653].

Hamilton, Roland. "Cobo, Bernabé (1580–1657)." In *Guide to Documentary Sources for Andean Studies, 1530–1900,* edited by Joanne Pillsbury, vol. 2: 152–55. Norman: University of Oklahoma Press, 2008.

■ ADRIANA VON HAGEN

A woman offers coca leaf to a visitor; scenes such as these are still common in the Andes. Guaman Poma de Ayala, Felipe. *El primer nueva corónica y buen gobierno*. Edited by John V. Murra and Rolena Adorno, 811/865. Mexico City: Siglo Veintiuno, 1980 [1615].

lems and high-altitude sickness. Because the leaves contain iron, phosphorus, vitamin A, and riboflavin, coca has nutritional value as well.

Coca's economic and political importance cannot be separated from its crucial role in Inca religion. The precious leaf was offered not only to other people, but to deities as well. Inca society was organized around sacred places (**huacas**) of various sorts, including heroes turned into stone, ancestral origin places, tombs of mummified forebears, and prominent landmarks. In **Cuzco**, the imperial capital, priests tended temples dedicated to the Sun, the Moon, Lightning, and the mummies of deceased emperors; while throughout the empire, ethnic communities paid homage to their own local *huacas* and ancestors (see **Deities; Religion**). To maintain positive relationships with these powerful entities, it was necessary to "feed" them with sacrificial offerings. Coca was an essential component of virtually all these sacrifices; it was burned with maize and shells, pulverized and blown as a powder, and even offered as a masticated quid. Coca was also used in **divination**; ritual specialists would burn a mixture of coca and llama fat and predict the future based on the appearance of the flames. The *Huarochirí Manuscript* (a narrative of native Andean religion, compiled around 1600; see **Avila, Francisco de**) recounts how that region's paramount *huaca*, Pariacaca, commanded the people to supply coca for his son (another local *huaca*) before chewing it themselves. Dancers performed for Pariacaca three times a year carrying large leather bags of coca contributed by their home communities. Presumably this coca was left with Pariacaca's priests for use in offerings as well as for their own consumption.

It is unclear to what extent access to coca leaf was controlled under Inca rule. Many Spanish chroniclers state that its consumption was strictly limited to the aristocracy, and the Incas clearly did try to control the cultivation and distribution of coca among their subject peoples. After conquering the Chillón valley on Peru's central coast, for example, they sent *mitmacuna* (colonists from other ethnic groups) to commandeer *tupa coca* plantations and cultivate them for the Cuzco nobility and priesthood of the Sun. Other *mitmacuna* were sent to coca-growing regions in Bolivia. On the other hand, eminent historians such as **John V. Murra** and **María Rostworowski** argue that the Incas were not completely successful in establishing a monopoly on coca.

Even under Inca subjugation, local polities maintained access to coca through long-standing exchange relationships. While people of higher status, such as *curacas* and priests, had more access to the leaf than people of lower rank, commoners did consume coca; in fact, the chronicler **Juan de Betanzos** says they always had it in their mouths. While **Felipe Guaman Poma de Ayala** depicts rulers, queens, and military leaders carrying coca bags, his chronicle also includes a drawing of simple horticulturalists sharing coca leaves. Travelers chewed coca to ward off fatigue, and when crossing a pass they would rub their coca quid on a ceremonial mound of stones (*apacheta*), asking for a safe and prosperous journey. If resting or sleeping overnight in a cave, they rubbed coca quid on the cavern ceiling, imploring, "Cave, do not eat me" (i.e., "do not collapse"). Another early chronicler, the priest Molina el Almagrista, also implies that coca chewing was a daily practice, commenting that whenever the Natives chewed coca they would offer some to the Sun; if they passed a fire, they would reverently throw in a few leaves as an offering.

The Spanish conquest had a profound effect on the political economy of coca. Although the Church discouraged its religious uses, production of coca leaf actually increased under Spanish rule; colonists conscripted native Andeans to work in mines and paid them in coca to increase their work output. Mining took a heavy death toll, as did punishing labor conditions on greatly expanded coca plantations in the upper Amazon. In 1860 a German chemist developed a method to refine pure cocaine from the leaves. For a time cocaine was touted as a wonder cure for a range of ailments and was used as anesthesia in surgical procedures; simultaneously its recreational use and abuse grew, and by the 1930s cocaine was banned or severely restricted throughout North America and Western Europe.

Although cocaine is distilled from coca leaf, the two must not be confused. Masticated or consumed as tea, the effects of coca leaf are roughly comparable to those of a cup of coffee or a cigarette. Coca is still consumed throughout the highlands of Peru and Bolivia to energize the body and focus the mind for work; it retains deep symbolic significance in native religious practices and has many medicinal uses. As in Inca times, sharing coca leaf signifies amity and a cooperative spirit. Guaman Poma's drawing of a country farmer courteously sharing his coca—"Take this coca, My Sister"—could (with a change in costume) just as well depict contemporary practice.

Further Reading

Allen, Catherine J. *The Hold Life Has: Coca and Cultural Identity in an Andean Community*. Washington, DC: Smithsonian Institution Press, 2002.

Betanzos, Juan de. *Narrative of the Incas.* Translated by Roland Hamilton and Dana Buchanan. Austin: University of Texas Press, 1996 [1551–1557].

Cobo, Bernabé. *Inca Religion and Customs.* Translated and edited by Roland Hamilton. Austin: University of Texas Press, 1990 [1653].

Guaman Poma de Ayala, Felipe. *Nueva corónica y buen gobierno.* Complete digital facsimile edition of the manuscript, with a corrected online version of Guaman Poma 1980. Scholarly editor Rolena Adorno. Copenhagen: Royal Library of Denmark, 2001 [1615]. http://www.kb.dk/elib/mss/poma.

Pacini, Deborah, and Christine Franquemont, eds. *Coca and Cocaine: Effects on People and Policy in Latin America.* Cambridge, MA: Cultural Survival, 1986.

Ramírez, Susan Elizabeth. *To Feed and Be Fed: The Cosmological Basis of Authority and Identity in the Andes.* Stanford, CA: Stanford University Press, 2005.

Rostworowski de Diez Canseco, María. *History of the Inca Realm.* Translated by Harry B. Iceland. Cambridge: Cambridge University Press, 1999.

Salomon, Frank, and George L. Urioste, trans. and eds. *The Huarochirí Manuscript: A Testament of Ancient and Colonial Andean Religion.* Austin: University of Texas Press, 1991.

Steele, Paul R. *Handbook of Inca Mythology.* Santa Barbara, CA: ABC-CLIO, 2004

■ CATHERINE J. ALLEN

COLLASUYU

The largest of all the *suyu* divisions, Collasuyu extended southward from Cuzco, embracing the southern highlands, Lake Titicaca, the temperate and tropical regions to the east of the lake, and down into what is today Chile, as far south as Santiago, and into northwestern Argentina. Collasuyu, along with **Cuntisuyu**, formed the *hurin*, or lower, half of Tahuantinsuyu, the Inca Empire. The city of **Cuzco** was also divided into four *suyus*, and the main plaza served as the axis of these territorial divisions as well as the nexus of the four roads leading to the territorial divisions. Collasuyu was also one of the four divisions of the valley's *ceque* system, the system of imaginary lines that radiated out from the **Coricancha**, the Sun temple. The *huacas*, or shrines, located along the 328 or so *ceques* were ranked accordingly.

The region of Lake Titicaca was one of the earliest targets of Inca expansion far beyond the Cuzco heartland; indeed, excavations of an Inca house south of Lake Titicaca revealed pottery predating the mid-fifteenth century (see **Chronology, Inca**). No doubt, the area's enormous herds of wild and domesticated camelids made it especially attractive to a people keen on procuring fiber to weave cloth, regarded by Andean peoples as one of the most valuable of commodities (see **Weaving and Textiles**). The Incas also focused on the region's religious shrines, in particular the **Island of the Sun** in Lake Titicaca, where a sacred rock marked the Sun's birthplace and featured in an Inca **origin myth** that claimed the founding Incas emerged from the lake. On the mainland at Copacabana, as well as on the Island of the Sun and the neighboring Island of the Moon, the Incas built temples, shrines, roads, and facilities for pilgrims—one of the most elaborate building schemes and reorganization of sacred space ever undertaken in Tahuantinsuyu. A long-distance *ceque* linked the lake to Cuzco and, via another *ceque*, to the Pacific Ocean. The *ceque* mirrored the path of the sun as it emerged from the lake and set into the sea.

To the east of Lake Titicaca, the temperate valleys of the Andean foothills are particularly well suited to maize production. This region was the target of an ambitious

Incallacta in Bolivia was part of Collasuyu, the empire's southern quadrant.
It contains one of the largest single-room roofed buildings ever built by the
Incas, seen here in the center of the photograph flanking a large double plaza.
Lawrence S. Coben.

resettlement program by the Inca emperor Huayna Capac in the Cochabamba valley.
Beyond Cochabamba, the Incas built an imperial installation at Incallacta, a monumental ceremonial site at Samaipata, and a chain of "forts" and other installations geared to
securing tropical resources from largely uncooperative tribes living along the empire's
eastern fringe, and defending the region from attacks by the feared Chiriguano people.

The Incas began expanding into Chile and Argentina by at least the early fifteenth
century. Faced with less centralized societies and an uneven distribution of natural and
human resources (in stark contrast to **Chinchaysuyu**), the approach was more gradual
and focused on Collasuyu's underground wealth: metallic ores, mainly copper, tin, and
silver. Tin was especially important because when alloyed with copper, it produces tin
bronze, the "stainless steel" of the Inca empire (see **Metallurgy**; **Mining**). The lack of
monumental architecture belies the intensity of Inca rule in this region, where the Incas
established relationships with dozens of local groups, built scores of settlements, and expanded the road network. Nonetheless, the region witnessed numerous revolts by powerful ethnic confederations up until the time of the Spanish invasion.

The Incas left their mark on the sacred landscape as well. Collasuyu is renowned
for the high incidence of human sacrifice on its snow-clad mountains, many towering
over 5,000 meters (16,400 feet) above sea level. Many peaks, most notably 6,739-
meter-high (22,110 feet) Llullaillaco in Argentina, have yielded astonishingly well-
preserved offerings of children and young women accompanied by rich grave goods
(see **Capac Hucha**).

Further Reading

Bauer, Brian S., and Charles Stanish. *Ritual and Pilgrimage in the Ancient Andes: The Islands of the Sun and the Moon.* Austin: University of Texas Press, 2001.

D'Altroy, Terence N., Veronica I. Williams, and Ana Maria Lorandi. "The Incas in the Southlands." In *Variations in the Expression of Inca Power,* edited by Richard L. Burger, Craig Morris, and Ramiro Matos, 85–134. Washington, DC: Dumbarton Oaks, 2007.

Reinhard, Johan, and Maria Constanza Ceruti. *Inca Rituals and Sacred Mountains: A Study of the World's Highest Archaeological Sites.* Los Angeles: Cotsen Institute of Archaeology, 2011.

■ ADRIANA VON HAGEN

CONQUESTS

The Incas conquered a large swath of the Andes, and the first Europeans in the region wondered how they were able to do so in just a few generations. One of the most astute writers, **Polo Ondegardo**, argued that Inca forces almost always succeeded because they were numerically superior—which raises the question of how they had allied with or conquered their neighbors in the Cuzco region to establish the momentum of imperial expansion. Archaeological and documentary evidence from the Cuzco region indicates that Inca power grew in the century or so before the first imperial campaigns, as rulers built stronger networks of regional allies and engaged in extended campaigns to conquer multiple resistant communities (see **Archaeology, Cuzco; Warfare**). The earliest expansion beyond the Cuzco valley focused on the incorporation of weaker groups, but by AD 1400 Inca rulers succeeded in conquering their most powerful local rivals and extending their domain along key corridors that connected Cuzco to other parts of the Andes.

The most reliable early chronicles describe the first Inca campaigns beyond the Cuzco region as rare events in which a ruler mustered all resources at his disposal to make Inca military power felt across a targeted region. The Incas advanced quickly in many regions because of local political decentralization and intergroup hostility, a common scenario in the central Andes at the time. As the Inca army approached an area, emissaries sought to convince local leaders to submit and become Inca vassals. Success in attracting a local ally often hardened the resistance of their local rivals, resulting in bloody battles.

The chronicler **Juan de Betanzos** describes generational campaigns in which the mobilization of the army coincided with the construction of infrastructure that facilitated future military incursions into a conquered region. The construction of **roads** and **bridges** enhanced the reach of Inca power, and Betanzos notes how the construction of the strategic bridge over the Apurímac River during an early campaign led immediately to the surrender of multiple groups living on the other side of that natural barrier. Betanzos and other chronicles describe Inca conquest ideology in the early years as motivated by respect for the ruler's title and for the Sun cult.

Imperial campaigns in the early fifteenth century involved universal conscription of an overwhelming force of Inca subjects, a peasant army under the direct strategic direction of the ruler and a few of his closest male relatives (see **Warfare**). Over time, the growing empire found it useful to raise troops more frequently, and by the middle of the fifteenth century it was not uncommon for multiple armies to be in the field at the same time, led by two or three brothers or sons of the ruler. Delegation of command allowed the Incas to expand along the axis of the Andean highlands while also making forays toward the Amazonian slope to the east and the Pacific coast to the west.

To a certain extent, rulers seem to have delegated command as they grew older and shifted their focus to ritual and administrative power seated at the capital. Vesting one's sons with military power was seen as a way of allowing potential future rulers to distinguish themselves, and to channel some of the negative effects of sibling rivalry from the capital into unconquered parts of the Andes. Some Inca princes perished on campaign, but those who returned victorious brought prisoners and spoils to offer to their father so that he could celebrate his victory—even when the ruler was so feeble that he had to be carried through the ceremony.

The speed of early Inca campaigns relied on attracting allies using intimidation as well as promises of marriage alliances and rich gifts for cooperative local leaders. Over time, many Inca allies rebelled, and the chronicles clearly link rebellion to periods of royal succession, which frequently came with factional violence in the Inca imperial heartland (see **Wars, Dynastic**). At such times, Inca military power was directed at itself, and the personal connections that local leaders had forged with a deceased ruler were no longer certain. Many chronicles identify the accession of Topa Inca Yupanqui as a time of pronounced rebellions that required costly campaigns of reconquest.

Suppression of revolts provided the empire with the opportunity to consolidate its administrative power, establishing networks of roads, way stations, and administrative centers that could facilitate the movement of information from provinces to the capital (and of soldiers to hot spots that developed). The Incas demilitarized their interior, except for key facilities, such as bridges. Topa Inca Yupanqui is generally acknowledged as a great consolidator in the central highland provinces, but he followed his campaigns of reconquest with an extended foray into the southern periphery of the empire, bringing some form of Inca rule to a huge territory that covers parts of what is today southern Peru and Bolivia, northern Chile, and northwest Argentina.

Inca military strategy developed as conquests extended into the northern Peruvian highlands and into Ecuador. The broken terrain and climate of the tropical highlands made it more difficult to divide and conquer local populations, and the Chachapoya and Cañari peoples proved to be especially difficult to incorporate. The empire restructured new provinces, resettling much of the indigenous population and drawing large numbers of permanent retainers (*yanacuna*), as well as households that served in a more permanent capacity as soldiers (see **Labor Service**). As the Inca advance slowed, the empire shifted from conscript armies to a standing frontier force, as well as strategically placed garrisons that protected the corridors from the highlands to the Amazonian slope (see **Fortifications**). There is archaeological evidence that local populations also built frontier forts to protect themselves from the Inca advance, and many groups were feared for their ability to penetrate Inca territory and wreak havoc on colonist populations that settled to consolidate imperial power. The emperor Huayna Capac spent decades living at the front to direct territorial expansion northward, moving his family there and establishing palaces and estates for their maintenance.

Accounts of the Inca army in the decade before the Spanish conquest describe a force that was unlike the army that set imperial expansion in motion, and the imperial motivation for conquest reflects a different set of targets. Instead of seeking local allies who led local populations that were at least partly autonomous, the Incas sought to push "uncivilized" frontier populations out of territory that the army held as new settlers colonized the land and took over broader economic networks. This militarized emphasis on civilizing the Amazonian and Ecuadorian frontier contrasts with the evidence for military action against the states and empires that ruled over the central and northern Peruvian coast.

Whereas the chronicler Betanzos offers vivid accounts of Inca armies in the Amazonian heart of darkness, he is silent about the incorporation of coastal civilizations. Some sources suggest that military conquest was necessary to annex the north coast Chimú Empire (see **Chronology, Pre-Inca**), and remove its paramount ruler from power, and that extended campaigns requiring new infrastructure and extended sieges brought kingdoms like Huarco in the Cañete valley on Peru's south coast, under Inca rule. Other sources emphasize the lack of conflict in the incorporation of some coastal societies.

A destructive civil war overtook the Inca Empire in the early 1530s, and it illustrates how much Inca military power changed over the course of a century. Atahualpa, the military governor of Quito, rose up against his half brother Huascar, who held ritual and administrative power in Cuzco (see **Wars, Dynastic**). Atahualpa's generals turned a seasoned frontier army onto the interior of the empire, using the roads and way stations to march on the capital. Huascar's generals were able to raise several conscript armies that reportedly outnumbered the Quito force, but they were cut to shreds and scattered repeatedly before the frontier troops arrived at the capital and laid waste to the households of royal lineages that had sided with Huascar. Pizarro's small expedition arrived shortly afterward, and made similar use of Inca infrastructure in their invasion, and, as they brought down the mighty empire, adding the support of unhappy Inca subjects and fighting in a manner that confounded Inca frontier and conscript armies (see **Invasion, Spanish**).

Further Reading

Bauer, Brian S., and R. Alan Covey. "Processes of State Formation in the Inca Heartland (Cuzco, Peru)." *American Anthropologist* 104, no. 3: 846–64, 2002.

Betanzos, Juan de. *Narrative of the Incas.* Translated and edited by Roland Hamilton and Dana Buchanan. Austin: University of Texas Press, 1996 [1551–1557].

Bram, Joseph. *An Analysis of Inca Militarism.* Seattle: University of Washington Press, 1941.

Covey, R. Alan. *How the Incas Built Their Heartland: State Formation and the Innovation of Imperial Strategies in the Sacred Valley, Peru.* Ann Arbor: University of Michigan Press, 2006.

Murra, John V. "The Expansion of the Inka State: Armies, Wars, and Rebellions." In *Anthropological History of Andean Polities,* edited by John V. Murra, Nathan Wachtel, and Jacques Revel, 49–58. New York: Cambridge University Press, 1986.

Ondegardo, Polo de. *Relación de los fundamentos acerca del notable daño que resulta de no guardar a los Indios sus fueros. Colección de Libros y Documentos Referentes a la Historia del Perú,* series 1, vol. 3: 45–188. Lima: Sanmartí, 1916 [1571].

Rowe, John H. "Absolute Chronology in the Andean Area." *American Antiquity* 10, no. 3: 265–84, 1945.

Sarmiento de Gamboa, Pedro. *The History of the Incas.* Translated and edited by Brian S. Bauer and Vania Smith. Austin: University of Texas Press, 2007 [1572].

■ R. ALAN COVEY

CORICANCHA

The principal Sun temple of Tahuantinsuyu, the Coricancha ("golden enclosure") lay in the southern part of Cuzco's ceremonial core, not far from the confluence of the city's two rivers, the Saphi and the Tullumayu (such locations, known as *tinkuys*, are considered auspicious). The temple served as the nexus of the valley's *ceque* system, the imaginary lines that underlay Cuzco's ritual organization. Because of the preeminence of Inti, the Sun god, and his human manifestation in the Inca ruler, the Coricancha ranked as the empire's most important shrine, acting as a conceptual model for a network of Sun temples across the realm. Sun temples received rich endowments of religious specialists, *aclla* (chosen women), land—much of it devoted to maize cultivation—as well as pastures to sustain large herds of camelids. Only the most devout could enter the Coricancha's inner sanctum after fasting and abstaining from salt, meat, hot peppers, and sex for a year; and they could only enter barefoot and carrying a burden, as a sign of submission and reverence.

Because of the temple's wealth and grandeur, many chroniclers devoted long passages to its description. **Cieza de León**, who saw it sixteen years after it was first ransacked by Spanish soldiers, called it one of the richest temples in the whole world. The complex housed the "hall of the sun" and several "chapels," according to the chronicler **Garcilaso de la Vega**. Other chroniclers say images of the Creator deity, the Sun, and Illapa, the thunder god, shared the Coricancha's main "altar," suggesting that the three may have been worshipped as different aspects of a single solar deity (see **Deities; Religion**). The *Villac Umu*, the high priest of the Sun, presided over the Coricancha. Every year, for instance, when the sovereign summoned portable versions of the empire's leading *huacas* (shrines) to Cusco for an oracular congress, the Villac Umu, the empire's highest ranking medium, served as the voice of the Sun (see **Oracles**).

The Spaniards built the church of Santo Domingo over the Coricancha, Cuzco's sun temple and one of the empire's holiest shrines. Jean-Pierre Protzen.

A single entryway led into the complex, which may have contained as few as four, and as many as seven, rectangular halls surrounding a central courtyard. (A Dominican church and cloister, built over and around the Coricancha in Colonial times, has obscured or destroyed many Inca walls.) The enclosing wall of the temple complex features one of the most superb constructions in Tahuantinsuyu, a curved wall of andesite. "In all Spain," wrote Cieza, "I have seen nothing that can compare with these walls" (Cieza 1959 [1553]).

Only three Spaniards, dispatched from Cajamarca to Cuzco in early 1533 to hasten the shipment of gold to secure the captured ruler Atahualpa's release, saw the temple before its plunder (see **Invasion, Spanish**). Some chroniclers would have us believe that gold sheet covered the entire compound, but the earliest account states that only the façade of the hall of the sun was sheathed in gold, while on the side that was shaded from the sun, the gold was "more debased." It is reported that the three Spaniards used crowbars to remove 700 gold plates from the hall of the Sun.

In the Coricancha's central courtyard, eyewitnesses observed a stone carved in the shape of a seat and covered in gold, a gold basin, and next to it an image shaped like a young boy, called *Punchao* (day, or young Sun), all made of gold. Dressed in a tunic of fine cloth and wearing the *mascaypacha*, the Inca "crown" and symbol of kingship, Punchao's hollow stomach contained the ashes of deceased rulers' internal organs. At a noon ceremony, women uncovered the seat and offered the image maize, meat, and **chicha** (maize beer). At night, Punchao "slept" in a small room on a seat covered in iridescent feathers. The Coricancha also housed a silver image of Quilla, the Moon goddess. The mummies of the deceased rulers and their queens were seated on benches at the Coricancha when they weren't attending ceremonies in the city's main plaza or visiting their country estates, attended by a woman who fanned away dust and flies (see **Mummies, Royal**).

A ceremonial garden faced the hall of the Sun, linking the Sun and the reigning Inca with maize, the empire's most important ritual crop and source of *chicha*, which was imbibed in great quantities at every ceremony. Three times a year—at sowing, at harvest, and when noble Inca youths were initiated into adulthood—the ruler cultivated this ritual garden, which had been planted with golden stalks of maize.

Further Reading

Bauer, Brian S. *Ancient Cusco: Heartland of the Inca.* Austin: University of Texas Press, 2004.

Farrington, Ian S. *Cusco: Urbanism and Archaeology in the Inka World.* Gainesville: University Press of Florida, 2013.

Hyslop, John. *Inka Settlement Planning.* Austin: University of Texas Press, 1990.

■ ADRIANA VON HAGEN

COSTUME

Like so many aspects of Inca culture, costume in Inca times did not differ markedly from the attire of immediate pre-Inca peoples, nor from that of contemporary societies conquered by the Incas. Rather, the Incas adopted popular styles of clothing and headdress and added embellishments and iconography as well as garments of a standardized size that distinguished the costume as Inca. In fact, as noted by a well-informed Spanish chronicler, **Bernabé Cobo,** the Incas required all peoples in the empire to wear their native headdresses, which allowed their ethnic affiliation to be identified at a glance. The bright colors and bold designs of Inca costume made it readily recognizable and imbued wearers with prestige, especially if it was a gift from the ruler.

Aside from clothing unearthed in coastal Inca-period graves and the rare cloud forest or highland cache, much of what we know about Inca costume is derived from descriptions in chronicles, especially that of Bernabé Cobo, and from the drawings in the illustrated chronicle of **Felipe Guaman Poma de Ayala.**

In the highlands, women wore a dress called an *acsu*, composed of a rectangular or square piece of fabric of cotton or camelid fiber wound around the body under the arms; the edges of the fabric went over the shoulders and were secured with *tupu* pins of gold, silver, or bronze. A wide cloth belt cinched the dress at the waist. The design of the fabric was quite simple, usually composed of color blocks woven in natural hues. Women also wore shawls, known as *liclla*, pinned at the breast with a *tipki* pin, which is generally smaller than a *tupu* pin. Like the fabric used for the dresses, that of the *lliclla*s was generally woven in stripes of solid colors.

Small holes in the *tupu* pins, which were worn with the points facing upward, served to secure a cotton cord attached to a tubular woven structure studded with various items ranging from the ornamental, such as palm seeds or shell carvings, to the utilitarian, such as combs, weaving utensils, and metal tweezers.

On their heads women displayed headbands or a headcloth folded several times known as a *pampacona* or a *ñañaca*, and they wore their hair loose or braided. Their feet were shod with sandals of *cabuya* (a fiber derived from the leaves of the fique plant, *Furcraea andina*), or moccasins of deer or camelid leather.

Men's attire consisted of a three-quarter-length sleeveless tunic known as an *uncu*, a breechcloth, a mantle, and a headband or other headgear. *Uncus* are one of the most

An *uncu* or man's tunic in provincial Chachapoya-Inca style, a classic example of the hybrid textiles produced in the Inca Empire. The iconography is Chachapoya, but certain technical features point to its Inca affiliation. Adriana von Hagen, courtesy Museo Leymebamba, Leymebamba, Amazonas, Peru.

distinctive garments of Inca men's costume and could be far more elaborate than the wraparound dresses worn by women. While many men wore plain-weave *uncus*, others, especially those donned by nobles and those that had been received as a gift (a common diplomatic overture by the Inca or his agents to the *curacas*, or headmen, of newly conquered peoples), could be quite exquisite. Many are of finely woven tapestry and the design repertory is so standardized that some scholars believe it may denote status, profession, or place of origin. Indeed, one classic Inca *uncu* design, a black and white checkerboard motif with a red yoke, is believed to have been worn by warriors. The tapestry designs usually take the form of small tapestry squares, known generically as *tocapu*. Many *uncus*, even plain-weave ones, have *tocapu*-decorated waistbands, another distinguishing feature. The standardized proportions, size, and finishing details are other distinctive traits.

Over their shoulders men wore mantles known as *yacolla*, which they wore loose or tied under the chin or at the shoulder. Larger than women's shawls, these too appear to have been generally undecorated. Breechcloths, *huara*, were usually plain weave. On the coast, however, loincloths were often decorated, as tunics were shorter. This unremarkable garment featured in an important coming-of-age ritual known as the *huarachicuy*,

This finely woven tapestry *uncu*, or man's tunic, of cotton and camelid fiber is decorated with small rectangles known as *tocapu*. Such designs are believed to have only been worn by people of royal or high rank. Dumbarton Oaks, Pre-Columbian Collection, Washington, D.C.

when noble youths received their first loincloth. The elaborate ritual culminated with an ear-piercing ceremony; large ear spools set the youths apart as nobles.

Headdresses served as ethnic markers and told knowledgeable observers about the ethnic identity, place of origin, and other essential social and political facts about the wearer. As the chronicler **Pedro de Cieza de León** remarked,

> If they were Yungas, they went muffled like gypsies; if Collas, they wore caps shaped like mortars, of wool; if Canas they wore larger caps and much broader. The Cañari wore a kind of narrow wooden crown like the rim of a sieve; the Huancas, strands that fell below their chin, and their hair braided; the Canchis, broad black or red bands over their forehead. Thus all of them could be recognized by their insignia. (Cieza 1959 [1553]).

The Inca ruler and the nobility, as well as **Inca by privilege**, donned standardized, often elaborate, headgear. Inca men wore a headdress known as a *llautu* that resembled a sling and was composed of a braided headband twisted around the head several times. Nobles wore a metal plaque attached to the *llautu*, along with a feather ornament. Instead of a metal plaque attached to the *llautu*, the ruler's badge of office was the *mascaypacha*, which consisted of a red fringe hanging down the center of his forehead to which were attached hollow gold tubes. Warriors sported feather headdresses (see **Feathers**).

Like women, men wore sandals and moccasins, and appear to have kept their hair short, although hair styles too appear to have served as ethnic markers, as Cieza noted in his description of the braids worn by the Huancas. Ear spools, known as *paku*, ranged from wood and tufts of wool to precious metals. The Spaniards referred to men wearing large ear ornaments as "*orejones*," or big ears. Nobles also wore gold or silver bracelets. Both men and women carried coca leaves in small woven bags; these were also common diplomatic gifts and could be quite elaborately woven or covered in feathers.

Further Reading

Cobo, Bernabé. *Inca Religion and Customs*. Translated and edited by Roland Hamilton. Austin: University of Texas Press, 1990 [1653].

Guaman Poma de Ayala, Felipe. *The First New Chronicle and Good Government: On the History of the World and the Incas up to 1615*. Translated by Roland Hamilton. Austin: University of Texas Press, 2009 [1615].

Murra, John V. "Cloth and Its Function in the Inca State." *American Anthropologist* 64, no. 4: 710–28, 1962.

Rowe, Ann Pollard. "Inca Weaving and Costume." *Textile Museum Journal* 34–35:4–53, 1995–1996.

■ ADRIANA VON HAGEN

CRIME AND PUNISHMENT

In general, the Incas applied codes of conduct and customs that would have been easily recognized by most Andean peoples. "These Indians," noted the chronicler **Bernabé Cobo**, "had many . . . laws which were very beneficial for governing their republic well" (Cobo 1979 [1653]). The Incas, however, introduced new regulations that were aimed at protecting state assets, the ruling class, and religious officials. People could be judged by

According to the native chronicler Poma de Ayala, those who committed the most serious crimes were thrown into an underground dungeon to be devoured by pumas, jaguars, bears, and snakes. Guaman Poma de Ayala, Felipe. *El primer nueva corónica y buen gobierno*. Edited by John V. Murra and Rolena Adorno, 277/302. Mexico City: Siglo Veintiuno, 1980 [1615].

someone of higher rank (but not the reverse), and the nobility enjoyed free rein in most matters; however, if they committed an especially heinous act they were punished, but not as severely as non-nobles. The punishments for crimes thus differed according to the social status of the transgressor.

The chronicler **Garcilaso de la Vega** notes that crimes were recorded on **quipus**, adding that knots of certain colors stood for the crimes punished, and small threads of various colors attached to the thicker cords showed the penalty meted out and the law that had been applied. Men and women did not receive the same punishment for the same crimes: men, for example, could be exiled to work in the coca fields of **Antisuyu** or dispatched to perform hard labor in the mines, while women were forced into temple service. Punishments ranged from public humiliation, exile, and torture, to death by hanging or by being thrown into a prison and mauled by wild animals.

Cobo provides us with a range of crimes and their punishments. Rape was punishable by having a stone dropped on one's back at the first offense; the second offense resulted in death. Robbery spelled certain exile to the coca fields of Antisuyu. If someone on duty at a *tambo* (way station) failed to turn over his load to the head of the *tambo*, then his village was punished, because the village was responsible for the service to that *tambo*. Stealing irrigation water before it was one's turn to water one's own fields got an "arbitrary punishment." Bridge burning was regarded as a serious offense (reflecting the strategic importance of river crossings), resulting in the death penalty. Changing one's costume

In this drawing from the chronicle of Martín de Murúa, a thief is whipped. Murúa, Martín de. *Códice Murúa—Historia y Genealogía de los Reyes Incas del Perú* (Códice Galvin). Madrid: Testimonio Compañía Editorial, S. A., 2004 [1590–1598].

and "insignia of birthplace," that is, masquerading as a person of an ethnic identity different from one's own, was considered a great transgression against the Inca, the nation, and the province whose dress had been adopted. Such an offender of the public order was "punished with rigor." If one removed a stone boundary marker, known as *topo*, or entered someone else's property without that person's permission, the criminal was given the stone punishment the first time and the death penalty the second time. Misuse of supernatural powers and sorcery were grave offenses and resulted in death. If a "governor" of a province failed to administer justice, or covered up anything because of bribery, the Inca himself punished that official, removing him from office.

According to Garcilaso, severe reprisals awaited the *curaca*, or local lord, who rebelled against the Inca. The chronicler also noted that seducing an *aclla*, or chosen woman, was regarded as an especially outrageous crime. The *aclla* was to be buried alive and her accomplice hanged. In addition, as violations of the sanctity of these young women who were in service to the state were considered so heinous, the guilty man's wife, children, and servants were to be killed, as were his kinsmen, neighbors, townsmen, and flocks, and his village was to be destroyed and strewn with rocks. But, Garcilaso adds, the punishment struck such fear in the hearts of the people that no one even contemplated committing such a crime.

Cobo writes of two prisons in Cuzco. One, in the parish of San Sebastian just south of Cuzco, was destined for thieves and other criminals. The wrongdoers were hanged upside down and left there until they died. The other prison was an underground dungeon where people who committed the "most atrocious offenses," such as treason against the king, were thrown to be devoured by pumas, jaguars, bears, and snakes.

Further Reading

Cobo, Bernabé. *History of the Inca Empire: An Account of the Indian's Customs and Their Origin, Together with a Treatise on Inca Legends, History, and Social Institutions.* Translated and edited by Roland Hamilton. Austin: University of Texas Press, 1979 [1653].

Garcilaso de la Vega, El Inca. *Royal Commentaries of the Incas and General History of Peru, Part One.* Translated by Harold V. Livermore. Austin: University of Texas Press, 1966 [1609].

■ ADRIANA VON HAGEN

CUISINE

What, how, and with whom we eat are among the most fundamental ways that humans define themselves as social beings. For this reason, food preferences, culinary practices, and commensal relations—all a part of what defines cuisine—constitute one of the strongest markers of social identity and group membership. Various recent anthropological studies underscore the political dimensions of culinary practices, highlighting the prominent roles food and feasting play in the emergence of social hierarchy and the negotiation of power. Imperial Inca "haute cuisine" can thus be seen as a key domain for the investigation of Inca statecraft. Analyzing Inca foodways, cooking practices, and culinary artifacts provides important insights into the close connections among food, politics, and gender in the context of empire building. For the Incas and their subjects, these connections were materially manifest in the elaboration of a distinctive ensemble of polychrome pottery serving, storage, and cooking vessels (see **Ceramics**). The evidence used to reconstruct imperial Inca culinary practices and cuisine is drawn primarily from ethnohistoric records, archaeology, and palaeoethnobotanical research, with contemporary Andean ethnographic data providing useful points of comparison and analogy.

The major food categories comprising the Andean diet in the late pre-Columbian era consisted of maize—served in both cooked and fermented states; a large variety of potatoes and other tubers; the high altitude grain-like crop, quinoa; a variety of beans; a rather limited amount of meat consisting mainly of guinea pig (*cuy*), camelids, and some wild game and fish (see **Animals, Domesticated; Foodstuffs, Domesticated**); and various herbs, including hot peppers (ají), and salt for flavoring. The most common method of food preparation involved boiling, and foods were quite often consumed in the form of stews or soups. Other widespread culinary techniques in the Andes included roasting, parching, and toasting. Food preparation was likely a very time consuming activity as many products required several stages of processing, which could include drying, soaking, rinsing, mixing, parching, boiling, and reheating.

Maize (corn) was by far the most highly esteemed crop in the Inca Empire. Virtually every sixteenth-century account of native subsistence lists it as one of the main elements of the pre-Columbian diet. After it was dried, maize could be prepared in a number of different ways that typically involved either boiling or toasting.

One of the most important uses of maize was for the production of *chicha*, or maize beer. *Chicha* preparation was a highly elaborate process involving multiple processing stages that included grinding, boiling, cooling, decanting, and fermentation. Besides being the daily beverage of the local population, *chicha* was an important element of social and ceremonial gatherings where ritual drunkenness was often obligatory. In general, the ethnohistoric sources convey the sense that maize was special, desirable, and even viewed as holiday food by the highland populations.

Various chroniclers offer hints as to what may have constituted Inca haute cuisine, though none address the matter directly. The Native author **Felipe Guaman Poma de Ayala**, for instance, states that the Inca ruler "ate selected maize which is *capya utco sara*, and *papas manay* [early potatoes], . . . and llama called white *cuyro*, and *chiche* [tiny fish], white *cuy*, and much fruit and ducks, and very smooth *chicha* which took a month to mature and was called *yamor aca*. And he ate other things which the Indians were not to touch upon pain of death" (Guaman Poma 2009 [1615]). Reports of royal gifts involving food offer further insight into the symbolic weighting of Andean dietary elements. The Inca ruler Atahualpa, for instance, is said to have sent llamas, cooked llama meat, dried ducks, maize bread (possibly *sanco*), and vessels of *chicha* to Francisco Pizarro as he made his way to Cajamarca (see **Invasion, Spanish**).

It is apparent from various sources that maize and meat were considered the food of the gods, and by extension, of the Inca nobility. Ethnohistoric sources clearly state that the nobility ate more meat and maize than their subjects, who dined primarily on tubers and greens. In addition to the types of foods consumed, another aspect of Andean haute cuisine seems to have revolved around the concept of variety. The ability to prepare and serve either a variety of different plates in a single meal or to prepare a single meal using a variety of ingredients was apparently key to the notion of "dining splendidly." There are also indications that the amount of time invested in the preparation of foods, as in the case of the *yamor aca,* or aged *chicha* mentioned above, the complexity of the dishes served, and the costliness of the ingredients all figured into the equation of what constituted an elite repast.

In sum, Inca haute cuisine does not appear to have differed radically from the baseline Andean diet in terms of elemental composition. Rather, it seems to have been defined on the basis of quality, quantity, and multiplicity of ingredients, and differences in modes of preparation, consumption, and disposal.

Further Reading

Bray, Tamara L. "To Dine Splendidly: Imperial Pottery, Commensal Politics and the Inca State." In *The Archaeology and Politics of Food and Feasting in Early States and Empires*, edited by Tamara Bray, 142–63. New York: Kluwer/Plenum Press, 2003.

Coe, Sophie. *America's First Cuisines*. Austin: University of Texas Press, 1994.

Goody, Jack. *Cooking, Cuisine, and Class*. London: Cambridge University Press, 1982.

Guaman Poma de Ayala, Felipe. *The First New Chronicle and Good Government: On the History of the World and the Incas up to 1615*. Translated and edited by Roland Hamilton. Austin: University of Texas Press, 2009 [1615].

Hastorf, Christine. "The Effect of the Inka State on Sausa Agricultural Production and Crop Consumption." *American Antiquity* 55, no. 2: 262–90, 1990.

Hastorf, Christine, and Sissel Johannessen. "Pre-Hispanic Political Change and the Role of Maize in the Central Andes of Peru." *American Anthropologist* 95, no. 1: 115–38, 1993.

Murra, John. "Rite and Crop in the Inca State." In *Culture and History*, edited by Stanley Diamond, 393–407. New York: Columbia University Press, 1960.

National Research Council. *Lost Crops of the Incas: Little-Known Plants of the Andes with Promise for World-wide Cultivation*. Washington, DC: National Academy Press, 1989.

■ TAMARA L. BRAY

CUNTISUYU

The smallest of the *suyu* divisions, Cuntisuyu extended south-southwest from Cuzco to the Pacific coast, bordered to the north by Lake Parinacochas and the bay of Chala, and to the south by the region of Arequipa. Cuntisuyu was also a quadrant of the city and of the valley's *ceque* system. Together with **Collasuyu**, this *suyu* formed part of the *hurin*, or lower, division of the Inca Empire. Some chroniclers claim that the Cuntisuyu road afforded the closet route between Cuzco and the Pacific coast and, if so, it probably served as the route that provided the Inca ruler with fresh fish.

The main road to Cuntisuyu left the city of Cuzco just below *puma chupan* (the "puma's tail," at the confluence of the Tullumayu and Saphi, below the Sun temple, **Coricancha**) marked by a *ceque* shrine known as Uxi and headed south-southwest for the mythic origin place of Pacariqtambo. Known today as Maucallacta (old town), Pacariqtambo was a settlement of some 200 structures said to have housed the founding Inca Manco Capac's oracle. According to legend, the cave of Tambo T'oco on a nearby stone outcrop marks the place where Manco Capac and his siblings emerged from below ground to found Cuzco (see **Myths, Origin**).

Vicuñas pause in the shadow of Coropuna in Cuntisuyu, regarded by the Incas as one of the empire's most sacred mountains. Coropuna's temple and oracle were located nearby. Adriana von Hagen.

While Cuntisuyu was the smallest of the *suyu* divisions, its size and apparent insignificance belied its importance, along with Collasuyu, as one of the richest ceremonial *suyus*, embracing important regional and empire-wide religious centers, ranging from Pacariqtambo to the snow-clad volcanoes of Arequipa with their human sacrificial offerings. Fertile *puna* grasslands provided pasture for vast herds of wild and domesticated camelids, and the few Spanish descriptions of the region also note rich gold mines.

A major feature of Cuntisuyu is the Colca valley, famed for its elaborate terracing systems, most of which predate Inca times. The valley served as a gateway to mountain-top shrines, among the most sacred in the empire, especially Coropuna, ranked by the chronicler **Pedro de Cieza de León** as the fifth most important sanctuary in the empire. The lofty, snow-covered peak is surrounded by more than thirty-five Inca sites, notably Maucallacta (not to be confused with the Maucallacta of Pacariqtambo), apparently the seat of Coropuna's **oracle** and temple.

Like Collasuyu, the region's sacred peaks served as destinations for elaborate processions bearing gifts as well as children and young women intended for human sacrifices (see **Capac Hucha**). The most famous of these is a young woman wearing fine garments and plumed headgear buried near the summit of Ampato.

Further Reading

Bauer, Brian S. "Pacariqtambo and the Mythical Origins of the Inca." *Latin American Antiquity* 2, no. 1: 7–26, 1991.
Reinhard, Johan. "Peru's Ice Maidens." *National Geographic* 189, no. 6: 36–43, 1997.

■ ADRIANA VON HAGEN

CUZCO

When the Spanish expedition led by Francisco Pizarro marched into Cuzco on November 15, 1535, they saw spread before them a city tucked into the end of a long valley, nestled against forested hills. "The city," noted Pizarro's scribe, Pedro Sancho, "is full of the houses of the nobles who are the illustrious people of the city. . . . There are many other buildings and much grandness; on both sides flow two rivers . . . [that] are paved so that the water runs clean and clear. . . . [T]here are bridges to enter the city" (Sancho 1917 [1532–1533]). Although Sancho compared Cuzco to the cities of Spain, Cuzco's plan echoed that of other Inca settlements, focused on a large open space, the dual plazas of Aucaypata and Cusipata. And like so many Inca plazas, an *ushnu* graced the center: a sugarloaf-shaped stone covered with a strip of gold, placed on a low, stepped platform (see **Ushnus**). Flanking the plaza of Aucaypata were the royal compounds of Inca kings and their lineages, built of finely fitted stone and adobe and topped by thatched roofs. To the south, where the ceremonial city core tapered at the confluence of the Saphi and Tullumayu rivers, rose the pitched roofs of the empire's holiest shrine, the Coricancha (golden enclosure; see **Coricancha**).

The plaza witnessed daily, monthly, and yearly rituals and functioned as the axis of the empire's territorial four-part *suyu* division and, by extension, the roads to the four *suyus*: **Chinchaysuyu** to the northwest, **Antisuyu** to the northeast, **Collasuyu** to the southeast,

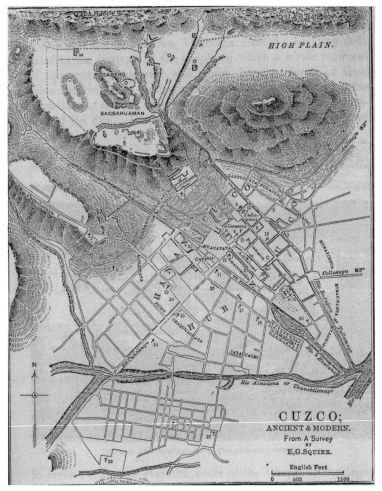

This nineteenth-century map of Cuzco shows the city's principal monuments: Sacsahuaman at the northern end and residential compounds and temples, including the Sun temple, in the central and southern part. Squier, E. George. *Peru: Incidents of Travel and Exploration in the Land of the Incas*. London: Macmillan, 1877.

and **Cuntisuyu** to the southwest. Non-Incas residing in Cuzco lived in the directions of their respective *suyus*. In turn, the dual divisions of *hanan*, upper, and *hurin*, lower, divided the city into two parts. *Hanan* Cuzco included Chinchaysuyu and Antisuyu while *hurin* Cuzco incorporated Collasuyu and Cuntisuyu. Scholars disagree over whether the southeast side of the plaza, or the confluence of the city's two rivers, the Saphi and Tullumayu just below the Coricancha, marked the division.

The ceremonial core of the city was quite small: just over a kilometer long and about half a kilometer wide at its broadest point, embracing some 40 hectares, or about 100 acres. Inca city planners earmarked some 12 outlying districts for residents known as **Incas by privilege** and provincial lords and their families; the latter were required to spend time in Cuzco, to be versed in Inca customs and in **Quechua**, the lingua franca. These outlying districts extended for some 11 kilometers (7 miles) below and on hill-sides surrounding the center. The city plan embraced not only the ceremonial core and surrounding districts, but also extended several kilometers beyond to include small agricultural estates, as well as hamlets for laborers, agricultural terraces watered by irrigation canals, and a dozen or so storage centers. The priest **Cristóbal de Molina** observed that the city had more than "forty thousand citizens" and 200,000 if one included the suburbs and outlying settlements. Though difficult to calculate, given the destruction of the city since Colonial times, greater Inca Cuzco's resident population probably numbered around 100,000 people, making it Tahuantinsuyu's largest settlement.

Nevertheless, it was not a city in which ordinary, subject peoples could reside. The center of Cuzco itself was sacred: those who entered had to carry a burden as a sign of humility and respect and no one could enter or leave the city at night. In the Chinchaysuyu quarter a gateway known as Huaca Puncu controlled those who came into the city; no doubt similar gateways existed on the other main roads leading into the city. Above all, Cuzco was the city of the Inca, his retinue and court officials, including his wives and children; the Willac Umu, high priest of the Sun; the *panacas* or lineages of past rulers and their attendant personnel; the chosen women or *acllacuna* and the retainers, *yanacuna*; imperial officials and *quipucamayoc*, who recorded the vital data of the empire on knotted-string *quipus*; the sons and daughters of conquered provincial lords; and specialized artisans who served the Inca.

Some chroniclers credit Cuzco's design to the Inca ruler Pachacuti, noting that he had the imperial capital built from the ground up, an effort that took 20 years. According to the chronicler **Juan de Betanzos**, Pachacuti named the whole city "puma's body." Some scholars read a puma shape into the ceremonial core of the city, with **Sacsahuaman**, the temple-fortress, serving as the puma's head, the Tullumayu river as its back, and the confluence of the city's two rivers as the puma's tail, an area in fact called *puma chupan* (puma's tail). But others interpret references in the chronicles to the puma as a metaphor of Inca kingship rather than as the town plan or the shape of the city.

While a single architect-ruler may not have designed and built the entire city in a mere 20 years, careful planning is nonetheless evident. Excavations in the city core reveal earlier Killke foundations (see **Chronology, Inca**), dismantled by Inca builders. Although an overarching grid plan is not readily discernable, there are at least two longitudinal streets traversed by at least five intersecting streets, forming irregular blocks. These blocks contained the *cancha* compounds, which varied in size. Sancho noted how the houses that composed the *canchas* were built of well-fitted stone with upper stories of adobe (mainly the gables, which reduced the weight of the building). Covered by roofs of thick thatch, the adobe gables weathered the rainy season. The streets were narrow, paved and often stepped, with a water channel running down the center. Sancho complained that these were too narrow, as only two horsemen could ride abreast.

Nevertheless, almost five centuries of wars, earthquakes, demolition, and remodeling make it difficult to imagine Cuzco in all its splendor. Almost immediately after their entry into the city, in 1534, the Spaniards began dividing *cancha* compounds into house lots, dismantling the walls or piercing them with doorways and streets. In fact, the surviving segments of Inca walls are generally retaining walls or enclosure walls of *cancha* compounds; the interior buildings were all razed. The Spaniards began to reduce the size of the dual plaza that so dominated the city plan, erasing the division of the great plaza by covering over the Saphi River to make way for houses. In addition, Inca walls served as convenient quarries for the Spanish settlers, who filched the stones to build their churches and residences. Attempts to reconstruct Inca Cuzco are further hampered by the confusing and contradictory descriptions by the first Spanish eyewitnesses to see the city before the 1536–1537 siege by Inca rebels. In May 1536, frustrated by the looting, ill-treatment, and awarding of house lots to Spaniards, Huayna Capac's son Manco Inca, who had been crowned ruler by the Spaniards, rebelled against the Spanish invaders. From the summit of **Sacsahuaman**, which rises above the city, Manco Inca's forces fired incendiary, red-hot sling stones wrapped in cotton cloth down onto the Spaniards, who were holed up in the city; the thatch smoldered for days, and the roof beams eventually collapsed, further destroying the Inca city.

In Inca times, a layer of coastal sand "two and a half palms" (about 50 centimeters [20 inches]) thick covered the main plaza. Inquiries by **Polo Ondegardo**, Cuzco's chief magistrate, revealed that the sand had been brought "out of reverence" for Ticsi Viracocha, the creator god linked to the Sun's daily journey from Lake Titicaca to the Pacific Ocean. In 1559, Polo ordered the sand removed after he discovered offerings of gold and silver figurines buried in it. More recently, excavations in the plaza uncovered not only some of the sand, but also camelid figurines fashioned in gold, silver, and Spondylus shell, as well as part of a wall, the probable remains of the plaza's *ushnu* platform. Unlike the monumental stepped *ushnus* of other Inca settlements, the one in Cuzco's main square was a more modest affair, a stone set on a low, stepped platform with a side basin for receiving libations. At night attendants covered the stone with a rounded wooden roof.

Several royal compounds surrounded the plaza of Aucaypata. A large terrace containing one or two large halls dominated the plaza's northeast side, today the site of the city's cathedral. One hall was converted into the Triunfo church, built to commemorate the apparition of the Virgin Mary, who was said to have materialized miraculously to extinguish the fires sparked by Manco Inca's incendiary sling stones. Any other constructions on the Aucaypata terrace were destroyed when construction began in 1559 on the cathedral, which also encroached onto the plaza itself. On the plaza's southeast corner stood the Hatun Cancha, the "great" or "large enclosure," entered by a single gateway facing the plaza. The city's largest compound, enclosing 5 hectares/about 12 acres, was the seat of the Acllahuasi, the "house of the chosen women" who attended Cuzco's religious shrines, served as custodians of the royal mummies, wove fine cloth, and brewed **chicha** beer for ceremonial consumption (see **Acllacuna**). The women worked in a building of many small cells located off a narrow alleyway; storage bins held the maize used to brew the *chicha*. Across from the Hatun Cancha, separated by one of the few extant Inca streets, stood the Amaru Cancha (Enclosure of the Serpent). Today occupied by the Jesuit Compañía church, in antiquity it contained a large hall, which functioned as a temporary shelter that was perhaps used by celebrants attending Cuzco's ceremonies, or (as archaeology has demonstrated in other places) as a public place for feasting. It is not known to whom this compound belonged, although some chronicles claim it was the town palace of Huascar.

On the northwest side of the plaza stood the Casana, the town palace of Huayna Capac and one of the few constructions reliably linked to a ruler. It too boasted a large hall with an open front, apparently so large that the chronicler **Garcilaso de la Vega** claimed it could hold 3,000 people. Sancho, Pizarro's scribe, called it Cuzco's "best," and it is no coincidence that the *conquistador* Francisco Pizarro chose it for himself when house lots began to be awarded. Two round, masonry towers roofed with thatch flanked the compound's entrance, which was painted red and white. A late sixteenth–early seventeenth century description of what may have been Huayna Capac's town palace notes it was divided into two parts, with elaborate doors or gateways providing access into each sector, both of which contained spacious courtyards. In the innermost sector were the "salons and rooms" of the Inca, "full of delights . . . planted with gardens and trees . . . and the royal lodgings were spacious and built with marvelous artistry" (Murúa 2001 [ca. 1590–1598]).

Further Reading

Bauer, Brian S. Ancient *Cuzco: Heartland of the Inca*. Austin: University of Texas Press, 2004.

Farrington, Ian S. *Cusco: Urbanism and Archaeology in the Inka World*. Gainesville: University Press of Florida, 2013.

Hyslop, John. *Inka Settlement Planning*. Austin: University of Texas Press, 1990.

Sancho de la Hoz, Pedro. "Relación." In *Colección de Libros y Documentos referentes a la Historia del Perú*, edited by Horacio H. Urteaga, vol. 5, 122–202. Lima: Sanmartí, 1917 [1532–1533].

■ ADRIANA VON HAGEN

D

DANCE

Dance in Inca times formed part of larger ritual celebrations that included music as well as various rites and offerings. Dance was almost always accompanied by song; therefore the Quechua term *taqui* usually refers to both song and dance together in ritual celebration or veneration (see **Music**).

Dances were used for work (harvest or sowing, for example), symbolized battle, and praised the Inca ruler. They were also performed during rites of passage such as the cel-

In this drawing by Felipe Guaman Poma de Ayala, men dressed in feathered tunics and plumed headgear dance as a woman plays a drum. Guaman Poma de Ayala, Felipe. *El primer nueva corónica y buen gobierno*. Edited by John V. Murra and Rolena Adorno, 301/326. Mexico City: Siglo Veintiuno, 1980 [1615].

ebration of a child's first haircutting (*chukcha rutuy*), which took place at weaning; entry into service of the Sun; and passage from boyhood to manhood (*huarachicuy*) when boys received their *huara*, or breechcloth. The Spanish priest **Cristóbal de Molina** describes the boys' dances as lasting six days and nights, when sacrifices were made to the creator god, Sun, Moon, thunder, and the ruling Inca, as well as to all the young men newly armed as warriors. One particular dance during *huarachicuy*, known as *coyo*, was said to have been invented by the Inca ruler Pachacuti Inca Yupanqui. It was performed to the beat of two drums from *hanan* (upper) Cuzco and two from *hurin* (lower) Cuzco. The dancers wore red tunics (*uncu*) with a white and red fringe.

Each area or cultural group had its unique dances and songs, which, according to the priest and chronicler **Bernabé Cobo**, changed with the introduction of Catholic festivals when people began to imitate dances from other regions. One hundred and twenty years after the Spanish invasion, Cobo wrote of a Corpus Christi festival in which dancers represented 40 "Indian nations."

Cobo described various dances: jumping masked men who carried the dried-out body of an animal (*guacon*); men and women with painted faces, donning gold or silver ribbons that hung from ear to ear across the face; farmer's work dances (*haylli*), performed by men with *chakitaqlla* (footplow) and women with *atuna* (adz); weapon-carrying war dances; and circle dances with both men and women (*cachua*). Forms of the *haylli* and *cachua* are still performed in the Peruvian Andes today.

The dance for the Inca king, *huayyaya*, was restricted to the nobility, some of whom bore royal standards. This dance could comprise up to two or three hundred men and women who joined hands in a line and processed two steps forward and one step back in a very solemn manner, to the beat of a large drum, until they eventually reached the Inca king. On special occasions the Inca king joined the dance. Another dance involved the Inca ruler flanked by two noble women, performing intricate turns and loops with continuously joined hands. The dancers moved rhythmically toward and away from the same place. The accompanying songs were festive praise of the Inca and his past exploits.

Funeral rites for an Inca king or *curaca* (ethnic lord) involved dirges accompanied by lamenting dances and days-long processions accompanied by drums, flutes, and sad singing that lauded the heroic deeds of the deceased. The death of an Inca king heralded particularly majestic, solemn dances performed by his elegantly adorned men and women servants. After vigorously dancing and drinking, the servants were strangled in order to accompany and tend to the soul of the Inca ruler in the afterlife. The songs relayed this continued servitude. Similarly, great dances and songs were performed to celebrate human sacrifices on occasions other than the death of a king.

Dances were staged during offerings and sacrifices to **huacas** (sacred places or objects). The priest Cristóbal de Molina describes the offerings to the *huaca* Anaguarque, two leagues (about 10 kilometers [6 miles]) south of Cuzco, with warriors standing still and holding their staffs (*yauri*), while the people performed the *taqui* called *huarita* with *huayliaquipas* (shell trumpets). When the *taqui* performances subsided, both women and men raced to nearby *huacas*, in representation of how the *huaca* Anaguarque had flown as fast as the hawk in the flood during the life of Manco Capac when all people perished (see **Myths, Origin**).

The chroniclers **Pedro Sarmiento de Gamboa**, **Pedro de Cieza de León**, Cristóbal de Molina, and Bernabé Cobo all write of a dance performed with a rope that took place at public festivities throughout the year. Molina describes it as having occurred during the *Camay Quilla* celebration in December in which men and women took opposite ends of a black, white, red, and tan rope and danced in homage to various *huacas* and deceased Inca kings. The dancers encircled Cuzco's main plaza with the rope and by joining both ends made various movements that coiled the rope into the form of a snail or snake. When the rope was finally dropped to the ground, it resembled a coiled snake, hence the dance was named *moro orco*. Sarmiento also describes the dance, although he called it *moroy urcu,* noting that a many-colored, 275-meter-long (900-foot-long) rope made by the Inca king Pachacuti Inca Yupanqui was taken out at four festivities throughout the year. The magnificently dressed dancers sang and completely encircled Cuzco's main square, the Aucaypata, with the rope. Cobo describes another version of this dance performed on the day of the ruler Huayna Capac's birth, when 200 people danced with a thick, long golden chain. He explains that the Inca prince Huascar received his name in memory of this chain (*huasca*).

Many dances were performed to the rhythm of a single, large or small, individually held *huancar* drum (hollow log drum covered with llama skin). Dancers wore ankle shakers made of large, colored beans (*zacapa*); silver and copper, cup-shaped bells (*chanrara*); and sea shells (*churu*). Cobo notes that these gave way to European bells, whose sound Andean peoples preferred. The native chronicler **Felipe Guaman Poma de Ayala** depicts ankle shakers worn by a *chunchu* dancer from **Antisuyu**, the tropical, forested quarter of the empire. Guaman Poma's drawing shows one of the few dances that has maintained continuity through time and is still danced today during patron saint festivals.

Further Reading

Cieza de León, Pedro de. *The Incas of Pedro de Cieza de León.* Translated by Harriet de Onis. Edited by Victor Wolfgang von Hagen. Norman: University of Oklahoma Press, 1959 [1553–1554].

Molina, Cristóbal de. *Account of the Fables and Rites of the Incas.* Translated and edited by Brian S. Bauer, Vania Smith-Oka, and Gabriel. E. Cantarutti. Austin: University of Texas Press, 2011 [1575].

■ HOLLY WISSLER

DEITIES

The Incas worshipped two kinds of deities: a few high gods of the sky and the sea, belonging to the state religious pantheon and decidedly political in nature, and myriad sacred entities of the terrestrial landscape, known as **huacas** and closely connected to the everyday and social life of individuals and groups. At the height of the Inca pantheon there was the triad formed by Inti (the Sun), Viracocha (a mythological figure ranging between a Creator and a civilizing hero), and Illapa (the god of Thunder and Lightning).

Inti was the tutelary god of the Empire. He was believed to be the ancestor of the Inca dynasty, and for this reason the Incas called themselves *Intip churin* (children of the Sun). He was also linked to the growth and maturing of crops, particularly maize, a major staple food of Andean people. The leading festivals in the Inca ritual calendar were held during the solstices and marked the growth cycle of maize. In the **Coricancha**, Inti's shrine in Cuzco, a small sacred field was devoted to maize and adorned with life-size, golden maize plants during the festivals marking sowing, harvest, and the annual initiation rites of noble Cuzco youths. A statue of Punchao (day, or young Sun), the most sacred image of the Sun in all of Tahuantinsuyu, occupied the *sanctum sanctorum* of the Coricancha. Many historical sources describe Punchao as a golden image of a seated boy, with solar rays emanating from his head and shoulders and whose hollow core contained a paste of gold dust and the ashes of the hearts of deceased kings.

Two other golden images accompanied Punchao in the Coricancha: those of Viracocha Pachayachachi (The Master of the World) and Illapa. Pucamarca Quisuarcancha, another major temple complex located midway between the Sun shrine and the main square of Cuzco, was expressly dedicated to these two deities (see **Cuzco**). The chronicler **Cristóbal de Molina** claims this shrine was built during a major reformation of the Inca religious system by the ruler Pachacuti, who placed a golden statue of Viracocha in the temple. The statue was the size of a ten year-old boy, with his right arm raised as a symbol of authority.

The Incas dedicated another major shrine to Viracocha in Cacha, some 100 kilometers (60 miles) southeast of Cuzco, in the heart of Canas territory. The Inca ruler visited Cacha during solemn pilgrimages held during the June solstice. According to Inca lore, the god Viracocha stopped here after emerging from Lake Titicaca and creating the Sun, the Moon and the stars, as well as the ancestors of all peoples, along with their languages and traditions (see **Myths, Origin**).

Viracocha also paused at a mountain bearing his name near the towns of Urcos and Huaro, some 50 kilometers (30 miles) southeast of Cuzco, where the chronicler **Juan de Betanzos** claims a shrine contained an image of Viracocha seated on a large golden throne. After walking across the Andes from the southeast to the northwest teaching people how to cultivate their crops and live in a civilized way, Viracocha finally reached the Pacific Ocean. (Accounts of where Viracocha disappeared into the sea range from **Pachacamac** on Peru's central coast to Manta in Ecuador.)

Given that Viracocha emerged from a lake and ended his earthly mission in the ocean, and since his name itself includes the term *cocha* (lake, sea), Viracocha seems to be closely connected with the sea, which the Inca pictured as a huge expanse of water that surrounded and supported the earth, and which surfaced through springs and lakes.

Illapa, who was also known as Chuqui Illa (Golden Light) or Inti Illapa (Thunder of the Sun), was a veritable "lord of atmospheric phenomena" whom the Inca called upon to plead for rain and ward off frosts and other adverse meteorological phenomena. The Jesuit priest **Bernabé Cobo** noted that Illapa was believed to be a man formed by the stars in the sky holding a sling in his right hand and a war club in his left one. His shining garments discharged lightning when he prepared to hurl his sling, and the cracking of his sling created claps of thunder. Rain was believed to be the water he drew from the heavenly river or Milky Way. Cobo also says that Inca Pachacuti was devoted to Inti Illapa, and had a shrine built in his honor in the Cuzco precinct of Totocachi. There he placed a golden statue of the god atop a litter also made out of gold, and he always carried it with him during military campaigns as his protective deity. The Inca frequently made human sacrifices to this image, so that the god would keep the king strong and ensure the power of the empire.

Sixteenth- and seventeenth-century sources give varying accounts of Inca oral traditions, in which the same mythical deed is indistinctly ascribed to either the Sun or Viracocha. Such is the case of the famed vision that prince Inca Yupanqui, the future ruler Pachacuti, had at the spring of Susurpuquio, prior to the decisive victory over the Chancas, which marked the beginning of Inca imperial expansion (see **Chronology, Inca; Conquests**). In the accounts of **Pedro Sarmiento de Gamboa** and **Cristóbal de Molina**, the god that appeared before Pachacuti is the Sun, whereas **Juan de Betanzos** notes it was Viracocha. Betanzos himself pointed out this (apparent) contradiction, remarking that the Inca indistinctly ascribed the nature of Creator sometimes to the Sun and sometimes to Viracocha.

One possible explanation is found in the 1608 Quechua dictionary of the Jesuit priest **Diego González Holguín** that defines *Viracocha*, as an epithet of the Sun god, suggesting that Inti and Viracocha were a single deity. This, along with the fact that the Thunder god was often called *Inti Illapa* (i.e., Thunder of the Sun), leads to the conclusion that the Incas in fact conceived of Inti, Viracocha, and Illapa not as three different entities, but as different aspects of a single solar deity that through its various manifestations ensured the existence of humanity. Indeed, many prayers in the state religion began precisely with a joint invocation to the Sun-Viracocha-Thunder triad, which the faithful addressed with a specific ritual veneration not used with any other deity.

Thus, the evidence suggests that the great religious reformation begun by Pachacuti and continued by his son Topa Inca Yupanqui consisted of the establishment of a highly institutionalized and theologically complex religion that focused on a multifaceted Sun god. To enhance the Sun's glory, prestige, and acceptance by conquered peoples, Inti assumed the powers and attributes of a series of ancient regional Andean deities—Huari, Tunupa, Llibiac, and **Catequil**—related to agriculture, water, and meteorological phenomena. Therefore, by subsuming all of the major powers of nature, Inti and his two alter egos, Viracocha and Illapa, embodied and expressed the power of Tahuantinsuyu and provided the ideological support required by the divine monarchy.

Other celestial deities in the state religious pantheon with significant political connotations were Mama Quilla (Mother Moon) and Chascaquyllor (Shaggy Star). Mama Quilla, the sister-wife of Inti and patroness of the *Coya*, the main wife of the Inca king, presided over the female universe. The Incas had a special regard for Mama Quilla because Cuzco's ceremonial calendar was essentially based on lunar months. Indeed, both the Coricancha and a Moon temple on the Island of Coati, part of the great Titicaca oracle (see **Oracles**), boasted two large gold and silver anthropomorphic images of the Moon. Chascaquyllor, the planet Venus in its manifestation as Morning Star, which fades at dawn when the Sun rises, was associated with the *curacas* or ethnic lords. According to a myth related to the shrine of Titicaca, when the Sun rose for the first time from the sacred rock of Titicala it defeated and overshadowed the Morning Star, whose light had until then lit the world. It is not hard to see in this account a metaphor of the supremacy the Inca, the son of the Sun, had over the ethnic lords, and a eulogy of the civilizing mission of Tahuantinsuyu. The Incas also worshipped the Pleiades, which were known as *Collca* (storehouse) and believed to be protectors of the crops, as well as a group of stars in the Lyra constellation called *Urcuchillay*, envisaged as a multicolored llama and master of the herds (see **Astronomy**).

But beyond the official cult of the major celestial and marine gods of the state religion, the daily social and religious life of Incas and other contemporary Andean peoples focused on the worship of sacred entities related to terrestrial landscape features, called *huacas*. Every family, social group, community, and ethnic group had a direct and privileged relationship with a specific *huaca*, which was considered their tutelary and ancestral divinity. A *huaca* could be a specific landscape feature, such as a rock, a spring, a mountaintop, or a cave, or an object such as an upright stone, statue, or mummy, believed to be infused with a life force known as *camaquen*. The possession of this force manifested itself through the capacity these supernatural entities had to communicate with humans. In fact, in order to be a *huaca*, these entities had to have the power of "speech," which materialized essentially in the sounds made by animals, music, or nature, such as thunder, bubbling water, or the cracking of ice. These sounds were conceived as a supernatural language that only certain specialists, in altered states of consciousness, could understand and translate into a verbal message that was intelligible to the faithful.

Essentially, Andean **religion** in Inca times was a system of representations and practices of a strongly aural nature, that is, one which focused on sensing and interpreting the "voices" emitted by the universe that surrounds humanity. The *huacas*, the manifestation as well as the fulcrum of this religion, were conceived as essentially sonorous sacred entities, and their shrines as spaces where one went to hear their "voices" (see **Oracles**). Inca shrines, located at strategic sites carefully prepared to heighten the perception of the sounds of nature as well as those produced by different devices and instruments, thus provided intense auditory experiences, creating, perhaps, the most perfect and generalized case of acoustic spaces and structures made by an ancient society. Indeed, one of the most common and striking characteristics of these sacred sites is that they are located in places that have some natural source of sound, or comprise structures meant to produce or amplify the sound of flowing water or wafting wind. In this sense, splendid monumental Inca oracular centers of a pan-Andean nature such as Titicaca or Pachacamac were simply the largest imperial manifestations of an institution—the *huaca*—that lay at the very heart of ancient Andean religion.

Further Reading

Curatola Petrocchi, Marco. "La voz de la *huaca*. Acerca de la naturaleza oracular y el trasfondo *aural* de la religión andina antigua," In *El Inca y la huaca*, edited by Marco Curatola Petrocchi and Jan Szeminski. Lima: Pontificia Universidad Católica del Perú, 2015.

Betanzos, Juan de. *Narrative of the Incas*. Translated and edited by Roland Hamilton and Dana Buchanan. Austin: University of Texas Press, 1996 [1551–1557].

Demarest, Arthur A. *Viracocha. The Nature and Antiquity of the Andean High God*. Peabody Museum Monographs 6. Cambridge, MA: Harvard University, 1981.

Itier, César. *Viracocha o el Océano. Naturaleza y funciones de una divinidad Inca*. Lima: Instituto Francés de Estudios Andinos and Instituto de Estudios Peruanos, 2013.

MacCormack, Sabine. *Religion in the Andes: Vision and Imagination in Early Colonial Peru*. Princeton, NJ: Princeton University Press, 1991.

Staller, John E., and Brian Stross. *Lightning in the Andes and Mesoamerica: Pre-Columbian, Colonial, and Contemporary Perspectives*, New York: Oxford University Press, 2013.

Steele, Paul R., and Catherine Allen. *Handbook of Inca Mythology*. Santa Barbara, CA.: ABC-CLIO, 2004.

Ziólkowski, Mariusz S. *La guerra de los Wawqui. Los objetivos y los mecanismos de la rivalidad dentro de la élite inka, siglos XV–XVI*. Quito: Ediciones Abya-Yala, 1997.

■ MARCO CURATOLA PETROCCHI

DISEASES, FOREIGN

The impact of the so-called Columbian Exchange transformed the Inca Empire. It was a biological exchange first and foremost, but also an economic and social one that changed traditional ways of doing things in profound ways. The exchange was two sided, as Old and New Worlds collided, shook, and ultimately transformed the globe. The exchange involved the movement across the Atlantic and Pacific Oceans of long-separated peoples, taking with them their plants and animals, and their pathogens.

Of the three principal elements of the Columbian Exchange, disease caused by pathogens, resulting in sickness and untimely death, had the greatest and most immediate impact on the peoples of the Americas. Pathogens are any foreign agents entering the body that can cause disease. Broadly the pathogens are viruses, bacteria, parasites, protozoa, and fungi. Just to list their names would consume several pages. With the coming of the agricultural revolution and rising populations, the peoples of linked Eurasia and Africa experienced the heavy impact of pathogens. It appears there was a greater diversity of pathogens in the Old World than in the Americas, and there was substantial regional specificity.

The New World was not a disease-free environment. It too went through the agricultural revolution and the rise of cities, and faced the impact of pathogens. A large number of autochthonous Andean diseases also debilitated or killed victims outright (see **Health and Illness**). Syphilis, tuberculosis, and *leishmaniasis* were endemic, and there were various hemorrhagic fevers. Parasites were ubiquitous. But the introduction of Old World disease as part of the Columbian Exchange caused exceptional mortality.

The principal early culprits were smallpox and measles—acute, easily communicable viruses that could spread rapidly, especially in areas of high population density. Both require a chain of infection, otherwise an epidemic will burn itself out. In densely populated areas of the Old World both diseases tended to be endemic, affecting mostly children. Measles, especially complications resulting from it, took 10–15 percent of victims, whereas smallpox wiped out 25 percent or more with each flare-up. Smallpox and measles survivors developed lifelong immunity. Some experienced subclinical infections (mild cases with no visible symptoms) that provided some immunity in future outbreaks, too. Infected individuals can carry the virus several days before the onslaught of sickness, therefore the infection can be carried in advance of any knowledge of it.

Smallpox and measles were relatively easy for Spanish physicians of the period to identify by their symptoms, and the differences were known and described as early as the tenth century in a medical text by the Persian physician Rhazes. The arrival of the vectored diseases, such as typhus, plague, malaria, and yellow fever, was delayed given the need for an American vector species capable of carrying it, or until the Old World vectors transported to the New World survived and prospered. Typhus, largely vectored by the body louse (*Pediculus humanus*), could be identified by early modern physicians, especially since it was well known in times of warfare and siege in late-fifteenth-century Europe. The bubonic plague, transferred from person to person, but mostly by infected fleas (*Xenopsylla cheopis*) on rodent hosts, was generally identified by its obvious symptoms. Malaria, caused by three strains of plasmodium with different rates of mortality, was primarily transported by *Anopheles* mosquitoes.

Direct physical contact between Spaniards and Incas took place almost four decades after exploration and scattered settlement of the Atlantic and Caribbean coasts. Record keeping in the Andean world differed from the European, so our knowledge of many things is imperfect. Oral history, recorded by Europeans years later, sheds some light on the events of the previous century, but the longer the passage of time from the actual event, the faultier that oral history is.

Smallpox may have been introduced into the Caribbean by Columbus's large second fleet as early as 1493, although it may not have reached the mainland. But the terrible pandemic that began on Hispaniola in 1518 did, and it devastated Mesoamerica and slowly but inexorably moved beyond. Deadly smallpox coincided with the conquest of the Aztec state, and in 1520 the epidemic was noted in Panama as well. Either from there or from sites of infection along the north coast of Colombia, the virus potentially moved southward deeper into the interior, as it passed from one group to another. Both smallpox and measles were present in the circum-Caribbean a decade or more before the Spanish arrival in Peru. Having never experienced smallpox or measles, all Native peoples were susceptible. Both diseases were highly contagious and affected all ages and sexes. The mortality rates were quite high in these initial epidemics.

When smallpox arrived in the mid-1520s, it swept away its indigenous victims prior to the penetration of Francisco Pizarro and his men. By 1531 smallpox was coupled with measles, as mentioned by early Spanish observers who looked to Native sources. The earliest information, taken from a group of *quipucamayocs* interviewed by Governor Cristóbal Vaca de Castro in the early 1540s, reports that Inca Huayna Capac died of a "pestilencia de viruelas" (disease of smallpox). At the end of the 1540s and in the early 1550s, two other Spaniards secured oral testimony concerning the death of the ruler. The chronicler **Juan de Betanzos** married an Inca *ñusta* (princess), and wrote a description of the Inca world based on accounts provided by her and her relatives. Betanzos noted that the Inca came down with an illness that at first made him delirious, followed by an eruption of scabies and what appeared to be leprosy (*sarna y lepra*), and he died within four days. Soldier **Pedro de Cieza de León**'s account, based on years of experience in the northern Andes and on the oral sources he consulted, composed a multivolume chronicle of the conquest of Peru. He wrote that the Quito area, following the completion of the Inca conquest of the north, was afflicted by a "great pestilence of *viruelas* (smallpox), so contagious that more than 200,000 died of it" (Cieza 1959 [1553]). When his symptoms appeared, the Inca Huayna Capac ordered sacrifices in all realms for his health, but efforts were in vain.

Although it is difficult to date Huayna Capac's death precisely, most observers and later historians believe it was sometime in 1524 or 1525. Certainly the impact was great on the Inca Empire. Huayna Capac's conquest of the northernmost reaches of the empire had just ended, but there was much native opposition to Inca domination. In Cuzco there was internal division and strife that was typical during transfers of authority following the death of the ruler (see **Wars, Dynastic**). We also know that many of Huayna Capac's relatives and children, including his designated heir, and many others in Tahuantinsuyu succumbed to sickness about the same time the ruler perished. The process of the preparation of his corpse and the ceremonial transfer of his mummified remains from the north to Cuzco led to new centers of infection. For the next half decade leading up to the Spanish arrival, there was a costly and deadly battle for leadership of the realm. The victory of Atahualpa over Huascar almost coincided with Pizarro's march from the Peruvian coast to **Cajamarca**. Such conditions of internal civil war, with a large toll in lives and disruption of the subsistence economy, were the perfect setting for a decline in nutrition with a simultaneous weakening of the human body's resistance to any type of pathogenic infection.

The initial introductions of first smallpox, and then measles in pandemic form were followed by subsequent introductions. Some were localized in nature, others pandemic. By the end of the sixteenth century epidemics fell into a more endemic pattern, although the two combined in a 1585–1591 pandemic to produce very high mortality. Other foreign pathogens were introduced before the end of the century. Typhus was probably the earliest in 1546, although it may have been plague. It was virtually impossible to distinguish between the two by their symptoms in their hemorrhagic forms. Based on demographic evidence taken from periodic native population counts and parish death and birth records, the cumulative impact of Old World diseases on the peoples of the Andean world by the second decade of the seventeenth century was a reduction of the population by approximately 90 percent.

Sixteenth-Century Epidemics in the Andean Region

1524–1528	smallpox
1531–1533	measles
1546	typhus and perhaps pneumonic plague
1557–1559	influenza, measles, smallpox
1566–1569	smallpox
1582	smallpox, measles
1585–1591	smallpox, measles, typhus, mumps
1589	influenza in Potosí
1597	measles

Further Reading

Alchon, Suzanne Austin. *New World Epidemics in a Global Perspective*. Albuquerque: University of New Mexico Press, 2003.

Cook, Noble David. *Born to Die: Disease and New World Conquest, 1492–1650*. Cambridge: Cambridge University Press, 1998.

———. *Demographic Collapse: Indian Peru, 1520–1620*. Cambridge: Cambridge University Press, 2004.

Cook, Noble David, and W. George Lovell. "*Secret Judgments of God:*" *Old World Disease in Colonial Spanish America*. Norman: University of Oklahoma Press, 1992.

Crosby, Alfred W. *The Columbian Exchange: Biological and Cultural Consequences of 1492*. 30th Anniversary Edition. Westport, CT: Praeger, 2003.

Livi-Bacci, Massimo. *A Concise History of World Population.* 4th ed. Oxford: Blackwell Publishing, 2007.
Newson, Linda A. *Life and Death in Early Colonial Ecuador.* Norman: University of Oklahoma Press, 1995.

■ NOBLE DAVID COOK

DIVINATION

Among the Incas and their Andean contemporaries, the habit of examining the signs left in the world by the gods or consulting them in oracular sanctuaries, resorting to a variety of soothsayers and divinatory techniques, was very widespread. The Incas believed that the will of the deities had to be respected in order to maintain a harmonious relationship: not understanding their wishes could result in dreadful consequences for individuals and their communities. For a highly complex, state-level society such as that of the Incas, which lacked a body of written norms, divination guaranteed correct choices and behavior, while at the same time, it objectified and legitimized the decision-making processes, thus assuring the broadest social and political consensus.

Specialists known as *hamurpa* (**Quechua** *hamurpayay* [to understand or consider in depth]) examined how llama fat or coca leaves burned, or how the blood of a disemboweled guinea pig spurted. They also scrutinized the legs of spiders enclosed in special containers, or observed how the juice of a wad of coca leaves spat onto the palm of the

In this image by Felipe Guaman Poma de Ayala, soothsayers practice divination by fire. Guaman Poma de Ayala, Felipe. *El primer nueva corónica y buen gobierno.* Edited by John V. Murra and Rolena Adorno, 250/277. Mexico City: Siglo Veintiuno, 1980 [1615].

hand drained through the fingers. Likewise, counting the number of small piles of maize kernels, beans, or small balls of llama dung was very common: even numbers were good omens; odd, unfavorable. Soothsayers frequently used black or colored pebbles, highly treasured and passed down from one generation to the next, in the belief that they were a gift and a sign of divine benevolence. Precise auguries were also obtained by observing the flight of birds.

The Incas held great faith in extipicy—the examination of the entrails of animals. In the *calpa* ritual, seers called *calparicuy* sacrificed a guinea pig, bird, or llama, pulled out its lungs and inflated them, "reading" the markings that appeared on the organ's surface. The chronicler **Pedro Sarmiento de Gamboa** narrates that the Inca Huayna Capac, while in Quito not long before his death, ordered a *calpa* ritual to find out which of his two sons, Ninan Cuyuchi or Huascar, would succeed him. The ritual, on that occasion, produced negative responses for both candidates.

Pyromancy, divination by fire, was an even more complex form of divination. Powerful and feared soothsayers called *yacarcas* foretold issues related to state security, such as how to prevent rebellions or attempts against the emperor's life. *Yacarcas* were part of the ruler's entourage and accompanied him on all his trips. According to Father **Bernabé Cobo**'s account, they used two large braziers, around which they placed dishes of the most exquisite food to attract and ingratiate supernatural entities. As they chewed coca leaves, sang, and wept, the *yacaracas* poked the fire and invited the deity to enter one of the braziers, "speaking" through the flames. If the response was unsatisfactory, they summoned another deity to enter the second brazier and confirm the prediction. This divinatory ritual, often attended by the *Sapa* **Inca** himself, was accompanied by many valuable offerings including the sacrifice of children and spotless white llamas.

The Incas also observed celestial bodies and constellations, in particular the Pleiades, called *Collca* (storehouse; see **Astronomy**). The intensity of the constellation's luminosity in the June sky was believed to be directly proportional to the amount of future harvests. People considered some celestial phenomena such as rainbows, solar or lunar eclipses, and the passage of comets to be evil omens. Inca astrologers interpreted solar eclipses as harbingers of a death in the royal family. In order to ward off the ill-fated presage, they made offerings and sacrificed children to the Sun god. The chronicler **Garcilaso de la Vega** states that during lunar eclipses, believed to signal the beginning of the world's end, the residents of Cuzco made as much noise as possible to ward off evil: they played musical instruments, children cried and screamed, and dogs were whipped to make them howl. According to a tradition recorded by Fernando de Montesinos, the Incas reacted in the same way when, following the appearance of two comets in the sky, the court astrologers stated that these had been sent by the god Viracocha to destroy the Moon and, with her, the entire world, as punishment for their sins.

The Incas paid close attention to dreams, interpreted by a class of seers called *moscoq*. They resorted to these specialists to avoid some ill-fated event that the dreams foretold. A series of dreamlike images were considered announcements of death or loss. The Andean chronicler **Felipe Guaman Poma de Ayala** mentions some of them: an image of a bird signified a fight; a river and a bridge, or a lunar or solar eclipse implied the

The reading of llama entrails to predict the future was a common practice in Inca times. Guaman Poma de Ayala, Felipe. *El primer nueva corónica y buen gobierno*. Edited by John V. Murra and Rolena Adorno, 826/880. Mexico City: Siglo Veintiuno, 1980 [1615].

death of a parent; the eruption of a tooth suggested the death of a father or a brother; a haircut, that of a husband; the sacrifice of a llama foretold one's own death. Some dream-visions, however, were favorable. In various Inca myths the Sun god or Viracocha appears in the dreams of a king or a future ruler, announcing victory in war and a glorious destiny.

But, above all, deities manifested themselves in dreams to priests. Indeed, this was one of the ways Andean divinities made their will and the future known, and answered the questions of those who visited their sanctuaries. More frequently, however, the gods communicated with the priests at night, in darkened chambers, "speaking" to them in esoteric, nonhuman languages of natural, musical, or animal sounds. In fact, many ancient Andean sanctuaries are located in places that provided natural sounds, and their spatial organization and architecture enhances the sound of musical instruments, flowing water, or whistling wind, offering mystical, aural experiences to the faithful (see **Deities**). The priests entered into trances induced by taking psychotropic substances that allowed them to hear the voices of the gods. This highly organized form of divination, which occurred in oracular sanctuaries, is a historical and cultural phenomenon shared by very few civilizations. In this sense, ancient Peru, at the time of the Incas, with its numerous and influential oracular centers, could be considered the "land of **oracles**" par excellence.

Further Reading

Cobo, Bernabé. *History of the Inca Empire: An Account of the Indian's Customs and Their Origin, Together with a Treatise on Inca Legends, History, and Social Institutions.* Translated and edited by Roland Hamilton. Austin: University of Texas Press, 1979 [1653].

Curatola Petrocchi, Marco. "Adivinación, oráculos y civilización andina." In *Los dioses del antiguo Perú.* Vol. 2, edited by Krzysztof Makowski, 223–45. Lima: Banco de Crédito del Perú, 2001.

Guaman Poma de Ayala, Felipe. *El primer nueva corónica y buen gobierno.* Edited by John V. Murra and Rolena Adorno. 3 vols. Mexico City: Siglo Veintiuno, 1980 [1615].

Rowe, John H. "Inca Culture at the Time of the Spanish Conquest." In *Handbook of South American Indians,* edited by Julian H. Steward, vol. 2, *The Andean Civilizations,* 183–330. Washington, DC: Smithsonian Institution, Bureau of American Ethnology, 1946.

Ziólkowski, Mariusz S. "Hanan pachap unanchan: Las 'señales del cielo' y su papel en la etnohistoria andina." *Revista Española de Antropología Americana* 15:147–82, 1985.

■ MARCO CURATOLA PETROCCHI

DUALISM

Although not exclusively Inca, as it had existed long before the emergence of Tahuantin-suyu, dualism was an integral part of Inca conceptions of time, space, and social relations. The most overt expression of dualism in the Inca state was at the level of the organization of space—that is, the division of communities into moieties (halves). An example was the division of the city of **Cuzco** into a *hanan*, or "upper" half, and a *hurin*, or "lower" half. According to the chronicler **Garcilaso de la Vega**, *Hanan* Cuzco was associated with the King (the *Sapa Inca*), while *Hurin* Cuzco was associated with the Queen (the *Coya*). Garcilaso states that the two halves of the city were equal, like brothers; however, the first was like the eldest brother and the second was like the younger brother. Garcilaso also likened *hanan* to the right hand and *hurin* to the left hand. He went on to note that divisions of this kind were made "in large and small villages throughout the Empire" (Garcilaso 1966 [1609]).

Another chronicler, **Juan de Betanzos**, states that the upper moiety was inhabited by the closest relatives of the Inca ruler while the Inca's secondary relatives lived in the lower moiety. Betanzos's testimony has been interpreted as evidence of the endogamous (i.e., marrying inside the social group) nature of these moieties, and it is thought by anthropologists that this was, in turn, the basis of the Inca system of political hierarchy. According to this system, particularly as it was formed through marriage ties, relatives from marriages inside the group were superior to those made with people outside the group.

Ethnohistorical reports of moieties in **Aymara**-speaking territories in Bolivia also display moiety divisions. For instance, in the case of the Lupacas of Chucuito, on the southwest shore of Lake Titicaca, as mentioned in the sixteenth-century **Visita** made by Garci Diez de San Miguel, the upper moiety, or *alasaa*, and the lower moiety, *massaa*, had separate, parallel leaders (Qari was the headman of the *alasaa* moiety, while Cusi headed *massaa*). As in Cuzco, Qari had political and ritual precedence over Cusi. In northern Potosí, Bolivia, this kind of mirror relationship between pairs (e.g., as in a pair of moieties) is referred to as a relationship of *yanantin*, which relates to a principle of complementary opposition between two elements, and is likened to the relationship between a man and a woman. There is an echo here of Garcilaso's statement that *Hanan* Cuzco was related to the King and *Hurin* Cuzco to the Queen.

In areas of the central Peruvian Andes, sixteenth- and seventeenth-century priests searching for native "idolatries" regularly reported that communities were divided between groups referred to as *Huari* and those called *Llacuaz*. Other Colonial historical documents note that the *Huaris* were commonly said to be autochthonous inhabitants of a locality while *Llacuazes*, who were characterized as foreigners, often were said to have migrated into the area from Lake Titicaca, far to the south. As the owners of the land, *Huaris* were farmers, while the *Llacuazes* were herders. Historians and anthropologists think that this kind of division was another expression of dualism that takes its basic features from the same principles that gave rise to the *hanan* and *hurin* division of Cuzco.

In the variety of formations and expressions noted above, Andean villages and whole regions have, paradoxically, fashioned unity on the basis of fundamental dual divisions of space, society, and political relations. This was as true for dualism in the Inca Empire as for many villages in the Andes down to the present day.

Further Reading

Duviols, Pierre. "Huari y Llacuaz, agricultores y pastores: Dualismo prehispánico de oposición y complementariedad." *Revista del Museo Nacional* 39:153–91, 1973.

Garcilaso de la Vega, El Inca. *Royal Commentaries of the Incas and General History of Peru, Part One.* Translated by Harold V. Livermore. Austin: University of Texas Press, 1966 [1609].

Murra, John. "An Aymara Kingdom in 1567." *Ethnohistory* 15, no. 2: 115–51, 1968.

Palomino, Salvador. *El Sistema de oposiciones en la Comunidad de Sarhua.* Lima: Pueblo Indio, 1984.

Platt, Tristan. "Mirrors and Maize: The Concept of Yanantin among the Macha of Bolivia." In *Anthropological History of Andean Politics,* edited by J. V. Murra, N. Wachtel, and J. Revel, 228–59. Cambridge: Cambridge University Press, 1986.

Zuidema, R. T. "The Moieties of Cuzco." In *The Attraction of Opposites: Thought and Society in the Dualistic Mode,* edited by David Maybury-Lewis and U. Almagor, 255–76. Ann Arbor: University of Michigan Press, 1989.

■ JUAN OSSIO ACUÑA

ECONOMY, HOUSEHOLD

Household economy refers to how a household obtains and uses resources. It is often contrasted with political economy, which refers to the production, distribution, and consumption activities of a political entity. The two are obviously related by the demands or constraints that a political system places on its constituent households. This entry will discuss how households directed their economic activities and how conquered groups lived vis-à-vis the Incas of Cuzco.

We define *household* as the most common component of social subsistence. Nevertheless, were households in Inca times comprised by a nuclear family, an extended family, or multiple families? Given the extraordinary variety of groups conquered by the Incas, households may have included any one of these, and combinations as well. Second, archaeologists do not excavate social units, they unearth the structures and artifacts that are the result of those units' activities. Thus, a household might occupy one structure or

An isolated farmhouse surrounded by potato fields in the southern highlands of Peru. Simón Quispe. TAFOS Photographic Archive/PUCP, Lima, Peru.

a group of structures; it may include storage features, have boundaries or lack them; or it may be tightly grouped or dispersed.

How did households function in **Cuzco**, the capital? In the heart of the city lay the palaces of the kings—large compounds with many structures inside that housed the royal families, their servants, and goods. The royal *panacas* (descent groups of deceased rulers) also maintained residences in central Cuzco, but we do not know what kind of compounds they occupied. Presumably, they must also have been large, as they had to support the family of the dead king. The 10 nonroyal *ayllus* lived outside the center, and beyond them lay the settlements of conquered peoples.

The basic unit of Inca **architecture** was the *cancha,* a single-roomed, rectangular structure. Several of these, surrounded by a wall with only one entrance, formed *cancha* compounds. The compounds often housed nuclear families, but a group of related families, such as a *panaca,* may have inhabited the same enclosure. Conquered craftspeople, who likely lived in separate communities, delivered the crafts to the households of their Inca lords. How goods were produced and distributed within greater Cuzco is not known, due to the destruction of the social and economic systems by the Spaniards.

The most impressive **royal estates**—private landholdings of the kings, their relatives, and their descendants—lay scattered in and around Cuzco, but every province in the empire set aside such holdings. The land could be used as a retreat or as a source of wealth. The estates included a wide range of environments, and sometimes thousands of retainers. Upon the death of a king, his *panaca* inherited the lands. Farmland on the estate sustained its occupants; the household economy of these estates thus functioned much like a village.

Unlike the citizens of Cuzco and environs, who generally benefited from the expansion of the empire, conquered people and their domestic economies often were compromised, sometimes severely, by the demands of the empire. A family typically was given enough land by its *ayllu* (kin group) to support its members; larger families received more land than smaller ones. Family members planted and harvested their own fields (see **Farming**; **Subsistence**). While most villages were self-sufficient, exchange and trade provided resources that were not readily accessible. Low-altitude crops could be exchanged for high-altitude resources, for instance, and sometimes colonies from a community moved to other environmental zones to grow crops for their home village.

As many scholars note, one of the major repercussions of the large numbers of *mit'a* workers (the rotational labor force) who were called up for army duty was the added burden it placed on those who stayed put (see **Labor**; **Warfare**). As crops have specific planting seasons, villagers had to tend to their crops as well as those of their absent neighbors.

The Huanca people of the upper Mantaro valley, in the highlands east of Lima, provide a window on their household economy before and after the Inca conquest. Residential household compounds were the basic units of production and consumption. All households used basically the same tools and carried out the same activities, regardless of whether they were commoners or elites (the two basic statuses identified in this population).

As for craft production, many of the basic tools used by local people before and after the Inca conquest were locally produced. Both elite and commoner households spun thread and wove cloth. Some crafts, however, were specialized, such as the stone blades that were quarried and worked into blanks by the villagers living closest to the quarry. Fine quality pottery too was produced at certain villages and then traded to the rest of the region. All households in these villages created specialized crafts—again, regardless of status.

Settlement locations, however, saw a marked shift after the Inca conquest. Whereas the Huancas located their settlements in highly defensible positions, the Incas depopulated many of their villages and relocated them to lower elevations to focus on maize production. Nevertheless, the domestic economy of commoner households remained essentially the same, except for an increase in cloth production, no doubt reflecting the demands of the Inca state. High-altitude households were more likely to be engaged in stone tool production (since they were located closer to the quarries) while low-altitude ones were more focused on maize production. Settlements nearer to the Inca administrative center of Hatun Jauja were more likely to be specialized than ones farther away, suggesting Inca interest in controlling craft activities nearer the center. Elite households, however, were incorporated more into the Inca sphere of influence, indicated by a decrease in agricultural activities and textile production of elite households.

Thus, the Huanca region shows how Inca policies affected local communities as well as leadership roles. The conquest of this region initiated a *Pax Inca* that saw previous conflicts between Huanca villages eliminated and populations resettled to increase maize production. The domestic economy, nevertheless, witnessed increasing social differences between native elites and their subjects. The former spent less time farming and weaving, while the latter continued these activities or intensified them. These changes apparently reflect the incorporation of native Huanca elites into the state bureaucracy.

Along the coast, most villages practiced **irrigation** agriculture. On the central coast, entire villages specialized in particular crafts. Villages exchanged their products for those of other villages; fishing and farming had become mutually exclusive activities that involved multiple social groups. These specialized domestic economies were the result of long-standing differences among the economic activities of coastal groups.

The Chimú of the north coast represent a special case of coastal household economy (see **Chronology, Pre-Inca**). The Chimú were among the most complex Andean society to contest Inca expansion. During Chimú times, from the extensive compounds that housed the Chimú kings and their families, the ruling elite controlled craft production at their capital, Chan Chan. An intermediate-level elite occupied smaller compounds that shared administrative features of the ruler's compounds. Low-status craft workers lived in simple structures scattered among the larger compounds, where they produced textiles and metal goods.

A complex system of irrigation canals sustained the crops produced by specialized villages in the Chan Chan hinterland. These rural sites consumed more marine resources while the city's urban lower class had access to camelid meat. When the Incas conquered the Chimú, they curtailed the power of the ruling elites and placed their own personnel in the highest administrative offices, though they left many of the Chimú lords in charge of the activities they had previously overseen.

The household economies of societies that existed prior to the Inca conquest varied considerably, from the highly specialized Chimú to the humble Uru of Lake Titicaca. The

Incas, however, transformed the household economies of their subjects to accommodate their own imperial needs. While the object was to leave conquered groups as unchanged as possible and extract their labor, this ultimately led to many transformations, especially among local elite households forced to serve the empire. Although such households gained access to more elite goods, especially Inca-produced ones, commoners often continued their pre-Inca way of life, with the added burden of their *mit'a* obligations.

Further Reading

D'Altroy, Terance. *Provincial Power in the Inka Empire.* Washington, DC: Smithsonian Institution Press, 1992.

Mackey, Carol. "The Socioeconomic and Ideological Transformation of Farfán under Inka Rule." In *Distant Provinces in the Inka Empire. Toward a Deeper Understanding of Inka Imperialism,* edited by Michael A. Malpass and Sonia Alconini, 221–59. Iowa City: University of Iowa Press, 2010.

Pozorski, Shelia. "Subsistence Systems in the Chimú State." In *Chan Chan. Andean Desert City,* edited by Michael E. Moseley and Kent C. Day, 177–96. Albuquerque: University of New Mexico Press, 1982.

Rostworowski de Diez Canseco, María. *Étnia y Sociedad: Costa Peruana Prehispánica.* Lima: Instituto de Estudios Peruanos, 1977.

Wilk, Richard R., and William L. Rathje. "Household Archaeology." *American Behavioral Scientist* 25, no. 6: 617–39, 1982.

■ MICHAEL A. MALPASS

ESTATES, ROYAL

Royal estates formed a critical part of Inca imperial life. They served as private retreats for the acting Inca ruler, as temporary capitals when the ruler was in residence, and as centers for the *panacas* (royal descent groups) after a king's death. Thus, royal estates reflected the personal interests of a ruler, the particularities of his reign, and the collective identity and power of his *panaca*.

In **Cuzco**, each ruler had a palace or royal compound that symbolized his authority and housed critical functions related to his life and rule. In rural areas, royal estates had similar associations and functions, and thus extended imperial and personal authority from the sacred capital to the countryside. Pachacuti, for instance, is reported to have had a royal complex in Cuzco called Condorcancha, but built at least three royal estates: Pisac, Ollantaytambo, and **Machu Picchu**. His son Topa Inca Yupanqui erected an urban compound called Calispuquio in Cuzco, but toward the end of his rule built Chinchero, a royal estate north of Cuzco overlooking the Urubamba valley. Pachacuti's grandson Huayna Capac had at least one Cuzco compound called Casana, but also constructed a lavish retreat in the Urubamba valley known variously as Yucay and Quispihuanca. Pachacuti's great-grandson Huascar, who rose briefly to power amidst a violent civil war, seized land in Cuzco for his urban compounds of Amarucancha and Colcampata yet still found the time to build his own royal estate at Calca (not far from where his great-grandfather Viracocha built his estate of Caquia Xaquixaguana). For the Incas, royal estates were not simple expressions of leisure, but instead, constructed to be the material manifestations of a potent leader beyond the imperial capital.

Tipón, a royal estate just south of Cuzco, featured elegant terracing and waterworks.
Adriana von Hagen.

These rural manifestations were not bounded and contained entities like their urban counterparts. Instead, they comprised a diversity of site types scattered across a larger landscape. The functions served by these royal settlements included ceremonial plazas, ritual shrines, meeting rooms, servant work areas, agricultural lands and terraces, storehouses, the ruling Inca's sleeping quarters, pleasure gardens, hunting lodges, and baths. The classic example is the magnificent site of Machu Picchu, in the Urubamba valley, northwest of Cuzco. In sum, the architectural installations of a royal estate were designed to collectively meet the needs of a temporary capital when the ruler was in residence.

This dispersed settlement pattern was typical of the Inca state, which placed discrete imperial installations at critical visual, spatial, and temporal junctures in order to emphasize the Inca ruler's authority in the Andes, whether economic, religious, political, or cultural. Inca roads and way stations carefully monitored access to these installations, stretching the imperial presence even farther across the landscape. Hence, royal estates were not diminished by the fact that they were made up of a series of individual sites laid out across a large landscape. On the contrary, their placement and modes of access aggrandized the real and perceived power of the ruler and the Inca state.

While the **architecture** of royal estates shared many features of Inca design and construction, their underlying message was deeply informed by the specific needs of the patron and the particularities of his rule. Pachacuti, for example, built his royal estates in recently conquered lands. The architecture of his estates emphasized natural landscape features that had religious resonance. By blurring the line between the "natural" and the manmade, the architecture of Pachacuti's royal estates called into question where (and when) the architecture of the *Sapa* **Inca** (sole, unique Inca) began and where the sacred

Terracing at Machu Picchu, a royal estate. Scholars believe that these terraces could not have sustained the settlement's residents and that they obtained most of their food from elsewhere. Adriana von Hagen.

landscape ended. For Pachacuti, the architecture of his royal estates conveyed visual and material messages of his conquest.

By contrast, the political concerns of his son, Topa Inca, were vastly different and were thus reflected in the architecture of his royal estate. When Topa Inca built Chinchero at the end of his life, his primary concern was not conquest, but instead, succession. His estate was designed as a statement of preference for a favorite secondary wife and their son over that of his principal wife and child. Since gaining the support of powerful Inca nobles was key to securing his favored successor, Topa Inca had the elaborate entrance to his royal estate face the *panaca* lands of his father, rather than Cuzco, the capital. Hence, for Topa Inca, the royal estate had little to do with imperial conquest, but everything to do with royal authority, both present and future.

While Topa Inca's efforts ultimately failed, the importance of the royal estate and its relationship to the powerful *panacas* continued to grow. When Huayna Capac finally came to power (after a contested, behind-the-scenes battle involving various noblemen and women), he was left with some of the poorest agricultural lands in the Urubamba valley for a royal estate. In response, Huayna Capac marshalled experts in hydraulic engineering to tame the meandering Urubamba River and convert wetlands into some of the richest farming lands in the region. In doing so, the architecture of his royal estate visually demonstrated his power to transform a weakened condition into a defiant victory.

While the power of the *panacas* increased over time, they always played a critical role in Inca royal estates. This is because in the eyes of his subjects an Inca ruler did not die but, instead, was transformed from a *Sapa* Inca into a venerated ancestor. In this new desiccated existence, the royal mummy continued to visit his royal estates, where he was feasted, celebrated, and consulted on important matters. As the royal mummies depended on the *panacas* to carry out their wishes, however, it was the *panacas* who took over the running of the royal estates. Thus, for most of their existence, Inca royal estates were the focal point of *panaca* identity, authority, and ceremony.

Further Reading

Bengtsson, Lisbert. *Prehistoric Stonework in the Peruvian Andes: A Case Study at Ollantaytambo.* Vol. 44, *Etnologiska studier.* Göteborg: Göteborg University, Department of Archaeology, 1998.

Burger, Richard I., and Lucy C. Salazar. *Machu Picchu: Unveiling the Mystery of the Incas.* New Haven, CT: Yale University Press, 2004.

Nair, Stella. *At Home with the Sapa Inca: Architecture, Space, and Legacy at Chinchero.* Austin: University of Texas Press, 2015.

Niles, Susan. *Callachaca: Style and Status in an Inca Community.* Iowa City: University of Iowa Press, 1987.

———. *The Shape of Inca History.* Iowa City: University of Iowa Press, 1999.

Protzen, Jean-Pierre. *Inca Architecture and Construction at Ollantaytambo.* New York: Oxford University Press, 1993.

Reinhard, Johan. *Machu Picchu: Exploring an Ancient Sacred Center.* Los Angeles: Cotsen Institute of Archaeology Press, 2007.

Wright, Kenneth R., and Alfredo Valencia Zegarra. *Machu Picchu: A Civil Engineering Marvel.* Reston, VA: ASCE Press, 2000.

■ STELLA NAIR

ETHNICITY

Ethnic grouping formed one of the dominant principles of social organization in the Inca Empire. In the social sciences, ethnicity refers to the beliefs and practices of a group of people who believe themselves to be unique, with distinct origins, values, traditions, and practices that distinguish them from others—and which, in turn, is viewed by other such groups as possessing those qualities. That is, ethnicity is a reciprocal status, depending not just on how a particular group views itself, but also on how it is viewed by others. Ethnicity is widely regarded by anthropologists and archaeologists to be particularly pronounced in, if not peculiar to, state-level societies, and it certainly was so in the case of the Incas.

According to chroniclers' accounts, the Incas insisted that the empire's different ethnic groups maintain the distinctive clothing and headdress styles of their particular ethnic identities. The members of the different groups were not allowed to remove their clothing or exchange them for the attire of other groups. Distinctive headdresses were the most common mode of ethnic signaling. According to the seventeenth-century chronicler **Bernabé Cobo**:

> The men and women of each nation and province had their insignias and emblems by which they could be identified, and they could not go around without this identification or exchange their insignias for those of another nation, or they would be severely punished. They had this insignia on their clothes with different stripes and colors, and the men wore their most distinguishing insignia on their heads; each nation was identified by the headdress. . . . They were so well known by these insignia that on seeing any Indian or when any Indian came before him, the Inca would notice what nation and province the

Indian was from; and there is no doubt that this was a clever invention for distinguishing one group from another. (Cobo 1979 [1653])

Cobo continues by identifying the distinctive headgear of different peoples in the empire. The Cañari, for instance, wore a round wooden crown; the Indians of Bonbon (Pumpu in the central highlands) wore red and yellow kerchiefs around their heads; while those of Andahuaylas wrapped their heads with woolen cords that came down under the chin; and the Incas of Cuzco wore a twisted wool band the width of a finger, called a *llauto* (see **Costume**).

The material evidence for *mitmacuna*—people who were moved from their home territory to another place to practice their particular expertise (farming or metalworking, for instance) or to pacify recalcitrant peoples, or for other political and/or economic purposes—is especially difficult to identify. The even more widespread dispersal of *ayllus*, the kin-based groupings that made up ethnic groups, to multiple ecological zones (see **Murra, John Victor**), resulted in the large-scale "mixing" of identity groups across the landscape. These circumstances have considerably complicated the task of archaeologists in defining the ethnic boundaries of Tahuantinsuyu, although a number of studies successfully describe and analyze the archaeological record of ethnicity in the Andes.

Further Reading

Cobo, Bernabé. *History of the Inca Empire: An Account of the Indian's Customs and Their Origin, Together with a Treatise on Inca Legends, History, and Social Institutions*. Translated and edited by Roland Hamilton. Austin: University of Texas Press, 1979 [1653].

Reycraft, Richard M., ed. *Us and Them: Archaeology and Ethnicity in the Andes*. Monograph Series no. 53. Los Angeles: Cotsen Institute of Archaeology Press, UCLA, 2005.

■ GARY URTON

ETHNOGRAPHY, AS A SOURCE

Ethnography is a written account of the lifeways of a group of people usually based on long-term residence by an ethnographer within a given community. As a basic methodology of study by anthropologists since the late nineteenth century, ethnography usually results from what is termed *participant observation*, in which the ethnographer lives, works, and studies over a long time within a community. While formal ethnographies did not begin in the Andes until the early part of the twentieth century, certain Colonial-era travelers and chroniclers produced works that bore some of the hallmarks of ethnography; these include the early traveler and chronicler **Pedro de Cieza de León**, the native chronicler **Felipe Guaman Poma de Ayala**, the mestizo chronicler **Garcilaso de la Vega**, and even to a certain extent **Pedro Sarmiento de Gamboa**. The latter, a Colonial official who was commissioned by the Viceroy Francisco de Toledo to write the first history of the Inca Empire, carried out an inquest of more than 100 *quipucamayocs* (the keepers of the knotted-string accounts; see **Quipus**). From the testimony of the cord keepers, Sarmiento fashioned an account of Inca history and cultural practices that had some of the elements of an ethnography.

The modern practice of ethnography in the Andes began with the Peruvian anthropologist-novelist José María Arguedas, a man of mixed (Spanish/indigenous) ancestry who grew up in the southern highlands of Peru. Like many ethnographers who followed in his footsteps, Arguedas recognized that many Andean villagers lived lives based on agriculture and herding, followed other cultural norms long documented in historical records, and spoke **Quechua**. These features represented what were commonly termed "continuities" with Inca practices and customs described in the early Colonial chronicles and documents. Thus the notion grew among anthropologists that studying the lifeways of contemporary Andean people could shed light on the lifeways of people in the Inca Empire. Much has been learned of the lifeways of highland Quechua- and **Aymara**-speaking populations of the central Andes through ethnographic studies. These have often been used as a lens through which to read Colonial accounts to inform our understanding of Inca-era habits, practices, and values.

Further Reading

Arguedas, J. M. "Puquio, una cultura en proceso de cambio." *Revista del Museo Nacional* 25: 184–232, 1956.

Arguedas, J. M., and J. Roel Pineda. "Tres versiones del mito de Inkarrí." In *Ideología mesianica del mundo andino*, edited by J. Ossio Acuña. Lima: Ignacio Prado Pastor, 1972.

MacCormack, Sabine. "Ethnography in South America: The First Two Hundred Years." In *Cambridge History of the Native Peoples of the Americas*. Vol. 3, pt. 1, *South America*, edited by F. Salomon and S. Schwartz, 96–187. Cambridge: Cambridge University Press, 1999.

Salomon, Frank. "Andean Ethnology of the 1970s: A Retrospective." *Latin American Research Review* 17, no. 2: 79–129, 1982.

———. "The Historical Development of Andean Ethnology." *Mountain Research and Development* 51, no. 1: 78–98, 1985.

■ GARY URTON

EXPANSION

The Incas conquered a vast network of provinces in just a few generations, growing from a centralized state with increasing regional influence around AD 1400 to a mighty empire that ruled over far-flung and diverse territories (see **Archaeology, Cuzco**). Early Spanish chroniclers debated the timing, methods, and justification of Inca conquests. These questions became central to challenging or justifying Spain's right to conquer the Inca king and rule over the Andes, and the portrayal of Inca conquests changed several times during the century that followed the Spanish conquest. A key distinction that helps to organize and discuss accounts of Inca expansion is between writers who credit only two or three Inca rulers with imperial conquests, and sources that state that all Inca rulers contributed to the growth of the empire.

The earliest narratives of Inca expansion belong to the "late expansion" group. Detailed narratives of Inca history first appeared in the 1550s and focused on the legendary deeds of a prince named Inca Yupanqui, who led the defense of Cuzco against an invading army and then turned Inca military power outward to conquer across the Andean highlands. Although Inca Yupanqui receives the credit for transforming Inca society—so much so that he is better known by the nickname Pachacuti (The Upheaval of the Universe)—the early chroniclers **Pedro de Cieza de León** and **Juan de Betanzos** describe campaigns of expansion outside the Cuzco valley a generation or two earlier. One proponent of a Pachacuti-led imperial expansion was Bartolomé de Las Casas, a staunch supporter of indigenous autonomy who portrayed Inca expansion as the benevolent spread of civilization and good government. For Las Casas, Pachacuti represented a culture hero who invented and spread good government through benevolent means.

By the 1560s, royal officials complained that Las Casas had misrepresented Inca expansion, overstating the legitimacy of Inca rule and in the process damaging Spain's legitimate interests in the Americas. These writers argued that the Incas were tyrannical newcomers in most parts of the Andes, and that they did not begin their conquests until the late 1400s. The most extreme proponents of a late expansion paradigm claimed that it was not until the reign of Topa Inca Yupanqui that proper imperial campaigns commenced. Many of these sources were written around 1570, as the Spanish Crown engaged in administrative consolidation in the Andes and sought to discredit the legitimacy of Inca sovereignty. **Pedro Sarmiento de Gamboa** is one of the better known of these chroniclers.

Although most European writers described the earliest Inca rulers as mythical ancestors or leaders with very limited local power, several sources from the 1600s focused on these personages as imperial conquerors. Some chroniclers claimed that Inca conquests began in the time of the first Inca ancestors, although a large body of archaeological evidence contradicts this interpretation of early and gradual expansion. These sources include chronicles by men of Andean descent, such as **Garcilaso de la Vega** and **Felipe Guaman Poma de Ayala**. They present imperial expansion as the outgrowth of the efforts of Manco Capac, the first Inca ruler, who founded Cuzco and consolidated administrative power and ethnic unity across the Cuzco region (see **Myths, Origin**).

The early and late models for Inca expansion coexisted throughout the period of Spanish Colonial rule, and it was only in the nineteenth century that scholars began to try to disentangle what really happened from ancient myths and Spanish propaganda. In rediscovering Colonial manuscripts and publishing them for the first time, scholars identified biases that raised questions about the accuracy of accounts. Clements Markham, for instance, published a translation of Sarmiento de Gamboa in 1907 in which he italicized passages that he thought misrepresented Inca rule. Around this time, archaeologists working in Peru were becoming aware of pre-Inca civilizations, and were forced to confront the fact that Inca accounts of their rise to power could not adequately explain the kingdoms and empires that had come before them (see **Chronology, Pre-Inca**).

In 1928, Philip Ainsworth Means published the first part of his *Biblioteca Andina*, a treatment of the corpus of sixteenth- and seventeenth-century sources on the Andes. Taking a cue from the great Spanish historian Marcos Jiménez de la Espada, Means distinguished between groups of chroniclers whom he called "Garcilasans" (after the chronicler) and "Toledans" (after the Viceroy Toledo, who commissioned Sarmiento de Gamboa's chronicle), which correspond roughly to the early and late expansion models discussed above. Means discounted the Toledan accounts as being either ill informed or vindictive, and he saw the Garcilasan group as consisting of better chroniclers whose description of gradual Inca expansion seemed more reasonable.

Means's promotion of an early expansion model set the stage for the current interpretive paradigm, which **John H. Rowe** presented in 1945. Rowe reframed the early/late expansion models by asking whether a source would answer "yes" or "no" to the question "Had the Incas conquered territory more than about fifty miles from Cuzco at the beginning of Pachacuti's reign?" Leaving aside the question of how and when the Incas conquered the Cuzco region—an inquiry to which he never seriously returned—Rowe looked at the archaeological evidence for Inca expansion in provincial regions, concluding that the most reliable chroniclers and the material remains supported the interpretation of late and rapid imperial expansion. This new approach to Inca expansion treated it as a historically documented process, and Rowe produced a map showing the territories conquered by Pachacuti, Topa Inca Yupanqui, and Huayna Capac.

Subsequent historiographic work has fine-tuned aspects of this map, but the overall portrait of Inca expansion presented by Rowe in 1945 remains more or less unchallenged. Archaeological research has begun to raise some interpretive questions about this paradigm, bringing radiocarbon dates into the reconstruction of Inca expansion processes. Archaeological dates are less precise than the calendar dates developed from the Colonial chronicles appear to be, but they have been instrumental in reconstructing the earliest expansion of the Inca state in the Cuzco region, and for identifying an Inca presence that substantially predates the expected conquest date found in the chronicles.

Inca expansion beyond the Cuzco valley began a century or more before the first imperial campaigns outside the Cuzco region (see **Archaeology, Cuzco**). Documentary accounts describe three or four generations of local expansion, which included alliance building and periodic warfare (see **Conquests**). Between AD 1200 and 1400, the Incas began to dominate small villages located to the north and south of the Cuzco valley, and they intensified raids against more powerful rivals, conquering them permanently by around 1400. By 1400, Inca rulers shifted their attention to dominating local leaders living farther afield, including groups speaking other languages. Very little archaeological work has been done in the area just beyond the Cuzco region, and it is possible that archaeological dates from the upper Vilcanota valley or the Abancay region will reveal Inca incursions prior to AD 1400.

Likewise, the accumulation of radiocarbon dates in some provincial sites has led some researchers to propose that the Inca conquest of some areas may have occurred a generation or two earlier than indicated by Rowe's conquest maps. Several dozen radiocarbon dates from the southern periphery of the empire have led researchers to suggest that the Incas carried out some sort of contact or conquest early in the fifteenth century, rather than around 1470–1480. As dates and data accumulate, archaeologists will continue to scrutinize dates that seem too early, and to remain appropriately critical about what the dates mean. The early presence of Inca-style pottery, for example, does not necessarily indicate imperial conquest.

One distinct problem with the current map of Inca expansion chronology is that it does not adequately reflect the reality of Inca conquest and rule. Territorial annexation did not always occur as a single event, and some parts of the Andes were too marginal to encourage any sort of imperial attention. In areas targeted for conquest, Inca armies sometimes simply raided local populations or created alliances or some degree of indirect rule, only establishing formal administrative infrastructure when these relations deteriorated. Rebellions were common in many regions and required heavy military investments to reestablish imperial dominion. As researchers continue to study Inca expansion, more attention is sure to focus on setbacks to imperial rule and on places across the Andes where Inca power never reached.

Further Reading

Covey, R. Alan. *How the Incas Built Their Heartland: State Formation and the Innovation of Imperial Strategies in the Sacred Valley, Peru*. Ann Arbor: University of Michigan Press, 2006.

D'Altroy, Terence N., Verónica I. Williams, and Ana María Lorandi. "The Inkas in the Southlands." In *Variations in the Expression of Inka Power*, edited by Richard L. Burger, Craig Morris, and Ramiro Matos Mendieta, 85–133. Washington, DC: Dumbarton Oaks, 2007.

Garcilaso de la Vega, El Inca. *Royal Commentaries of the Incas and General History of Peru, Part One*. Translated by Harold V. Livermore. Austin: University of Texas Press, 1966 [1609].

Guaman Poma de Ayala, Felipe. *The First New Chronicle and Good Government: On the History of the World and the Incas up to 1615*. Translated by Roland Hamilton. Austin: University of Texas Press, 2009 [1615].

Las Casas, Bartolomé de. *Las antiguas gentes del Perú*. Colección de Libros y Documentos Referentes a la Historia del Perú, series 2, vol. 11. Lima: Librería Imprenta Gil, S. A. 1939 [1550s].

Means, Philip Ainsworth. "Biblioteca Andina—Part One." In *Transactions of the Connecticut Academy of Arts and Sciences* 29:271–525, 1928.

Pärssinen, Martti. *Tawantinsuyu: The Inca State and Its Political Organization*. Studia Historica 43. Helsinki: Finnish Historical Society, 1992.

Rowe, John H. "Absolute Chronology in the Andean Area." *American Antiquity* 10, no. 3: 265–84, 1945.

■ R. ALAN COVEY

F

FARMING

Farming in the Andes dates back millennia. Although the Incas neither added to the technological repertoire nor domesticated new plants, they did take agriculture to a scale never before seen in the Andes, thanks largely to an enormous labor force that built the terraces and irrigation systems and harvested the fields.

Farming was done in a variety of ways, especially in the highlands. People practiced agriculture in three main zones, corresponding to altitude and regimes of temperature and rainfall. The lowest zone was the *yunga,* where warm temperature crops such as cotton, manioc, and sweet potato thrived. **Irrigation** was usually required for such crops as rainfall was insufficient or irregular. Mid-altitude crops of the *quechua* zone included maize, quinoa, squashes of many varieties, beans of even more varieties, chili peppers, and other crops. The *puna* zone saw the cultivation of hardy plants such as potatoes, of several hundred varieties; *oca* and *ullucu,* two other native tubers; and other types of plants. The

Fields in the *altiplano* of Ayaviri, Puno, Peru, prepared for sowing potatoes. Eusebio Quispe. TAFOS Photographic Archive/PUCP, Lima, Peru.

136

puna also provided pasture *par excellence* for llamas and alpacas. Some farmers grew crops at altitudes that exceeded 4,000 meters (13,000 feet), higher than in other regions of the world (see **Andes, Central**; **Foodstuffs, Domesticated**).

In the highlands, farming systems adapted to the local geography. In valleys where the three zones were located relatively close to each other, farmers placed fields in the different zones to grow a variety of plants. In addition, they spaced their fields to avoid losing their entire crop to a hailstorm, pest infestation, or early frost. Where flat land was at a premium, **terracing** was developed to increase farming outputs. Rainfall dictated whether irrigation systems were needed.

In regions where the three ecozones were spaced far apart, such as the *altiplano* of southern Peru and Bolivia, other means existed for procuring the resources of distant zones. Using llama caravans, people exchanged produce between villages located in the different zones. This system is still in use today in southern Peru where people from the *altiplano* exchange dried meat and *puna* crops such as potatoes with other groups in mid-altitudes for maize, beans, and other local crops; they also trade with coastal groups for dried fish, seaweed, and low-altitude crops. After trading on the coast, the *altiplano* people return to their villages, collecting their local products along the way. No doubt this is an ancient, probably pre-Inca practice.

Andean peoples also developed another mechanism to meet the challenges of distant resources. In this system, villages in one zone sent family members to live in another zone to produce the necessary crops. The Incas expanded this concept to include entire villages that they moved to grow crops of interest to them (see **Labor Service**).

In addition to the three main zones, people also cultivated the *ceja de montaña* (eyebrow of the jungle), a region of high rainfall and warmer temperatures that lies between the high-altitude *puna* and the tropical forest of Amazonia along the eastern flanks of the

Men preparing a field for planting using the *chakitaclla*, or foot plow, in Ayaviri, Puno, Peru. Sebastián Turpo. TAFOS Photographic Archive/PUCP, Lima, Peru.

Andes. An essential crop grown in this zone was **coca** leaf, so vital to both domestic and ceremonial life. People chewed coca leaves with a small amount of lime or potash, which released the active alkaloid ingredients causing mild numbness and reducing fatigue and hunger. In a challenging environment like the highlands, coca was an asset for agriculturalists. Coca also had ceremonial importance and was a frequent offering to the gods.

An underappreciated aspect of Andean agriculture was the practice of freeze-drying food. Meat, fish, and plant foods could all be processed to remove moisture and improve storage. Potatoes, for instance, are freeze dried by soaking them in running water and allowing them to freeze at night, followed by drying in the intense sun during the day. By doing this over the course of a week or so, the moisture is eliminated. This made the food lighter, easier to transport and preserve. Inca storehouses at major administrative centers such as Huánuco Pampa housed vast amounts of freeze-dried food.

Maize was the most important crop to the Incas, and was used both as a food and a drink when fermented into *chicha*. Like coca, chicha had ordinary and ritual uses: it was both a beverage to slake one's thirst and a ceremonial drink. Vast fields of maize were cultivated in all regions of the empire, and new fields were often opened up specifically for its production (see **Cuisine**).

The relatively flat topography of the coastal plains allowed people to work large fields, but the fields required irrigation due to lack of rainfall. Cultivated crops included maize, beans, squashes, manioc, and cotton. Before the Incas, local lords controlled the fields (see **Economy, Domestic**), but after their conquest of the coastal valleys, the Incas either continued to use the existing political system, if it was present, or installed their own lords to oversee farming and other activities.

Farming was the economic basis of the Inca Empire. Planting crops was an important complement to herding and fishing, but it played a more central role. The kinds of plants cultivated, the different systems of agriculture, and the processing of the products all contributed to the success of the Incas in feeding the millions of workers who served the empire.

Further Reading

Murra, John. "El 'control vertical' de un máximo de pisos ecológicos en la economía de las sociedades andinas." In *Visita de la Provincia de Léon de Huánuco*, by Iñigo Ortíz de Zúñiga, vol. 2: 429–76. Huánuco, Peru: Universidad Hermilio Valizán, 1972.

Masuda, Shozo, Izumi Shimada, and Craig Morris, eds. *Andean Ecology and Civilization: An Interdisciplinary Perspective on Andean Ecological Complementarity.* Tokyo: University of Tokyo Press, 1985.

■ MICHAEL A. MALPASS

FEASTS, STATE-SPONSORED

Anthropologists have long recognized the prominent role of food and feasting in the emergence of social hierarchies and the negotiation of power and identity. Centering on the communal consumption of food and drink, feasting is a form of extraordinary public activity that is distinguished in some way from day-to-day commensal events. Feasts are often differentiated from everyday meals on the basis of the types or quantities of foodstuffs served, the methods of preparation employed, the tableware used, the location or context of the event, excessive consumption or inebriation, or the presence of entertainment, such as singing, dancing, or oratory. It is the broader public and communal aspects of feasts and feasting that make them significant arenas of political and social action. The fact that feasts are typically hosted—be it by an individual, a clan, a community, or a governing elite—at once establishes both social relations and social hierarchy. The recognition that feasts are often aimed at the acquisition or maintenance of social or economic power is articulated by the notion of commensal politics, which has been employed by archaeologists to good effect in a variety of studies focused on early states and empires.

The processes and practices of feasting are amenable to archaeological detection due to the fact that many of the activities associated with feasting, including especially food preparation, consumption, and disposal, leave behind significant material remains. The different types of archaeological data that have been brought to bear in the investigation of commensal politics and state-sponsored feasting include paleobotanical and zooarchaeological remains; culinary equipment; architectural, osteological, and funerary remains; soil geochemistry; spatial and contextual data; and iconographic and epigraphic materials. Ethnohistoric and ethnographic data also provide useful sources of information and analogy for the investigation of feasting as a significant cultural practice within early states.

In the Andean context, food presentation and feasting have long been seen as critical to the consolidation of power. Archaeological studies of the Inca's imperial predecessors, the Huari and the Tiahuanaco, have provided insights into the importance of ritual feasting and large-scale *chicha* (maize beer) consumption during the Middle Horizon (see **Chronology, Pre-Inca**). These earlier Andean states promoted new culinary and commensal traditions that saw the creation of new and distinctive ritual feasting wares. The Middle Horizon approaches to empire-building in the Andes arguably laid the groundwork for the political practices developed by the Inca several centuries later.

For the Inca, the importance of reciprocity, hospitality, and feasting as key components of imperial statecraft was first discussed by **John V. Murra**. The **labor service** owed the state by local communities (*mit'a*) was typically appropriated under the rubric of reciprocity. An important aspect of labor exchange in the Andes was the understanding that the work party would be fully provisioned by the sponsor in terms of raw materials, tools, food, and drink. Such ethnographically derived insights have been borne out archaeologically at Inca administrative centers such as Huánuco Pampa, where enormous quantities of imperial Inca jar and plate fragments, suggesting large-scale *chicha* consumption and food-serving activities, were recovered in structures flanking the main plaza. Archaeological mapping of Inca administrative centers together with analysis of spatial layouts and architecture make clear that the characteristic large, central plazas were the focal points of these sites, rather than any specific buildings. The size and configuration of these plaza spaces, in conjunction with the evidence provided by the artifacts, suggest that these spaces were likely sites of state-sponsored feasting. The physical features of Inca administrative sites underscore the centrality of commensal politics to the imperial agenda.

A complementary line of archaeological research focusing on imperial state ceramics offers further support for the idea that state-sponsored feasting was a key strategy of Inca state expansion. The elaboration of a specific repertoire of service, storage, and cooking vessels provides another indication of the importance of the relationship between food and politics for the Inca. The richly embellished polychrome wares produced by the imperial state were stylistically and morphologically distinct from both their historical antecedents and contemporaneous local wares in the provinces (see **Ceramics**). In addition to the superlative aesthetic quality of Inca state pottery vis-à-vis most local wares, the specific vessel forms comprising the imperial assemblage indicate a clear emphasis on serving and consumption (as opposed to "behind-the-scenes" cooking). It is noteworthy that the most common Inca vessel by far, the tall-necked jar or *aríbalo*, is clearly associated with the storage and serving of the fermented maize beverage, *chicha*. The widespread distribution of this vessel form around the empire, together with the rest of the imperial assemblage, highlights the significance of state-sponsored drinking, and feasting, in general. Both the archaeological and ethnohistoric evidence point to the fact that commensal politics was a key component of imperial Inca statecraft and one of the primary methods employed toward the dual ends of promoting state allegiance and creating class difference.

Further Reading

Bray, Tamara L. "Inca Pottery as Culinary Equipment: Food, Feasting, and Gender in Imperial State Design." *Latin American Antiquity* 14, no. 1: 1–23, 2003.
———. "The Role of Chicha in Inca State Expansion: A Distributional Study of Inca Aríbalos." In *Drink, Power, and Society in the Andes*, edited by Justin Jennings and Brenda Bowser, 108–32. Gainesville: University of Florida Press, 2009.
Bray, Tamara L., ed. *The Archaeology and Politics of Food and Feasting in Early States and Empires.* New York: Kluwer/Plenum Press, 2003.
Dietler, Michael. "Theorizing the Feast: Rituals of Consumption, Commensal Politics, and Power in African Contexts." In *Feasts: Archaeological and Ethnographic Perspectives on Food, Politics, and Power*, edited by Michael Dietler and Brian Hayden, 65–114. Washington, DC: Smithsonian Institution Press, 2001.
Dietler, Michael, and Brian Hayden, eds. *Feasts: Archaeological and Ethnographic Perspectives on Food, Politics, and Power.* Washington, DC: Smithsonian Institution Press, 2001.
Morris, Craig, and Donald Thompson. *Huánuco Pampa: An Andean City and Its Hinterland.* London: Thames and Hudson, 1985.
Murra, John V. *The Economic Organization of the Inka State.* Greenwich, CT: JAI Press, 1980 [1955].

■ TAMARA L. BRAY

FEATHERS

Feather cloth and ornaments featured among the most spectacular of Inca textiles (see **Costume**; **Weaving and Textiles**), reserved for dressing kings, nobles, and soldiers; decorating gateways, palaces, and temples; and offered in sacrifice. The Inca emperor crowned his *mascaypacha*—the headdress that symbolized Inca kingship—with black and white feathers, carried a wooden staff festooned with colorful plumes, and was borne on a litter bedecked with parrot feathers, gold, and silver.

The Spaniards marveled at the quantities of desiccated birds and feathers warehoused in Cuzco. **Pedro Pizarro**, one of the few Spaniards to see **Cuzco** before the 1536 siege, noted, "There were deposits of iridescent feathers, some looking like fine gold; others of

A feathered headdress found on the summit of Llullaillaco in Argentina. It accompanied the tomb of a young woman. Johan Reinhard.

a shimmering golden green color. These were very small feathers, from birds a little larger than cicadas [hummingbirds]. . . . They made clothing from these feathers, and they amazed one, for where could they find such amounts of iridescent [feathers?] There were many other feathers of various colors used to make the clothing worn at the fiestas by the lords and ladies, and not by others" (Pizarro 1921 [1571]).

The empire often reserved the finest garments, especially feather cloth, for its soldiers. The description by **Bernabé Cobo** of soldiers' attire indicates that the men carried shields "covered on the outer side with a piece of fine cotton, wool or feather cloth," and over their defensive gear they "would usually wear their most attractive and rich adornments and jewels; this included wearing fine plumes of many colors on their heads" (Cobo 1990 [1653]).

Feathers also featured in ritual sacrifices, especially the **Capac Hucha** sacrifices found on snow-clad mountains in southern Peru, Chile, and Argentina. A sacrificed boy excavated on Mt. Aconcagua in Argentina wore a tunic made of feathers that had been dyed red and yellow. The figurines accompanying the boy wore headgear composed of toucan and scarlet macaw feathers. One of the sacrificed girls found on the summit of Llullaillaco in Argentina wore a headdress of white plumes attached to a woolen skullcap, echoing the feathered headdress topping a silver figurine accompanying the young girl; her tomb also contained a coca bag covered in red feathers (see **Collasuyu**; **Capac Hucha**).

Feathers were not only reserved to dress the living and the dead, but also to decorate architecture. South of Cuzco, on the **Island of the Sun** in Lake Titicaca, the Incas established one of the empire's most important shrines (see **Oracles**). Feathers covered two of the gateways leading to the sanctuary. One of these, Kentipuncu, was covered with hummingbird feathers, while another, Pillcopuncu, was adorned with the green feathers of a bird called *pillco*, a trogon with red and brilliant green feathers.

The Incas used feathers from an extensive array of birds found in a wide range of habitats. These include flamingos, native to the Peruvian highlands and the coast, and rheas (the South American ostrich) that live in the desert *puna* of Peru down to Chile and Argentina. According to Cobo, Spaniards used rhea feathers for parasols and feather dusters. In addition, ancient weavers used the feathers of water birds such as cormorants, herons, and ducks, also found in the highlands and on the coast, and birds of prey (hawks, eagles, cara caras) and carrion feeders (vultures, condors) with wide-ranging habitats.

The most sought after bird species were those from the cloud forest and lowland, tropical rainforest. According to the chronicler **Garcilaso de la Vega**, hunters trapped birds using nets strung up between trees. These nets probably served to capture small birds such as hummingbirds while larger birds may have been caught by using birdlime, a sticky substance spread on branches. The Incas not only controlled the production and distribution of feather cloth and ornaments, but also the sources of feathers, using trade networks that had been established centuries earlier. As the empire grew, the number of tropical regions supplying feathers grew accordingly.

Further Reading

Cobo, Bernabé. *Inca Religion and Customs.* Translated and edited by Roland Hamilton. Austin: University of Texas Press, 1990 [1653].

King, Heidi. *Peruvian Featherworks: Art of the Precolumbian Era.* New York: Metropolitan Museum of Art, 2013.

Pizarro, Pedro. "Relation of the Discovery and Conquest of the Kingdoms of Peru." Translated and annotated by Philip Ainsworth Means. 1921 [1571]. https://archive.org/stream/relationofdiscov 00pizauoft/relationofdiscov00pizauoft_djvu.txt.

Reina, Ruben E., and Kenneth M. Kennsinger, eds. *The Gift of Birds: Featherwork of Native South American Peoples.* Philadelphia: University Museum of Archaeology and Anthropology, University of Pennsylvania, 1991.

■ ADRIANA VON HAGEN

FOODSTUFFS, DOMESTICATED

By the time groups living in and around the Cuzco valley became part of the Inca empire, people had been living in the Andes, along the western coast of the South American continent, and in the Amazon basin for at least 10,000 years, and domesticating a diverse range of plants and animals (see **Animals, Domesticated**).

Women in Ocongate, south of Cuzco, sort potatoes, an Andean native and staple. Several hundred varieties of potatoes are cultivated today. Juan de Diós Choquepuma. TAFOS Photographic Archive/PUCP, Lima, Peru.

These ecologically diverse environments spurred experimentation. Ecological geographers have shown that certain regions of the world became hot spots for domestication as people persisted through various climatic shifts. The main criteria conducive to domestication are annual seasonality, wet and dry seasons, and plant diversity. The greater Andean region has these characteristics. It is no surprise that this region witnessed many plant domestications, some of which have spread around the globe since the Age of Exploration and the Conquests. The most commonly consumed domesticated plants from this region are the potato (*Solanum* spp.) and the sweet potato (*Ipomoea batatas*). Important dietary additions include a variety of beans (*Phaseolus* spp.), chili peppers (*Capsicum* spp.), squashes (*Cucurbita* spp.), peanuts (*Arachis hypogaea*), and manioc (*Manihot esculenta*). Less well known are quinoa (*Chenopodium quinoa*), oca (*Oxalis tuberosa*), ulluco (*Ullucus tuberosus*), mashua (*Tropaeolum tuberosum*), and jicama (*Pachyrhizus erosus*). This region also yielded animal domesticates: the camelids (llamas and alpacas), the guinea pig (*Cavia porcellus*), and the Muscovy duck (*Cairina moschata*), whose use as food has not spread outside of this region. Such a diverse and useful range of foods clearly allowed the Incas and their predecessors—Huari, Tiahuanaco, and Chimú, among others—to make and sustain their conquests across diverse ecological zones, peoples, and territories. Although the timing of these domestications is still a focus of study, we believe that these plants and animals have all been domesticated for at least 4,000 years, and some have been cultivated for 7,000 years.

The Incas focused their early conquests on peoples living in intermontane valleys. Long before the rise of the Incas, most of the familiar Andean crops and animals had been in regular production, with many regional variations bred and selected for local microclimate, productivity, flavor, and yield. In addition, a range of plants native to Central America entered into the region, just as some of the Andean domesticates traveled north. The most important dietary and cuisine species introduced from central America were maize (*Zea mays*) and avocado (*Persea americana*). Andean people also consumed many wild plants and animals, most prominently fish from the ocean, lakes, and rivers; a variety of wild cactus fruits; fruits such as chirimoya (*Annona cherimola*) and lúcuma (*Pouteria lucuma*); and wild herbaceous plants. They also domesticated nonfood plants, most prominently gourds (*Lagenaria siceraria*), for storage, as fishing net floats and for transporting liquids; cotton (*Gossypium barbadense*) for nets, bags, and clothing; **coca** (*Erythroxylum coca*) and tobacco (*Nicotiana* spp.) for psychological transformation. In fact, it is quite likely that mind-altering and spicy plants were some of the earliest South American domesticates.

Food is a fundamental building block of biological, ecological, and economic human systems. It is also a symbol; a means for communicating highly condensed, powerful statements about the political, cultural, and religious systems of a given society. Many studies demonstrate that people do not eat all things that are edible. Additionally, people eat inedible and even poisonous things. The Incas were no exception. Their culinary interests were based on a long history of Andean food traditions, linked to productivity, cooking styles, tastes, textures, and life ways (see **Cuisine**; **Feasts, State-Sponsored**). They built their empire on what they considered good food—meat and potatoes— which was reflected in their forms of cultivation and farming.

What was proper food for Inca people and their leaders? What was sacred food, state food, or lowly, everyday food? While many of the ingredients overlapped among these scenarios, the Inca leadership clearly preferred special foods for specific political settings. People across the empire were identified by domesticated varieties in addition to clothing styles and dialects. The Incas encouraged these differences to help account for the myriad groups that they codified in their hierarchical record keeping, with the local leaders reporting to Inca administrators via *quipus*, the knotted strings that listed all stored food and other goods in the royal storage buildings, called *collcas* (see **Storage**).

Most people ate two main meals a day. The first was consumed in the mid-morning, a thick soup with varying amounts of potatoes, quinoa, maize (and at times, fine soil for added minerals), depending on the elevation of the farm. On the coast this soup likely contained sweet potato, manioc or maize, with lima beans. At dusk, the highland evening meal was usually solid food of boiled potatoes with beans and a spicy sauce of chili peppers and wild herbs, eaten out of a common cooking jar or from a woven cloth. Meat was sometimes included, though it was usually only eaten on feast days. Camelid or guinea pig was the main meat source; less often, deer, wild ducks, rabbits, or other wild animals. Along the coast, fish, shellfish, and seaweed would have been common, spiced with chili peppers and wild herbs.

All social events were marked with food exchanges. Feasting activities occurred with the conquest of new peoples, and also at all religious ceremonies. Agriculture was core to Inca life. To plant, men had to make the holes in the ground as women placed the seeds in the earth. For all participating in the planting or harvest, *chicha* (maize beer), was provided to all workers with a hot, midday meal, primarily of potatoes.

When the Incas reached the borders of a group they wished to conquer, they sent emissaries to ask if the group wanted to join or fight the Incas. If the group chose to join, a date would be set for incorporation and on that day, Inca military leaders would arrive in the territory bearing gifts of fine clothing, elaborate imperial ceramics, and jewelry for the new local leaders to use as the emblems of the Inca state. If the local leaders accepted these gifts, a feast celebrated their incorporation into the empire, marked by the drinking of fermented beer, *chicha*. These state feasts focused on specific ingredients, ceramics, and performance. The Incas used three standardized receptacles to present food at these state occasions: ceramic jars and plates, and a drinking cup or *kero*, made of ceramic, wood, or metal (see **Ceramics; Keros**). The jars held and served a liquid, usually *chicha*. Andean peoples used many plants to make chicha, but the strongest was made of the fruit of the Peruvian pepper tree (*Schinus molle*), which thrived in warm valleys and on the coast. The most valued *chicha*, however, was from maize. The plates—used to present dried camelid meat (*charqui*), boiled potatoes, or toasted maize kernels—were an innovative way to present dry food in the Andes, allowing the Inca leadership to display state iconography. Outside of the imperial Inca feasts, such dried foods would have been presented on woven cloth, as is still done in the countryside today. The Inca controlled hunting of large game—primarily two kinds of deer (*loyco*, white-tailed deer; and *taruka*, northern, or Andean deer) and guánaco, a wild camelid—for their pleasure, making these animals a less common foodstuff than in earlier times.

In fact, maize became the staple plant crop of the empire, as the Incas focused many of their conquests on warmer intermontane valleys and the coast, where it grew well. They built **terraces** to grow maize in the mountainous regions, while on the flat lands they created state farms out of indigenous arable land. The value of domestic crops was so central to the Inca political and religious structure that at the start of the planting and rainy season between September and November, the **Sapa Inca** himself would lead the planting ceremony by making the first hole in the ground in a sacred field for maize plants. Royal food centered on maize and meat. Not only were these two foods the focus of Inca food production, they became the core foodstuff at all ceremonies. While the armies supposedly were given maize beer and meat, the historical evidence suggests that they lived mainly on starches, such as potatoes or sweet potatoes.

Inca deities were omnivorous, but they too appreciated beer and meat. In addition, they feasted on animals, *chicha*, maize, coca leaf, chili peppers, dried camelid meat, cactus fruit, humans, tubers, metals, textiles, Spondylus shell, quinoa, and fruit. While *chicha* and meat were the symbolic foods of the Incas, the empire really survived on potatoes and other starchy tubers, the true Inca domestic foods.

Further Reading

Bray, Tamara L. "To Dine Splendidly: Imperial Pottery, Commensal Politics and the Inca State." In *The Archaeology and Politics of Food and Feasting in Early States and Empires*, edited by Tamara L. Bray, 93–142. New York: Plenum Publishers, 2003.

Cook, Anita, *Feasting in the Andes: To Eat for Others* [To eat splendidly—Ñauraycuna *mizquimicuy*], *Food and Feasting in the Andes*. Washington, DC: Pre-Columbian Society of Washington, D.C., 2004.

Murra, John V., "Rite and Crop in the Inca state." In *Culture in History*, edited by S. Diamond, 393–407. New York: Columbia University Press, 1960.

Rowe, John H. "Inca Culture at the Time of the Spanish Conquest." In *Handbook of South American Indians,* edited by J. H. Steward, vol. 2, *The Andean Civilizations*, 183–330. Washington, DC: Smithsonian Institution, 1946.

Salomon, Frank, and George L. Urioste, trans. and eds. *The Huarochirí Manuscript: A Testament of Ancient and Colonial Andean Religion*. Austin: University of Texas Press, 1991.

Sauer, Carl. *Agricultural Origins and Dispersals*. New York: American Geographical Society, 1952.

■ CHRISTINE A. HASTORF

FORTIFICATIONS

The Incas used a form of fortification that had been perfected thousands of years earlier in the Andes: hillforts with concentric walls and narrow entrances, strategically located on passes and natural routes of travel. In the rugged Andean landscape of hills, sweeping views, and constrained routes of travel, such hillforts offered significant defensive advantages. But the Incas relied on them less than many Andean societies in the preceding centuries. Inca fortifications are rare in the heartland, perhaps because of the rapid and aggressive growth of the empire. In the earliest phase of Inca expansion, some new fortifications and encircling walls were built at recently subjugated centers in the Cuzco region: Raqchi, War'qana, Wat'a, and Pumamarca. Most sites we can confidently call Inca forts, however, are found at strategic points and passes near the edges of the empire, suggesting that investment in frontier defenses was a relatively late development. (Exceptions are northern Chile near the Atacama region, which may correspond to an earlier frontier or to an area where special vigilance was necessary, and the Calchaquí

The hilltop fortress of Quitaloma formed part of a chain of forts overlooking
the basin of Quito, Ecuador, and witnessed battles between Inca and Cayambe
warriors over several decades. Photo courtesy of Samuel Connell and Chad Gifford.

area in Argentina, where Inca forts safeguarded valuable metallic ore extraction and
production; see **Metallurgy**; **Mining**).

The distribution of Inca forts is uneven, with some frontiers much more heavily fortified than others: the northern frontier in Ecuador, the eastern rim of the highlands in
Bolivia, some distance within the southeastern frontier in Argentina, and near the southern limits of Tahuantinsuyu in Chile. Forts have not been reported on the poorly studied
eastern frontier in Peru. In some cases, the Incas reutilized earlier native forts after their
capture; this pattern is particularly common in the southern empire. In other cases, they
built new fortifications, as in Ecuador. The patchy distribution of Inca strongholds shows
they were not built as a blanket policy, but as needed, to support difficult campaigns of
expansion or counter threats by hostile unconquered people. For instance, cordons of
forts in Ecuador's Guayllabamba, Chilo, and Manchachi valleys correspond to documentary descriptions of the Inca offensive campaign against hostile Cayambe and Caranqui
peoples late in the empire's history.

During the period of hostilities, garrison forces were stationed at the larger forts more
or less permanently. Architectural complexes at some forts would have accommodated
sizable populations, who might have included not just soldiers, but their wives or families
as well. For instance, evidence of weaving and textile-working at Rumicucho in Ecuador
suggests that women were present. *Mitmacuna* (colonists from elsewhere in the empire)
are routinely mentioned in the chronicles as garrison populations, placed both in frontier

forts and in provinces whose loyalties were suspect. Interior garrisons in the provinces have been hard to identify archaeologically. A hilltop garrison of *mitmacuna* in the Lurín valley near Lima kept watch for trouble, and Inca complexes on recaptured rebel hill forts in the Titicaca basin were probably garrisoned. But many interior "garrisons" of loyal *mitmacuna* may not have been fortified at all; their mere presence would have discouraged sedition, and formed the first trip wire of alarm in case of rebellion.

Inca forts varied considerably in construction, size, layout, and defensibility. Construction sometimes showcased elaborate Cuzco-style masonry, but more often reflected regional traditions and conditions, perhaps making use of local labor. For example, shoot holes are found in Inca forts in the southern empire, but not in the central or northern Andes, while trenches are found in the north and not in the south.

An important functional distinction can be made between small outposts with little internal architecture, and larger, architecturally complex, permanently occupied installations. Small outposts are often found near a larger fort, supporting and extending the geographic reach of its military functions, providing extra vigilance and a base for flanking attacks. This "defense in depth" strategy is superbly illustrated at the Pambamarca hill range northeast of Quito, Ecuador, where several subsidiary watch posts bearing little sign of occupation are interspersed among larger, heavily fortified, permanently occupied forts with stockpiles of slingstones.

In this drawing by Felipe Guaman Poma de Ayala, Native troops storm a *pucara*, or fortress. Guaman Poma de Ayala, Felipe. *El primer nueva corónica y buen gobierno*. Edited by John V. Murra and Rolena Adorno, 51/63. Mexico City: Siglo Veintiuno, 1980 [1615].

While some forts were highly defensive, at others, ceremonial and administrative priorities largely dictated site layout. Indeed, Inca forts did more than defend routes into Inca territory; they were strategically placed nodes for exchange and gift giving, where interaction with frontier populations could be managed and ritualized. Features such as **ushnus** and plazas, along with feasting debris, suggest that some large Inca forts served as secure embassies for ceremonial diplomacy and the dissemination of imperial goods and mores to (semi-) independent native groups, and that ceremonial sectors were often an integral part of fort function. For instance, Incallacta in Bolivia, protected by a parapeted zigzag wall with baffled entrances, offered elaborate facilities for ceremonial performance, including a huge plaza with an *ushnu* and one of the largest *callancas* in the empire.

Thus, Inca military construction was expedient and flexible, since frontiers were dynamic and variable. Often occupied for only a short time, forts were abandoned once they outlived their usefulness. Inca forts on the eastern frontier were overrun by hostile Guaraní people shortly before the Spanish arrival, then recaptured and strengthened by the Incas. Some sites securely known to have been Inca military bases, such as Incahuasi in the Cañete valley on Peru's central coast, are not fortified at all. That is not to mention the important military functions of unfortified provincial centers in the interior, such as Huánuco Pampa.

All this suggests that categories of "fortification" and "fort" do more to serve archaeological convenience than to capture Inca realities. This is particularly evident at high-status royal and ceremonial sites in the Cuzco heartland that cannot comfortably be called "forts," but nonetheless demonstrate a concern for barring dangerous and unwanted people. Thick walls, such as the massive perimeter at Cacha, blocked local populations from entering Inca precincts. Sites converted from old fortified outposts, like the royal estate at Tipón, retained a defensible design. New **royal estates,** such as Pisac, Ollantaytambo, and Machu Picchu, incorporated defensive and exclusive elements: ridgetop locations, high walls and steep terraces, condor's-eye vantages, and tight control points. Above all, the magnificent ceremonial complex and fortress of **Sacsahuaman** above Cuzco was highly defensive: massive zigzag walls provided salients for flanking fire, and the bottom course of masonry blocks was too enormous to be scaled. The complex saw action in the 1536 siege of Cuzco (as did Ollantaytambo early the following year; see **Vilcabamba**). This is not to deny the symbolic and psychological impact of Sacsahuaman, or its valence as a sacred place, aspects that must have entered into its design as much as defensive considerations. For the Incas, there was apparently no contradiction between these functions.

Further Reading

Alconini, S. "The Dynamics of Military and Cultural Frontiers on the Southeastern Edge of the Inka Empire." In *Untaming the Frontier in Anthropology*, edited by B. J. Parker and L. Rodseth, 115–46. Tucson: University of Arizona Press, 2005.

Almeida Reyes, E. *Estudios Arqueológicos en el Pucara de Rumicucho (II Etapa)*. Quito: Museos del Banco Central de Ecuador, 1999.

Arkush, E. N. *Hillforts of the Ancient Andes*. Gainesville: University Press of Florida, 2011.

D'Altroy, T. N. *The Incas*. 2nd ed. New York: John Wiley & Sons, 2014.

D'Altroy, Terence N., Verónica I. Williams, and Ana María Lorandi. "The Inkas in the Southlands." In *Variations in the Expression of Inka Power*, edited by Richard L. Burger, Craig Morris, and Ramiro Matos Mendieta, 85–134. Washington, DC: Dumbarton Oaks Research, 2007.

Hyslop, John. *Inka Settlement Planning*. Austin: University of Texas Press, 1990.

Plaza Schuller, F. *La incursión Inca en el septentrional andino ecuatoriano*. Otavalo, Ecuador: Instituto Otavaleño de Antropología, 1976.

Raffino, R., and Stehberg, R. "Tawantinsuyu: The Frontiers of the Inca Empire." In *Archaeology in Latin America*, edited by G. G. Politis and B. Alberti, 168–83. London: Routledge, 1999.

■ ELIZABETH ARKUSH

G

Born of a Spanish father and an Inca mother, Garcilaso's chronicle of the Incas is one of the few accounts written by a *mestizo*. Although his given name was Gómez Suarez de Figueroa, he later took the name of his father, Sebastian Garcilaso de la Vega, and added "El Inca," to distinguish him from his father. Garcilaso was born in Cuzco in 1539 only a few years after the Spanish invasion. He spent his early years in the former Inca capital, playing with other youths in the city, speaking his mother's language (**Quechua**), and hearing stories about the Inca past—all experiences that later informed his writing about his homeland and his mother's people. In 1560, at the age of 21, Garcilaso left for Spain, where he sought to be compensated for his father's service to the Crown. He lived out the rest of his life in Spain, never to return to Peru. He studied in Spain and died in Córdoba in 1616. Before embarking on his magnum opus, Garcilaso authored several manuscripts, most notably *La Florida del Inca*, a history of Hernando de Soto's expedition to Florida and the southeastern United States.

It is the *Royal Commentaries of the Incas* for which Garcilaso is best known. The first part of the work, a history of the Incas, was completed in 1609. The second part, a general history of Peru, which deals with the Spanish conquest, the civil wars, and the **Vilcabamba** campaigns, culminating with the death of Túpac Amaru I in 1572, was posthumously published, in Córdoba, in 1617.

Garcilaso based his account of the Incas on several sources. Foremost were his memories of growing up in the former Inca capital. In his chronicle, he often laments the ongoing destruction of Cuzco by the Spaniards who pilfered Inca stones to build their churches and mansions. His mother, Chimpu Ocllo, and her family, descendants of the ruler Topa Inca, gave the young Garcilaso privileged information and access to descendants of former Inca nobility that few other chroniclers could claim. Once in Spain, Garcilaso kept abreast of events in his home country by letters from his childhood friends. In addition, and in keeping with the fashion of the times, he borrowed freely from other chroniclers, namely **José de Acosta**, **Pedro de Cieza de León**, and especially from the notes of another Peruvian *mestizo*, **Blas Valera**. Garcilaso cites long passages from Blas Valera, especially those concerning events in the northern empire, an area of which Garcilaso had no personal knowledge, as well as details of many incidents that transpired after Garcilaso had left for Spain.

Garcilaso's chronicle portrays the Incas as benevolent rulers, rather than as the tyrants and illegitimate rulers of Tahuantinsuyu, as depicted in **Pedro Sarmiento de Gamboa**'s chronicle published a few decades earlier, in 1572. In celebrating the Incas, however, Garcilaso often glossed over the less pleasant aspects of Andean culture, denying, for instance, that the Incas had practiced human sacrifice (see **Capac Hucha**). Admired for his eloquent writing style and an account filled with rich details, Garcilaso has also been criticized over the years for his hyperbole and some clear inaccuracies, although he has enjoyed a revival in recent years.

Further Reading

Garcilaso de la Vega, El Inca. *Royal Commentaries of the Incas and General History of Peru, Part One.* Translated by Harold V. Livermore. Austin: University of Texas Press, 1966 [1609].

———. *Royal Commentaries of the Incas and General History of Peru, Part Two.* Translated by Harold V. Livermore. Austin: University of Texas Press, 1966 [1617].

———. *Comentarios Reales de los Incas.* 2 vols. Edited by Carlos Araníbar. Lima: Fondo de la Cultura Económica, 1995 [1609, 1617].

Mazzotti, José Antonio. "Garcilaso de la Vega, El Inca (1539–1616)." In *Guide to Documentary Sources for Andean Studies, 1530–1900*, edited by Joanne Pillsbury, vol. 2, 229–41. Norman: University of Oklahoma Press, 2008.

■ ADRIANA VON HAGEN

GONZÁLEZ HOLGUÍN, DIEGO

The great **Quechua** lexicographer and grammarian commonly referred to solely by his matronym, or mother's surname, Holguín, was born in Cáceres, Spain, in 1552. He arrived in Peru in 1581, traveling on the same ship as his Jesuit colleague and author of works on the Aymara language, **Ludovico Bertonio**. Both men studied their respective languages in Juli, on the south shore of Lake Titicaca, which was the principal Jesuit center for the teaching of indigenous Andean languages at the time. Holguín studied both Quechua and **Aymara** while in Juli, but his later publications of grammars and vocabularies pertained to Quechua. While most of his time was spent as parish priest in Cuzco, he served initially as parish priest in Juli and, after his time in Cuzco, as vice rector of the Jesuit college in Quito, Ecuador. Holguín died in Mendoza, Argentina, in 1618.

Holguín's first work on Quechua was his *Gramática y arte nueva de la lengua general de todo el Perú, llamada lengua qquichua, o lengua del Inca* (New Grammar and Art of the General Language of All of Peru, Called the Quechua Language, or the Language of the Inca), which was written in the late 1590s but not published until 1607. Throughout his *Grammar*, Holguín systematically compares and contrasts Quechua grammar to that of Latin and Castilian Spanish, concluding that Quechua was superior grammatically to both European languages. The *Grammar* contains highly useful sections on kinship terms and Quechua numerals.

Better known and more widely used by students of Quechua and Inca civilization is the companion work to his *Grammar*, the *Vocabulario de la lengua general de todo el Perú llamada lengua qquichua, o del Inca*, published in 1608. This great dictionary of Quechua and Spanish—with 375 double column pages of Quechua–Spanish, and 332 pages of Spanish–Quechua—is the largest and most comprehensive Colonial dictionary of the Quechua language, the *lingua franca* of Inca administration in Tahuantinsuyu. (Holguín's is not the earliest dictionary, however; that honor goes to the Dominican friar Domingo de Santo Tomás's *Lexicón, o vocabulario de la lengua general del Perú*, written in 1560.)

Holguín states that he worked closely with native informants in Cuzco in constructing the *Vocabulario*, and he credits those individuals as the principal authors of the work. The work is structured primarily, though not strictly, alphabetically, as he often inserts terms related to a certain term by virtue of their being "sons and relatives" of that term. This makes for a highly contextualized and richly nuanced reading of many entries. In addition, unlike Santo Tomás's earlier *Lexicón*, which includes very few Spanish admixtures with Quechua, Holguín's *Vocabulario* contains many definitional phrases employing Spanish terms, thus attesting to the process of linguistic mixing that was ongoing in the Andes in the seventeenth century.

By any measure, the *Vocabulario* is a tremendously rich source of historical and ethnographic information on the Quechua language of the time, and it has been used to great advantage (and some abuse) by generations of students of Inca culture and civilization.

Further Reading

González Holguín, Diego. *Vocabulario*. Instituto de Lenguas y Literaturas Andinas-Amazónicas (IL-LA-A). 2007 [1608]. http://www.illa-a.org/cd/diccionarios/VocabularioQqichuaDeHolguin.pdf.

Mannheim, Bruce. *The Language of the Inka since the European Invasion*. Austin: University of Texas Press, 1991

———. "González Holguín, Diego (1552–1618)." In *Guide to Documentary Sources for Andean Studies, 1530–1900*, edited by Joanne Pillsbury, vol. 2, 252–54. Norman: University of Oklahoma Press, 2008.

Porras Barrenechea, Raúl. "Prólogo." In Diego González Holguín, *Vocabulario de la lengua general de todo el peru llamada lengua qquichua o del inca*, v–xliv. Lima: Universidad Nacional Mayor de San Marcos, 1952.

■ GARY URTON

GUAMAN POMA DE AYALA, FELIPE

The author of what is arguably the most influential work in the florescence of Inca studies through the twentieth century, *El primer nueva corónica y buen gobierno* (The First New Chronicle and Good Government), Guaman Poma was a descendant of native nobility from the southern highlands of Peru. It is thought that he was born sometime around 1535–1550, most likely in the Huamanga region in the northern part of the present-day department of Ayacucho. Guaman Poma was a member of the Guaman/Tingo clans (*ayllus*) of Huamanga. He was a native speaker of at least three varieties of **Quechua** and a few varieties of Aru, a language related to **Aymara**. Some of what we know about his later life and activities comes from documents involving a long legal struggle with people from Chachapoyas over land rights in the region of Chupas, near the town of Huamanga. His date of death is equally uncertain, but from evidence in his chronicle, it is estimated to have occurred around 1616.

It is clear from his writings that Guaman Poma received a fairly good education, and that he was exposed for some time to a wide range of European manuscripts, illustrations, and other printed material. It is fairly certain that he worked as an aide to clergy involved in the suppression of indigenous religious practices and the destruction of **huacas** and other native "idols." He claims to have served the ecclesiastical inspector (*visitador*) **Cristóbal de Albornoz** in that priest's 1569–1570 campaign through the territory of Huamanga. He also appears to have been involved in Viceroy Francisco de Toledo's 1571 *visita*, or inspection tour, of the Huamanga region. Guaman Poma also knew and for some time worked closely with the Mercedarian friar and chronicler, **Martín de Murúa**. It is clear, for instance, that Guaman Poma produced a few of the drawings in the manuscript known as the Galvin manuscript.

The manuscript of Guaman Poma's chronicle, *El primer nueva corónica y buen gobierno*, now in the Royal Library of Denmark, contains 1,190 pages of which 398 are full-page drawings produced by the author. The manuscript is written in Spanish but with a heavy admixture of Quechua and Aru terms and grammatical structures. Broadly, the substance of the work begins with a detailed historical account of the land of the Incas before the time of the Spanish conquest, followed by a middle section recounting the major events of the conquest itself, and ending with Guaman Poma's plaintive detailing of the destruction and ongoing deterioration of his Andean homeland under Spanish colonialism.

Guaman Poma's primary intended audience for the work was the king of Spain, Philip III, and his objective in producing the work was to argue to the king why it was essential that the conquest and colonization be brought to an end and that governance of the land be returned to its natural rulers, the descendants of the Incas and those of high ranking lineages. In order to make his argument (in his own eyes) to the king of Spain, Guaman Poma understood himself, first, to be writing "the first new chronicle," in the sense that he was contesting those chronicles written by Europeans up to his time, which he saw as unsympathetic to Andean peoples; and second, that he was, in his chronicle, detailing the "good governance" that had existed in the land, under the native lords, before the arrival of the Spaniards.

Guaman Poma's account contains a tremendous amount of detailed ethnographic information on Andean life before and up to the time of the writing of the chronicle. This information includes accounts of many on-the-ground realities of life in Andean communities, such as agricultural practices, agricultural and ritual calendars, the tending of crops and herds of camelids, the production of textiles, and other such matters. At a higher, public level, Guaman Poma discusses public administration and the relationship between Inca administration and local administrative officials, the system of decimal administration and census taking, the hierarchies of state administrative and religious officials, and a wide range of religious beliefs and practices, both indigenous and Christian. Both his text and his drawings are particularly insightful concerning ongoing transformations in civil and ecclesiastical administration, in which Natives had begun to take on the dress and duties of the various offices introduced by the conquerors.

Felipe Guaman Poma de Ayala's imagined presentation of his illustrated chronicle, *El Primer Nueva Córonica y Buen Gobierno*, to King Philip III of Spain. The presentation actually never occurred. Guaman Poma de Ayala, Felipe. *El primer nueva corónica y buen gobierno*. Edited by John V. Murra and Rolena Adorno, 897/960. Mexico City: Siglo Veintiuno, 1980 [1615].

Guaman Poma was also deeply concerned about the newly emergent *mestizo* (Native/European) identity, which he saw as detrimental to Andean civil society. Particularly troubling to him was the fact that *mestizos*, whether living in rural communities or in the emerging cities, were not subject to tribute obligations. He generally saw this new class of individuals as highly disruptive of Andean life ways, often portraying them as much given to drunkenness, prostitution, and other forms of behavior that had baleful effects on indigenous communities. All of these matters are covered not only in the author's text, but in the drawings as well. On this and a host of other issues addressed in his chronicle, Guaman Poma's work is rich in nuance, deeply informative, and highly effective in its interplay between image and text.

Further Reading

Adorno, Rolena. *Guaman Poma: Writing and Resistance in Colonial Peru*. Austin: University of Texas Press, 2000 [1986].

———. *Guaman Poma and His Illustrated Chronicle from Colonial Peru: From a Century of Scholarship to a New Era of Reading*. Copenhagen: Museum Tusculanum Press, University of Copenhagen, 2001.

———. "Guaman Poma de Ayala, Felipe (ca. 1535–1550–ca. 1616)." In *Guide to Documentary Sources for Andean Studies, 1530–1900*, edited by Joanne Pillsbury, vol. 2: 255–72. Norman: University of Oklahoma Press, 2008.

Guaman Poma de Ayala, Felipe. *The First New Chronicle and Good Government: On the History of the World and the Incas up to 1615*. Translated by Roland Hamilton. Austin: University of Texas Press, 2009 [1615].

The Guaman Poma Website, Royal Library, Copenhagen, Denmark. http://www.kb.dk/permalink/2006/poma/info/en/frontpage.htm.

■ GARY URTON

H

HEALTH AND ILLNESS

Even before the European diseases introduced by the Spanish conquistadors during their invasion of the Inca Empire decimated the populations of the Central Andes, the Incas contended with and survived rare and endemic diseases and ailments, as well as the typical afflictions of many living peoples (see **Diseases, Foreign**). The most direct line of evidence of Inca health and illness comes from skeletonized and mummified human remains, but ethnohistorical sources have also provided complementary details about health and illness that are not recorded on Inca human remains.

Inca health and illness varied widely by geographic location and proximity to the Inca capital, either within the core of the Inca Empire, the periphery of the Inca heartland, or in the provinces some distance from the capital. Because Inca imperial policies and practices varied within and between different regions, some communities may have benefited from greater access to foodstuffs and dietary diversity and from lower tribute demands and workloads, which would have contributed to positive health outcomes and stronger immunity to diseases. Other communities may have had reduced access to dietary diversity and foodstuffs and higher tribute demands, which may have negatively affected their health and increased their susceptibility to disease. Bioarchaeological investigations of human remains from Cuzco have demonstrated that these people were generally very healthy with few skeletal indicators of physiological stress, and no evidence of nutritional deficiencies, chronic diarrheal disease, or parasitic infections. The people from Cuzco, however, did show higher frequencies of one type of skeletal indicator of physiological stress: osteoperiostitis, a nonspecific inflammation of the outer tissue surrounding bone (periosteum), which may have resulted from the more urban and crowded conditions in Cuzco.

In contrast, communities from the peripheries of the Inca heartland showed slightly higher frequencies of skeletal indicators of physiological stress, as well as higher frequencies of degenerative joint disease. This suggests that labor demands by the Inca state may have been higher for these peripheral communities, but that physiological stress was not significantly greater. The few bioarchaeological investigations of communities living in the provinces of the Inca empire show higher frequencies of all types of skeletal indicators of physiological stress, but it appears that Inca imperial practices did not dramatically impact diet or health in the communities studied to date. Bone chemistry studies of carbon and nitrogen in the diets of people from one provincial community indicate that diet was nutritionally adequate. Human remains from the provinces show significantly higher frequencies of degenerative joint disease in comparison to people from the core and peripheries of Cuzco, which suggests that workloads and tribute demands may have been higher in the provinces.

Broken bones were fairly common during Inca times and were typically caused by accidents or occupational hazards. Nonlethal and healed injuries to the cranium indicate that some people may have participated in ritualized battles or intergroup conflicts, but lethal perimortem injuries, which would have occurred around the time of death and were often associated with pitched battles and warfare, are relatively rare in the Cuzco region and only slightly more common in the provinces.

Accounts by the chroniclers detail how Inca medical specialists applied herbs and poultices to fractures and stitched or set these injuries. The Incas were also adept at the surgical removal of part of the cranium, a practice known as trepanation, that has been studied extensively and which was likely undertaken to treat cranial trauma, infection of the mastoid of the temporal bone, epilepsy, and non-epileptic seizure disorders. Cuzco Inca practitioners of trepanation had success rates of approximately 80 percent and they were more successful in their surgeries than pre-Inca surgeons. Their success was likely due to the use of antiseptics, such as balsam, saponins, cinnamic acid, and tannins, as well as their standardized surgical methods and advanced knowledge of cranial anatomy. Cuzco trepanations were typically two of the four common types observed in the Central Andes, either circular grooving or scraping methods. In circular grooving, a circular or ovoid incision was made and a round plug of cranial bone would be removed. With the scraping method, a wide swath of cranial bone was scraped from the ectocranial surface and a smaller portion of bone was scraped from the endocranial surface.

Similar to other Central Andean prehistoric peoples, the Incas likely suffered from chronic and acute infectious diseases, such as tuberculosis, the non-venereal forms of treponemal disease, and different forms of pneumonia. Probable cases of tuberculosis and treponemal disease have been differentially diagnosed from bioarchaeological investigations of Inca skeletons, but they have not been confirmed with other lines of evidence. Soft tissue evidence of Chagas' disease, common in some regions of modern Peru, is an infection caused by the protozoan parasite *Trypanosoma cruzi* and was found in an Inca mummy from Cuzco. It is likely that many people suffered from Chagas' disease, but unfortunately the disease does not leave diagnostic evidence on the skeleton. Although they have not been observed on Inca human remains, several diseases endemic in modern-day Peru, Carrion's disease (bartonellosis) and leishmaniasis, also likely afflicted people and probably caused considerable illness among the Incas. Endoparasites, such as intestinal worms, and ectoparasites, such as lice, probably also plagued the Incas and may have weakened an individual's immune response and increased susceptibility to nutritional deficiencies and diarrheal disease. Soft-tissue and bony tumors have also been observed in mummies and skeletons, so the Incas likely suffered from these conditions as well, although not as commonly as the infectious diseases discussed.

Several chroniclers speak of the use of medicinal plants and herbs to treat illness and cure various ailments. Various preparations and applications of the fruit, leaves, bark, and resin of the molle tree (*Schinus molle*), for example, were used to treat gout, leishmaniasis, wounds, eczema, joint pain, and bladder and stomach ailments, among other afflictions.

Maize, quinoa, and **coca** leaf were also used medicinally. Ethnobotanical research among modern medical specialists and healers from the Central Andes list hundreds of medical plants and herbs, so it is likely that the Incas used far more medical plants and herbs than those that were recorded by the chroniclers.

Prior to the devastating impacts of epidemic diseases, such as smallpox, introduced by the Spaniards (see **Diseases, Foreign**), the Incas were afflicted by, and often survived, numerous endemic and rare diseases and ailments. Bioarchaeological research indicates that communities closer to the Inca capital of Cuzco were healthier than people living on the peripheries of the Inca heartland and those in the distant provinces.

Further Reading

Allison, Marvin. "Paleopathology in Peruvian and Chilean Populations." In *Paleopathology at the Origins of Agriculture*, edited by Mark N. Cohen and George J. Armelagos, 515–29. New York: Academic Press, 1984.

Andrushko, Valerie A. *The Bioarchaeology of Inca Imperialism in the Heartland*. PhD diss., University of California, Santa Barbara. Ann Arbor: UMI, 2007.

Andrushko, Valerie A., and Elva C. Torres. "Skeletal Evidence for Inca Warfare from the Cuzco Region of Peru." *American Journal of Physical Anthropology* 146:361–72, 2011.

Andrushko, Valerie A., and John W. Verano. "Prehistoric Trepanation in the Cuzco Region of Peru: A View into an Ancient Andean Practice." *American Journal of Physical Anthropology* 137:4–13, 2008.

Cobo, Bernabé. *Inca Religion and Customs*. Translated and edited by Roland Hamilton. Austin: University of Texas Press, 1990 [1653].

Elferink, Jan G. R. "Ethnobotany of the Incas." In *Encyclopedia of the History of Science, Technology, and Medicine in Non-Western Cultures*. 2nd ed. Edited by Helaine Selin, 840–45. New York: Springer, 2008.

Fornaciari, Gino, Maura Castagna, Paolo Viacava, Adele Tognetti, Generoso Bevilacqua, and Elsa Segura. "Chagas' Disease in Peruvian Inca Mummy." *Lancet* 339:128–29, 1992.

Garcilaso de la Vega, El Inca. *Royal Commentaries of the Incas and General History of Peru, Part One*. Translated by Harold V. Livermore. Austin: University of Texas Press, 1966 [1609].

Guaman Poma de Ayala, Felipe. *The First New Chronicle and Good Government*. Translated by Roland Hamilton. Austin: University of Press, 2009 [1615].

Murphy, Melissa S., Catherine Gaither, Elena Goycochea, John W. Verano, and Guillermo Cock. "Violence and Weapon-Related Trauma at Puruchuco-Huaquerones, Peru." *American Journal of Physical Anthropology* 146:636–49, 2010.

Rowe, John H. "Inca Culture at the Time of the Spanish Conquest." In *Handbook of South American Indians*, edited by Julian Steward, vol. 2, *The Andean Civilizations*, 183–330. Washington, DC: Smithsonian Institution, Bureau of American Ethnology, 1946.

Verano, John W. "Advances in the Paleopathology of Andean South America." *Journal of World Prehistory* 11 no. 2: 237–68, 1997.

Williams, Jocelyn S., and Melissa S. Murphy. "Living and Dying as Subjects of the Inca Empire: Adult Diet and Health at Puruchuco-Huaquerones." *Journal of Anthropological Archaeology* 32:165–79, 2013.

■ MELISSA S. MURPHY

HUACA

Often glossed as "sacred place," *huaca* is a term used frequently by the Spanish chroniclers to invoke a concept that they clearly understood to be a core principle, or value, of Inca and Andean peoples' religious beliefs and practices, as well as their senses of being and place. It was a concept that should be understood as a central ontological (i.e., concerning the nature of being, or reality) principle in the Inca concept of the universe and the place of humans within it.

The central problem in understanding this important religious concept is that the characterizations of it come largely by way of the Spanish Colonial authors, virtually all of whom were steeped and heavily invested in Spanish Catholic religious beliefs and values—not to mention grammatical constructions. The challenge then is to "read back" through the Spanish chronicles, with the aid of the few indigenous texts available to us (e.g., the Huarochirí Manuscript; see **Avila, Francisco de**), to try and capture whatever indigenous essence and meaning we may attribute to the term. In short, as we will see, *huaca*-being was not a petrified, stable, nor fixed state of things; rather, it was a status, value, and quality constructed over time in the worship and tending of an object, the feeding of it, the conversing with it, and the attending to its needs and wishes. The *mestizo* (half-indigenous/half-Spanish) chronicler **Garcilaso de la Vega** produced the following characterization:

> *Huaca* . . . means "a sacred thing," such as . . . idols, rocks, great stones or trees which the enemy [i.e., the devil] entered to make the people believe he was a god. They also gave the name *huaca* to things they have offered to the Sun, such as figures of men, birds, and animals. . . . The same name is given to all those things which for their beauty or excellence stand above other things of the same kind. . . . On the other hand they give the name *huaca* to ugly and monstrous things . . . everything that is out of the usual course of nature, as a woman who gives birth to twins . . . double-yolked eggs. (Garcilaso 1966 [1609])

As Garcilaso's account suggests, virtually any object could be bestowed with *huaca* identity and, thereby, be accorded the respect and worship, including sacrifices, appropriate to this status. The object, however, had to be a particularly striking, unusual, or wondrous example of its type in order to be considered to possess the supernatural quality of *huaca*. That is, not just an ear of corn, but a double ear of corn; not just a stone, but a stone believed to be possessed by special powers, such as the gift of making oracular pronouncements (via a human medium devoted to the care and feeding of the stone; see **Oracles**); not just a human, but a human with a harelip; and not just a bend in a canal, but a point in the landscape attached to wondrous mythological events. Such objects and places were named; accorded regular sacrifices (i.e., they were regularly "fed" specific objects, such as feathers, ground Spondylus shell, llama fat, etc.); endowed with herds and agricultural fields; considered to have kinship relations with a host of other such entities; and attended by devotees dedicated to their well-being and the care of their property.

The chronicler **Bernabé Cobo** wrote the most detailed account of the *huaca* network that composed Cuzco's *ceque* system. This was an arrangement of some 328–350 named *huacas* located along 41 imaginary lines (*ceques*) radiating outward from the Temple of the Sun, the **Coricancha**, throughout Cuzco and the surrounding valley. The care and tending of these *huacas*, one per day, by members of Cuzco's different **panacas** and **ayllus** provided the framework for the city's annual **ritual calendar.**

Further Reading

Bray, Tamara L., ed. *The Archaeology of Wak'as: Explorations of the Sacred in the Pre-Columbian Andes*. Boulder: University Press of Colorado, 2015.

Cobo, Bernabé. *Inca Religion and Customs*. Translated and edited by Roland Hamilton. Austin: University of Texas Press, 1990 [1653].

Garcilaso de la Vega, El Inca. *Royal Commentaries of the Incas and General History of Peru, Part One*. Translated by Harold V. Livermore. Austin: University of Texas Press, 1966 [1609].

Salomon, Frank. "Introductory Essay: The Huarochirí Manuscript." In *The Huarochirí Manuscript: A Testament of Ancient and Colonial Andean Religion*. Translated and edited by Frank Salomon and George L. Urioste, 1–38. Austin: University of Texas Press, 1991.

■ GARY URTON

INCA BY PRIVILEGE

"Incas by privilege" were indigenous non-Inca people of the Cuzco region to whom the Incas awarded special, hereditary status. Incas by privilege held an intermediate status position between provincial commoners and Incas of royal blood, who claimed to be direct descendants of the first Inca sovereign. The Inca ruling class conferred this privileged status by marrying Inca noblewomen to local lords or headmen (*curacas*) from Cuzco region ethnic polities. Consequently, the Incas considered the Incas by privilege to be secondary relatives and referred to them as *huaccha* Inca, which meant "poor Inca" and signified a seminoble status. Incas by privilege administered the lands of Cuzco and the provinces, participated in exclusive ceremonies that affirmed Inca authority, and served as loyal subjects who colonized new terrain or fought alongside Inca royalty in military engagements.

Spanish and indigenous chronicles state that the Inca by privilege status was as old as the Inca Empire itself. Some chronicles claim that the Incas by privilege accompanied the mythic Inca ancestors as they journeyed toward Cuzco on their divine mission to civilize and rule the Andes (see **Myths, Origin**). Others hold that Manco Capac, the first Inca ruler, created the Inca by privilege status when he established the city of **Cuzco**. Still others contend that Pachacuti Inca Yupanqui, the ninth Inca ruler, granted this special status to the lords who aided him in the defense of Cuzco and then helped him to rebuild the city as a monumental, imperial capital. Though these chronicles are not literal histories of the empire, the stories that they contain often reflect Inca ideas of hierarchy and social difference. Despite their discrepancies, then, the stories of Incas by privilege suggest that the Incas sought to naturalize the social differences of their realm by declaring that they had existed since time immemorial.

By creating the Incas by privilege status, the Incas crafted a hierarchical social landscape that they envisioned as a vast kin network. During the height of Inca rule, kinship with the Inca ruler and status within the imperial hierarchy decreased with distance from Cuzco. While Inca royalty lived in the center of the city, the Incas by privilege inhabited the edges of the Cuzco region. Marriage bonds served to connect these inner and outer areas. The *curacas* of the Cuzco region's ethnic groups took the Inca ruler's actual and nominal sisters as their wives and, in so doing, became secondary kin of the Inca. These *curacas* contributed their sisters and wives (*iñacas*) to the Inca ruler, and these women then became mothers of his lower status children (*huaccha concha*). Because the Incas by privilege were socially and geographically close, and by implication loyal, to the royal families in Cuzco, the Incas often asked them to settle and govern newly appropriated territory.

Though select *curacas* became Incas by privilege, they could never become Inca. Their subordinate status was permanent—it was marked on their bodies, renewed in major ceremonies, and gouged into the land. Cuzco's ritual pathways (**ceques**) and shrines (**huacas**) normalized differences between Inca and Inca by privilege. The *ceques* demarcated the boundaries between the land of the Incas and Incas by privilege, while the segregation of *huacas* and their attendant ritual practices worked to distinguish the essential spaces and rites of Cuzco's royal houses (**panacas**) from those of the Incas by privilege. During Cuzco's cleansing ceremony (*citua*), Incas of royal blood demonstrated their centrality to Inca society as they ran from Cuzco's center to its margins, and from these places, Incas by privilege performed their subordinate roles as they continued the ceremony by running to the farthest reaches of the Cuzco region. During the *Capac Raymi* initiation ceremony, the Incas forced some of the Incas by privilege to leave Cuzco. And at *Inca Raymi Quilla*, the Incas pierced the ears of the Incas by privilege with earspools that were smaller than the ones the Incas wore and therefore accentuated the semi-noble role of the Incas by privilege. Similarly, the Incas adorned the Incas by privilege with clothes and insignia that both mirrored the high elite and denoted a lesser status.

Historians and archaeologists have long defined the Incas by privilege according to information gleaned from the chronicles. But knowledge of the Incas by privilege remains limited because so few chroniclers mention them, and those who do, cast them as passive subjects or vanquished foes. Current research, however, is beginning to look beyond the chronicles and investigate how Cuzco's ethnic groups helped to forge the Inca state and extend its power. Archaeologists have demonstrated that ethnic groups, such as the Quilliscachi, became Inca authorities and subjects as they labored to convert their own ancestral ceremonial centers into places that manifested Inca ideals of order. Ethnohistorians have revealed that, during early Spanish colonization, Incas by privilege, such as the Mascas, sought to assume a noble status and avoid taxation by reinventing Inca mythic histories. Such studies, which concentrate on local actors and histories rather than Inca visions of imperial order, indicate that the Incas by privilege actively sought to bolster their status and negotiate their authority during and after the Inca reign.

Further Reading

Bauer, Brian S. *Ancient Cuzco: Heartland of the Inca*. Austin: University of Texas Press, 2004.

Betanzos, Juan de. *Narrative of the Incas*. Translated and edited by Roland Hamilton and Dana Buchanan. Austin: University of Texas Press, 1996 [1551–1557].

Cobo, Bernabé. *History of the Inca Empire: An Account of the Indian's Customs and Their Origin, Together with a Treatise on Inca Legends, History, and Social Institutions*. Translated and edited by Roland Hamilton. Austin: University of Texas Press, 1979 [1653].

Garcilaso de la Vega, El Inca. *Royal Commentaries of the Incas and General History of Peru*. Translated by Harold V. Livermore. Austin: University of Texas Press, 1966 [1609].

Guaman Poma de Ayala, Felipe. *The First New Chronicle and Good Government: On the History of the World and the Incas up to 1615*. Translated by Roland Hamilton. Austin: University of Texas Press, 2009 [1615].

Urton, Gary. *The History of a Myth: Pacariqtambo and the Origin of the Inkas.* Austin: University of Texas Press, 1990.

Zuidema, R. Tom. *Inca Civilization in Cuzco.* Austin: University of Texas Press, 1990.

■ STEVE KOSIBA

INVASION, SPANISH

The seemingly unlikely "conqueror" of the Inca Empire was an unschooled, illegitimate son of a lower-level noble from Extremadura, Spain. Without much of a future in Spain, Francisco Pizarro emigrated to America, where he spent time in the Caribbean and joined Vasco Núñez de Balboa's 1513 march across the isthmus of Panama. Thereafter, he was present at the founding of the city of Panama and was rewarded for his aid in the wars with the Natives and other services to the king with an *encomienda* (grant of Native labor and tribute), making him a well-to-do settler.

After Captain Pascual de Andagoya explored the south of Panama, rumors circulated about a distant Native kingdom. Pizarro formed a partnership with Diego de Almagro and the priest Hernando de Luque to reconnoiter the coast. With capital supplied by Luque, Pizarro led a small expedition south in 1524, but returned after experiencing considerable challenges from the hostile Natives, starvation, and other hardships. A second expedition in 1526 encountered similar difficulties. Landing on the Island of Gallo in the

The Inca ruler Atahualpa, imprisoned in Cajamarca, awaits the arrival of a ransom of gold and silver to secure his release. Guaman Poma de Ayala, Felipe. *El primer nueva corónica y buen gobierno.* Edited by John V. Murra and Rolena Adorno, 359/387. Mexico City: Siglo Veintiuno, 1980 [1615].

Tumaco estuary, the expeditionaries decided that, while Almagro returned to Panama for supplies and reinforcements, Pizarro and a band of 13 volunteers would remain. After Almagro's return some months later, they continued. En route, their pilot, Bartolomé Ruiz, captured a large, oceangoing balsa raft with fine cotton sails carrying 20 Native sailors adorned with gold and silver ornaments. The vessel also came loaded with quantities of stone beads, pottery, tightly woven wool and cotton textiles, and other fineries that the men traded for crimson and orange sea shells valued as a sacrifice to their gods (see **Sámano Account**; **Seafaring**; **Wealth**). This chance meeting motivated the Spaniards to continue. They eventually landed near Tumbes, a northern ceremonial center where they saw evidence of advanced civilization—monumental temples, extensive roads, and state storehouses. They eventually sailed as far south as Santa and Virú, on Peru's north coast, before returning to Panama.

At this point, Pizarro crossed the Atlantic to negotiate a contract (*capitulación*) with Charles I, licensing further exploration. The terms gave Pizarro the title of *adelantado* (the Crown's advance agent) and captain-general for life of what he explored. The 13 men who remained on the Island of Gallo were ennobled. Almagro, not present at the negotiations, received the title of governor of Tumbes. The disparity in positions later caused friction between the two partners and led eventually to the civil wars of the 1540s. Before embarking on the return voyage to America, Pizarro stopped in Extremadura to encourage his brothers, cousins, and acquaintances to accompany him.

The third expedition captained by Pizarro with fewer than 200 men and 27 horses sailed in late December 1530. Almagro promised to follow with reinforcements and supplies. Reaching Tumbes, Pizarro found the monumental architecture he had seen on his earlier voyage in ruins and the population absent. Continuing south, Pizarro eventually established the first Spanish settlement in Peru, the city (*villa*) of San Miguel de Piura, and he awarded *encomiendas* to its citizens. It was soon after that the Spanish made contact with a representative of the Inca Empire.

As they marched on, skirting the western flanks of the Andes, they learned that the populace had already suffered an exotic disease. This epidemic killed many, including "the Cuzco," later identified as the emperor Huayna Capac and his named successor (see **Diseases, Foreign**). The ruler's death provoked a succession crisis between two half brothers (see **Wars, Dynastic**). Disease and civil war contributed to the Spaniards' success in gaining control of the Andean population in the coming months.

Other factors of note are the Spaniards' superior weapons (e.g., cannon, harquebus, and metal pikes, swords, and spears), horses, and tactics (e.g., the ambush); the help of Native allies who resented Inca domination; and the Native views and practices, which led them to believe fleetingly that the invaders were gods or emissaries of the god Viracocha (see **Religion**) who had come to settle the disagreement between the two brothers. Another related factor was their belief that the proper way to greet a visitor was to drink large quantities of **chicha**, maize beer; this no doubt dulled the judgment and sensibilities of Atahualpa as he entered the plaza of **Cajamarca**. The deceptively small Spanish force also blinded the ruler to the danger they posed to his own safety and sovereignty.

From the coastal Zaña valley, Pizarro and his band began the climb into the mountains on November 8, 1532, reaching Cajamarca a week later. They were unnerved when they saw the tents of Atahualpa's forces that extended a league (about five kilometers) across the valley. Yet, a small contingent of mounted ambassadors found Atahualpa at the nearby hot springs of Cónoj and eventually received his word to come to Cajamarca the next day.

That night, the Spaniards hardly slept. Pizarro placed most of his men and horses out of sight in the buildings that lined three sides of the plaza. Some mounted pieces of artillery on the small "fortress" (an **ushnu**, or ceremonial platform) on one side of the plaza. Atahualpa, riding on his litter, arrived, as promised, very late the next afternoon, surrounded by a few thousand of his brightly attired retainers and servants. There in the plaza of Cajamarca, the friar Vicente de Valverde, with Bible or breviary in hand, tried to communicate the essence of the *requerimiento* (literally, the requirement, a document that justified making war on and enslaving Natives who resisted Spanish hegemony and evangelization) to Atahualpa through a young interpreter, a Native who had been captured on the second voyage and taken to Spain where he learned the rudiments of the Spanish language. Atahualpa understood imperfectly that Valverde's message was contained in the book, no doubt likening it to the **oracles** he frequented and that offered advice. Valverde handed him the tome, but when it did not "speak" to Atahualpa, he became annoyed and threw it to the ground. An indignant Valverde shouted to Pizarro to attack. At the prearranged signal, the Spaniards emerged from hiding and fired into the surprised crowd, while the cavalry charged, knocking Natives down. The shocked ranks of Atahualpa's escort turned and fled in terror, stampeding toward an adobe wall that enclosed the plaza. Many fell and were crushed. The troops waiting beyond the plaza fled. The Spanish pursued them and massacred or wounded many. Meanwhile, despite his bearers' valiant efforts to keep his litter aloft, Atahualpa was captured and placed under house arrest. At that point, Atahualpa's forces temporarily ceased their resistance, fearing that any onslaught would result in Atahualpa's immediate execution.

In the following months, Atahualpa negotiated with the Spaniards for his release, eventually promising to fill rooms with gold and silver in return for his freedom. Huascar, who had been taken captive by Atahualpa's generals, was executed for fear that the Spaniards would deem him the rightful ruler after he promised to match and better Atahualpa's ransom.

As the days passed, gold and silver from throughout the empire arrived daily in Cajamarca, where it was melted down and distributed, making even infantrymen incredibly wealthy by peninsular standards. The Natives brought approximately 13,000 pounds of gold and nearly twice that weight in silver. Pizarro gave leave to a few who were old or sick to return to Spain with their newly won riches. This proved a shrewd move as the parade of veterans from Peru encouraged a gold-rush that brought more Spaniards and new energies to his side. Almagro and the reinforcements arrived after the partition. They received paltry sums, only exacerbating the simmering resentment between the two partners and their parties.

With the Cajamarca treasure divided, the Spaniards eagerly awaited a continuation of their march south toward the ceremonial complex identified as the center of the realm. Atahualpa became a problem, solved when a rumor circulated that he had ordered the massing of his armies. This became the justification for Atahualpa's execution by garroting. Pizarro soon appointed Túpac Hualpa as his successor and pushed south. After

In this imaginary encounter between the ruler Huayna Capac and a Spaniard, an incredulous Inca wonders if the Spaniard eats gold. Guaman Poma de Ayala, Felipe. *El primer nueva corónica y buen gobierno*. Edited by John V. Murra and Rolena Adorno, 343/369. Mexico City: Siglo Veintiuno, 1980 [1615].

Túpac Hualpa died, Manco Inca was named (see **Vilcabamba**). Before reaching their destination, the Spanish forces battled Atahualpa's forces and defeated them with the aid of Native allies.

The center called the "city of 'the **Cuzco**'" yielded more treasure that was divided among the men. But, still desirous of more, Almagro left with Manco Inca on an expedition into what is today Chile. Pizarro returned north to found a capital on the coast, the "city of Kings," known today as Lima, a corruption of the indigenous name *Rimac*. It took additional decades for the Spaniards, often seeking El Dorado (the golden one), to explore the rest of the Inca domain.

Further Reading

Cieza de León, Pedro de. *The Discovery and Conquest of Peru: Chronicles of the New World Encounter*. Edited and translated by Alexandra Parma Cook and Noble David Cook. Durham, NC: Duke University Press, 1998 [1554].

Hemming, John. *The Conquest of the Incas*. New York: Harcourt Brace Jovanovich, 1970.

Lamana, Gonzalo. *Domination without Dominance: Inca-Spanish Encounters in Early Colonial Peru*. Durham, NC: Duke University Press, 2008.

Pizarro, Pedro. *Relation of the Discovery and Conquest of the Kingdoms of Peru*. Translated by Philip A. Means. Boston: Milford House, 1972.

Prescott, William H. *History of the Conquest of Peru*. Philadelphia: J. B. Lippincott, 1902.

Puente Duthurburu, José de la. *El Marqués Gobernador*. Lima: Editorial Brasa, S. A., 1993.

Sancho, Pedro. *An Account of the Conquest of Peru*. Translated by Philip A. Means. Boston: Milford House, 1972.

Titu Cusi Yupanqui, Diego de Castro. *History of How the Spaniards Arrived in Peru*. Translated by Catherine Julien. Indianapolis: Hackett Publishing Company, 2006 [1570].

Zárate, Agustín de. *The Discovery and Conquest of Peru*. Baltimore, MD: Penguin Books, 1968.

■ SUSAN ELIZABETH RAMÍREZ

IRRIGATION

Irrigation brings water to fields from a source other than rainfall. It is used when natural rainfall is too scarce or irregular to depend on or where greater yields are desired. The Incas made extensive use of irrigation largely to increase harvests; the surplus supported the state and the religion. Irrigation technology predates the Incas by several millennia, and so by the time the Incas emerged as a distinct culture in the Cuzco valley, irrigation was widespread throughout the Andes. Irrigation systems in the Inca Empire ranged from small, local community-sponsored systems, to vast valley-wide ones along the north coast of Peru co-opted by the Incas when they conquered the region.

At its simplest, irrigation involves cutting a channel for water to flow from a source of water to the fields. In practice, it includes careful analysis of several factors: the kinds of crops to be watered, the slope of the canal, the length of the canal, and the characteristics of the canal (such as shape, whether it is paved or merely lined with soil or clay, etc.).

Sources of irrigation water along the coast rely exclusively on the rivers that tumble down the western flanks of the Andes. Many of these rivers have water only a few months of the year, when rains fall in the adjacent highlands. Thus, irrigation was critically important to distribute the limited water to as many people and their fields as possible. Due to the relatively flat topography of the coastal plain, primary canals could be tens of kilometers long, with secondary, tertiary, and quaternary canals dividing the water for field systems. Due to evaporation and loss of water through the unpaved canals, as much as 85 percent of the water was lost before it reached its destination. The distribution of water was a major concern for polities that formed in these valleys, and for the Incas as well.

Because of the extreme aridity of the coastal zones of Peru and Chile under Inca control, irrigation was a requirement. Societies along the north coast of Peru were among the largest of those conquered by the Incas, and their large-scale irrigation systems were one major reason for their success. The Chimú Empire, for instance, boasted three major canals that delivered water to fields throughout the Moche valley, heartland of the empire. Problems such as irregular rainfall in the adjacent highlands and the steady, albeit slow, rate of coastal uplift affected irrigation. The latter led to a continuous downcutting of rivers, often stranding the canal intakes. Such issues were ongoing problems for both the Chimú and Incas.

The Incas conquered the Chimú during the latter part of the fifteenth century, if not earlier, and installed Inca bureaucrats to administer these massive irrigation systems. At the regional center of Farfán in the Jequetepeque valley, for instance, local administrators retained positions of authority. Maintaining local irrigation systems was one of their administrative tasks, along with others such as craft production. As cotton was an important local crop—vital to textile production—irrigation was critical.

In the highlands, the amount of irrigable land is more limited, so canals were shorter, although some could still be quite long. Sources of water included springs, rivers, and permanent snowfields above valleys. The irrigation systems of the Incas in the Cuzco region were particularly impressive. Dozens of laborers toiled to straighten the meander plain of the Urubamba River between Pisac and Yucay, for example, increasing field systems on either side of the river, while irrigation of the contour terraces above Pisac involved long canals that snaked around hillsides. Tipón, a royal estate just south of Cuzco, has a sophisticated set of irrigation features as well as beautiful fountains that suggest the movement of water was more than just utilitarian.

Immediately prior to the Inca conquest, irrigation canals in the highlands supported the fields of local communities. When the Incas conquered them, however, the communities were required to provide the labor used to produce agricultural surpluses. In order to maximize this production, irrigated terrace systems were developed that augmented harvests (see **Terracing**).

Irrigation was thus critical to the success of the Inca Empire. In the Cuzco region, it bolstered the agricultural surpluses that fed the city's residents. On royal estates, it supported the retainers and *mit'a* labor that made these royal lands function. In the vast hinterland of the empire, irrigation supported the agricultural surpluses required for state activities such as warfare and craft production. It is evident that Inca specialists were well aware of the technology that made such systems operate effectively. The fact that many of these systems continue to function today is a tribute to their creators.

Further Reading

Mackey, Carol. "The Socioeconomic and Ideological Transformation of Farfán under Inca Rule." In *Distant Provinces in the Inka Empire: Toward a Deeper Understanding of Inca Imperialism,* edited by Michael A. Malpass and Sonia Alconini, 221–59. Iowa City: University of Iowa Press, 2010.

Shimada, Izumi. *Pampa Grande and the Mochica Culture.* Austin: University of Texas Press, 1994.

Wright, Kenneth R. *Tipón: Water Engineering Masterpiece of the Inca Empire.* Reston, VA: ASCE Press, 2006.

■ MICHAEL A. MALPASS

ISLANDS OF THE SUN AND THE MOON

According to an Inca **origin myth**, the Sun emerged from a sacred rock on the Island of the Sun in Lake Titicaca to illuminate the world. The nearby Island of the Moon housed a shrine to Quilla, the Moon goddess. On the Islands of the Sun and Moon the Incas embarked on one of the most ambitious building schemes and reorganizations of sacred geography ever undertaken in Tahuantinsuyu, the Inca Empire—converting a mythical place of origin into a pilgrimage shrine. So revered was the shrine that it ranked among the empire's most sacred, after Cuzco's holy of holies, the **Coricancha** Sun temple and the pilgrimage center and oracle of **Pachacamac,** on Peru's central coast.

The sacred rock is a sandstone outcrop measuring 5.5 meters (18 feet) in height and 80 meters (260 feet) in length. The rock, according to chroniclers, was once covered in gold sheet on the plaza-facing side and fine cloth on the side overlooking the lake. Ex-

A triple-jamb niche at Pilco Kayma, a two-story structure on the Island of the Sun in Lake Titicaca. Once plastered and painted, triple-jamb niches such as this one are extremely rare and were reserved for use in buildings that commemorated places of origin. Joe Castro/Guía del Caminante.

cavations revealed the remains of a stone-lined canal leading from the sacred rock across the plaza, probably to drain the libations that the chronicler **Bernabé Cobo** says were poured into a basin in front of the rock. Constructions on the Island of the Sun included a Sun temple, an Acllahuasi, and storerooms. The temple of Iñak Uyu on the Island of the Moon apparently housed the statue of Quilla, the Moon goddess that Cobo described as made of "gold from the waist up and silver from the waist down."

The Incas resettled the islands' original residents on the mainland and replaced them with *mitmac* colonists from all over the realm to serve the shrines and the pilgrims, both on the islands and on the mainland. At the Copacabana peninsula on the mainland, an administrative center controlled the flow of pilgrims, who came from afar bearing offerings of llamas, gold, silver, Spondylus shell, feathers, coca, and fine cloth. Storehouses contained provisions and clothing for attendants and pilgrims. Before reaching Copacabana, pilgrims had to pass through a gate with watchmen and guards. Prior to embarking for the islands, the pilgrims fasted, abstaining from salt, meat, and hot peppers, and visited and prayed at local shrines. They sailed for the islands in reed boats, continuing via paved roads to the sanctuaries.

The chronicler Ramos Gavilán, writing in around 1618, said that pilgrims approaching the sacred rock had to pass through three gateways, each increasingly sacred. The final gateway marked the boundary of the precinct, which was surrounded by a low wall. Pilgrims removed their shoes to enter the plaza, but not everyone could approach the sacred rock; lower-status pilgrims probably only went as far as the first entry gate. From the plaza, pilgrims observed solstice sunrises and sunsets. Those not allowed into the plaza could observe the sun setting over the rock and plaza from an observation platform outside the sacred precinct.

Given the importance of the islands, it is surprising that the Incas did not use their famous dressed and fitted stone masonry for the main buildings on the Titicaca islands. Rather, the buildings are constructed of fieldstone joined with mud mortar, covered with a thick layer of earthen stucco.

Further Reading

Bauer, Brian B., and Charles Stanish. *Ritual and Pilgrimage in the Ancient Andes: The Islands of the Sun and the Moon.* Austin: University of Texas Press, 2001.

■ ADRIANA VON HAGEN

KEROS

Keros are wooden versions of an important type of Inca drinking vessel; gold or silver *keros* are called *aquillas*. They were also made in ceramic for which no Quechua term has been recorded. These vessels had either an hourglass or a cylindrical shape with the circumference widest at the lip and tapered toward the base. *Keros* and *aquillas* have a long history in Andean art, dating back at least a thousand years prior to the Incas. Inca *keros* and *aquillas* seem to be derived directly from vessels used by the Tiahuanaco and Huari peoples (see **Chronology, Pre-Inca**). Moreover, *keros* continued to be one of the most important media of artistic expression throughout the Colonial period (1532–1821) and into the Republican era (1821–present).

The differences between their size (from 2.5 centimeters [1 inch] in height to 78.2 centimeters [2.5 feet] in height) and the materials of *kero* and *aquilla* were symbolically

A pair of wooden Inca-style *keros*, or drinking vessels, found at Laguna de los Cóndores in Chachapoyas, northern Peru. Inca officials presented *keros* such as these to local lords. Adriana von Hagen, Museo Leymebamba, Leymebamba, Amazonas, Peru.

important to the Incas as *keros*, *aquillas*, and ceramic examples were used in almost all Inca rituals held throughout the empire, including as **Capac Hucha** offerings. The material— gold, silver, wood, or ceramic—denoted hierarchy in Inca political culture. Gold vessels were given to the most important individuals in the empire whereas wooden ones were offered to high-ranking local chiefs, or *curacas*. The vessels were always made in nearly identical pairs so that they could be used to offer a toast in equal amounts to a companion or a divinity such as the Sun. Each one of the pair was also recognized as being either *hanan* or *hurin* (upper half/lower half in the Inca system of duality; see **Dualism**) and they were used together in community feasts to express social and political solidarity through a series of exchanged toasts. They were also used to drink with the ancestors. The illustrated chronicle of **Felipe Guaman Poma de Ayala**, for example, includes several images in which the living are shown offering a drink to the body of a deceased ancestor using a pair of *keros*. Among other things, *keros* still form an important link between contemporary Andean peoples and their ancestors.

The drink that was usually offered was **chicha**, fermented corn beer. This was an extremely important ritual beverage that is today still offered to *apus,* or mountain divinities, and sometimes Colonial or even Inca *keros* are used in contemporary offerings to the mountain gods.

Like much of Inca art, *keros* and *aquillas* were decorated with abstract geometric designs. The designs on *keros* were carved into the surface of the wood and the contrast between the surface and the incised lines revealed the geometric forms. The designs of *aquillas* were revealed by both incised and repoussé techniques (hammering from the reverse side to create low relief designs). *Keros* and *aquillas* were decorated with the same types of designs. Some consisted of a series of concentric rectangles while others included a series of repeated zigzag lines that went around the vessel's circumference. One particular type of design shows a highly schematized series of arms and decapitated heads decorating the rim. Some Chimú-Inca and also Colonial *keros* were even shaped in the form of human heads.

The decapitated head design, as well as the vessels in the form of human heads, demonstrate the importance of *keros* and *aquillas* as objects used in negotiations between the Incas and peoples whom they wished to incorporate into Tahuantinsuyu. *Keros* or *aquillas* as well as textiles were offered to leaders and if the gifts were not accepted, the Incas would attack and the heads of the leaders were converted into drinking cups. In fact, the first objects presented by the Inca ruler, Atahualpa, to the Spaniards as they made their way to Cajamarca were two sets of *aquillas*. Unfortunately the Inca ruler's offer was not accepted and eventually he was captured and executed (see **Invasion, Spanish**). Although this event marked the beginning of the end of the Inca Empire, both *keros* and *aquillas* not only continued to be made by Andean peoples, but they saw a florescence in the Colonial period.

The *kero*, in particular, became an extremely important medium of Colonial Andean artistic expression, continuing until today. Nevertheless, the decoration and designs found on the Colonial vessels are radically different from their Inca predecessors. Colonial artisans filled in the incised wooden surfaces with colors mixed with a resin-based substance. In addition, the designs shifted from the abstract geometric ones of the Inca period to pictorial forms arranged in increasingly complex narrative compositions.

One of the earliest painted *keros* was found in an early Colonial, Inca-style grave at Ollantaytambo in the Urubamba valley in Cuzco. It has a small jaguar painted in red with gold and silver highlights with a series of incised concentric rectangles placed in the center. A number of other Colonial *keros* combine Inca incised designs with painted figural motifs. The majority of the images on these *keros* are either animal figures, such as the jaguar on the Ollantaytambo pair, or insects such as butterflies.

As Spanish artistic norms began to spread throughout the Andes, some Native artists transferred their new skills and pictorial techniques to the *keros* and *aquillas*. As a result, artisans decorated the vessels with more complex pictorial scenes, many of which depict the human figure, dressed in archaic imperial Inca dress. The more complex scenes often depict Inca ritual ceremonies in which *keros* and *aquillas* were used.

Only a few Colonial *aquillas* have survived, in part because the monetary value of their gold or silver made them vulnerable to sale or theft. In comparison, a large number of Colonial painted *keros* remain in private and public collections throughout the world. Their beauty and imagery have made them popular with collectors since the eighteenth century. In fact, several examples were sent to King Charles III in 1773. Most *keros* have remained in Andean communities over the centuries, and they appear to have been almost mass-produced during the later Colonial period. They began to be collected in greater numbers at only the beginning of the twentieth century so that some indigenous communities have been able to keep *keros* as prized possessions. They are carefully wrapped in textiles and on special ritual occasions are brought out as heirlooms, passed down from father to eldest son.

Further Reading

Cummins, Thomas B. F. *Toasts with the Inca: Andean Abstraction and Colonial Images on Quero Vessels.* Ann Arbor: University of Michigan Press, 2002.

Howe, Emily, Emily Kaplan, Judith Levinson, and Ellen Pearlstein. "Análisis técnico de qeros pintados de Períodos Inca y Colonial." *Iconos: Revista peruana de conservación, arte y arqueología* no. 2, 30–38, 1999.

Ochoa, Jorge Flores, Elizabeth Kuon Arce, and Roberto Samanéz Argumedo. *Qeros: Arte Inka en Vasos Ceremoniales.* Lima: Banco de Credito, 1998.

Rowe, John. "The Chronology of Inca Wooden Cups." In *Essays in Pre-Columbian Art and Archaeology,* edited by S. Lothrop et al., 317–41. Cambridge, MA: Harvard University Press, 1961.

■ THOMAS B. F. CUMMINS

KING LIST

Most scholars describe the Inca dynasty as composed of 12 male monarchs who passed a royal office (**Sapa Inca**, sole or unique Inca) from father to son from the time of the founding ancestor until the 1530s. The list currently used (see table) comes from chronicles written from the 1550s until the 1570s, but king lists recorded before or after that period differ from the "official" dynasty used today. Many early sources only mention the last three or four rulers, and accounts tracing the Incas from their creation myth to the conquest present early rulers in different order and include individuals who were omitted in the 1570s list. **Pedro de Cieza de León**, for example, names Inca Urcon as the ninth ruler, whereas later lists omit him. The king list that was established by the 1570s differs from the later account of Antonio Vázquez de Espinosa, which reflects the Inca lineages that were recognized by the Spanish crown throughout the Colonial period.

Inca Rulers and Their Colonial Descendants

	Name	Colonial Lineage
1	Manco Capac	Chima
2	Sinchi Roca	Raora
3	Lloque Yupanqui	Hahuanina
4	Mayta Capac	Usca Mayta
5	Capac Yupanqui	Apu Mayta
6	Inca Roca	Vicaquirao
7	Yahuar Huaccac	Aucaylli
8	Viracocha Inca	Sucsu
	Inca Urcon	
9	Pachacuti Inca Yupanqui	Hatun
	Inca Yupanqui	Iñaca
10	Topa Inca Yupanqui	Capac
11	Huayna Capac	Tomebamba
12	Huascar	
	Atahualpa	
	Túpac Hualpa	
	Manco Inca	
	Sayri Túpac	
	Titu Cusi Yupanqui	
	Túpac Amaru I	

Before describing the development of the king list used today, it is important to consider whether a list of 12 male monarchs adequately reflects Inca power. Some scholars have noted the strong patterns of dual organization in Andean communities, and have taken descriptions of chroniclers such as **José de Acosta** as evidence that the Incas governed with corulers from both of the royal moieties, or halves, known as *hanan* and *hurin* (see **Cuzco**; **Dualism**; **Planning, Settlement**). Although such an approach contradicts most Colonial sources, which describe the Inca monarch as a peerless lord, there is ample evidence of royal power sharing, including temporary delegation of military command and administrative responsibilities.

The Inca ruler had a female counterpart, and some chronicles describe the royal female title, *Coya*, or queen, as a unique paramount office that belongs in the discussion of the king list. Multiple chronicles state that some Inca women received royal funerary honors and that their mummies circulated after death like those of kings (see **Mummies, Royal**; **Women**). Several chroniclers, such as **Pedro Sarmiento de Gamboa** and **Felipe Guaman Poma de Ayala**, recorded the names of Inca queens, although there is less consistency in the dynastic list of queens than of kings.

The *Sapa Inca* was not an absolute monarch, but rather, with his *Coya*, a cofounder of a royal household that interacted with other royal lineages to staff the highest positions in the military and administrative hierarchy. The descendants of earlier rulers were key players in the succession of new rulers and their success on the throne. As noted above, these individuals sometimes ruled in the place of a king when he was away from the capital, and some sources describe regents who coruled for a young emperor before he was of the age to govern on his own. Inca nobles could extend the scope of royal power, but they could also challenge it, and there are accounts of usurpers and palace coups that installed rulers who are not included in the 12-ruler king list.

The rulers included in Colonial king lists represented surviving noble Inca lineages, and royal mummies and "brother" (*huauque*) statues of rulers offered a material way of organizing and performing the dynastic history (see **Kingship, Divine**). The Spanish Crown used the 12-ruler dynasty to recognize who was, or was not, an Inca noble, and by the end of the sixteenth century there was an emphasis on male descent back to a recognized ruler on the royal genealogical tree. The king list that continued into the seventeenth century considered Huayna Capac to be the last ruler to found a royal descent group (*panaca*), effectively treating the dynasty as ending in the civil war between Huascar and Atahualpa (see **Wars, Dynastic**). These rulers were recognized as descendants of Huayna Capac, as were other Inca rulers up to 1572—Túpac Hualpa, Manco Inca, Sayri Túpac, Titu Cusi Yupanqui, and Túpac Amaru (see **Vilcabamba**).

Archaeology has a difficult relationship with the modern Inca king list. Some scholars treat the palaces and properties supposedly belonging to a ruler as material evidence of the dynasty. Documentary research has identified country estates belonging to the later (*hanan* [upper moiety] Cuzco) rulers, and archaeologists have investigated the monumental ruins still surviving at Pisac, Ollantaytambo, **Machu Picchu**, and other sites with royal affiliation (see **Estates, Royal**). Archaeological dates from these sites suggest that they were not all built at one time, making it difficult to develop a chronology of estate construction that could be checked against the chronology of the king list. At present, archaeology cannot determine whether the royal lineages laying claim to country estates in the early Colonial period were the families who built the estates, or whether estates changed hands as new factions gained power. At the same time, archaeologists and historians are shifting their attention from a line of male rulers to try to understand how the men and women of royal Inca families extended and contested power in the Inca heartland and beyond.

Further Reading

Cieza de León, Pedro de. *The Second Part of the Chronicle of Peru.* Translated and edited by Clements R. Markham. London: Hakluyt Society, 1883 [1553].

Covey, R. Alan. "Chronology, Succession, and Sovereignty: The Politics of Inka Historiography and Its Modern Interpretation." *Comparative Studies in Society and History* 48, no. 1: 166–99, 2006.

Duviols, Pierre. "La dinastía de los Incas: ¿Monarquía o diarquía? Argumentos heurísticos a favor de una tesis estructuralista." *Journal de la Société des Américanistes* 66, no. 1: 67–83, 1979.

Guaman Poma de Ayala, Felipe. *The First New Chronicle and Good Government: On the History of the World and the Incas up to 1615.* Translated by Roland Hamilton. Austin: University of Texas Press, 2009 [1615].

Niles, Susan A. *The Shape of Inca History. Narrative and Architecture in an Andean Empire.* Iowa City: University of Iowa Press, 1999.

Sarmiento de Gamboa, Pedro de. *The History of the Incas.* Translated by Brian S. Bauer and Vania Smith. Austin: University of Texas Press, 2007 [1572].

Vázquez de Espinosa, Antonio. *Compendium and Description of the West Indies.* Translated by Charles Upson Clark. Washington, DC: Smithsonian Institution, 1942 [1528].

■ R. ALAN COVEY

KINGSHIP, DIVINE

The Incas held that the monarch was the son of the Sun (*Inti*), and therefore a divine being with a legitimate mandate to rule the world. He was simultaneously a deity on earth, political leader, and military commander. The chronicler **Garcilaso de la Vega** wrote that his titles included *Sapa Inca* (unique or sole lord; see **Sapa** Inca), *Intip Churin* (son of the Sun), *Capac Apu* (powerful lord), and *Huaccha Ccoyac* (lover and benefactor of the poor). His divinity lay at the core of state ideology, along with the Sun's supremacy over all other deities. Those paired ideas allowed the Incas to assert a right to dominate relationships between humanity and the other beings of the cosmos. Despite the apparent inconsistency, the Incas also claimed that the ruler was a direct descendant of the primordial brother-sister pair, Manco Capac and Mama Huaco/Ocllo (see **Myths, Origin**).

The ruler was considered to have exceptional powers, especially his ability to intervene with the Sun, and thus shower beneficence on humanity. He presided over the empire's most sacred activities, such as breaking the soil to inaugurate the agricultural season, and hosted Cuzco's daily feasts, when affairs of state were conducted. No one was allowed to approach the ruler without offering a gift, or to touch him, and visitors were required to keep their eyes downcast in his presence. The ruler's sanctity was displayed in a variety of forms. It is not clear if his substance was thought to be present simultaneously in multiple physical things, or if his power was simply extended through a range of other objects. In either case, several items were treated precisely as if they were the ruler, in both his mortal and immortal states. Each ruler had a named brother icon (*huauque*) made of stone or gold. It accompanied him in life and death, and could stand in for him in official acts. The icon of the founder, Manco Capac, was known as "falcon," Pachacuti's was "lightning" or "viper," and Topa Inca Yupanqui's was "happy son." Pachacuti's icon was found by the Spaniards at his death house, called Patallacta (likely the site of Kenko, near Cuzco), where it stood guard over his mummy. Although the chronicler Acosta wrote that those shapes were representational, he never saw one, and it seems most likely that it was the essence of the icons that was most important, not their appearance.

Because the ruler's physical being was divine, his exuviae, including his hair and nail clippings, were protectively curated. Over time, they were incorporated into another icon, called a *bulto* (Spanish, bundle) in the Colonial era. That concept was analogous to the idea that any material has an essence, whatever state it may be in, much as gold (tears of the Sun) was the Sun god materialized on earth. It may be telling that no identifiable image of a ruler has been found that dates securely to the pre-Hispanic era, perhaps because an image could be subject to magic. The ruler's potency extended to all of the items that he touched during his lifetime. The Spaniards observed that idea in practice while holding Atahualpa captive in Cajamarca (see **Invasion, Spanish**). His attendants collected leftovers from his meals and other objects that came into contact with him, with the intent to burn them at the end of the year. People believed that his power, or perhaps even his persona, was diffused into those items, and that they could be used in witchcraft if they fell into malevolent hands.

The divinity of the ruler continued after death. Select internal organs were extracted for incineration, before the remainder of the body was mummified for perpetual veneration (see **Mummies, Royal**). The ashes were deposited in the belly of the golden idol of a small boy (*Punchao*, i.e., day; the young Sun), who was the incarnation of the Sun in Cuzco's main temple (**Coricancha**). That act reunited the essence of the Inca ancestral line with the golden substance of Inti. One organ (probably the heart) of Huayna Capac was retained in Ecuador, where he had died, and a rebellious cult was built around its veneration.

The mummies were treated as if they were living beings, plied with food and drink, and consulted on matters of state. Their estates, theoretically maintained in perpetuity by their offspring, formed cult centers for the deceased. A single Quechua word, *mallqui*, meant mummy, sapling, and sprout ready for planting. The logic was that society's continual regenesis arises from the ancestors, much as the sprout yields the mature plant. In this light, the original two ancestors, Manco Capac and Mama Huaco, were illustrated by one early author of Andean heritage (**Pachacuti Yamque**) as saplings with roots (see **Worship, Ancestor**).

In major ceremonies, the mummies of the deceased rulers and their wives were brought forth on litters and arrayed by rank in Cuzco's main plaza. According to an eyewitness, Pedro Sancho, Francisco Pizarro's secretary, if no mummy had been preserved (e.g., Manco Capac), a clay, plaster, or stone persona stood in, which could incorporate their hair and nail clippings. The conquistador **Pedro Pizarro**, a relation of Francisco Pizarro, noted that the mummies were carefully tended by pairs of male and female attendants, who served as their voices for public pronouncements. The mummies were typically kept in state in one of their several manors. Spanish eyewitnesses reported, for example, that Huayna Capac was comfortably seated in his urban residence facing the main plaza in **Cuzco**. When two royal mummies were burned by the Spaniards (Viracocha) and Incas (Topa Inca Yupanqui), their followers gathered the ashes in jars and venerated them as if they were still living.

Further Reading

Cobo, Bernabé. *Inca Religion and Customs,* Translated and edited by Roland Hamilton. Austin: University of Texas Press, 1990 [1653].

MacCormack, Sabine. *Religion in the Andes: Vision and Imagination in Early Colonial Peru.* Princeton, NJ: Princeton University Press, 1991.

Molina, Cristóbal de. *Account of the Fables and Rites of the Incas.* Translated and edited by Brian S. Bauer, Vania Smith-Oka, and Gabriel E. Cantarutti. Austin: University of Texas Press, 2011 [1575].

■ TERENCE N. D'ALTROY

L

LABOR SERVICE

The Incas were unusual among preindustrial empires in relying on labor service (*mit'a*) as the fundamental source of economic support for imperial activities. While labor taxes were widely used in early empires, most of them drew upon a mix of revenue sources, including levies of money, tribute, tax in kind, and labor service. At the time that the Incas forged their realm, however, highland Andean societies did not depend on money or markets, or have notions of capital, investment, or profit (see **Wealth**). While aware of the use of semi-monetary goods among the peoples whom they ultimately dominated, the Incas did not use specie, or currency, in the state economy, instead preferring to foster specialization in labor services. The Incas' dependence on labor thus required the massive mobilization of labor by both general taxpaying households and, over time, cadres of specialists. The system worked in large part because so many people were already skilled artisans (*camayoc*), who could be called on to craft whatever material goods the state required.

The institutionalization of labor service arose from three features: (1) existing economic practices, (2) the Incas' rationale for the legitimacy of their rule, and (3) an overarching concept of socialized relations between humanity and the world. The structure of Inca labor service was grounded in widespread, and probably long-standing, relationships within highland Andean societies. An ethic of mutuality drove many activities within the basic corporate units (*ayllu*) of those societies. Most productive resources were jointly owned, including agricultural land, water, and pasturage; they could not be bought, sold, or otherwise transferred. In this context, labor exchanges among families or people of equal status (*ayni*) fostered networks of joint obligation and support. Between people of different statuses, such as lord and commoner, labor service (*minca*) was reciprocated by various forms of leadership, whether political, martial, or ceremonial. As **John V. Murra** described in his foundational thesis on the Inca economy, the existing relationships of inequality, in which labor was exchanged for leadership, provided the rationale for the Inca taxation system. Taxpayers did not render anything from the community's resources or from their own production, but were obligated to work for the Incas as a condition of keeping their own resources.

The relationship between humanity and the land also had a direct effect on the implications of labor service. Many features of the landscape were considered animate beings, forming their own society, with whom people maintained active relationships. Among

Men and women provided their labor to the empire by tilling fields and sowing seeds. Guaman Poma de Ayala, Felipe. El primer nueva corónica y buen gobierno. Edited by John V. Murra and Rolena Adorno, 1050/1153. Mexico City: Siglo Veintiuno, 1980 [1615].

those beings were the living ancestors, often identified with a particular place or feature, along with mountain peaks, rock formations, and springs (see **Worship, Ancestor**). Both water and the earth itself had vitality. As a result of this perspective, people and the land's sentient actors were integrated into a single social framework. Labor performed to yield products was not a simple exploitation of raw materials; it was a perpetually negotiated relationship, among humans and between people and the living landscape. In this context, the Incas' exaction of labor service was part of an effort to dominate humanity's relationship with the other forces of their world.

The general taxpaying populace owed about two to three months of service annually. The range of services required was broad, but can be grouped as follows: agropastoral production, extraction of raw materials, manufacture of material goods, construction or maintenance of the physical infrastructure, and labor that yielded a service, like military and guard duty or portage. Agriculture and military duty appear to have been the most heavily applied taxes. In some instances, military service took people away from their homes for years or even permanently. The proportion of individual societies thus affected could be a third or more of the populace (such as occurred among the Colla of the *altiplano* on the shores of Lake Titicaca, for instance), while other societies claimed wholesale commitment to military duty (e.g., the Charkas of Bolivia or the Chachapoya of the cloud forest of northern Peru). The Incas also favored certain groups because of their special talents—Rucanas as litter-bearers and Chumbivilcas as dancers, for example. The chroniclers Falcón, **Martín de Murúa**, and **Felipe Guaman Poma de Ayala** provided general lists of 30–40 duties, sometimes distinguishing between coastal and highland peoples. Spanish inspections of the early Colonial era also recorded the labors owed by particular ethnic groups. The table lists both Falcón's highland categories and the obligations owed by the Chupachu people of Peru's north-central highlands.

State personnel determined the amount of labor service to be provided on an annual basis. According to the chronicler **Bernabé Cobo**, the nature and kind of service was assigned according to the anticipated needs of the state, without a fixed amount having been set. That approach required a systematic, periodically updated **census**; knowledge about regional resources, both human and natural; and regular communications between provincial and central officials. Typically, provincial governors oversaw application of the labor tax, but lower-tier officials, generally from subject societies, seem to have had the discretion to select the taxpayers who were assigned to specific duties. While scant, the available evidence for mobilizations from particular provinces suggests that labor-yielding services may have been assessed by proportions of units of 1,000 households, while labor that yielded ecologically targeted products was taxed by proportions of 100 households. A strict proportionality may have been applied in the kinds of products to which people were dedicated, as the Chupachu textile producers were 10 times the number of pottery-makers and other less prestigious manufactures.

Labor obligations were discharged at places of the state's choosing. Craft production could take place at provincial centers, such as Huánuco Pampa, where the state maintained housing for upward of 10,000 temporary personnel. In such cases, people could be required to travel for days and stay for months, discharging their duties while living off state supplies. In many places, the Incas established farms, mines, or artisan communities at locations with suitable productive resources. Colonists or temporary workers were brought in to staff the production centers (see below). In all cases, the Incas supplied the raw materials and the people provided their expertise and labor. Thus, women used state fiber to produce one shirt a year while working at home. The products were typically stored in warehouse facilities erected near state centers and support stations, for use against future need.

Both general chronicles and Spanish provincial inspections reported that the Incas resettled as much as a third of the Andean populace as internal colonists (*mitmacuna*). That figure, if correct, means that the Incas relocated upward of four to five million people, for economic, political, military, and ideological purposes. They were committed to agropastoral production, artisanry, and staffing both frontier forts and internal garrisons. The largest farms included those established at Abancay and the Mantaro valley (Peru), Cochabamba (Bolivia), and Coctaca-Rodero (Argentina). At Cochabamba, 14,000 permanent and temporary workers grew maize for the army, while at Abancay, farmers cultivated cotton, hot peppers, and other warm weather crops. Skilled weavers and potters staffed facilities at Milliraya, on the northeast side of Lake Titicaca.

In addition to the broadly applied labor taxes, the Incas committed significant numbers of people to specialized statuses or institutions. Among the most important were the women's orders, the *acllacuna* and the *mamacuna* (see **Acllacuna**). *Aclla* were girls

Falcón (1567) list	Chupachu Labor Service in 1549	
Highland Service Categories	Assignment	Taxpayers
human sacrifice administrators	gold miners: 120 men, 120 women	120
guardians of the Sun?	silver miners: 60 men, 60 women	60
servants of dead Incas	construction (Cuzco area)	400
gold specialists	agriculture (Cuzco area)	400
silver specialists	retainers of Huayna Capac (Cuzco)	150
copper (?) specialists	guards for body of Topa Inca Yupanqui	150
pigment (?) specialists	guards for weapons of Topa Inca	10
guardians of sacred objects/locations	Yupanqui (Cuzco)	
feathered-cloth weavers: fine, ordinary	garrison in Chachapoyas	200
weavers: four classes	garrison in Quito	200
sandal makers: fine, ordinary	guards for body of the Inca (Cuzco)	20
hunting noose specialists	feather workers	120
guards for women of the Sun	honey gatherers	60
oca farmers	weavers of tapestry cloth	400
potato farmers	dye makers	40
coca farmers	herders of Inca's flocks	240
llama keepers: two kinds	guards for maize fields	40
ash/lime loaf makers	pepper cultivators	40
aji specialists	salt miners (varied: 40, 50, 60)	50
salt specialists	coca cultivators	60
maize sprout specialists	hunters for royal deer hunt	40
early maize specialists: two kinds	sandal makers (Cuzco, Huánuco)	40
potters: fine, ordinary	wood workers, products to Cuzco	40
orchard keepers	potters, products to Huánuco	40
river (?) specialists	guards for Huánuco Pampa	68
bridge keepers	porters carrying loads to Huánuco	80
masons	guards for women of the Inca	40
messengers	soldiers and litter bearers	500
earspool makers	cultivators of Inca lands	500
lead cord makers (bolas?)	makers of weapons and litters (Cuzco)	*
colonists	processors of dried, salted fish	*
agricultural workers for Inca	snare makers for the hunt	*
agricultural workers for lords	women in service to the Inca	*
laborers on other public works: temples,		
roads, bad passes, bridges, houses,	Total	4,108
corrals, buildings		
porters	* new unquantified categories	
	mentioned in 1562 reinspection	

Note: The types of labor services provided by highland peoples appear in the first column, and the labor obligations of the Chupachu of the north-central highlands in the second column.

Terence D'Altroy

reaching adolescence, who lived in sequestered quarters at state installations. There, they learned the finer arts of weaving and brewing **chicha**, maize beer, before being awarded in marriage to distinguished men or selected for sacrifice (see **Capac Hucha**). The *mamacuna* were a religious grouping of mature women dedicated to weaving the finest textiles, and to activities surrounding worship of the Moon and ritual hospitality, among other things. *Yanacona* made up another specialized labor category: individuals cut off from their home societies, often as a punishment, and committed to life-long service for the state or aristocrats.

The Inca aristocracy also benefited from dedicated labor service. Each emperor ostensibly had an estate in every province, staffed by individuals and families resettled for that purpose. Because the emperor's descendant kin held his estates in perpetuity, each successive ruler created his own sets of workers. The scale could be enormous, as Topa Inca Yupanqui installed 1,000 gold miners and 5,000 support families in just one mine in Bolivia. Estates in the Urubamba valley near Cuzco also boasted thousands of workers, not just farmers and household servants, but metalsmiths and weavers as well, among other specialists.

Floor mats being carried to the bridge of Queshuachaca, (see **Bridges**) during the annual rebuilding of the bridge. In Inca times, people such as the *chacacamayoc*, or bridge master, served the empire by providing their labor and expertise. Adriana von Hagen.

Further Reading

D'Altroy, Terence N. "Remaking the Social Landscape: Colonization in the Inka Empire." In *The Archaeology of Colonial Encounters*, edited by Gil Stein, 263–95. Albuquerque, NM: SAR Press, 2005.
Julien, Catherine J. "How Inca Decimal Administration Worked." *Ethnohistory* 35, no. 3: 257–79, 1988.
Murra, John V. *The Economic Organization of the Inka State*. Greenwich, CT: JAI Press, 1980 [1956].

■ TERENCE N. D'ALTROY

LEGACY, INCA

In the wake of the Spanish explorer Vasco Núñez de Balboa's sighting of the Pacific Ocean, in 1513, rumors soon began to swirl among the Spaniards of a wealthy kingdom located south of the Gulf of Darien. Balboa organized an expedition in search of the fabled land. Unfortunately, his plans floundered because of rivalries with other Spaniards, particularly his father-in-law, Pedro de Arias Dávila, known as Pedrarias, who had him beheaded. Pedrarias subsequently organized two expeditions; Francisco Pizarro, the future conqueror of Peru, participated in one of them. Serious Native resistance would ultimately foil both these attempts at locating the fabled rich kingdom in the south.

The first expedition, led by Pascual de Andagoya, only reached 50 miles south of Panama, to a river known as *Virú*. According to several historians, this was the first name given to the territory the Spanish planned to conquer. In the course of time *Virú* became *Peru*.

In fact, the names of Native entities were matters of considerable confusion at the time. When the Spaniards first heard of the conflict between the brothers and rival claimants to the throne, Huascar and Atahualpa, they understood that what they were competing for, identified in the term *Cuzco*, was recognition as the leader of the realm, equivalent to a "king" (see **Wars, Dynastic**). Only later did **Cuzco** refer to the capital of the empire.

When did the terms *Inca* or *Ynga* become commonplace, and when was the term *Tahuantinsuyu* first recorded? The earliest evidence for *Inca* or *ynga* occurs in a 1540 fact-finding mission, or **visita**, undertaken in Cajamarca. *Tahuantinsuyu* as a name for the Inca Empire as a whole, is first mentioned in **Polo Ondegardo's** chronicle of 1571, although references to the four *suyus* (which made up Tahuantinsuyu) were noted earlier, by **Pedro de Cieza de León,** in 1553, and by **Juan de Betanzos**, in 1557. The fact that these terms were employed by indigenous informants should not be taken as an indication that a sense of unity existed among the myriad ethnic groups then dominated by the Incas. The early Spanish chronicles are filled with accounts of revolts against the Incas. It seems that the sense of cohesion implied by terms such as Tahuantinsuyu only began with an awareness of the dire implications for the indigenous world of the Spaniards' presence.

The Taki Onqoy movement of 1564 and the chronicle, *El Primer Nueva Córonica y Buen Gobierno*, by the Native chronicler **Felipe Guaman Poma de Ayala**, provide us with evidence for the development of cohesion among Andean peoples vis-à-vis their new Spanish overlords. The Taki Onqoy was a messianic movement that erupted in the south-central Andes, around present-day Ayacucho, in which Natives were possessed by the spirits of the **huacas**, dancing and singing wildly on mountaintops, away from Spanish eyes. They called for a return to the care and tending of the indigenous *huacas* and a complete rejection of the Spaniards and their Christian religion. Followers of the Taki Onqoy movement believed that the Incas had been defeated because the Spanish God was more powerful than their *huacas*. Nevertheless, the adherents of Taki Onqoy agitated for a *Pachacuti* (turning around/upside-down of the earth) that would overwhelm the Christian God.

In his account, *Nueva Córonica,* the indigenous chronicler Guaman Poma represents Andean peoples and Spaniards as occupying opposite moieties, or halves. To enhance the internal unity of each group in their separate realms, Guaman Poma imagined a space for each divided in four parts by a configuration of five elements—that is, with one element located at the center and the other four arrayed around it—in a pattern that reproduced the unity of Tahuantinsuyu, with the Inca ruler and Cuzco as the center/mediator among the four *suyus* of the empire. By the early Colonial period, this image of ideal order had been disrupted in Guaman Poma's view because Andean peoples and Spaniards, who should have remained in their separate worlds, had intermingled, producing a *Pachacuti*, a cosmic cataclysm that had turned the world upside down.

For Guaman Poma and many of his fellow Andeans, the nostalgic image of the **Sapa Inca**, the sovereign of Tahuantinsuyu, served as a unifying principle. Guaman Poma, however, knew that Atahualpa, one of Huayna Capac's potential successors, had been captured, ransomed and (in popular belief) beheaded at Cajamarca. Atahualpa was replaced by the King of Spain, whom Guaman Poma regarded as the Monarch of the World who held the power of the world in his hands.

The image that emerged of the last Inca was the figure known as *Inkarrí* (derived from Spanish, "Inca Rey," or Inca king). This mythical figure was based on Atahualpa who, it was believed, was beheaded and his body hidden in a cave. When he regrew his head and body, Inkarrí would reemerge and the Inca Empire would be reestablished. Some scholars have viewed Guaman Poma's chronicle as the first manifestation of nostalgia for the Inca and the restoration of Tahuantinsuyu, sentiments that have over the centuries fostered a succession of messianic movements beginning in the sixteenth century and continuing, at least in Peru, down to the present time.

The mestizo chronicler **Garcilaso de la Vega** became a staunch defender of Native Andeans and especially of the Incas. He described Inca rule as a kind of Christian utopia that had prepared the terrain for facilitating the introduction of Catholicism. Garcilaso's *Royal Commentaries of the Incas* enjoyed widespread readership after it was first published, in 1609. Through their reading of Garcilaso and other chroniclers, Europeans became transfixed by the image of the Incas, not only for their gold and silver but also for such achievements as their road system and the spectacular architecture of **Cuzco** and the megalithic "fortress" of **Sacsahuaman**. These views, however, were tempered by the influence of works produced under the Viceroy Toledo, especially the chronicle of **Sarmiento de Gamboa**, in which many Inca accomplishments were characterized as having been constructed under the "tyranny" of the Incas.

Despite the critics of the Inca rulers, Europe soon fell under the sway of the image of this great American empire, especially as recounted by Garcilaso. Soon, imaginary engravings of the city of Cuzco began to appear, as well as portraits of Inca rulers and idealized descriptions of Inca political organization and cultural achievements. During the eighteenth century, such was the popularity of Inca achievements that in France they inspired an opera-ballet, titled *Les Indes Galantes* (The Noble Indies) and the well-known *Lettres d'une Peruvienne* (Letters from a Peruvian Woman), a romantic novel written by the French woman Françoise de Graffigny, in which **quipus** played a leading role in a delightful love story. This work in particular attracted the attention of an Italian, Raimundo de Sangro, Count of Sansevero, who created drawings of knotted cords, heavily annotated with a series of largely imaginary symbolic elements.

Near the end of the eighteenth century, an Indian rebellion that aimed to restore Tahuantinsuyu shook the southern Andes. Its principal leader, José Gabriel Condorcanqui, known by his *nom de guerre* Túpac Amaru II, named himself after an Inca ruler who had held sway in the neo-Inca stronghold of **Vilcabamba**. Spanish officials suspected that Garcilaso's *Royal Commentaries* might have helped stir up this rebellion, and his chronicle was banned in the Viceroyalty of Peru.

Awareness of past neo-Inca movements saw a resurgence at the same time that liberalism began to promote ideas of independence, at the beginning of the nineteenth century. Soon, the influence of Túpac Amaru II's rebellion and a series of political circumstances undermining Spanish rule motivated Argentinian leaders, such as Generals Manuel Belgrano and José de San Martin, to advocate for independence from Spain. From early on, these moves were accompanied by calls for the restoration of an Inca monarchy. Although many people in the future Andean nations were sympathetic to these views, once independence was gained (which occurred in Peru in 1821), these nostalgic calls for the rebirth of an Inca state were abandoned in favor of a Republican political order under Simón Bolívar.

The attraction of the earlier historians of the Incas continued with renewed strength in Republican times, motivating the publication of new editions of several works, as well as the production of secondary works, some of which combined archival research with visits to archaeological sites. Garcilaso retained his popularity among historians such as William Prescott, who, in his *Conquest of Peru* (1847) characterized the Inca government as mildly despotic.

Given the utopian nature of Garcilaso's chronicle, other writers of the mid-to-late nineteenth century saw similarities between the Inca Empire and real or imagined socialist states. The Peruvian intellectual José Carlos Mariátegui even applied this idea to contemporary Peruvian politics, asserting that this form of organization was deeply rooted in the Andean past.

Ideas like those espoused by Mariátegui underlay the emergence in the twentieth century of the *Indigenista* movement, which celebrated and promoted indigenous values and styles in art, literature, politics, and the social sciences. Anthropology in Peru and in other Andean countries was born under the influence of *Indigenismo*. Because this movement blamed the large land-owners for the poverty of the Indians, the idea of agrarian reform became pervasive, spurred on in part by guerrilla movements promoted by Cuba. President Fernando Belaúnde Terry made a minor attempt at agrarian reform during his first administration, but he was ousted in 1968 in a military coup d'etat led by General Juan Velasco Alvarado.

The Velasco regime initiated a more radical agrarian reform than that envisioned by Belaúnde, disenfranchising virtually completely the agrarian aristocracy whose power rested on enormous land holdings. Together with agrarian reform, many other reforms were carried out that increased state control of production and labor. Nationalism played a dominant role in this movement, supported by images derived from historical and mythic Indian figures, such as Túpac Amaru II and Inkarrí. In tune with such sentiments in support of indigenous peoples—who were now officially designated *campesinos* (peasants) by the Velasco administration—**Quechua**, the *lingua franca* of the Inca Empire, was made an official language of Peru.

As the decades passed, many of the reforms carried out during the 1970s proved to be ineffective in dealing with the changes taking place in Peru and the world. By the mid-1990s, neoliberalism had begun to replace socialism. Many agricultural cooperatives founded during the Velasco regime were dismantled and the associates were given the opportunity to privatize small parcels of land. When Alejandro Toledo came to power as president of Peru, in 2001, symbols associated with Tahuantinsuyu were resurrected. Toledo was sworn-in as president not only in Congress, but also at **Machu Picchu**.

Further Reading

Betanzos, Juan de. *Narrative of the Incas*. Translated and edited by Roland Hamilton and Dana Buchanan. Austin: University of Texas Press, 1996 [1551–1557].

Cieza de León, Pedro. *Del señorío de los Incas*. Madrid: Imprenta de Manuel Gines Hernandez, 1880 [1553]. http://archive.org/stream/segundaparte00ciezrich#page/n0/mode/2up.

Garcilaso de la Vega, El Inca. *Royal Commentaries of the Incas and General History of Peru*. Translated by Harold V. Livermore. Austin: University of Texas Press, 1966 [1609].

Guaman Poma de Ayala, Felipe. *The First New Chronicle and Good Government: On the History of the World and the Incas up to 1615*. Translated by Roland Hamilton. Austin: University of Texas Press, 2009 [1615].

———. *Nueva corónica y buen gobierno*. Complete digital facsimile edition of the manuscript, with a corrected online version of Guaman Poma 1980. Scholarly editor Rolena Adorno. Copenhagen: Royal Library of Denmark, 2001 [1615]. http://www.kb.dk/elib/mss/poma/.

Mariátegui, José Carlos. "El Problema del Indio." In *Siete ensayos de la Realidad Peruana*. Lima: Biblioteca Amauta, 1928. http://www.marxists.org/espanol/mariateg/1928/7ensayos/index.htm.

Molina, Cristóbal de. "Relación de las Fábulas y Ritos de los Ingas." In *Fábulas y mitos de los incas*, 47–159. Cuzco: CBC, 1989 [1575?].

Ossio, Juan M. *Los Indios del Perú*. Madrid: Mapfre, 1992.

Pizarro, Pedro. *Relacion del descubrimiento y conquista del Peru*. Lima: PUCP, 1978 [1571]. http://es.scribd .com/doc/50568747/PIZARRO-Pedro-1571-1978-Relacion-del-descubrimiento-y-conquista -del-Peru.

Prescott, William. *The History of the Conquest of Peru*, Philadelphia: J. B. Lippincott, 1874.

■ JUAN OSSIO ACUÑA

M

MACHU PICCHU

The most iconic of all Inca settlements, Machu Picchu perches on a granite ridge amid lush cloud forest high above the roaring Urubamba River, northwest of Cuzco. In this spectacular setting, with distant views of the sacred, snow-clad peaks of the Urubamba and Vilcabamba ranges, Machu Picchu's builders combined a remarkable landscape with brilliant site planning, creating one of the world's most renowned examples of harmony between architecture and sacred geography.

Although the earliest map to include Machu Picchu dates to 1874, the settlement came to public attention only after 1911, when the American explorer **Hiram Bingham** stumbled upon it after a local guide led him on a tough slog up a steeply forested mountain. Bingham was searching for **Vilcabamba**, the "lost city of the Incas," which in fact he found at a place called Espíritu Pampa (Plain of the Spirits) only a month after exploring Machu Picchu. By 1930, and despite overwhelming evidence to the contrary, Bingham proclaimed Machu Picchu to be Vilcabamba. Since Bingham's landmark discovery, however, exploration and mapping have shown that the Incas did indeed found their last capital of Vilcabamba at Espíritu Pampa, which left open the questions: Who built Machu Picchu? And what was its significance?

We shall never be entirely certain of Machu Picchu's function. Was it, along with other settlements strung along the narrow, stone-paved "Inca Trail," located high above the Urubamba River valley as it descends toward the tropical forest, built to commemorate conquests and dominion over the region? The overall quality of Machu Picchu's stonework and several double-jambed entryways (a feature reserved for only the most elite buildings; see **Architecture**) indicate that it was more than an Inca outpost. Did its seemingly inaccessible location high above the river, with surrounding walls, a drawbridge, easily blocked approach roads, single inner gateway, and dry moat restrict access to a site populated by a highly religious elite, thereby demarcating the sacred from the profane? Alternatively, was it designed to deter incursions by hostile groups of jungle dwellers, known as Antis?

Research suggests that Machu Picchu may have transformed over the period of its occupation from a defensive outpost near a frontier, in the early years of its founding, to serve in its heyday as the showpiece of a ruler's **royal estate**. Indeed, a document from 1568 indicates that all of the lands from Torontoy, downriver from Ollantaytambo,

Machu Picchu sits high above the Urubamba River surrounded by forested peaks. It may have served as a royal estate managed by the lineage of the Inca ruler Pachacuti. Walter Wust.

to Chayllay, downstream from Machu Picchu, once formed part of a densely occupied area of Inca towns and agricultural complexes earmarked as properties of the ruler Pachacuti Inca Yupanqui's **panaca**. The document mentions a place called "Picho" and notes that "Indians" from Picho paid tribute to Spanish officials in coca leaves. Although some scholars believe that Picho refers to Machu Picchu, *picho* or *picchu* means "peak" in **Quechua** and could signal any number of places.

Building Machu Picchu was an enormous undertaking, requiring large numbers of workers to move great quantities of earth to create its terraced plaza, where archaeologists have recorded up to 2.5 meters (almost 8 feet) of fill. An onsite quarry provided the white granite for its walls. Carved stones, boulders, and outcrops as well as fountains, or baths, are central to the site's design. Sculpted rocks flank burial caves, enhance structures or patios, or mimic the shapes of distant mountains. The so-called Intihuatana stone (Quechua: "hitching post of the sun") caps a terraced platform and is aligned with sacred mountains and the cardinal directions. The first bath in a chain of 16 spring-fed fountains flanks a building with a curved wall known as the *Torreón*, which may have served as a Sun Temple. Built over a stone outcrop and a cave graced with elaborate stonework, the Torreón may also have been used as an observatory for viewing the June solstice sunrise and the rise of the Pleiades, two astronomical observations that were central to the regulation of the Inca **calendar**, in Cuzco. Due to its sweeping views of distant mountain peaks, some scholars claim that Machu Picchu served as an important central place in an elaborate cosmological scheme embracing numerous sacred mountains (such as Salcantay, to the south) within the region.

Some scholars suggest that Machu Picchu's residential remains could have housed some 750 people, while others claim that only about 300 people could have lived there. While the site is flanked by agricultural terraces, which protected it from erosion, the extent of terracing was insufficient to produce enough crops to sustain its residents. Machu Picchu's inhabitants probably relied on foodstuffs brought in from farms on the valley bottom and neighboring settlements. Pollen studies indicate that farmers grew maize as well as potatoes and a type of legume. Some of Machu Picchu's inhabitants engaged in metalworking, as revealed by the discovery of pure tin and copper sheet, alloyed to produce tin bronze, and cast to create tools and decorative items. Spindle whorls and bone weaving tools point to cloth production.

Bingham and his crew discovered over 100 burial caves containing the remains of 174 individuals. A reappraisal of these skeletal remains and their burial offerings signal that they were mostly low-status *mitmacuna* laborers (see **Labor Service**), who occupied temporary residences at the site. (The settlement's more elite residents lived in elegant, finely built compounds.) Distinct types of cranial deformation indicate that some of the laborers came from the Titicaca area while others originated on Peru's central and north coast. Studies of pottery offerings imply that other residents came from the northern reaches of the empire—Chachapoyas in northern Peru and the land of the Cañari, in Ecuador. Contrary to a report produced by Bingham's expedition, which claimed that the majority of skeletal remains were those of females, the skeletal material in fact reflects a balanced female-male ratio. The presence of infants and newborns among the burials, along with evidence that some of the women gave birth, signals that Machu Picchu was not, as Bingham claimed, "the home of a considerable number of the Virgins of the Sun" (H. Bingham 1979 [1930]).

Further Reading

Bingham, Alfred M. *Portrait of an Explorer: Hiram Bingham, Discoverer of Machu Picchu.* Ames: Iowa University Press, 1989.
Bingham, Hiram. "In the Wonderland of Peru." *National Geographic* 24, no. 4, 1913.
———. *Machu Picchu: A Citadel of the Incas.* New York: Hacker Art Books, 1979 [1930].
Burger, Richard L., and Lucy C. Burger, eds. *Machu Picchu: Unveiling the Mystery of the Incas.* New Haven, CT: Yale University Press, 2004.
Reinhard, Johan. *Machu Picchu: Exploring an Ancient Sacred Center.* Los Angeles: Cotsen Institute of Archaeology Press, 2007.

■ ADRIANA VON HAGEN

METALLURGY

The Incas were not innovators of metallurgical technologies. By the first quarter of the fifteenth century AD, when they began their expansion that culminated in the establishment and administration of Tahuantinsuyu, the Inca Empire, they had inherited close to a millennium of highly sophisticated metallurgies practiced by communities, newly incorporated into the Inca Empire, from the central Andes of Peru and the south-central Andes of Bolivia and northwest Argentina. The metallurgies the Incas encountered and appropriated, though they differed locally, shared common technological and cultural foundations. The Incas relied on this pan-Andean quality in the production and significance of metal, just as they did with cloth (see **Weaving and Textiles**; **Costume**). Inca metallurgy was an imperial metallurgy that served the purposes of state.

Metallurgical technologies that involved mining metallic ores, the extraction of the metallic component of the ores through smelting, and the subsequent production of metal objects from solid metal ingots or by casting molten metal into ceramic or stone

A long-haired llama made of crimped silver sheet metal, 23.8 centimeters (9.4 inches) tall. These special llamas provided unusually long, fine fiber. American Museum of Natural History, NY, Catalogue No. B/1619, Courtesy of the Division of Anthropology, American Museum of Natural History.

molds, were initiated and highly developed by Moche societies located on the north coast of Peru (see **Chronology, pre-Inca**). During the prior Initial Period and Early Horizon Andean smiths practiced metalworking, taking advantage of the malleability of native metals (metals that occur in the earth's crust in metallic, not in mineral, form) to shape them into objects. Native metals included gold, silver, copper, and native alloys such as electrum (the natural alloy of gold and silver).

Central Andean metallurgical technologies centered on the metals gold, silver, and copper, and on the binary (2-element component) and ternary (3-element component) alloys these metals form when melted. Both Andean and Mesoamerican pre–Hispanic metallurgies were nonferrous; iron ores were not smelted in the Americas prior to the European invasion in the sixteenth century. In the Andes, copper became the primary and necessary component of almost all the alloys developed there.

The melting together of smelted copper metal and smelted silver metal over a wide range of proportions (by weight) of the two components, produced what are likely the earliest alloys in the central Andes and the most important alloys throughout Andean prehistory. Central Andean metalsmiths preferred to handle metal as a solid, often hammering and annealing (intermittent heating) the metal into thin sheets that they shaped and joined subsequently into three-dimensional objects. Copper-silver alloys provided excellent solders for joining an assemblage of thin sheets of gold or of copper. (Modern industry uses these same solders to assemble components of electronic circuit boards.) Of greater significance are the mechanical and physical properties that copper confers to silver when the two metals are alloyed and shaped through mechanical means, such as hammering. Thin sheets of copper-silver alloy are mechanically tough (they resist fracture), maintain sufficient malleability to undergo continued deformation and annealing to produce the final form, and they are stiff enough to retain their shape under normal conditions of use.

The physical properties of these alloys were of equal importance to their mechanical enhancement. For Moche smiths, color was the most salient physical property of the metal objects they crafted. Regardless of the proportions of copper to silver in an alloy, during the annealing of thin sheet metal, copper atoms at the surfaces of the sheet oxidize, leaving on the surfaces a layer of almost pure silver to confer a silver color to the sheet. In this regime, copper within the alloy, or inside the object, provides a mechanism for transforming the surface color of the alloy and for exhibiting that color as a key manifestation of the object. Similarly, the Moche prepared ingots of ternary copper-silver-gold alloys that, when rendered into thin sheet, displayed richly golden surface colors after chemical treatments of the surfaces eliminated both the copper and silver alloy components. These techniques are often referred to as depletion silvering and depletion gilding—surface enrichment of culturally desired color through depletion of selected alloy elements.

On the north coast of Peru, the Moche were followed by Sicán, and Sicán by Chimú (see **Chronology, pre-Inca**). Each of these societies continued the sheet metal, enrichment-coloring traditions established by the Moche, with increasing production of large, shiny, elite, silver- and gold-colored objects that the Inca encountered upon their conquest of the kingdom of Chimor ca. AD 1476. The Incas dispatched Chimú metalsmiths to Cuzco and other leading Inca centers to continue their specialized craft as retainers of the state. When the invading Spaniards in the sixteenth century carried out assays of bullion melted in Peru and in Spain from the great quantities of gold and silver objects they ransomed or looted from the Incas (see **Invasion, Spanish**), they expressed surprise at finding that most of the silver and much of the gold was impure, containing significant concentrations of copper and other metallic components.

Throughout Andean prehistory, items in metal served primarily to convey social status, to demonstrate political power, and to generate awe inspired by religious or political ritual enactments. The Andean metal inventory was tool-poor. Small tools such as needles, spindle whorls, depilatory tweezers, chisels, and axes were made of copper or from a variety of bronze alloys. But the purpose of body and clothing ornaments such as earspools, nose rings, and mouth masks, or of ritual paraphernalia, staffs of office, military regalia, and drinking vessels was to communicate messages of social significance. Such objects carried and imparted information through their form, their color, and by the technological processes by which they were made.

Archaeological data from elite tombs of Moche lords and priestesses suggest strongly that gold, silver, and copper metals carried gender: gold/male, silver/female, and copper/female. Ethnohistoric studies of Colombian communities that continue to curate and to wear ornaments made of ternary copper-silver-gold (*tumbaga*) alloys consider these materials, in alloyed, inseparable association, as representing generative or procreative forces. Sixteenth-century Spanish chronicles that report Inca origin myths relate that the first member of the Inca royal *ayllu* was the progeny of the wedding of the Sun and the Moon (see **Myths, Origin**). The Inca described the metal gold as the sweat of the Sun, silver as the tears of the Moon. These two metals were the birthright of the Inca. When alloyed alone or with copper they reinforced the continued generation of the royal **panacas** and their celestial beginnings.

The notable change that accompanied Inca metallurgy is evident in the scale of imperial operations, in both the mining and processing of ore and the production of metal objects. Gold and silver, the sacred metals and the prerogative solely of the royal *panacas*, sheathed interior palace walls and were shaped into large discs to represent Inti, the Sun god at the center of the state **religion**. Inca expansion from Cuzco deep into the south-central Andes was stimulated, in part, by the presence there of rich gold, silver, and cassiterite (tin oxide) ores—the latter indispensable for the production of tin bronze (see **Mining**).

During the Andean Middle Horizon (AD 540–900) a variety of bronze alloys was in widespread use throughout the Andean zone: copper-arsenic alloy bronzes in the central Andes, copper-tin alloy bronzes in the south-central Andes. The specific elements in a bronze alloy were a direct consequence of the kinds of metallic ores that were present and accessible in each region. Metalworkers in the south-central Andes produced bronze by alloying copper with tin. The cassiterite fields that run from the Bolivian highlands into northwest Argentina are the unique occurrence of tin ore in South America and constitute one of the richest sources of tin in the world.

Tin bronze objects in the south were shaped by casting molten bronze into ceramic molds. Large, circular discs often weighing as much as 33 kilograms (72.8 pounds), heavy bells measuring over 30 centimeters (11.8 inches) in height, and massive, elaborate axe heads or composite axe-and-handle castings completed a suite of three items of ritual paraphernalia that also served as sumptuary goods for political elites.

The Inca appropriated this metallurgical complex, entirely new to them, that combined tin bronze alloys and intricate casting techniques. They, alone, controlled the source of tin. Having rejected the religious and ritual connotations associated with the southern castings, the Inca designed a set of small, imperial bronzes that archaeologists encounter disseminated widely throughout Tahuantinsuyu: cast *tumi* knives with cylindrical handles and flaring blades, lobed mace heads, small axe heads, and a combination mace-and-axe head. No member of this set was a tool or an instrument of war. They were state issue, markers of imperial presence made from an imperial alloy.

Further Reading

González, Luis R. *Bronces Sin Nombre: La Metalurgia Prehispánica en el Noroeste Argentino*. Buenos Aires: Fundación CEPPA, 2004.

Hosler, Dorothy. *The Sounds and Colors of Power*. Cambridge, MA: Massachusetts Institute of Technology, 1994.

Lechtman, Heather. "The Inka, and Andean Metallurgical Tradition." In *Variations in the Expression of Inka Power*, edited by Richard L. Burger, Craig Morris, and Ramiro Matos Mendieta, 314–55. Washington, DC: Dumbarton Oaks, 2007.

———. "Andean Metallurgy in Prehistory." In *Archaeometallurgy in Global Perspective: Methods and Syntheses*, edited by Benjamin Roberts and Christopher Thornton, 361–422. New York: Springer, 2014.

■ HEATHER LECHTMAN

MINING

Mining and metallurgy formed an integral part of the Inca political economy. The Incas mined copper, gold, silver, lead, tin, and possibly zinc as well as a variety of other minerals such as turquoise, obsidian (a volcanic glass), and cinnabar (an ore of mercury). The objects

created from these minerals included small tools, weapons, and a variety of personal ornaments and ritual items. While many of these objects had practical uses, all were imbued
with social and religious significance, as were the very acts of mining and smelting. The
practical, political, and ideological were thus intrinsic aspects of the production of metal
and other materials won from the earth.

No systematic survey of the location of mines throughout the Inca realm has been
conducted, but a number of regional surveys have been done. In Peru, Inca mines and
mineral processing sites have been identified on the coast and the western shores of Lake
Titicaca. The most thorough surveys have been conducted in the mineral-rich southern
Andes where archaeologists estimate that 50–80 percent of the Inca sites identified in
northwestern Argentina and northern Chile are associated with mining or metallurgical
activities. These figures indicate not only the intensity of Inca mining, but also suggest
that access to minerals was a primary factor motivating Inca expansion into the region.

The organization of Inca mining was shaped by imperial policies, as well as by technological requirements and local socioeconomic conditions. Mining and agriculture were
organized in a similar fashion, with the state claiming dominion over all mineral deposits,
but allowing less productive mines to be worked by local leaders. These provincial rulers
were expected to offer silver and gold to their imperial overlords, and following Andean
norms of reciprocity, also received such gifts from the Inca. The exchange of metal items
thus played an important part in the imperial political economy.

Inca mines were closely supervised by state personnel. Workers included nearby populations complying with the *mit'a,* the rotating, state-imposed labor draft (see **Labor
Service**), and *mitmacuna,* colonists who were permanently relocated in order to supply a
self-sufficient labor force. *Yanacuna,* specialized retainers who worked for the Inca, were
probably employed to perform skilled tasks such as smelting. Workers were often drawn
from communities already familiar with mining, and in all cases, couples, rather than individual men, would have been recruited by the state.

The Incas took over previously established facilities and constructed new mining centers in sparsely populated areas; in both cases the way in which production was organized
appears to have been similar. El Abra, a copper and turquoise mine in the Atacama region
of northern Chile, is one of the best preserved examples of an Inca mining complex. It
consists of six sites, including a mine, an area for separating ore from waste rock, a place
to load and unload llamas, housing for workers, storage, and ritual platforms.

Inca mines usually consisted of open pits, although narrow tunnels that only admitted
a single individual at a time were also constructed. Ore was removed using hafted stone
axes and shovels and put into bags or baskets that were dragged to the surface by the
miner. The ore was then further separated from the waste rock using hammerstones and
anvils, often on a terrace adjacent to the mine. Additional processing, including grinding,
smelting, and refining, took place at sites located at a distance from the mine. Smelting
of both copper and silver was conducted in *huayrachinas.* These small wind furnaces were
made of clay or cobbles and had holes pierced in their sides to allow the wind to stoke
the charge of fuel and ore. Huayrachinas were introduced to northern Chile prior to the
Inca conquest and were later extensively employed by the Incas. The final production of

metal objects probably took place in provincial centers or in Cuzco itself as evidence for metalworking is absent from mining sites, with the exception of Tarapacá Viejo, Chile.

The Incas also appropriated and transformed local belief systems and ritual related to mining. The brilliance of gold and silver was intimately linked to the vital force of the sun that was embodied by the Inca himself. Large gold nuggets and pieces of high grade silver were considered *mamas* or *illas* that, like unusually large or uniquely shaped potatoes and maize cobs, were viewed as embodiments of this fertile power and were venerated in order to increase productivity. These were sometimes elevated to regional status. Such was the case in southern Bolivia, where a regional cult centered on the silver mine at Porco was located. The idol, or *huaca*, of this mine was a large piece of silver ore called "Tata Porco," and it, as well as the mine and the mountain where it was located, were revered not only for their relationship to the Sun but also to Illapa, the deity of lightning and warfare.

A number of scholars have suggested that some of the high-altitude Inca sanctuaries on mountain peaks in the southern Andes were also related to mining. These shrines were constructed by the Incas as part of their ritual conquest of the region, one that went hand-in-hand with the appropriation of material and human resources for imperial use (see **Capac Hucha**).

Further Reading

Berthelot, Jean. "The Extraction of Precious Metals at the Time of the Inca." In *Anthropological History of Andean Politics*, edited by John Murra, Nathan Wachtel, and Jacques Revel, 69–88. Cambridge: Cambridge University Press, 1986.

D'Altroy, Terence N., Ana María Lorandi, Veronica I. Williams, Milena Calderari, Christine A. Hastorf, Elizabeth DeMarrais, and Melissa B. Hagstrum. "Inca Rule in the Northern Calchaquí Valley, Argentina." *Journal of Field Archaeology* 27, no.10: 1–26, 2000.

Petersen, G. Georg. *Mining and Metallurgy in Ancient Peru*. Special Paper #467, translated by William E. Brooks. Boulder, CO: Geological Society of America, 2010.

Zori, Colleen, Peter Tropper, and David Scott. "Copper Production in Late Prehispanic Northern Chile." *Journal of Archaeological Science* 40, no. 2: 1165–75, 2013.

■ MARY VAN BUREN

MUMMIES, ROYAL

Although ancestor worship in the Andes is an ancient practice predating the Incas by several millennia, it is best known from the Inca cult of the royal mummies, thanks in large part to Spanish eyewitnesses who saw the mummies playing an active role in the lives of the living. *Panacas* (the royal descent groups established during a ruler's lifetime) were responsible for preserving the memory of their ancestors as well as "the cult of his body and the sustenance of the family," according to the chronicler **Bernabé Cobo**, and they "adored the body as a god" (Cobo 1979 [1653]). The *panacas* owned vast tracts of land in Cuzco and environs (see **Estates, Royal**), causing Huascar, Atahualpa's brother, to complain that the dead had the best of everything in the land. When the mummies were

Born in Baeza, Jaén, Spain sometime earlier than 1529 (d. 1585), Molina arrived in Cuzco before 1556. He served in the *Hospital de los Naturales* (Hospital for Native People) and was the first priest of the hospital parish, founded in 1572, during the administration of Viceroy Francisco de Toledo. Toledo may also have appointed Molina general preacher (*predicador general*) of the Natives of Cuzco. The Bishop of Cuzco commissioned Molina to write a history of the Incas and an account of their religion. Molina wrote the former sometime around 1572 and the latter around 1576. Only his account of Inca religion survives, a work titled *Relación de las fábulas i ritos de los Ingas* (Account of the Fables and Rites of the Incas).

Some have argued that Molina's role as both priest and author of a treatise on Inca religion skewed his work so much that he portrayed certain aspects of Inca religion as being compatible with Christianity. This included a possible notion of a trinity of sacred identities that together composed the principal Inca deity, Viracocha (see **Religion**). Molina also included a number of prayers (*oraciones*) to Viracocha, which have been important texts for the study of Inca verse and poetry.

Molina's chronicle is an important source of information on the annual religious festivals and ceremonies of the Incas in Cuzco. His account has been used by numerous scholars over the years to attempt to reconstruct the sequences of events and astronomical periodicities (especially those of the moon) regulating the capital's ritual calendar. Molina gives detailed accounts of the festivals of Aymoray, a harvest festival in April-May; Inti Raymi, the winter solstice (in the southern hemisphere) festival in June; Citua, a festival aimed at cleansing the city of ills, in August-September; and Capac Raymi, the great festival of the sun linked to male initiation rituals at the time of the austral summer solstice, in December.

Further Reading

Molina, Cristóbal de. *Account of the Fables and Rites of the Incas.* http://muse.jhu.edu.ezp-prod1.hul.harvard.edu/books/9780292729995.
———. "An Account of the Fables and Rites of the Yncas." Translated and edited by Clements R. Markham, 3–64. Works issued by the Hakluyt Society, no. 48. London: Hakluyt Society, 1873. New York: Burt Franklin, 1963, 1964, and 1969.
———. *Relación de las fábulas y ritos de los incas.* Critical edition by Paloma Jiménez del Campo, paleographic transcription by Paloma Cuenca Muñoz. Madrid: Iberoamericana, 2010.
———. *Account of the Fables and Rites of the Incas.* Translated and edited by Brian S. Bauer, Vania Smith-Oka, and Gabriel. E. Cantarutti. Austin: University of Texas Press, 2011 [1575].
Urbano, Henrique Osvaldo. "Molina, Cristóbal de (ca. 1529–1585)." In *Guide to Documentary Sources for Andean Studies, 1530–1900*, edited by Joanne Pillsbury, vol. 3, 427–28. Norman: University of Oklahoma Press, 2008.
Zuidema, R. T. "The Sidereal Lunar Calendar of the Incas." In *Archaeoastronomy in the New World*, edited by Anthony F. Aveni, 59–107. Austin: University of Texas Press, 1982.

■ GARY URTON

The mummy of Huayna Capac, who died in Ecuador apparently of smallpox, is borne on a litter to Cuzco along with the bodies of his wife and son. Guaman Poma de Ayala, Felipe. *El primer nueva corónica y buen gobierno*. Edited by John V. Murra and Rolena Adorno, 350/377. Mexico City: Siglo Veintiuno, 1980 [1615].

not holding court at Cuzco's Sun temple or engaged in celebrations in the city's main square, they retired to their country estates.

In fact, the mummies were viewed as **oracles**, and interceded and interfered—through mediums—in the running of the empire, offering their opinions on successions and other important matters of state. On especially solemn occasions, attendants carried the mummies into Cuzco's main square, seating the five kings of upper (*hanan*) Cuzco on the right side of the plaza and the five kings of lower (*hurin*) Cuzco on the left side. There, the attendants offered them food and drink, "and the dead toasted each other and the living, and the living toasted the dead" (Pedro Pizarro 1921 [1571]). Since each attendant had to drink for two, these drinking binges became drunken affairs and the plaza's drains "ran with urine throughout the day" (Estete 1938 [ca. 1535–1540]). The mummies made one of their last public appearances in December 1533 for the investiture of Manco Inca, one of Huayna Capac's sons.

After Manco Inca's failed siege of Cuzco in 1536, however, the mummies' public appearances became more sporadic and, when Spanish officials declared the cult idolatrous, their attendants took them into hiding. In 1559, the then viceroy instructed Cuzco's chief magistrate, **Juan Polo Ondegardo**, to put an end to the idolatrous worship of the mummified ancestors and to find the mummies, which had been concealed in and around the city. Within a few months, Polo succeeded in discovering several mummies of Inca kings along with their substitute statues (which ruling kings and queens had made of themselves in wood, gold, or silver), as well as the mummified remains of several queens. The fact that the mummies were accompanied by lavish offerings, such as goblets of gold and other "treasure," made their discovery especially rewarding. Polo Ondegardo had some of the bodies secretly buried and dispatched four mummies to Lima, where they went on display.

Before the mummies left Cuzco, however, the chronicler **Garcilaso de la Vega** saw them, and his account sheds some light on how the mummies may have been prepared, "without the loss of a hair of the head or brow or an eyelash." He described how they were seated, dressed "as they had been in life," with their hands across their breasts and their eyes lowered. Another eyewitness, **José de Acosta,** who saw them in Lima in 1590, wrote that Pachacuti's body was so well preserved that he appeared to be alive, and that it was covered with a certain "resin." Nevertheless, he did not discover how the body had been embalmed. Garcilaso believed that the bodies had been taken above the snow line and kept there until their flesh dried, after which they were covered with the "resin" mentioned by Acosta. The chronicle of **Juan de Betanzos** provides a telling clue. He noted that when Huayna Capac died in Ecuador the nobles who accompanied him had the body opened, and removed the entrails, "preparing him so that no damage would be done to him and without breaking any bone." Then he was "prepared" and "dried" in the sun and the air, dressed in "costly clothes" (Betanzos 1996 [1551–1557]), placed on a litter adorned with feathers and gold, and carried to Cuzco.

While no royal mummies have been discovered, Inca-period mummies uncovered in tombs in the cloud forest of Chachapoyas in northern Peru provide some insight into how the Inca royals may have been embalmed. Embalmers controlled decomposition by emptying the abdominal cavity through the anus, sealing the orifice with a plug of cotton cloth. Fly casings found in the mummy bundles indicate that the mummification process must have taken some time. The skin appears leathery, apparently treated with some as-yet-unidentified substance or substances, perhaps the "resin" or "balsam" mentioned by the chroniclers. Unspun cotton placed under the cheeks, in the mouth, and in the nostrils preserved facial features. Some of the Chachapoya-Inca mummies were placed in a seated position with their arms crossed over their breasts, much like the ones Garcilaso saw in Cuzco. Most of the Chachapoya mummies, however, have their hands tucked under their chins or placed across their faces, which prevents the jaw from slacking open. Just like the mummies seen by Garcilaso in Cuzco, the Chachapoya-Inca ones weigh very little, "so that any Indian could carry them in his arms."

In Cuzco the Incas observed a mourning ceremony called *purucaya*, a rite of passage that took place a year after the ruler's death and celebrated the feats of the deceased. It may also have marked the completion of the mummification process.

Further Reading

Bauer, Brian S. *Ancient Cuzco: Heartland of the Inca.* Austin: University of Texas Press, 2004.

Betanzos, Juan de. *Narrative of the Incas.* Translated and edited by Roland Hamilton and Dana Buchanan. Austin: University of Texas Press, 1996 [1551–1557].

Cobo, Bernabé. *History of the Inca Empire: An Account of the Indians' Customs and Their Origin, Together with a Treatise on Inca Legends, History and Social Institutions.* Translated and edited by Roland Hamilton. Austin: University of Texas Press, 1979 [1653].

Born in Odessa, Russia, Murra (1916–2006) grew up in Romania and immigrated to the United States in 1934. He attended the University of Chicago where he earned a BA degree in Sociology, in 1936. In February 1937, Murra traveled to France on his way to Spain to fight in the Spanish Civil War, on the side of the Republic, as a member of the Abraham Lincoln Brigade. With the end of the war in Spain, Murra returned to Chicago where, switching from sociology to anthropology, he earned an MA in 1942 and a PhD in 1956. He subsequently taught at the University of Puerto Rico (1947–1950), Vassar College (1950–1961), Yale (1962–1963), and the University of San Marcos, in Lima (1964–1966), before taking up a long-time teaching position at Cornell University (1968–1982). He died at his home in Ithaca, New York, in 2006.

Murra made a number of critical contributions to Inca studies over the course of his professional life. While early in his career he carried out some ethnographic research in the central Andes, around Huánuco, where he was also involved in archaeological research at the site of Huánuco Pampa, his major work and contributions derived from his intense study of administrative documents produced by Spanish Colonial administrators during the first half century or so following the European invasion of the Inca Empire. Murra's initial interest concerned the economic organization of the Inca state, the subject of his PhD dissertation. The Andean economy writ large (i.e., in pre-Inca and early Colonial times) remained a central focus of his research over his long career.

From close readings of the Colonial administrative documents, Murra developed what became the dominant paradigm of the twentieth century for explaining how the Inca—and more generally, the highland Andean—economy worked to maintain self-sufficiency in a heterogeneous, unpredictable, and vertical environment. This centered on what he termed "vertical archipelagos." In this scheme, an individual highland community dispatched settlers—members of its own kin group (*ayllu*)—to colonize distant ecological zones, whose resources were unavailable to the nuclear group, at altitudes above and below the nuclear *ayllu* settlement. These colonies constituted permanent "islands" of kinfolk who exchanged the products of their zone with the nucleus. By this arrangement, the geographically discontinuous community (i.e. the *ayllu*), consisting of a nucleus and its island outliers, dispersed by altitude and ecozone throughout the landscape, functioned as a "vertical archipelago," combining people and resources into one political and economic macrosystem. Without the aid of markets (which Murra argued did not exist in the Andes before Spanish contact), the archipelago arrangement accomplished the distribution of the myriad products available in the Andes across entire social networks . While Murra's model is subject to some debate by ethnohistorians today, it still represents a major interpretive approach to the study of the Incas, their ancestors, and their early Colonial descendants.

Murra formulated the core principles of the vertical archipelago economic model primarily from his reading and study of Colonial *visitas*. These administrative documents resulted from systematic "visits" by Spanish Colonial officials to different regions and settlements in the Andes and were aimed at conducting censuses, inquiring into local forms of social and political organization, gauging the size of vast herds of llamas and alpacas, and the forms of local land tenure, as well as investigating Inca practices of governance, including the levying and redistribution of tribute and other practices. Murra was responsible for the publication of several *visitas*, including those conducted at Huánuco (1562), Chucuito (1567), and Sonqo (1568–1570). Many of his most important contributions were initially published in Spanish.

Over the course of his career, Murra trained numerous PhD students who have gone on to make fundamental contributions to the study of the Inca—and broader, longer-term Andean—economy, as well as a wide range of issues in Andean cultural history.

Further Reading

Murra, John V. *The Economic Organization of the Inca State*. Greenwich, CT: JAI Press, 1980. Publication of the original PhD diss., University of Chicago, 1955.

———. "'El Archipélago Vertical' Revisited." In *Andean Ecology and Civilization: An Interdisciplinary Perspective on Andean Ecological Complementarity*, edited by Shozo Masuda, Izumi Shimada, and Craig Morris, 3–13. Tokyo: University of Tokyo Press, 1985.

———. "The Limits and Limitations of the 'Vertical Archipelago' in the Andes." In *Andean Ecology and Civilization: An Interdisciplinary Perspective on Andean Ecological Complementarity*, edited by Shozo Masuda, Izumi Shimada, and Craig Morris, 15–20. Tokyo: University of Tokyo Press, 1985.

———. "Did Tribute and Markets Prevail in the Andes before the European Invasion?" In *Ethnicity, Markets, and Migration in the Andes*, edited by B. Larson and O. Harris, 57–72. Durham, NC: Duke University Press, 1995.

———. *El mundo andino*. Lima: Pontificia Católica del Perú, 2002.

Van Buren, Mary. "Rethinking the Vertical Archipelago: Ethnicity, Exchange, and History in the South Central Andes." *American Anthropologist* 98, no. 2: 338–51, 1996.

■ GARY URTON

Estete, Miguel de. "Noticia del Peru." In *Los cronistas de la conquista*, selection, prologue, notes and concordances by Horacio H. Urteaga, 195–251. Biblioteca de la Cultura Peruana, no. 2. Paris: Desclée, de Brouwer, 1938 [ca. 1535–1540].

Garcilaso de la Vega, El Inca. *Royal Commentaries of the Incas and General History of Peru*. Translated by Harold V. Livermore. Austin: University of Texas Press, 1966 [1609].

■ ADRIANA VON HAGEN

Little is known about the life of the Mercedarian friar Martín de Murúa (also spelled *Morúa*). While his birthdate is unknown, he claimed to have been from Guipúzcoa, in the Basque country of northern Spain. He arrived in the Andes sometime before 1585, serving as parish priest in Capachica on Lake Titicaca and perhaps in Curahuasi, near Cuzco as well as in Arequipa. He was an acquaintance of the indigenous chronicler **Felipe Guaman Poma de Ayala**, although the exact nature of their relationship is unclear. Both men wrote chronicles detailing myriad aspects of life in the Andes under the Incas and in the early Colonial period. Both men's works included copious drawings, and it is certain that Guaman Poma produced a few of the drawings that appear in at least two of Murúa's manuscripts. The two men had a falling out following their collaboration, and, in his chronicle, Guaman Poma derided Murúa's character and qualities as a historian. Murúa returned to Spain where, in 1616, he sought license to publish a chronicle about the Incas and Peru. He died a few years later, at an unknown date, probably in Spain.

Describing Murúa's "chronicle" is challenging, as it took different forms over time as he reworked the manuscript. Murúa's narrative survives today in two manuscript versions, which may represent different stages in the production of a history of the origin and genealogy of the kings of Peru. The earliest manuscript, titled *Historia del origen, y genealogía real de los reyes ingas del Piru* (History of the Origin and Royal Genealogy of the Inca Kings of Peru), dates to 1590–1598. This manuscript is held in the Galvin collection, Ireland. The second manuscript, titled *Historia general del Perú* (General History of Peru), dates to 1611–1616. Formerly known as the Wellington manuscript, this manuscript is now held at the J. Paul Getty Museum, Los Angeles. A third manuscript, titled *Historia del origen y genealogía real de los reyes Inças del Perú*, is largely a nineteenth-century copy of the Galvin manuscript, but with additional, later material. This version is known as the "Loyola manuscript," as it is held at the convent of Loyola, Azpeitia, Guipúzcoa, Spain.

The Murúa manuscripts are differentiated by the number, quality, and artist of their respective illustrations. The Galvin manuscript contains 113 illustrations; the Getty manuscript has 37 watercolors; and the Loyola manuscript includes five line drawings. A few of the illustrations in the Galvin and Getty manuscripts were drawn by Guaman Poma. Murúa himself probably produced the rest of the illustrations. In the two colorfully illustrated manuscripts, the drawings are extremely important and useful for their view into the dress, ritual paraphernalia, and symbolism associated with the kings, queens, and assorted officials—both civil and ecclesiastical—in the Inca Empire.

The manuscripts of Murúa's history and genealogy of the Incas contain a tremendous amount of information about the lives and deeds of the Incas; the institutions and practices of Inca governance; religious beliefs, practices, and rituals and ceremonies both of the Incas and of people in the countryside; and a host of other matters. Scholars argue that the Galvin manuscript in particular draws heavily from Andean oral traditions that must have been collected by Murúa from informants, one of whom may have been Guaman Poma de Ayala.

Further Reading

Ballesteros Gaibrois, Manuel. "Dos cronistas paralelos: Huaman Poma y Murúa (Confrontación de las series reales gráficas)." *Anales de literatura hispanoamericana* (Madrid) 9, no. 10: 15–66, 1981.

Cummins, Thomas B. F., and Barbara Anderson, eds. *The Getty Murúa: Essays on the Making of Martín de Murúa's "Historia General del Piru," J. Paul Getty Museum Ms. Ludwig XIII, 16*. Los Angeles: Getty Publications, 2008. http://d2aohiyo3d3idm.cloudfront.net/publications/virtuallibrary/0892368945.pdf.

Mendizábal Losack, Emilio. "Las dos versiones de Murúa." *Revista del Museo Nacional* (Lima) 32: 153–85, 1963.

Ossio, Juan M. "Murúa, Martín de (?—ca. 1620)." In *Guide to Documentary Sources for Andean Studies, 1530–1900*, edited by Joanne Pillsbury, vol. 3, 436–41. Norman: University of Oklahoma Press, 2008.

"Scientific Investigation of Martín de Murúa's Illustrated Manuscripts." The Getty. http://www.getty.edu/conservation/our_projects/science/coll_res/murua_manuscripts.pdf.

■ GARY URTON

MUSIC

The Quechua word *taqui* encompassed song, dance, drinking feasts, and celebrations that included song and/or dance. Inca music and dance were part of larger ritual complexes and celebrations that included rites, sacrifices, special dress, offerings, and consumption and exchange of ceremonial **chicha** (maize beer) and **coca** leaves, the mildly narcotic stimulant. This is still the case with the music of many indigenous Andean communities today.

The Incas used song and music for many purposes: to record oral history; to praise the great deeds of living and deceased Inca kings; to commemorate battle victories; in large gatherings of nobles from around the empire; in initiation ceremonies of new *orejones* (young men with newly pierced ears); in processions carrying statues and figures to *huacas* for veneration by Incas, *orejones*, and accompanying people; to solemnize human and animal sacrifice; and in calendric events throughout the year for planting, harvesting, purification, and praises to the creator god, the Sun, and water (especially in the form of rain, rivers, and lakes).

The chronicler **Pedro de Cieza de León** wrote about the intergenerational oral transmission of history through narrative ballads, which told of events that occurred as many as 500 years before the Spanish invasion. The Inca ruler ordered the creation of ballads, sung during large ceremonial gatherings of nobles from around the empire, that extolled his feats. The select composers would also create accounts that were sung at marriage festivities and joyful celebrations. Ballads of praise were also sung around the deceased Inca's statues, which were placed in the Aucaypata, Cuzco's main square, for ceremonies of veneration, when food and drink were offered. The death of an Inca king was commemorated by prolonged

A woman beats on a large drum as men from Collasuyu play flutes in this drawing by Felipe Guaman Poma de Ayala. Guaman Poma de Ayala, Felipe. *El primer nueva corónica y buen gobierno*. Edited by John V. Murra and Rolena Adorno, 299/324. Mexico City: Siglo Veintiuno, 1980 [1615].

mourning and weeping, when elders sang ballads of the king's great deeds and accomplishments. According to Cieza de León, the *quipucamayocs* recorded the sung praises on *quipu*, which could then be read and performed at later festivities. In this way, the *quipucamayocs* kept accounts of many events throughout the empire that could be relayed by select experts in ballad-style. The *harawi* was another type of song used to express pain and tribulation, either individually or collectively. This pre-Hispanic custom of sung weeping and improvisational storytelling through song is still expressed today in remote communities, such as among the Q'eros cultural group of the southeastern Andes.

A song recorded by the chronicler **Juan de Betanzos** conveys the spirit of Inca songs. This is said to have been sung by Pachacuti Inca Yupanqui on his deathbed: "Since I bloomed like the flower of the garden, up to now I have given order and justice in this life and world as long as my strength lasted. Now I have turned to earth" (Betanzos 1996 [1553]). Songs lauding the chosen people who gave up their lives to serve the gods were chanted just before human sacrifice at key worship locations such as the **Coricancha**, Cuzco's Sun temple, and the sacred hill of Huanacauri. During the *huarachicuy* rite of passage from boyhood to manhood, boys received loincloths (*huara*) and red tunics with white stripes, and sang the *huari taqui* repeatedly during the celebration. It was believed that this particular *taqui* was bestowed by the creator god when the first Inca, Manco Capac, emerged from the cave of Tambo T'oco (see **Myths, Origin**). Because of this auspicious origin, the *huari taqui* was sung at this ritual and no other.

Although some chroniclers carefully wrote detailed descriptions of *taqui* celebrations, very little is known about what Inca music actually sounded like. Specifics such as types of scale, for example, are only inferred from chroniclers' descriptions of celebrations, postconquest ethnographic research, and modern studies of pitches produced on extant Inca musical instruments. The theory that the five-note (pentatonic) scale prevailed in Inca times has been debunked by recent scholars for lack of evidence; many of the ancient musical instruments, in fact, produce microtonal scales. In addition, while melodies composed of three pitches (tritonic scale) are often associated with ancient Andean rituals such as animal fertility and *marcación* (the marking of herd animals), we can also only infer that this scale has its roots in pre-Hispanic times.

What is more evident is the type of instruments employed in celebration. Inca instruments were variations of flutes and drums. String instruments were introduced by the Spaniards, or are later adaptations of Spanish prototypes. Cieza de León describes golden drums, some with semiprecious stones, which were played by women and used to accompany the singing of *mamaconas* (chosen women; See **Acllacuna**) during the 20-day feast of Hatun Raymi in celebration of the August harvest of maize, potatoes, coca, and quinoa.

Cobo wrote about *huancar*, small and large drums made of hollow logs with llama skin membranes at both ends and played with a stick by men and women. A small tambourine, *huancar tinya*, was played by women to accompany their singing.a

The Native chronicler **Felipe Guaman Poma de Ayala** depicts various instruments played during Inca times, which allows researchers today to track continuity: *pingollana* flute players playing "Inca songs"; *chasqui* runners blowing the *pututu* conch shell to announce events; deer skulls and antlers played during a **Chinchaysuyu** festival; *antara* (single-row pipes) and seed shakers attached to the ankles of a *chunchu* dancer from **Antisuyu**; and a woman playing a *tinya* and a *huancar*.

Inca flutes included bamboo cane or condor bone *pinkuyllu* and *quenaquena*, both vertical notched flutes, as well as a variety of single-row and double-row cane, ceramic, and human bone panpipes, which were played both in large ensembles and to accompany singing and dancing. Double-row pipes were most likely played in interlocking style (each row of pipes has half of the melody notes), as they are today. An *antara* (single-row pipes) made of an enemy's bones, as well as a drum made of his skin, were important instruments of the Inca king (see **Warfare**).

From approximately 1564 to 1571 the southern highlands of Peru experienced the *Taqui Oncoy* movement (disease of the song/dance). Distressed and starving spirits of the *huacas* rose to life again by possessing the Native Indians, causing them to enter into a trance that included song and dance, believing they would eventually defeat Spanish rule and Catholicism and secure the return of the Incas and the *huacas*.

Further Reading

Cieza de León, Pedro. *The Incas of Pedro de Cieza de León.* Translated by Harriet de Onis. Edited by Victor Wolfgang von Hagen. Norman: University of Oklahoma Press, 1959.

Molina, Cristóbal de. *Account of the Fables and Rites of the Incas.* Translated and edited by Brian S. Bauer, Vania Smith-Oka, and Gabriel. E. Cantarutti. Austin: University of Texas Press, 2011 [1575].

■ HOLLY WISSLER

MYTHS, ORIGIN

The Inca myths of origin that have come down to us are preserved in the Spanish chronicles, a fact that is important to bear in mind, as the chroniclers often gave their own, Catholic flavor and interpretation to the recorded events. Catherine Julien attempted an original and highly interesting critical reading of the early chronicles in an effort to interpret the form and content of these recorded myths in their original versions (and recordings in the knotted-cord *quipus*).

There are two main origin traditions: one focuses on Lake Titicaca, located on the border between present-day Peru and Bolivia; the other centers on the site of Pacariqtambo, an archaeological site (now known as Maucallacta) located some 26 kilometers southwest of Cuzco. A few origin myths combine these two sites into a hybrid story, recounting the origin of the universe and humanity at Lake Titicaca and ending with the emergence of the Inca ancestors from a cave in Pacariqtambo.

The myths set at Lake Titicaca recount first the origin of the sun, moon, and stars from the lake, at the urging of the Andean creator deity, Viracocha. After creating the universe, Viracocha set about creating humanity. This was done in five different episodes, the first four of which ended when the creator deity, displeased with some aspect

A watercolor in the chronicle of Martín de Murúa shows the founding of Cuzco by the mythical Inca ruler Manco Capac. *Los Retratos de los Incas en la Crónica de Fray Martín de Murúa* (Wellington Ms.). Edited by Eduardo Jahnsen Friedrich. Lima: COFIDE, 1985.

or the behavior of the beings he had created, destroyed them. It was only after the fifth creation that Viracocha was satisfied with his work. He then scattered the peoples he had created under the ground at the places where they would later emerge onto the earth. These ancestral peoples claimed their place of origin (e.g., a cave, or a spring or some other place) as the unique *pacarina* (place of dawn/origin) of their respective lineages. Viracocha was aided in the task of "seeding" people in their home territories by his two sons. One son passed through the sky from Lake Titicaca toward the northwest, over the coast; the other son passed through the sky to the east of the Andes toward the northwest; Viracocha himself went straight over the central Andean corridor. After completing their work, all three deities passed over the ocean, to the northwest of Puerto Viejo, on the coast of Ecuador. At Viracocha's call, the many different Andean peoples emerged from their places of origin and began to inhabit their own particular locales in the Andean world. The ancestors of the Incas, referred to in the Spanish texts as the *Hermanos Ayares* (Ayar siblings), came out of a cave called Tambo T'oco (inn of the slit/window), at Pacariqtambo (inn of dawn/origin).

It should be noted before passing on to the Pacariqtambo myths that the Incas revered Lake Titicaca as their place of origin and carried out annual pilgrimages there. These ceremonies focused principally on the **Islands of the Sun and the Moon**, located within Lake Titicaca, as well as at the site of Tiahuanaco, home of the pre-Inca Tiahuanaco culture, just southeast of the lake. Notable Inca period ruins can be seen at the Island of the Sun today. Rising near these ruins is a great rock with a split through the center, which is said to be where the sun emerged at the beginning of the universe (see **Oracles; Religion**).

The origin myth centering on Pacariqtambo not only accounts for the emergence of the Inca ancestors from the earth, but also explains the subsequent actions of the royal ancestors, culminating in their founding of what would become the capital of Tahuantinsuyu, Cuzco. As recounted in numerous chronicles, at the beginning of time (for the Inca state) the founder of the Inca Empire, Manco Capac, emerged from the cave of Tambo T'oco at Pacariqtambo along with his three brothers and four sisters, referred to as the Ayar siblings. The Inca ancestors enlisted the aid of a local people, the Tambos, and set off in search of a place where they could take up residence. They moved around the countryside and, with a golden bar, tested the soil at each place they came to looking for fertile soil. Various events occurred along the way, including an episode in which one of the brothers, Ayar Cachi, who was very unruly and troublesome, was sent back to the cave of Tambo T'oco on a ruse, to try to get rid of him. Once inside the cave, the other siblings rolled a large boulder into the mouth of the cave, trapping Ayar Cachi inside for all time.

The ancestors continued their search for a homeland, eventually coming to a high mountain, Huanacauri, overlooking the Cuzco valley. One of the brothers threw the golden bar down from the mountain of Huanacauri into the valley, and it sank into the rich soil. Knowing that this was a sign that they had found their long-sought-after home, the siblings descended from Huanacauri into the valley. At that time there was a small settlement in the valley, home of the Huallas peoples. The Incas defeated the Huallas and then set about transforming Cuzco into their capital, beginning with the founding of the **Coricancha**, the Temple of the Sun. From that time forward, Cuzco became the home of the Inca dynasty and the capital of what would later become Tahuantinsuyu.

A later myth that accounted for the transformation of the Incas from local lords to the kings of an expansive empire centered on relations between the Incas and peoples to the northwest, the Chancas. As told in the chronicle written by **Pedro Sarmiento de Gamboa**, the Chancas were a very aggressive people who continually threatened the Incas and other people in the region. At the time of what most chroniclers identify as the eighth Inca king, Viracocha Inca, the Chancas began advancing on the city of Cuzco. Viracocha was frightened by the Chanca attack and retreated to a nearby valley, leaving his son, Pachacuti, to defend the city. The Chancas then attacked Cuzco and Pachacuti and the few men and women who remained by his side fought fiercely to defend the city. It is said that the stones in the Cuzco valley, which were called *pururaucas*, transformed into warriors and came to the aid of Pachacuti. With the help of the *pururaucas*, Pachacuti and his followers ended the Chanca siege and pursued them back to their homeland.

From then on, the Incas began to expand, culminating in their domination over most of the central Andes. Inca expansion and Tahuantinsuyu itself came to an end only with the Spanish invasion. The Spanish conquest, in 1532, was the beginning of the entry of Inca mythical history, or mythohistory, into world history.

Further Reading

Bauer, B. S. "Pacariqtambo and the Mythical Origins of the Inca." *Latin American Antiquity* 2, no. 1: 7–26, 1991.

Bauer, B. S., and C. Stanish. *Ritual and Pilgrimage in the Ancient Andes: The Islands of the Sun and the Moon.* Austin: University of Texas Press, 2001.

Bouysse-Cassagne, T., and P. Bouysse. *Lluvias y cenizas: Dos pachacuti en la historia.* Biblioteca Andina, 4. La Paz: HISBOL, 1988.

Duviols, P. "Huari y llacuaz, agricultores y pastores: Un dualismo prehispánico de oposición y complementaridad." *Revista del Museo Nacional, Lima* 39:153–91, 1973.

Julien, C. J. *Reading Inca history.* Iowa City: University of Iowa Press, 2000.

Salomon, F., and J. Urioste, eds. and trans. *The Huarochirí Manuscript: A Testament of Ancient and Colonial Andean Religion.* Austin: University of Texas Press, 1991 [1598–1608].

Sarmiento de Gamboa, P. *The History of the Incas.* Translated by B. S. Bauer and V. Smith. Austin: University of Texas Press, 2007 [1572].

Urbano, H. *Wiracocha y Ayar: Héroes y funciones en las sociedades andinas.* Cuzco: Centro Bartolomé de las Casas, 1981.

Urton, G. *The History of a Myth: Pacariqtambo and the Origin of the Inkas.* Austin: University of Texas Press, 1990.

———. *Inca Myths: The Legendary Past.* Austin: University of Texas Press, 1999.

Zuidema, R. T. "Myth and History in Ancient Peru." In *The Logic of Culture,* edited by I. Rossi, 150–75. South Hadley, MA: Bergin and Garvey Publishers, 1982.

■ GARY URTON

O

ORACLES

Oracles—sanctuaries where deities, through their spokespersons, gave answers to those who consulted them—represented one of the most important and original Inca institutions. Tahuantinsuyu included myriad oracular sanctuaries. Some, such as **Titicaca**, on the Bolivian *altiplano*, and **Pachacamac**, on Peru's central coast, were the focus of pan-Andean pilgrimages. Others were of regional and interregional importance, while the majority served as local shrines. In fact, every Andean sociopolitical unit, such as an *ayllu* or an ethnic group, had its own oracle, represented by an upright stone (*huanca*) identified with the mythical founder of the group, by the mummified body (*mallqui*) of an ethnic lord's ancestor, or by a particular feature in the landscape—a rock, spring, cave, or mountain peak (*pacarina*), from whence people believed the first ancestors emerged. All these sacred entities and any object, idol, or place of worship identified with supernatural beings and powers were known as *huacas* and all of them were, at least potentially, oracles.

If it was the aural nature of the Andean religion that spurred the development of oracular practices in the Andes, it was under the Incas that this phenomenon reached its greatest development and diffusion. Indeed, the creation of large oracular centers represented one of the principal concerns of the Inca rulers. The emperor Pachacuti built the **Coricancha**, the Temple of the Sun in Cuzco. His son Topa Inca Yupanqui transformed two ancient regional sanctuaries, Titicaca and Pachacamac, into impressive oracular centers of pan-Andean renown; and his son, Huayna Capac, adopted the oracle of **Catequil** as his protective deity and spread its worship throughout northern Tahuantinsuyu.

In fact, Inca rulers did not make any decisions without first consulting the Sun god in the Coricancha. For the most important state matters, the ruler usually dealt directly with the sacred image of the Sun, *Punchao* (the day, or young Sun), a small, seated anthropomorphic figure of gold, whose hollow interior contained the ashes of the hearts of former Inca rulers. According to the chronicler **Felipe Guaman Poma de Ayala**, the Inca knelt in the middle of the temple and queried the Sun idol, who unfailingly answered him. The only other person who could communicate with the Sun god was the Willac Umu (the soothsayer who relates, who announces), the head priest of Inca religion. The Willac Umu lived in the Coricancha, assisted by a number of priests and hundreds of "chosen women" (*mamacunas*) and servants (*yanacunas*). He cared for Punchao, and served as his spokesperson. The Willac Umu appointed oracular priests throughout Tahuantinsuyu and,

Every year the images of conquered provincial *huacas* were summoned to Cuzco to foretell the future. Guaman Poma de Ayala, Felipe. *El primer nueva corónica y buen gobierno*. Edited by John V. Murra and Rolena Adorno, 235/261. Mexico City: Siglo Veintiuno, 1980 [1615].

as the Sun god's spokesperson, proclaimed who was destined to be the next ruler. The chronicler **Pedro Sarmiento de Gamboa** described how then prince Pachacuti, after defeating the Chancas (see **Myths, Origin**), asked the Sun who would be the next Inca, and the god, through the high priest, told him that he would be the new king. As a matter of fact, what the Sun god manifested in Coricancha was not just the religious support of any decision and step of some importance taken by the Inca, but it was the very origin of his legitimacy as ruler.

Next to the Coricancha, a plaza called Rimacpampa (the plaza of he who speaks) served as the setting for a solemn ceremony attended by the chief lords and the priests of the empire's major *huacas*. There, proclamations of new emperors took place and oracular pronouncements were made public.

While the Coricancha oracle was reserved only for the Inca ruler, Huanacauri (the rainbow) served as the oracle of the Inca nobility in general. Its sanctuary was located near the peak of the eponymous hill that dominates Cuzco to the southwest. Huanacauri had been the main deity of the pre-imperial Incas and remained the oracle *par excellence* of the lords of Cuzco until the arrival of the Spaniards. According to Inca tradition, it was from the mountain of Huanacauri that Manco Capac, the mythical founder, glimpsed the valley of Cuzco for the first time (see **Myths, Origin**). The apparition of a double rainbow over a mountaintop, as well as the outcome of divination rites held there, were interpreted by the Inca as signs that this was the appropriate valley where he should settle with his people and found Cuzco. Furthermore, one of Manco's brothers transformed into a *huanca* (upright stone) on the summit of Huanacauri. From that elevated spot, he maintained direct communication with the Sun, speaking with him and interceding in favor of his people, so that the god would protect them. This privileged relationship with the Sun god explains why an agricultural field near the Coricancha was devoted to the shrine of Huanacauri.

The importance of Huanacauri is underscored in a famous drawing by Guaman Poma that shows the Inca Topa Yupanqui speaking to the images of different *huacas*. Among them Huanacauri, the only one identified by name, stands out due to its dominant position. Guaman Poma's drawing illustrates the oracular *huaca* congress that took place in Cuzco at the annual festival of Capac Raymi, celebrated during the austral summer solstice, in December. It suggests that the ceremony was instituted by Topa Inca Yupanqui, the divine king who not only spoke to the *huacas*, but also had the power to make them speak when he wished.

The chronicler **Pedro de Cieza de León** noted that each year the Inca summoned the principal *huacas* to Cuzco. Entourages of priests and servants accompanied the *huacas*, which were received with considerable pomp. On the designated day, they gathered in the main plaza and as the ruler, the people of Cuzco, and the delegations looked on, each one made predictions about the coming year. In general, the *huacas* were invited to opine on whether there were to be good harvests and increase of livestock or if, on the contrary, famine or plagues would affect the people and the flocks; if the Inca would enjoy good health; if there would be peace in Tahuantinsuyu, or if there would be conflict and rebellion. The Inca priests, under the direction of the Willac Umu, asked the questions and each *huaca's* priest replied. They heard the voices of their gods as they drank abundant amounts of **chicha** (corn beer) mixed with psychotropic substances. The *huacas* "spoke" to them directly or through dreams. The Inca priests recorded each answer, and the following year assigned the sanctuaries of the *huacas* whose prophecies came true with rich gifts and endowments. The *huacas* that had given inexact or wrong predictions lost prestige, however, and their shrines received neither benefits nor privileges.

As noted, Topa Inca Yupanqui was associated above all with the great oracles of Titicaca, located on an island in the eponymous lake, across from the Copacabana peninsula, and **Pachacamac**, situated at the mouth of the Lurín River, just south of Lima. The development of Titicaca and Pachacamac as large oracular centers of pan-Andean prominence reflected the strategic plans of Topa Inca Yupanqui, who was determined to expand and consolidate the Empire. In both places, the Incas applied the same measures of forced "Incanization," which entailed the mobilization of labor and resources on an unprecedented scale, at least for religious centers outside of Cuzco. These sanctuaries also saw the implementation of analogous forms of worship, pilgrimages, human sacrifices, and offerings of valuable and prestigious goods, carried out according to the Inca ceremonial calendar, particularly during Capac Raymi, the summer solstice festival (see **Calendar, Ritual**).

Without doubt, the sanctuary of Titicaca was one of the empire's most sacred shrines, on which more resources were lavished than on any other. During the reign of Topa Inca Yupanqui, the Incas transformed a regional shrine into the destination of long-distance pilgrimages. According to Inca tradition, the Sun had appeared there for the first time, emerging from a cavity at the base of a rock, called *Titicala*, which represented the *sanctum sanctorum* of the oracle. This sacred rock, considered the dwelling place of the Sun god, was covered in fine cloth (*cumbi*) and the hollow whence it emerged was completely sheathed with gold and silver. Furthermore, the entire sanctuary, which included the nearby Island of Coati, where the Moon, wife of the Sun, was worshipped, tangibly expressed the glory and power of the Sun god, with its monumental buildings in which myriad priests, *mamacuna*, and a variety of servants lived and worked as caretakers and to welcome pilgrims.

The great majority of pilgrims who reached the island of Titicaca were not allowed to approach the rock of *Titicala*. The faithful could only see it from a gateway called Intipuncu (gateway of the Sun), located some two hundred steps from the rock, where they delivered their offerings to the priests. The chronicler Ramos Gavilán noted three successive portals. Possibly each gateway represented the limit that pilgrims could reach, according to their rank. At each doorway, Inca priests waited for the pilgrims to "confess," interrogating them about the faults that they and their communities may have committed in the observance of the Inca state religion and other obligations. Hiding any failures was considered a grave sin, leading to the most terrible punishments for them and their people by the all-powerful and omniscient Sun god.

Evidently, oracles such as Titicaca were formidable centers of information gathering. Through the ritual of confession the pilgrims told oracular priests what went on in their communities. This information, duly processed and collated with analogous testimonies and data, lent a high degree of accuracy to the oracle's predictions, above all in those of a political nature, increasing people's levels of trust in them. In turn, this trustworthiness, conditioning, and influencing the process of decision making of people and therefore their actions, increased the possibilities that oracular predictions come true.

It is likely that Titicaca's three gateways corresponded to the various patios and thresholds seen in the temple of Pachacamac (the one who animates the world), the oracle of oracles, located on the central coast of Peru, just south of Lima. There, as on Titicaca, the Incas invested enormous resources and energy in remodeling and expanding a preexisting sanctuary, known until then as Ychsma. The Incas constructed an impressive Sun temple, a complex for the *mamacunas*, an enormous plaza with an **ushnu** (platform and altar) to receive pilgrims, a palace for the Inca governor, three large perimeter walls, new access roads, and numerous other monumental structures. Thus, they transformed the shrine of Pachacamac into a magnificent sacred city visited by lords from the farthest reaches of the Inca Empire. When the Spaniards arrived, the sanctuary covered more than 50 hectares (123 acres).

According to the accounts of the first Spaniards who set foot in the sanctuary, pilgrims had to fast for several weeks before entering the lowest patio of Pachacamac's temple, and they had to wait even longer to be admitted into the highest patio, where the main priest officiated. Generally, only the most important ethnic lords could reach this final patio, querying the priest, who received them seated and with his head covered with a blanket. Afterward, other priests, called *yanac,* the "servants" of Pachacamac, took over, entering and walking backward into the chamber that housed the god's wooden idol, in order to "speak" to him. The consultations generally took place at night. In the darkness of the chamber, maintaining their backs to the idol, the *yanac* posed their questions to the god, who answered with a whistle or a hair-raising shriek.

The chronicler **Garcilaso de la Vega** wrote that the Incas removed minor deities from Pachacamac, and restricted access to the oracle to "kings and great lords." The elitist nature acquired by the oracle is reflected by the fact that burial in the area surrounding the temple was an honor reserved exclusively for the bodies of high-ranking lords and priests. People of lower status could be buried in the sanctuary of another important oracle, Rimac (he who speaks), located on the left bank of Lima's river, where the Spaniards later built the Church of Santa Ana. Coastal ethnic groups worshipped and consulted Rimac about important matters. The Incas themselves revered it; Huayna Capac, for instance, consulted it before setting off to conquer the island of Puná, in Ecuador.

Huayna Capac established a privileged relationship with the oracle of **Catequil**, an ancient deity of the northern highlands of Peru, linked to Thunder. He spread the cult of Catequil to Ecuador, where various sacred places associated with springs are located. In this way, Catequil became one of the most important oracles in Tahuantinsuyu. It was considered the most "talkative" of all the oracles, and it was believed to have the faculty to give speech to *huacas* who didn't know how to speak. On the eve of the Spaniards' arrival, the sanctuary of Catequil, located on a mountain peak in the Inca province of Huamachuco, was destroyed by the Inca Atahualpa, after the god predicted that Atahualpa would lose to his brother Huascar (see **Wars, Dynastic**). Atahualpa's extreme reaction responded to the need to silence the oracle so that its prophecy would not be repeated to the delegations of peoples from all over the empire who regularly visited the sanctuary. Such an unfavorable prediction would have led them to side with Huascar, changing the outcome of the war of succession.

Other famous Inca oracles included Apurimac, Vilcanota, and Coropuna. The sanctuary of Apurimac (the lord who speaks) was located near the eponymous river, to the southwest of Cuzco, and was under the care of a priestess of noble Cuzco blood. The oracular idol was represented by a thick wooden staff in the shape of a human figure, and placed in a small chamber decorated on the outside with polychrome paintings and inside immersed, like Pachacamac, in complete darkness. The oracle of Vilcanota (**Aymara**, house of the Sun) was located south of Cuzco at the La Raya pass, which separates Cuzco from the *altiplano* region where Lake Titicaca is located. People took this oracle's predictions as absolute truth. The Incas used to offer Vilcanota large quantities of camelids and, on occasion, human beings.

According to Cieza de León, the sanctuary of Coropuna, located near a large snow-capped volcano in the Inca province of Cuntisuyu, was always crowded with pilgrims from across Tahuantinsuyu. The empire's leading lords visited this oracle with considerable frequency, since it answered their questions year round, and not only during particular festivals, as was the case with many of the other oracles. Thanks to the high attendance of pilgrims, who left precious offerings, and to the benefits and endowments granted by the Incas, Coropuna became a primary religious center, with a number of priests, *mamacunas* and *yanacunas*, an enormous treasury, and considerable resources consisting of large flocks of camelids and rich agricultural fields. Likely, the sanctuary of Coropuna corresponds to the sprawling, 45-hectare (111-acre) settlement, located at 3,600 meters (11,811 feet) above sea level on the southern side of the mountain of Coropuna and known today as *Maucallacta* (Old Town), with more than two hundred monumental stone buildings, plazas and large ceremonial structures.

Further Reading

Bauer, Brian S., and Charles Stanish. *Ritual and Pilgrimage in the Ancient Andes: The Island of the Sun and the Moon.* Austin: University of Texas Press, 2001.

Cieza de León, Pedro de. *The Incas of Pedro de Cieza de León.* Translated by Harriet de Onís. Edited by Victor Wolfgang von Hagen. Norman: University of Oklahoma Press, 1959 [1553–1554].

Curatola Petrocchi, Marco. "¿Fueron Pachacamac y los otros grandes santuarios del mundo andino antiguo verdaderos oráculos?" *Diálogo Andino* 38:5–19, 2011.

Curatola Petrocchi, Marco, and Mariusz Ziólkowski, eds. *Adivinación y oráculos en el mundo andino antiguo.* Lima: Pontificia Universidad Católica del Perú/Instituto Francés de Estudios Andinos, 2008.

Gose, Peter. "Oracles, Divine Kingship, and Political Representation in the Inka State." *Ethnohistory* 43, no.1: 1–32, 1996.

Patterson, Thomas C. "Pachacamac—An Andean Oracle under the Inca Rule." In *Recent Studies in Andean Prehistory and Protohistory. Papers from the Second Annual Northeast Conference on Andean Archaeology and Ethnohistory*, edited by D. Peter Kvietok and Daniel H. Sandweiss, 159–76. Ithaca, NY: Cornell University Latin American Studies Program, 1985.

Topic, John R., Theresa Lange Topic, and Alfredo Melly Cava. "Catequil. The Archaeology, Ethnohistory, and Ethnography of a Major Provincial Huaca. " In *Andean Archaeology I: Variations in Sociopolitical Organization*, edited by William H. Isbell and Helaine Silverman, 303–36. New York: Kluwer Academic/Plenum Publishers, 2002.

■ MARCO CURATOLA PETROCCHI

P

PACHACAMAC

This term referred to two different, but ultimately interrelated, identities and concepts in Tahuantinsuyu: first, a pilgrimage center on the central coast of Peru, and second, a deity in the Inca pantheon.

The archaeological ruins that were the site of the great **oracle** and pilgrimage center of Pachacamac are located on the north bank of the Lurín River, whose waters flow into the Pacific Ocean. The Lurín River is the first major river valley south of the Rimac River, the location of present-day Lima. The lower Rimac and Lurín valleys formed the heartland of a pre-Inca kingdom, known as the *Señorío de Ychsma* (Kingdom of Ychsma). As the site of a powerful oracle, Pachacamac had served as a major pilgrimage center since long before the time of the Incas, and perhaps even of the Ychsma peoples themselves, going back at least to the late Middle Horizon (around AD 600–900; see **Chronology, Pre-Inca**).

The oracle of Pachacamac attracted adherents and suppliants from the coast and highlands of the central Andes. The oracle itself, a tall, elaborately sculpted wooden image, was located in a small chamber at the heart of the site. An early Spanish visitor, Miguel de Estete (see **Chronicles, Cajamarca**), described the room as "a very dark chamber with a close fetid smell. Here there was a very dirty idol made of wood and they say that this is their God who created them and sustains them." The Spaniards promptly set about destroying the idol.

The Incas were intent on controlling Pachacamac from the earliest decades of their expansion beyond the Cuzco basin. Their objective seems to have been not only to control and perhaps benefit from the great wealth of tribute brought to the oracle by pilgrims, but also to establish a place for their own deity, Inti, the Sun, adjacent to the powerful oracle and to win the hearts and minds of conquered peoples who worshipped Pachacamac. Though they built a massive Temple of the Sun at the western edge of Pachacamac, they allowed the old oracle of Pachacamac to continue to function and to receive suppliants. To accommodate the influx of pilgrims, the Incas built a so-called Plaza of the Pilgrims, a large rectangular space that may have been designed to receive the pilgrims and their caravans of camelids carrying offerings for the oracle. The Incas built other structures, including storehouses and an Acllahuasi (house of the chosen women).

As for the meaning of Pachacamac, the deity, the term is composed of two Quechua roots. The first, *pacha-*, may be glossed as "space/earth/time"; The root *camac*—the agentive form of the verb *camay*—may be glossed as "maker, organizer, or 'vivifier' (i.e., one who gives life, or organizes matter/s)." A "camac" entity is a generative force, one that gives life, and organizes matters to arrive at a productive state of affairs. The combination of these glosses, which suggests a power to shape and reshape earth and time, in the name of a deity—Pachacamac—helps us to understand why this was the identity of the great and powerful Andean earthquake deity. In one of our few indigenous sources on Native Andean religion, the *Huarochirí Manuscript* (see **Avila, Francisco de**), it was said of Pachacamac—and may also have implicated the powerful oracle that bore his name—that "When he gets angry, earth trembles / When he turns his face sideways, it quakes / Lest that happen he holds his face still / The world would end if he ever rolled over" (Avila 1991 [1598–1608]).

Therefore, one may speak of *Pachacamac* the pilgrimage center and of *Pachacamac* the oracle and earthquake deity; however, it is important to recognize that the two referents of this title inform or implicate one another, attesting to the wide-ranging significance and importance of this concept in the Andean and Inca universe.

Further Reading

Eeckhout, Peter. "Reyes del Sol y Señores de la Luna: Inkas e Ychsmas en Pachacamac." *Chungará, Revista de Antropología Chilena* 36, no. 2: 495–503, 2004.

———. "Inca Storage and Accounting Facilities at Pachacamac." *Andean Past* 10:213–39, 2012.

Patterson, Thomas C. "Pachacamac—An Andean Oracle under Inca Rule." In *Recent Studies in Andean Prehistory and Protohistory: Papers from the Second Annual Northeast Conference on Andean Archaeology and Ethnohistory*, edited by D. Peter Kvietok and Daniel H. Sandweiss, 159–76. Ithaca, NY: Cornell University Latin American Studies Program, 1983.

Rowe, John H. "The Origins of Creator Worship among the Incas." In *Culture in History*, edited by Stanley Diamond, 408–29. New York: Columbia University Press, 1960.

Salomon, Frank. "Introductory Essay: The Huarochirí Manuscript." In *The Huarochirí Manuscript: A Testament of Ancient and Colonial Andean Religion*. Translation from the Quechua by Frank Salomon and George L. Urioste, 1–38. Austin: University of Texas Press, 1991.

Shimada, Izumi. "Pachacamac Archaeology: Retrospect and Prospect." In Max Uhle, *Pachacamac: A Reprint of the 1903 Edition*. University Museum Monographs 62. Philadelphia: University Museum of Archaeology and Anthropology, University of Pennsylvania, 1991.

■ GARY URTON

PANACA

Panaca is a general term used in Inca social, political, and ritual organization primarily in Cuzco to designate royal *ayllus*, or kin groups, made up of the descendants of a deceased Inca king, with the exception of his successor. The formation of the *panaca* kin group, which functioned as a kind of corporation that maintained and managed the estate of a dead king, was grounded in a practice of Inca succession referred to as "split inheritance." According to this practice, when a king died, he was replaced by the most capable

This indigenous, probably **Aymara**-speaking Andean man, who will be referred to herein as Pachacuti Yamqui, was a native of a village southeast of Cuzco, in the region known as Orcosuyu, between the provinces of Canas and Canchis. It is not known what year he was born. He claimed to be a descendant of local nobility, and he also made clear that he and many of his family members had adopted Christianity. He is the principal author of one text, the *Relación de antigüedades deste reyno del Pirú* (The Account of Ancient Things of This Kingdom of Peru). The date is unknown but it may have been written after 1613. Pachacuti Yamqui was probably educated and received lessons in reading and writing Spanish by clergy. He accompanied at least one famous priest (**Avila**) on inquests aimed at investigating and destroying indigenous "idols" in Native communities.

In his chronicle, Pachacuti Yamqui constructed a history of the Incas, interspersed with accounts of Inca rites and ceremonies, that is outside of the norm—in tone, content, and structure—of most of the Spanish chroniclers' accounts. He is one of our only sources for songs, or hymns, which were presumably sung at the Inca's court. The *Relación* includes seven hymns, all in **Quechua** (or a Spanish-modified Quechua) as well as three drawings, each accompanied by text. These drawings have been the subject of much speculation by modern students of the Incas. Pachacuti Yamqui's motive for writing the chronicle and the significance it has for Inca studies have been interpreted from two very different perspectives.

One interpretation seeks to read the chronicle, with its hymns and drawings, as an account that offers deep insight into Inca symbolism, cosmology, and history writing that, while deflected through an indigenous (thus foreign to Westerners) mentality, is a critical, firsthand look at Inca cosmology and the indigenous, Andean mode of making meaning. Thus, a drawing, presented by Pachacuti Yamqui, that shows imagery evoking the sun, moon, stars, humans, rainbows, and so forth, is interpreted by this school as explaining everything from the Inca view of the cosmos, to the structure of Inca kinship and marriage.

The other interpretation focuses on Pachacuti Yamqui's commitment to the Christian God and his attempts to show that the Incas had a tumultuous, back-and-forth history of adoring many gods under some kings, and recognizing monotheism under others. According to this view, Pachacuti Yamqui depicted objects as idolatrous images that some (his favored) Incas had overcome, or rejected, in favor of a single Andean deity. Pachacuti Yamqui named this deity Viracocha Pachayachachic. This school of interpretation argues that Pachacuti Yamqui promoted the view that the monotheism focusing on Viracocha Pachayachachic both foretold and paved the way for the Christian God in the Andes.

Both these interpretive traditions are valuable. That is, while a rejection of pre-Christian deities, rituals, and symbols may have been Pachacuti Yamqui's own motive in producing both his text and his drawings, he nonetheless provides us with such information from the perspective of an early-seventeenth-century Aymara speaker of the Cuzco region; that perspective is valuable for approaching an interpretation of Inca realities of an earlier time.

Further Reading

Duviols, Pierre. "Pachacuti Yamqui Salcamaygua, Joan de Santa Cruz (seventeenth century)." In *Guide to Documentary Sources for Andean Studies, 1530–1900*, edited by Joanne Pillsbury, vol. 3, 488–96. Norman: University of Oklahoma Press, 2008.

Harrison, Regina. "Modes of Discourse: The *Relación de antigüedades deste reyno del Pirú* by Joan de Santacruz Pachacuti Yamqui Salcamaygua." In *From Oral to Written Expression: Native Andean Chronicles of the Early Colonial Period*, edited by Rolena Adorno, 65–99. Foreign and Comparative Studies, Latin American Series, no. 4. Syracuse, NY: Maxwell School of Citizenship and Public Affairs, Syracuse University, 1982.

Itier, César. "Las oraciones en quechua de la *Relación* de Joan de Santa Cruz Pachacuti Yamqui Salcamaygua." *Revista Andina* (Cuzco) 12:555–80, 1988.

Pachacuti Yamqui Salcamaygua, Joan de Santa Cruz. "An Account of the Antiquities of Peru" (English translation). Internet Sacred Text Archive. http://www.sacred-texts.com/nam/inca/rly/rly2.htm.

Pease, Franklin. "El mestizaje religioso de Santa Cruz Pachacuti." *Revista Histórica* (Lima) 28: 125–31, 1965.

■ GARY URTON

among his sons by one of his several wives. The naming of a successor was an intensely politicized affair, with contests among the dead king's kinfolk, wives, and their children. The successor to the Inca ruler assumed the throne, but he did not inherit the property or wealth acquired by the king during his life; rather, the king's estate was inherited by another of his sons along with his descendants, with the exception of his successor-son. That is, one son inherited the kingship; another son became the head of a corporate-like body that inherited the king's wealth. In short, the two resources that made up a king's inheritance: (1) kingly power, authority, and the presumption of divine descent from the Sun, and (2) the king's earthly resources and wealth—were split between two of his descendants upon his death.

At the time of the European invasion, the social, political, and ritual organization of the capital, **Cuzco**, was structured around 10 *panacas* (i.e., royal *ayllus*) and 10 nonroyal *ayllus*. The former are generally referred to by the chroniclers as *panacas* (although in a few cases they are, confusingly, referred to as *ayllus*, while the latter are only referred to as *ayllus*). The members of each *panaca* resided in the king's old residence within the city and managed not only that property, but also any other estates outside the city built and maintained by the sovereign before his death. Each *panaca* was also associated with a particular **ceque** of Cuzco's *ceque* system, and the members of the *panaca* were responsible for making sacrifices at the several **huacas** that defined that *ceque*. Each of the 10 nonroyal *ayllus* were also responsible for a *ceque* and its constituent *huacas*. These links between royal and nonroyal kin groups (respectively, *panacas* and *ayllus*) and their relations to each other

PEASE, FRANKLIN

Born in Lima in 1939, Franklin Pease was a Peruvian historian who specialized in the study of Andean Peru, with special emphasis on the world of the Inca. His initial studies, which focused on the final years of Tahuantinsuyu, the Inca Empire, were groundbreaking as they helped scholars to envision Tahuantinsuyu as an ancient Andean society immersed in myth and religion—that is, on its own terms, and not as a somewhat secular society that would have easily fit in the mold of early modern Europe.

The study of the conflicting claims presented in the chronicles—the accounts written by the Spaniards in the sixteenth and seventeenth centuries—as well as their silences made Pease realize that these accounts were based on myths recounted by Native informants from Cuzco. To counteract the Cuzco bias of the sources, Pease turned to Colonial administrative documents and studied the relationship between the imperial center and local polities and populations. Furthermore, although the chronicles were usually considered independent accounts, it was obvious that many authors had borrowed freely from each other. Pease therefore turned to the study of Colonial sources and sought to publish critical editions (an ongoing effort cut short by his untimely death in 1999) in order to determine their originality, as well as to establish the chronology of the image the Spaniards gradually developed of the Incas, and to determine the European influences that shaped their accounts.

Further Reading

Pease, Franklin. *Los últimos Incas del Cuzco*. Lima: P. L. Villanueva, 1972.
———. *Del Tahuantinsuyu a la historia del Perú*. Lima: Instituto de Estudios Peruanos, 1978.
———. *Las crónicas y los Andes*. Rev. ed. Lima: Fondo de Cultura Económica, 2010.

■ JAVIER FLORES ESPINOZA

and to the living Inca lay at the heart of the core structures and relations that made up the social, political, and ritual organization of the capital, Cuzco, in the time of Tahuantinsuyu.

Further Reading

D'Altroy, Terence N. *The Incas*. 2nd ed. Chichester, UK: John Wiley & Sons, 2014.
Pärssinen, Martti. *Tawantinsuyu: The Inca State and Its Political Organization*. Studia Historica 43. Helsinki: Finnish Historical Society, 1992.
Rowe, John H. "La constitución inca del Cuzco." *Histórica* 9, no. 1: 35–73, 1985.
Zuidema, R. Tom. *The Ceque System of Cuzco: The Social Organization of the Capital of the Inca*. Leiden, Netherlands: E. J. Brill, 1964.

■ GARY URTON

Born around 1513 in Toledo, Spain, Pedro Pizarro is often regarded as the *conquistador* Francisco Pizarro's cousin, but although the two families were apparently closely related, their exact relationship is not clear. Pedro Pizarro joined Francisco Pizarro's expedition as a young page. He was an eyewitness to the lead-up to the tumultuous events in Cajamarca, and the subsequent march by Francisco and his troops from Cajamarca to Cuzco and the Spaniards' entry into Cuzco. He wrote a vivid account of the pillaging by the Spaniards of the treasures in Cuzco and of the subsequent siege of Cuzco by Manco Inca, in 1536.

Pedro Pizarro was awarded several *encomiendas* (a grant of Native labor and tribute) in Cuzco, Tacna, and Arequipa by Francisco Pizarro. Pedro died, however, an impoverished man in Arequipa, in 1587, as the income from his *encomiendas* dwindled because the number of available Native laborers had decreased drastically. Although his chronicle, the *Relación de los descubrimientos y conquista de los reinos del Peru* (Account of the Discovery and Conquest of the Kingdoms of Peru) is narrated as an eyewitness account, it was in fact written decades after the events unfolded. The manuscript was completed in 1571 and dispatched to Spain to be presented to Philip II. Like his fellow soldier and eyewitness Diego de Trujillo, Pizarro may have been commissioned to write his account by Francisco de Toledo, fifth Viceroy of Peru (1569–1581), who urged the aging conquistadors to write their memoirs.

Pizarro's account is critical to our understanding of the behavior and stature of Atahualpa, one claimant to the throne at the time of the Spanish invasion, and of the deference with which Inca royalty were treated by their attendants. He notes the obsequiousness of Atahualpa's retainers, the food he ate and the manner in which his retainers served him, and the clothing he wore (most notably a cloak made of bat skins). Pizarro remarked that everything that had been touched by Atahualpa, including his clothing, which was only worn once, was discarded and burned. His description of the rituals in Cuzco's main plaza, especially the procession of the royal mummies and the food and drink they were served by their retainers, was copied by many chroniclers, particularly **Bernabé Cobo**. Pizarro also marveled at Cuzco's storehouses and the feather cloth he saw—passages also subsequently plagiarized by Cobo.

But most astute of all is Pedro Pizarro's acknowledgment that if the Spaniards had not found Tahuantinsuyu embroiled in a bloody civil war, Francisco Pizarro and his men would not have succeeded in toppling Tahuantinsuyu, unless "over a thousand Spaniards had come simultaneously" (Pizarro 1921 [1571]).

Further Reading

Pizarro, Pedro. "Relation of the Discovery and Conquest of the Kingdoms of Peru." Translated and annotated by Philip Ainsworth Means. 1921 [1571]. https://archive.org/stream/relation ofdiscov00pizauoft/relationofdiscov00pizauoft_djvu.txt.

Varón Gabai, Rafael. "Pedro Pizarro (ca. 1513–1587)." In *Guide to Documentary Sources for Andean Studies, 1530–1900*, edited by Joanne Pillsbury, vol. 3, 524–28. Norman: University of Oklahoma Press, 2008.

■ ADRIANA VON HAGEN

PLANNING, SETTLEMENT

As Tahuantinsuyu expanded, the Incas launched a massive construction program, building works of infrastructure as well as new settlements. The new infrastructure included an extensive **road** network, innumerable agricultural **terraces**, and wide-ranging **irrigation** systems. The Incas spanned canyons and rivers with ingenious suspension **bridges**, a technology hitherto unknown to the Europeans. In conjunction with works of infrastructure, the Inca built fortresses, *tambos* (way stations), administrative centers, **royal estates**, and religious sanctuaries. At *tambos* and administrative centers, in particular, they built large **storage** facilities holding a variety of goods from food, to clothing, and weaponry, among other things, that provided for the needs of the traveling Inca ruler and his entourage, the army on the move, the state religion, and the local population.

Several Spanish chronicles suggest that Inca planners made clay models to visualize their concept of new settlements. In developing their concepts the Incas took into account a number of factors: location, function, terrain, landscape, and orientation, among others. Most settlements were strategically located along an Inca road. Many were built on vacant land; in other cases the Inca adopted and transformed existing settlements. Way stations were typically spaced about a day's travel apart; administrative centers appear to have been placed near concentrations of local ethnic groups; most royal estates were focused on the Cuzco heartland; sanctuaries, devoted almost exclusively to religious activities, were state installations at recognized Andean holy places.

A settlement could serve more than one function. For example, an administrative center could also be a *tambo*, a sanctuary, or even a stronghold, determining its size and organization. Some settlements were built on relatively flat land, while others, on very rugged terrain. The latter often required extensive remodeling of the terrain with ter-

The so-called "Intihuatana sector" at Pisac above the Urubamba River features finely fitted masonry. The stone outcrop surrounded by a semicircular wall (center, right) may have served as a Sun temple. Adriana von Hagen.

racing to accommodate the buildings. (**Machu Picchu** is an excellent example of this.) The surrounding landscape played an important role in the layout and orientation of a settlement. To the Incas, Mother Earth, Pachamama, was sacred, thus at many sites one finds the integration of views of distant mountain peaks, waterfalls, and other natural features, as well as the incorporation within the settlement of rock outcrops and other *huacas*, or sacred objects.

As a result, the settlements are so diverse in their physical layout, or plan, that no obvious pattern emerges. As archaeologist John Hyslop noted, "No two Inka state settlements are identical. There were no universal principles followed in . . . planning the layout of major Inka settlements" (Hyslop 1990). Architects Graziano Gasparini and Luise Margolies, in their study of Inca architecture, suggested that similarities between site plans should not be searched for in the physical form, but instead "in the meaning and the functions of the form." They argued that, if one disregards physical form, one will note that certain elements are "repeated with considerable insistence" (Gasparini and Margolies 1980). What these elements are is derived from early accounts of **Cuzco**, the center of the Inca Empire, by Spanish chroniclers and from archaeological research at Cuzco and other Inca settlements.

The core of Cuzco occupied a low ridge between two rivers, the Huatanay to the southwest and Tullumayo to the northeast. To the northwest, on a hillside above the city and dominating it, is the formidable complex known as **Sacsahuaman**. A number of distinct residential districts surrounded the settlement. The streets in the core are straight and cross at right angles, yet the street pattern was designed to adapt to the topography. As a consequence the street blocks vary in size and shape. Religious and residential

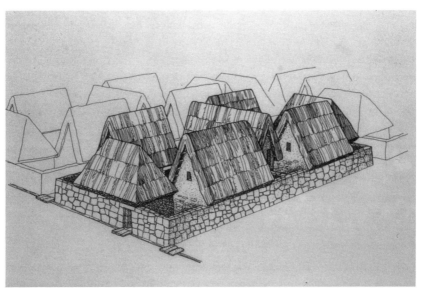

A typical *cancha* layout composed of four buildings surrounding a central courtyard. The house in the center had a common wall, but the two *canchas* were not connected. Drawing by Robert Batson, courtesy Jean-Pierre Protzen.

compounds, *cancha,* occupied the blocks. A *cancha* consists of three or more single-room, rectangular buildings arranged more or less symmetrically around an open court and is often surrounded by a wall with only a single entryway.

The center of urban Cuzco was a *plaza* divided into two parts by the Huatanay River with the eastern part called Aucaypata and the western one Cusipata. Aucaypata was the place for religious ceremonies and rituals, initiation rites, ancestor worship, and other festivities. An important element in Aucaypata was the **ushnu**, a sugarloaf-shaped stone set in a basin with a drain atop a small bench onto which offerings were made. To the northwest and southeast the Aucaypata was bordered by *canchas* identified as royal palaces. Also facing the plaza was at least one great rectangular hall with many doorways on its long side, today commonly called a *callanca*. *Callancas* served primarily public functions, where celebrants took refuge on rainy days. Near the southeastern corner of Aucaypata was another compound, the Acllahuasi, or the house of the chosen women, whose job (among others) was to brew maize beer, or **chicha**, and weave fine cloth. Among the city's religious compounds the most prestigious one was the **Coricancha**, the Temple of the Sun, the center of Inca state religion. Distributed throughout Cuzco and its surroundings were a great number of holy places, **huacas***,* arranged along imaginary lines, **ceques***,* radiating out from the Coricancha. Another imaginary line at the Coricancha divided the settlement into *hanan* (upper) and *hurin* (lower) Cuzco. This division was a social one and the concept of **duality** has ancient Andean roots. Additional elements are extensive waterworks, both utilitarian and sacred (fountains and baths), terraces for gardens and agriculture, and storehouses.

The *cancha* is the single most distinguishable element at almost every type of Inca settlement, small or large, outside of Cuzco. Another recurrent feature at administrative centers and many way stations in the provinces is a major plaza with an *ushnu. Ushnus* at some of these settlements differ dramatically from the one at Cuzco. The sugar-loaf stone, its basin and drains were placed atop impressive platforms, which, in addition to their ceremonial and ritual functions, also served as thrones and reviewing stands from which the Inca lord interacted with the conquered population. Intriguingly, there are no *ushnu* platforms at royal estates in the Cuzco heartland. Some of these estates, however, feature elaborate complexes with a carved living rock, called *intihuatana*, which some researchers believe were just another form of *ushnu*. More likely, *intihuatana* played an astronomical role in determining specific dates for ceremonies, planting and harvest seasons, and other events.

Discernible at many way stations, administrative centers, and military settlements are the *callancas* facing the main plaza. There they served not only for festivities, but also as temporary accommodations. Administrative centers were said to have included a palace, an *acllahuasi*, and a Temple of the Sun. Without specific historic or archeological data, it is difficult to know whether a *cancha* is a palace, a residence, or an administrative or religious compound, since they hardly differ in design. The few positively identified *acllahuasi*, on the other hand, are so dramatically different from each other that they provide even fewer clues for the identification of other such structures.

Extensive storage facilities were primarily associated with administrative centers, although storehouses existed at many other settlement types. Integral to many settlements are terraces, both for agricultural production and for the support of buildings, as well as

Tambo Colorado in Peru's Pisco valley is one of the best preserved Inca coastal
settlements. Built of adobe, its walls still retain traces of red, yellow, and white
paint. A low *ushnu*, or ceremonial platform, graces the western end of the plaza.
Jean-Pierre Protzen.

waterworks for utilitarian and ceremonial purposes. The construction of terraces often
required massive movement of earth. Yet, gigantic as these transformations were, the
terraces did not destroy the landscape but rather accentuated the topography. The most
elegant terraces and most elaborate waterworks dedicated to the cult of water are found
at royal estates in the Cuzco heartland.

Although the *hanan/hurin* division most likely was applied to most, if not all, settlements, its identification remains speculative; there are no architectural features defining
it. Equally speculative is the existence of *ceque* systems at sites outside of Cuzco. Specific
astronomical alignments of buildings and other elements, on the other hand, have been
demonstrated to exist at many sites.

Inca settlement planning played a strategic role in the expansion and governance of
the Inca Empire. It allowed Cuzco to keep in contact with far away settlements, facilitated
the swift movement and provision of the armies, the political integration and control of
local populations, and supported the economy of the state. The settlements were a symbol
and reminder of the power of the Inca.

Further Reading

Agurto Calvo, Santiago. *Estudios acerca de la construcción, arquitectura, y planeamiento inca*. Lima: Camera
    Peruana de la Construcción, 1987.
Canziani Amico, José. *Ciudad y territorio en los Andes: Contribuciónes a la história del urbanismo prehispánico*.
    Lima: Fondo editorial, Pontífica Unviersidad Católica del Perú, 2009.
Gasparini, Graziano, and Luise Margolies. *Inca Architecture*. Translated by Patricia Lyon. Bloomington:
    Indiana University Press, 1980.

Hardoy, Jorge E. *Ciudades Precolombinas*. Buenos Aires: Ediciones Infinito, 1964.

Hyslop, John. *Inka Settlement Planning*. Austin: University of Texas Press, 1990.

Morris, Craig. "State Settlement in Tawantinsuyu: A Strategy of Compulsory Urbanism." In *Contemporary Archaeology*, edited by M. P. Leone, 393–401. Carbondale: Southern Illinois University Press, 1972.

von Hagen, Adriana, and Craig Morris. *The Cities of the Ancient Andes*. London: Thames and Hudson, 1998.

■ JEAN-PIERRE PROTZEN

PUQUINA

Puquina is a language that has been extinct since around the second half of the nineteenth century, and is known only from a handful of pastoral materials compiled in the late sixteenth century by the Franciscan Jerónimo de Oré and published in 1607. As with **Quechua** and **Aymara**, the name of the language was coined by the Spaniards, based on the name of the ethnic group who spoke it, and could be formally reconstructed as *puqi-na*, although the meaning, apart from the ethnic group, remains obscure.

The scant available documentation indicates that it was an agglutinative language, in which words were created by adding suffixes. For a long time, it was confused with the Uru language of the islands of Lake Titicaca and Lake Coipasa. But thanks to new information about the Uru language, which survives in the Bolivian *altiplano*, they are now recognized as different. Some grammatical elements of the language, particularly possessives, are formed using quasi-prefixes in a system reminiscent of the Arawak languages (as described by Raoul de la Grasserie in 1894), leading some experts to suggest that they are related, although that is difficult to prove because of the lack of available materials.

According to Colonial documents, and based on place-name evidence that has come to light in recent years, it appears that the language was spoken over a wide area that centered on the region around Lake Titicaca and extended northward to what are now the provinces of Canas and Canchis in the department of Cuzco, Peru; westward over the western slope of the Andes to the Pacific coast, from Cailloma, in the Peruvian department of Arequipa, to Tarapacá in Chile; and eastward across the piedmont of the eastern mountains in what are now the provinces of Carabaya and Sandia in the Peruvian department of Puno, and in Bolivia to northwestern La Paz and the regions of Cochabamba and Sucre, reaching Potosí in the south. Such vast coverage, still apparent in the sixteenth century (although somewhat fragmented) led the Colonial authorities to declare it one of the "general languages" of Colonial Peru, along with Quechua and Aymara. Nevertheless, Colonial sources indicate that by the time the Spaniards arrived, the highly fragmented language was already being replaced by Aymara and Quechua. That could at least partly explain why the Spanish evangelizers never wrote grammars or vocabularies for the language.

Unlike the Quechua and Aymara people, Puquina speakers have essentially been erased from Colonial historical accounts. Although some sources refer to Collas and Puquinas as related ethnic groups, most eventually reflected the idea that the Collas should be understood to be Aymara speakers. The Incas might have been responsible for that confusion, because after the bloody battle with the Colla chief in his stronghold of

Born in Valladolid, Spain, about 1520 and arriving in Peru in 1544, Polo Ondegardo was a noted jurist, viceregal functionary, owner of a grant of *encomienda* (protector of Natives with rights to collect tribute from them), as well as a prodigious producer of legal, historical, and cultural documents. Polo Ondegardo spent years in Lima, Cuzco, and Charcas (in central Bolivia, near the mining town of Potosí) from the mid-1540s until his death, in 1575. He knew a great deal about the Andean world during the period beginning a decade after the Spanish conquest, particularly as he was commissioned to carry out inquests on a variety of matters—including *encomienda* rights, mining, Inca mummies, and the **ceques** of Cuzco—for Peruvian viceroys beginning with La Gasca, in the late 1540s, to Toledo, in the 1570s.

While Polo Ondegardo produced copious documents on administrative and historical matters, few of them actually contain his signature, or were issued under his name. He appears to have been a major source of information for contemporary chroniclers and for those who followed the administration of Viceroy Toledo (1569–1581). Most notably, Polo Ondegardo studied the ritual organization of Inca Cuzco by means of the *ceques*, and he appears to have been the author of a "chart of the *ceques*," which has never been found but which is thought to have been the source for the chronicler **Bernabé Cobo**'s detailed description of that system.

Polo Ondegardo's most informative work relevant to the study of the Incas was his *Errores y supersticiones de los indios* (Errors and Superstitions of the Indians), which was completed in 1559 and was included in the documents published by the Third Lima Provincial Church Council, of 1583. Polo Ondegardo was in Cuzco assisting Viceroy Toledo and his historian, **Pedro Sarmiento de Gamboa**, in their investigation of the Inca past; some of the information he gathered, such as that on Inca mummies, was incorporated in Sarmiento's *Historia Indica* (History of the Incas), completed in 1572.

Further Reading

Polo Ondegardo, Juan. "Report by Polo de Ondegardo." In *Narratives of the Rites and Laws of the Yncas*, translated and edited by Clements R. Markham, 149–71. Works issued by the Hakluyt Society, no. 48. London: Hakluyt Society, 1873. New York: Burt Franklin, 1963, 1964, and 1969.

———. *El Orden del Inca: Las contribuciones, distribuciones y la utilidad de guardar dicho orden (s. XVI)*. Edited by Andrés Chirinos and Martha Zegarra. Lima: Editorial Commentarios, 2013.

Presta, Ana María, and Catherine Julien. "Polo Ondegardo (ca. 1520–1575)." In *Guide to Documentary Sources for Andean Studies, 1530–1900*, edited by Joanne Pillsbury, vol. 3, 529–35. Norman: University of Oklahoma Press, 2008.

■ GARY URTON

Hatuncolla, they used that landmark event to give the name **Collasuyu** to the region around that capital, which was populated by Aymara chiefdoms. As the Puquina language gave way to Aymara, the Colla ethnic group became equated with the Aymara language, consigning the Puquina-Colla peoples to oblivion, as recent ethnohistorical research has indicated.

Regarding the historical and sociocultural context, once Aymara was ruled out as the language of Tiahuanaco, Puquina remained as the possible language of that civilization, based on the geographic coverage indicated in the documents that exist and on onomastic research, which supports that hypothesis. The traditional idea that *altiplano* place names derived mostly from Aymara, therefore, is not supported, as recent onomastic investigation shows that place names that can be attributed to Puquina coincide almost perfectly with the territory that archaeologists postulate for Tiahuanaco.

If the hypothesis that Puquina was the language of Tiahuanaco is accepted, then it follows that the "particular language" of the Incas, which Colonial sources say was different from Aymara and Quechua, could have been a form of Puquina spoken by descendants of the *altiplano* migrants who, after the collapse of the Tiahuanaco civilization, moved toward Cuzco in search of better land. Linguistic, documentary, and archaeological evidence in recent years appears to support that hypothesis. It would not be surprising, therefore, if much of the cultural and institutional vocabulary of the Inca Empire, incorporated into Quechua and/or Aymara, could only be explained by Puquina etymology. This would indicate that the primordial language of the ancestors of the mythical Incas could have been Puquina, a minority language replaced, by the second or third generation, by Aymara, which was the predominant language at the time in the Cuzco valley.

Further Reading

Adelaar, Willem, with Pieter Muysken. "Puquina and Callahuaya." In *The Languages of the Andes*, edited by Willem Adelaar with Pieter Muysken, 350–62. Cambridge: Cambridge University Press, 2004.

Bouysse-Cassagne, Thérèse. "Apuntes para la historia de los puquina hablantes." In *Boletín de Arqueología PUCP* no. 14: 283–307, 2011.

Cerrón-Palomino, Rodolfo. "Unravelling the Enigma of the 'Particular Language' of the Incas." In *Archaeology and Language in the Andes*, edited by Paul Heggarty and David Beresford-Jones, 265–94. Cambridge: Oxford University Press, 2012.

Domínguez, Nicanor. "Para una cartografía de la lengua puquina en el altiplano colonial (1548–1610)." *Boletín de Arqueología PUCP* 14:309–28, 2011.

Torero, Alfredo. "Puquina." In *Idiomas de los Andes. Lingüística e historia*, by Alfredo Torero, 389–456. Lima: Editorial Horizonte e IFEA, 2002.

■ RODOLFO CERRÓN-PALOMINO
(TRANSLATED BY BARBARA FRASER)

Q

QUARRYING AND STONECUTTING

Although the majority of Inca structures are built of uncut stone assembled with clay mortar, of adobe brick, or both, the architectural style is still best known for its tightly fitting cut stone masonry assembled without mortar. This masonry style has been marveled at ever since the Spanish conquerors first saw it. One eyewitness, for example, said, "And what one admires most is that, even though these [stones] . . . are not cut straight, but differ in size and shape, they fit together with incredible precision without mortar" (Acosta 1962 [1590]).

How Inca builders—who lacked iron tools and the wheel—cut stone, achieved the tight fit, and transported and hoisted the stones (some of which weigh over a hundred metric tons) has been the subject of wild speculation. These conjectures range from the intervention of extraterrestrials to the use of laser-like tools—and even the application of

This abandoned stone in a field was destined for the Inca settlement of Ollantaytambo in the Urubamba valley and came from the rockfalls of Kachiqata, 5 kilometers (3 miles) distant on the opposite bank of the river. Adriana von Hagen.

stone-softening herbs. More down-to-earth answers to these questions are now emerging from recent research.

To obtain their stone, the Incas either picked suitable blocks out of a rockfall or broke them off a fractured rock face. An example of the first is the quarry of Kachiqhata, the source of the reddish rhyolite for some of the structures on the Temple Hill at Ollantay-tambo (see **Estates, Royal**); an example of the second is the quarry of Rumicollca, the source of much of the andesite used in the construction of Cuzco. The Incas used and quarried other varieties of stones, for example, granite at **Machu Picchu,** and limestone and diorite near Cuzco.

At Kachiqhata, high up on a mountainside about 5 kilometers (3.1 miles) from Ollan-taytambo, the selected blocks, most of which weigh from 40 to over 100 metric tons (44 to over 110 short tons), were roughly trimmed and shaped before they were sent to the construction site. At Rumicollca, some 35 kilometers (22 miles) south of Cuzco, even the densest and best bedrock is fissured enough so that blocks can easily be broken out of the rock face. To break out the stone, quarry workers may have used copper or bronze pry bars such as those exhibited in various museums in Peru or they may have used wooden or metal wedges. The stones quarried at Rumicollca are much smaller than those at Kachiqhata; they weigh 50–600 kilograms (110.2–1,323 pounds). Unlike the Kachiqhata stones, the ones at Rumicollca have been nearly finished in the quarry.

Several authors suggest that the Incas may have broken up big stones or detached them from bedrock by cutting grooves along a desired fracture line. They worked oblong holes into these and inserted wooden wedges. The evidence for this technique at the quarries is rather scant, however, and by no means conclusive.

Detail of stone wall at the coastal site of Paredones in the Nazca valley on Peru's south coast is a rare example of finely fitted stonework at a coastal settlement. Adriana von Hagen.

Detail of a finely fitted stone wall at Hatunrumiyoc in Cuzco reveals the pit marks left by stone hammers. The smaller, finer pit marks along the edges of the building blocks show that smaller hammer stones were used to cut the edges.
Jean-Pierre Protzen

To rough out, cut, and dress stone, the Incas used simple river cobbles as hammers. These tools and their fragments are found in abundance in the ancient quarries scattered among roughed-out building blocks and in the quarrying waste. The hammerstones are easily distinguished from other stones by both their shape and their petrological characteristics; they are rounded stones of materials significantly different from the quarried stone and the surrounding bedrock. The hammers come in many sizes: some are as small as an egg and weigh under 500 grams (17.6 ounces); others, the size of a football or larger, weighing up to 8 kilograms (17.6 pounds) or more.

Stone masons used the largest of these hammerstones to break up and roughly shape the raw stone, while the medium-sized ones served for dressing the faces of the building blocks, and the smallest ones, for drafting and cutting their edges and corners. The technique involved is exactly as the chronicler **Garcilaso de la Vega** described it: "Stonemasons similarly worked their stone with some black pebbles called hihuana [*sic* for hihuaya], with which they pounded rather than cut" (Garcilaso 1966 [1609]).

When hitting the workpiece straight on with a hammerstone, the rock is crushed, producing little more than dust. But if the angle of impact is increased to about 15–20 degrees, little chips flake off. By further increasing the angle to some 45 degrees by imparting a twist to the hammer just before impact, even larger chips can be removed, accelerating the process considerably. The impact of the hammer leaves a small pit mark on the workpiece. Such pit marks can be observed on every face of every building block in every Inca wall of cut stone, regardless of the building blocks' material. Smaller, finer pit marks found along the edges of the building blocks indicate that smaller stones were used to cut the edges. This particular edge-cutting technique requires that the edge be

Detail of a terrace wall at Tarahuasi, west of Cuzco, composed of stones fitted in the polygonal style. Adriana von Hagen.

shaped by hitting the workpiece with grazing blows directed away from the workpiece, resulting in corners with dihedral angles larger than 90 degrees. It is these obtuse angles that account for the characteristic beveled joints of Inca cut stonemasonry.

Extensive experiments have demonstrated that the process is effective and precise, and not as time consuming as one might assume. Twenty quarry workers laboring side by side could rough out a block 4.5 meters long, 3.2 meters wide, and 1.7 meters high—the dimensions of one of the largest building blocks in the ancient Inca quarry of Kachiqhata—in fewer than 15 days. Smaller blocks, like those at Rumicollca, can be shaped in about two hours.

The most intriguing question about Inca cut stonemasonry concerns the precision fitting of the blocks. It has been repeatedly argued that Inca stonemasons ground the blocks into place using a mixture of sand and water. The evidence, however, does not support this hypothesis. Where walls have been dismantled or fallen apart one finds the exact imprint of the stones that have been removed or fallen off. The shape of an imprint determines a unique position for the stone that it once accommodated. To grind in a stone, however, requires that the stone can move freely along a path in at least one direction. Thus, the ground stone would fit in any, and not just one, position along that path. Furthermore, if the stones had been ground into place, the joints should show signs of abrasion, but they do not. Instead one finds the typical pit-marks, which result from pounding.

Unfinished walls reveal that Inca stonemasons left the top face of every new course uncut until it was ready to receive the next course. First, masons cut the bottom and lateral faces of the block of the new course. A matching bedding joint to receive the already cut block was then carved out of the top of the course already in place. A similar approach was used for the rising joints; it is the side of the block already *in situ* that was carved to

A dismantled wall at Ollantaytambo shows the exact imprint of the stones that have been removed or fallen off. The imprint determines the unique shape and position of the stone that once occupied it. Jean-Pierre Protzen

match the precut shape of its new neighbor. The technique is one of trial and error. By trying the fit time and again the masons obtained a perfect match.

The trial and error technique is perhaps not very convincing if one considers megalithic building blocks weighing several dozen tons. Nevertheless, it works and does not postulate the use of tools and machinery of which no traces have been found. The Incas had plenty of time and manpower at hand. Since they moved huge blocks over many kilometers, it is not inconceivable that they were capable of setting up a stone several times to achieve the desired fit.

It is, of course, also conceivable that the Inca stonemasons knew of another technique to transfer the shape of one stone to another without actually trying it in successive steps. Architect Vincent Lee has in fact proposed such a technique. Inspired by log cabin builders, Lee suggests that the shape of one stone was scribed onto the other with an ingenious but simple device consisting of a stick and a plumb bob. Although experiments have shown the technique to work, there is as yet no evidence that the Incas actually used it.

The Incas often had several construction crews working simultaneously and side-by-side on the same wall. Where two crews met in a course, the final gap was closed with a "wedge" stone introduced into the masonry bond from the front of the wall. Wedge stones fit to their neighbors only along a very narrow band near the face of the wall and slightly overlap the neighboring stones. Once one knows what to look for, it is relatively easy to spot wedge stones in an Inca cut-stone wall and to determine the construction sequences.

How did the Incas transport and heave enormous building stones? Evoking bas-reliefs discovered at Nineveh in Iraq and el-Bersheh in Egypt that depict people hauling colossal statues, some have suggested that the Incas may have moved their big stones on rollers, on sleds, or with both. The Near Eastern bas-reliefs show large numbers of people pulling the statues with ropes attached to the statues or to the sled.

Excavations under abandoned blocks near Ollantaytambo failed to prove the use of either rollers or sleds; they suggest, rather, that the blocks were dragged on a pre-pared roadbed. Such roadbeds can still be observed all the way from the quarries of Kachiqhata to Ollantaytambo's Temple Hill. Rough abrasion marks found on many rhyolite building blocks at Ollantaytambo confirm that the stones were dragged along the ground. From these marks it is even possible to determine the direction in which the blocks traveled. The dragging of big stones is consistent with chroniclers' reports, such as this one by Pedro Gutiérrez de Santa Clara: "These Indians used to move very large stones with muscle power, pulling them with many long ropes of lianas and leaf fibers . . . and they [the stones] are so big that fifteen yokes of oxen could not pull them" (Gutiérrez de Santa Clara 1904–1929 [1603]). Indeed, a modern experiment at Ollantaytambo showed that a crew of 180 people could drag a block of some 10 metric tons (11 short tons) with relative ease.

To hoist big blocks up onto a wall under construction the Incas built ramps perpen-dicular to the wall, raising the ramps as the wall grew higher. Such a ramp, leaning against an unfinished burial tower, can still be seen today at Sillustani near Lake Titicaca. This technique is further confirmed by the Jesuit priest and chronicler **Bernabé Cobo**, who observed this in Cuzco:

> And since they had no cranes, wheels, or apparatus for lifting them, they made a ramp of earth next to the construction site, and they rolled the stones up the ramp. As the structure went up higher, they kept building up the ramp to the same height. I saw this method used for the Cathedral of Cuzco which is under construction. Since the laborers who work on this job are Indians, the Spanish masons and architects let them use their own methods of doing the work. (Cobo, 1979 [1653])

According to some chroniclers, notably **Pedro de Cieza de León**, the smaller stones from Cuzco's Rumicollca quarries were not only transported to the capital itself, but may have been shipped all the way to Tomebamba in Ecuador, some 1,700 kilometers (1.056 miles) to the north. Recent research lends credibility to Cieza's claim: the geochemical composition of Inca andesite stones from the area of Tomebamba very closely matches the rock of Rumicollca. How and why did the Incas haul stones over such large distances? It is generally assumed that they carried the stones on litters or suspended from poles. But when it comes to the choice of a specific rock type, the Incas considered more than just the structural quality of the rock. To them rocks also had symbolic, even religious, significance. They frequently incorporated bedrock outcrops into their buildings; the buildings literally grow out of the bedrock on which they stand. Throughout the Inca landscape there are many rock outcrops regarded as *huacas* (sacred places or objects) that the Inca venerated. Some outcrops were left in their natural state; others were elaborately carved. The Inca stonemasons very likely understood each stone as a piece of Pachamama, Mother Earth, who had to be treated with respect and reverence.

Further Reading

Acosta, José de. *Historia natural y moral de las Indias.* Biblioteca Americana, 38. Mexico: Fondo de Cultura Económica, 1962 [1590].

Cieza de León, Pedro de. *The Incas of Pedro de Cieza de León.* Translated by Harriet de Onis. Edited by Victor Wolfgang von Hagen. Norman: University of Oklahoma Press, 1959 [1553–1554].

Cobo, Bernabé. *History of the Inca Empire: An Account of the Indian's Customs and Their Origin, Together with a Treatise on Inca Legends, History, and Social Institutions.* Translated and edited by Roland Hamilton. Austin: University of Texas Press, 1979 [1653].

Dean, Caroline. *A Culture of Stone: Inka Perspectives on Rock.* Durham, NC: Duke University Press, 2010.

Garcilaso de la Vega, El Inca. *Royal Commentaries of the Incas, and General History of Peru.* Translated by Harold V. Livermore. Austin: University of Texas Press, 1966 [1609].

Gutiérrez de Santa Clara, Pedro. *Historia de las guerras civiles del Perú (1544–1548) y otros sucesos de las Indias.* Colección de Libros y Documentos Referentes a la Historia de América, tomos 2, 3, 4, 10, 20, 21. Madrid: Librería General de Victoriano Suárez, 1904–1929 [1603].

Lee, Vincent. "The Building of Sacsayhuaman." *Ñawpa Pacha,* no. 24:49–60, 1986.

Ogburn, Dennis. "Evidence of Long-Distance Transportation of Andesite Building Blocks in the Inca Empire." *Latin American Antiquity* 15 no. 4: 419–39, 2004.

———. "Variation in Inca Building Stone Quarry Operations in Peru and Ecuador." In *Mining and Quarrying in the Ancient Andes: Sociopolitical, Economic, and Symbolic Dimensions,* edited by Nicholas Tripcevich and Kevin J. Vaughn, New York: Springer, 2013.

Protzen, Jean-Pierre. "Inca Quarrying and Stonecutting." *Journal of the Society of Architectural Historians* 44, no. 2: 161–82, 1985.

———. "The Fortress of Saqsawaman: Was It Ever finished?" *Ñawpa Pacha,* no. 25–27: 49–60, 1987–1989.

———. *Inka Architecture and Construction at Ollantaytambo.* New York: Oxford University Press, 1993.

■ JEAN-PIERRE PROTZEN

QUECHUA

Quechua is a linguistic family made up of dialects that are very different from each other, to the extent that people who speak one may not understand another. One of those forms became the "common language" toward the end of the Inca Empire, disappearing after the Spanish conquest and the subsequent dismantling of the political and administrative system that had sustained and promoted it. An agglutinative language, in which words are formed by adding suffixes, Quechua is very similar to **Aymara**, not because of a genetic relationship, but because of contact between speakers of the two, so that Quechua was molded by Aymara.

As in autocratic societies such as the Inca Empire, the language did not have its own name; terms such as Quechua or *runa-simi* (meaning "language of the *runas*" or Indians) were coined later, after the Spanish conquest had given rise to an established Colonial power. The name Quechua appears in early lexical and grammatical treatises written in the second half of the sixteenth century. The term *runa-simi* appeared during the period of the viceroyalty, and set the language apart from the "language of Castille," spoken by the Spaniards, by designating it the "language of the Indians," or *runas.* The term *runa-simi* is not the original name, as is often believed, because it was coined by the Spaniards in a context of Colonial domination. Quechua also is not the original name. That word means "land of temperate climate," referring, both ethnically and ecologically, to the people living in the area. Many places therefore bear the name *Quechua,* in different phonetic versions, depending on the local dialect. According to the tradition recorded by the Spaniards, however, the original speakers of the language were the historical ethnic group known as the Quechuas, whose language the Incas may have learned during the **conquests** that took place during imperial expansion.

The birthplace of the Quechua language is traditionally considered to be the Cuzco valley, and it was believed to be the native language of the founders of the Inca Empire. Documentary evidence from the sixteenth century, however, as well as early onomastic (mainly place names) and linguistic material contributed by researchers in the second half of the twentieth century, not only ruled out that possibility, but also showed that the language probably originated outside Cuzco. Quechua, therefore, could not have been the native language of the Incas, let alone of their legendary ancestors. The hypothesis most widely accepted today is that the language originated in the central Andes, along Peru's central highlands and coast, an area with great dialectal fragmentation.

Once Quechua is ruled out as the primordial language of the Incas, two questions remain: when did the rulers of Cuzco learn Quechua, and what might their ancestral tongue have been? Answers to those questions must be based on an examination and rereading of Colonial sources from the sixteenth century, some of which only came to light in the last few decades of the twentieth century. It appears that the Incas may have learned the language from the Quechuas, their first allies in the war against the Chancas, as described in oral tradition recorded by the Spaniards and retold in the chronicle of **Cristóbal de Albornoz** in 1581 (see **Myths, Origin**). The language that the Incas adopted after their victory over the Chancas and in their wars of conquest toward the northwest (the region later called **Chinchaysuyu**) would gradually replace the form of Aymara that until then had been the principal language of the fledgling empire. The best evidence of this is the hymn that the Inca Pachacuti composed to commemorate his victory over the Soras, one of the first groups subjugated in the conquests launched by the Inca ruler. The piece is written entirely in Aymara, although the chronicler **Juan de Betanzos** apparently did not realize that when he recorded it in 1551 as if it were a Quechua text.

The Aymara spoken by the Incas was a specific variety, different from *altiplano* Aymara, which would later disappear as it was replaced by Quechua. Even that form of Aymara was not the Incas' original language, however, or at most it might have been the language of the Incas of the mythical period. Linguistic and philological evidence suggests that their legendary ancestors may have spoken **Puquina** as their native language. Colonial sources indicate that Quechua became the official language of the Inca Empire under the last Inca rulers, Topa Inca Yupanqui and Huayna Capac. There is speculation that one of the main reasons why the Incas might not only have changed languages, but also have seen the strategic need to make it the official language of the empire, might have been that it was used, although in different dialects, throughout Chinchaysuyu, either as the only language or as the most prestigious one in places where it competed with others.

The form of Quechua adopted by the Incas became extinct after the Spanish conquest. It appears indirectly in the earliest chronicles, reflected in the Incas' cultural and institutional lexicon, and in the sporadic recording of phrases and expressions. It also appears in the earliest grammatical and lexical treatise, which was written by the Dominican friar Domingo de Santo Tomás of Seville in 1550 and published in Valladolid, Spain, in 1560. Compared with current varieties of the language, the Quechua of the Incas had notable exclusive phonological and lexical characteristics, although its grammar did not differ much from modern dialects of what is known as "southern Quechua," particularly the form spoken in Ayacucho. Once recognized as the official language, it had to compete with other languages that had existed since before the expansion of the Inca Empire (Aymara and Culli in the south-central and northern highlands, respectively, but also with native languages in Ecuador's inter-Andean valleys)—unless it was imposed in territories conquered by the last Inca rulers (in Cochabamba, Bolivia, for example). In many places, such as on Peru's northern coast, however, it did not have time to become well established before the sudden collapse of the empire.

Such was the "general language" to which the chroniclers refer—particularly Santo Tomás, in his *Dedicatoria al Rey* (Dedication to the King), who describes Quechua as a "tongue that was used and is used throughout the dominion of the great ruler known as Guaynacapa [Huayna Capac], which covers an area that is more than one thousand leagues in length and more than one hundred in breadth. In all of that [land] it was generally used by the leaders and most important people and by a large number of the common folk" (1995 [1560]). This common variety, disseminated by the Incas throughout Tahuantinsuyu, was celebrated by the conquistadors because of its extraordinary functionality for widespread communication, despite the linguistic diversity and many dialects of the empire. It would die out by the second half of the sixteenth century, succumbing to Spanish in Lima and the surrounding areas, and to the languages of peoples recently incorporated into the empire or to dialects of the same family (such as the Quechua of Cuzco) which Spanish Colonial civil and church authorities promoted.

Further Reading

Adelaar, Willem, and Pieter Muysken. "The Quechuan Language Family." In *The Languages of the Andes*, edited by Willem Adelaar with Pieter Muysken, 195–233. Cambridge: Cambridge University Press, 2004.

Cerrón-Palomino, Rodolfo. "Esbozo gramatical." In *Lingüística quechua*, edited by Rodolfo Cerrón-Palomino, 249–319. Cuzco: Bartolomé de Las Casas, 1987.

———. "Quechua." In *Voces del Ande*, 33–49. Lima: Fondo Editorial de la Pontificia Universidad Católica del Perú, 2008.

Itier, César. "What was the *Lengua General* of Colonial Peru?" In *History and Language in the Andes,* edited by Paul Heggarty and Adrian J. Pearce, 63–85. New York: Palgrave Macmillan, 2011.

Parker, Gary. *Trabajos de lingüística histórica quechua.* Edited by Rodolfo Cerrón-Palomino. Lima: Fondo Editorial de la Pontificia Universidad Católica del Perú, 2013.

Santo Tomás, Domingo de. *Gramática o arte de la lengua general de los Indios de los reynos del Perú.* Introductory study and notes by Rodolfo Cerrón-Palomino. Monumenta Linguistica Andina, no. 5. Cuzco: Centro de Estudios Regionales Andinos "Bartolomé de las Casas," 1995 [1560].

Torero, Alfredo. "La familia lingüística quechua." In *Idiomas de los Andes. Lingüística e Historia*, 55–108. Lima: Editorial Horizonte and Instituto Francés de Estudios Andinos, 2002.

■ RODOLFO CERRÓN-PALOMINO
(TRANSLATED BY BARBARA FRASER)

QUIPU

Quipu (knot) was the term used for the knotted-string device employed in record keeping throughout the Inca Empire. Spanish chronicles and documents from the Colonial era contain a host of information on the uses of these devices in Tahuantinsuyu, the Inca Empire, both on the basis of testimony from surviving officials—called *quipucamayocs* (knot makers/organizers)—who used these devices in state administration before the Spanish conquest, as well as from observations of their continued use in early Colonial times. The Spanish sources inform us that *quipus* were used primarily in the recording of administrative information, including the keeping of **census** and tribute records, although they were apparently also used to record information for the recitation/performance of narrative accounts, such as myths, life histories of the Inca kings, and so forth (see **Music**). Modern study of surviving *quipus*, of which there are some 870 samples in museum collections around the world, began in earnest early in the twentieth century.

Quipus are composed of a number of spun and twisted threads, called *pendant cords*, or strings, attached by means of half-hitch knots to a thicker cord, the latter of which is termed the *primary cord*. *Quipus* carry as few as one and as many as 1,500 pendant cords; the average number of pendant cords on samples, as determined by Harvard's Quipu Database Project, is 60, while the median number is 27. On about a third of the *quipus*, pendant cords have second-order cords attached to them, called *subsidiary cords*. Subsidiary cords may have third-order cords attached, and so on down to several levels of subsidiaries. The deepest level of subsidiary attachments recorded to date is on a sample from Arica, Chile, which has pendant cords with six levels of subsidiaries.

A *quipu*, or knotted-string accounting device, found at Laguna de los Cóndores in the cloud forest of Chachapoyas, northern Peru. Gary Urton, courtesy Museo Leymebamba, Leymebamba, Amazonas, Peru.

Quipus are made of either cotton fibers or camelid hair, although the vast majority—some 85 percent —are of cotton. They are generally quite colorful, as a result of the use of differently colored camelid fibers (these vary in hues of white, beige, brown, black) or cotton fibers. (Ancient Andean domesticated cotton varies greatly in color: white, and various hues of brown from light brown to chocolate.) In addition to these material-based sources of color differences, camelid threads were often dyed with vegetal dyes. It is thought that differences in cord color were one of the principal ways of signifying the identities of objects recorded in the *quipus*.

Three major types of knots were tied into *quipu* pendant, subsidiary, and top cords. The three knot types are referred to as *figure-eight knots*, whose final shape is indicated by the name of this knot—*long knots*, which are made by turning the cord between two to nine times inside the body of the knot; and *single* or *overhand knots*, which were used to sign increasing powers of 10. These three knot types were central elements in the signing of quantitative information in the decimal-based system of imperial administration (see **Administration, Decimal**). That is, the three types of knots were tied in tiered clusters along pendant cords to indicate values going from units, at the bottom of cords, to increasing powers of ten, the latter of which were signed by successively higher tiered clusters.

A watercolor portrait of a *quipucamayoc* and his *quipu* in the illustrated chronicle of Martín de Murúa. Murúa, Martín de. *Códice Murúa—Historia y Genealogía de los Reyes Incas del Perú* (Códice Galvin). Madrid: Testimonio Compañía Editorial, S. A., 2004 [1590-1598].

The cord-keepers, *quipucamayocs*, of the imperial administration were organized in a hierarchy, from those who served the court in Cuzco; to provincial cord-keepers in regional administrative centers; down to local, village-level cord-keepers. Some evidence for the standardization of recording techniques is provided by Spanish chroniclers, who state that a school for administrators was set up in Cuzco. The curriculum involved a four-year program, the last two years of which involved the study of *quipu* recording and reading methods. The *quipucamayocs* were responsible for maintaining records of all matters that concerned the state, including census records, tribute accounts, and records of goods stored in and redistributed from state storehouses.

The Spaniards were highly impressed by the record-keeping capacities of the *quipu*. One early chronicler, **Cieza de León**, states,

In each provincial seat there were accountants called quipu-keepers who, by their knots, had the record and accounting of what was owed as tribute by the people from that district, including silver, gold, clothing and livestock down to firewood and other, lesser items, and by means of the quipu, arriving at the end of the year, or of 10 or 20 years, in the accounting of the one who was commissioned to make the accounting, there would not be lost [from the accounting] even one pair of sandals. . . . And in each valley today they keep such an accounting, and there are always in each place of habitation as many accountants as there are lords and every four months they close out [rectify] their accounts in the aforesaid manner. (Cieza de León 1967 [1553])

The Spanish Colonial administrators recognized from the earliest days following the conquest that the *quipucamayocs* retained in their knot records a host of information that was critical to the reorganization and running of the Spanish Colonial administration. Therefore, they had transcriptions made of many of the *quipu* accounts from Native cord keepers' readings that were translated into Spanish and recorded by scribes. Researchers are at work today studying the surviving *quipu* transcriptions in an effort to try to understand how the original knot-based information may have been recorded.

Further Reading

Arellano Hoffmann, C., and G. Urton, eds. *Atando Cabos*. Lima: Ministerio de Cultura, Museo Nacional de Arqueología, 2011.

Ascher, M., and R. Ascher. *Mathematics of the Incas: Code of the Quipu*. Mineola, NY: Dover Publications, 1997.

Brokaw, G. *A History of the Khipu*. Cambridge Latin American studies, 94. Cambridge: Cambridge University Press, 2010.

Cieza de León, Pedro de. *El Señorío de los Incas*. Lima: Instituto de Estudios Peruanos, 1967 [1553].

Julien, Catherine J. *Reading Inca History*. Iowa City: University of Iowa Press, 2000.

Locke, L. L. *The Ancient Quipu or Peruvian Knot Record*. New York: American Museum of Natural History, 1923.

Mackey, C., H. Pereyra, C. Radicati di Primeglio, H. Rodríguez, and O. Valverde, eds. *Quipu y yupana: Colección de escritos*. Lima: Consejo Nacional de Ciencia y Tecnología, 1990.

Murra, J. V. "Las etnocategorías de un khipu estatal." In *Formaciones económicas y políticas en el mundo andino*, 243–54. Lima: Instituto de Estudios Peruanos, 1975.

Pärssinen, M., and J. Kiviharju, eds. *Textos Andinos: Corpus de Textos de khipus incaicos y coloniales*. Vol. 1. Madrid: Instituto Iberoamericano de Finlandia and Universidad Complutense de Madrid, 2004.

Pereyra Sánchez, H. *Descripción de los Quipus del Museo de Sitio de Pachacamac*. Lima: Centro de Producción Editorial e Imprenta de la Universidad Nacional Mayor de San Marcos, 2006.

Quilter, J., and G. Urton, eds. *Narrative Threads: Accounting and Recounting in Andean Khipu*. Austin: University of Texas Press, 2002.

Urton, G. *Signs of the Inka Khipu: Binary Coding in the Andean Knotted-String Records*. Austin: University of Texas Press, 2003.

———. "The Inka Khipu: Knotted-Cord Record Keeping in the Andes." In *Handbook of South American Archaeology*, edited by H. Silverman and W. Isbell, 831–44. New York: Springer, 2008.

———. Khipu Database Project, Harvard University. http://khipukamayuq.fas.harvard.edu/.

■ GARY URTON

RELIGION

Inca religion can be defined in two ways. First, it embraced the beliefs and ritual practices of the inhabitants of the Cuzco valley, composed of the "Incas-by-blood," descendants of the mythical founding ancestor, Manco Capac, and the **Incas by privilege**, who were not direct descendants of noble Inca lineages. Second, it was the religious doctrine of the empire, which saw many adjustments as it merged and incorporated the beliefs of the scores of ethnic and linguistic groups under the imperial yoke. This doctrine was made manifest and spread through feasts and rituals that legitimated the rule of the ***Sapa*** **Inca** (the sole, unique Inca), and his representatives.

The Incas' tutelary god was Inti, the Sun god, from whom the Inca rulers believed they descended. Guaman Poma de Ayala, Felipe, *El primer nueva corónica y buen gobierno*. Edited by John V. Murra and Rolena Adorno, 232/258. Mexico City: Siglo Veintiuno, 1980 [1615].

237

RELACIONES GEOGRÁFICAS

In 1577, the Spanish Crown drew up a set of 50 questions that were intended to elicit information on Crown holdings in the New World. The questions covered a range of issues concerned with history, geography, and economy. The questionnaire was motivated by the fact that Crown territories in the New World were still fundamentally unknown to administrators and members of the Council of the Indies, which oversaw all Colonial policies and practices in the New World. The hope was that a systematic investigation of all aspects of life in the communities governed by Spain would lead to a more enlightened administration in those far-flung holdings, both in the Viceroyalty of New Spain and that of Peru. The written responses to the questionnaire take the form of what are referred to today as the *Relaciones Geográficas de Indias* (Geographical Relations/Accounts of the Indies).

Within a decade of the printing of the questionnaire, copies had made their way to the Viceroyalty of Peru and were being implemented in inquests undertaken by administrative governors (*corregidores*) or priests in the various regions of the viceroyalty. Some 21 of the *Relaciones Geográficas de Indias* that returned to Spain and were published pertain either to the *Audiencia* (judicial region) of Lima or that of Quito. In both cases, the information elicited by the questionnaire related not only to the actual circumstances of Andean communities, but concerned conditions during the Inca domination of the region as well.

These documents are a source of exceptionally important information for researchers today trying to reconstruct provincial organization under the Incas. This includes such matters as the nature of settlements in a given region, the resources (e.g., minerals, plants, animals, sources of water) available, as well as the types of infrastructure (e.g., roads and storehouses). Many questions of a more explicitly cultural nature were also included, such as: What languages were spoken in a given town? How were towns governed? How were the houses built? Some questions were quite specific in asking about Native culture and customs, often reflecting the presumptions and prejudices of Crown officials. For instance, "Who were their rulers in heathen times? What rights did their former lords have over them? What did they pay in tribute? What forms of worship, rites, and good or evil customs did they practice?" Respondents were also encouraged to draw maps of the layouts of towns, or, in the case of towns along the coast, of the islands off the coast. Unfortunately, in only a handful of cases did respondents take the time to draw town maps or ones that depicted the geographical setting of a town or a group of settlements.

In any case, the *Relaciones Geográficas de Indias* are exceptionally important sources of information for understanding the world of the Incas and the nature of some of the major transformations following the Spanish conquest.

Further Reading

Cline, Howard F. "The Relaciones Geográficas of the Spanish Indies, 1577–1586." *Hispanic American Historical Review* 44, no. 3:341–74, 1964.

Mundy, Barbara E. "Relaciones Geográficas." In *Guide to Documentary Sources for Andean Studies, 1530–1900*, edited by Joanne Pillsbury, vol. 1, 144–59. Norman: University of Oklahoma Press, 2008.

■ GARY URTON

Our knowledge of Inca religion comes mainly from Spanish chronicles written in the sixteenth century, reflecting the lack of indigenous sources and religious imagery. The origin of these sources has had a marked impact on the quality of the information. In the case of priest-chroniclers, they were often convinced of the original good intentions of Native peoples and that their early notion of the existence of the Christian God was corrupted by the Devil. Indigenous chroniclers, such as **Felipe Guaman Poma de Ayala** and **Joan de Santa Cruz Pachacuti Yamqui Salcamaygua**, even went a step further and made supposed preconquest evangelizations the cornerstone of their writings. On the other hand, **Garcilaso de la Vega** idealized the pre-Hispanic past by pointing out the similarity between the Andean and Mediterranean belief systems. Many chroniclers clearly exhibited an interest in highlighting Andean concepts and ideas that appeared similar to the principles of the Christian faith in attempts to facilitate evangelization. Some of these analogies include the apparent, to their minds, similarity between the concept of "transgression" (*hucha*) and "sin," the existence or inexistence of confession in Andean rituals, the Holy Trinity, and the idea of creation. As a consequence, and despite the richness of Inca myths and rites included in these accounts, information about the Cuzco elites' thoughts of the divine and how they conceived of their gods remains scant and overly simplified. Yet another difficulty in trying to reconstruct Inca beliefs stems from the translation from **Aymara** and **Puquina** to either **Quechua** or Spanish. Translations undoubtedly changed the original meanings of several religious concepts. The people of Cuzco were in fact Aymara speakers and it is likely that the Incas originally spoke Puquina. This has great implications for the etymologies of deities' names and some place names.

Scholarship concerning Inca religion over the last century has revolved around two main issues: the nature of the supreme deity—creator *versus* animator or demiurge; and the name of the deity and his relationship with the other deities—the Creator (Viracocha Pachayachachi, see **Deities**) versus the Sun (Inti, Punchao), Thunder (Illapa), and Apu Huanacauri. Another major topic of concern has been the religious reform reportedly undertaken by the Inca ruler Pachacuti, who instilled the solar cult at the expense of Viracocha. Nevertheless, despite these debates, there was never any doubt about the existence of a supreme deity within a system that believed in one god but accepted the existence of other gods.

A new approach to the problem of Inca religion has gained strength since the 1980s. It is based on archaeological and ethnohistorical studies of sacred places or *huacas*, many of which surrounded Cuzco and were described by the chronicler **Bernabé Cobo** as part of the *ceque* system. Documents based on Native accounts became increasingly important, particularly the Huarochirí Manuscript (see **Avila, Francisco de**). Although inherent problems arise when comparing the recent ethnographic record with Colonial accounts, it is nevertheless true that Quechua- and Aymara-speaking communities maintained or reinvented rituals and practices that were deeply engrained in their cosmovision, despite some borrowings from Christianity.

One of the core beliefs of ancient Andean peoples, including the Incas, was the animated nature of the environment. Mountain peaks, lakes, springs, and rock outcrops were given life and agency, with the inherent capacity to influence human destiny and to speak and foretell the future (see **Divination**). This power was also attributed to the mummies of certain ancestors, especially those of the dead Inca rulers and their doubles (bundles and *huauques;* see **Worship, Ancestor**; **Kingship, Divine; Mummies, Royal**). Many inanimate objects were considered *huacas*, or sacred, and therefore could act. Among them were the *sayhuas* and *sucancas*, stone pillars used to observe solar movements; as well as *huancas*, standing stones regarded as petrified ancestors. *Huacas* also included movable objects such as *conopas* and *illas*—miniature images of camelids or maize, for instance—that insured the fertility of the herds and bountiful harvests. *Huacas* also legitimated rights over land and water.

Each river basin was integrated and organized around the axis of water circulation and divided into four parts in relation to the main river course, which was a reflection in each basin of the celestial river—the Milky Way, *Mayu*. The waterway divided each basin into two halves, each one on a different bank. The earthly river, which echoed the mythical celestial river, interconnected these two halves, or *sayas*: the upper one (*hanan*) with snow-covered peaks or *apus*, lakes, and canals that irrigated the pastures and crops; and, the lower one (*hurin*). Andean people believed that water circulated between the ocean in the underworld and the sky, uniting in the foremost confines of the earth. There was a biannual irrigation rhythm determined by the change in seasons: a wet and hot season, and a cold and dry one. Agrarian and pastoral rituals took place on specific dates noted in ceremonial calendars and the main goal was to make sure that water reached fields and pastures alike on time and in sufficient quantities. These rituals were also incorporated into the Inca state cult.

Inhabited space in Tahuantinsuyu was organized by river basins and regions, *suyus*. Each watershed had its own tutelary deities. The sacred geography of Cuzco included 328 or 350 *huacas* and followed the principles discussed above, with the valley's Huatanay River as its axis (see **Ceques**; **Temples**). According to the **origin myths**, Cuzco's first settlers, later venerated as ancestors, came from a *pacarina*, or origin place, usually a lake or a cave with a known location within the watershed. The Inca ancestors, for instance, emerged from the cave of Tambo T'oco, in Pacariqtambo.

In this sense, Inca religion lacked the characteristics of revelation religions such as those of Asia and Europe; instead, it possessed many of the particular traits regarded as animistic. The rural landscape surrounding Cuzco and public and residential spaces were filled with sacred places and mobile objects, which were also considered deities. Most of the nonmobile *huacas* were related to rivers and canals. Others (such as *sucancas*) were related to places for astronomical observations at sunrise and sunset. None of the principal deities seems to have had the nature of a creator god. The capacity to animate, to give life—*camaquen* in Quechua—was shared by all divine beings, including the **Sapa Inca**, regardless of hierarchy.

Despite the fact that the Inca religious system was described as polytheistic because of the multiplicity of sacred beings it included, Andean deities were not like their counterparts in Greco-Roman mythology. They lacked an anthropomorphic persona, or a nature or craft, which would describe their essence as gods of fire, air, water, war, or the arts. Their powers overlapped and complemented each other. They had no single material expression because they transformed, unfolded, and multiplied their very being. They could appear as birds, eggs, rocks, a constellation of stars, a dark spot in the Milky Way, or even as human beings. The conceptualization of the Andean *numen* was expressed in the idiosyncrasy of the farmer and herder who fought for survival in an extreme environment. From their perspective, every supernatural capable of animation must also combine the forces of sun and water at the appropriate time of the annual cycle in order to make barren lands fertile.

This interrelation is expressed through the identity of the four main male gods of the Inca state pantheon. Their differences reflect whether they controlled the sky or the earth. In the world inhabited by mortals, the daytime sky was under the domain of the Sun—Inti—tutelary deity of the *Sapa* Inca and the empire. On the other hand, Apu Huanacauri, one of Cuzco's most revered mountains, represented the lineage of the Ayar siblings, the founding ancestors of the Incas-by-blood (see **Myths, Origin**). The mythical account of the siblings' arrival and the founding of Cuzco was revived during rituals on Huanacauri. Meanwhile, the god Viracocha ruled over the waters of the universe and the origin of life itself. Illapa, Thunder, was imagined as a resplendent warrior brandishing a slingshot; he ruled the nighttime sky. Deceased Inca rulers were considered incarnations of Illapa, while the living sovereign represented the Sun—Punchao—among the mortals. There is evidence to support the notion that each of these gods could unfold to attend to both halves of the animated universe. The feminine counterpart was represented in the Inca pantheon by, respectively, the Moon, Quilla; the morning and evening stars; the earth, Pachamama; and the sea and the lakes, Cochamama. The mummy bundles of *Coyas*, the queens and principal wives of the Inca ruler, were worshiped in Quilla's sacred chamber in the temple of **Coricancha** in Cuzco.

The main festivities in the Inca ceremonial calendar (see **Calendar, Ritual**) were dedicated to the Sun, Inti. Two festivities were dedicated to the Sun and took place just outside of Cuzco. Capac Raymi honored the Sun at the December solstice, or *huayna Punchao*, the young Sun. Inti Raymi, on the other hand, was consecrated to the Sun of the June solstice, or *Inca Punchao*. In addition to observing the movement of the sun, the ceremonies also included the ritual movement of people along the rivers. One of these movements was upriver during the Mayucati feast, following Capac Raymi, the feast celebrating the December solstice. The second took place during Inti Raymi, at the time of the June solstice, when the priests made their pilgrimage downriver. Both ceremonies also featured visits to the solar temples and to the summit of Apu Huanacauri. The ancestor Sun, Apu Punchao, was worshiped during a third ceremony, known as Citua; in this ceremony, rituals were performed in the plaza flanking the Sun temple, Coricancha. Its main purpose was to rid Cuzco of "evils" in order to prepare it for a new agricultural year; all the *ayllus* and *panacas* were present, each carrying the mummy bundle of their ancestors. This festivity was related to another one dedicated to the Quilla (Moon), known as Colla Raymi. Even though some of the rituals were led by specialized priests, all of Cuzco took part in these and other ceremonies of the ritual calendar. Particularly important rituals took place during the rainy season, when noble young warriors were initiated by participating in races. After receiving their ear spools, the warriors of opposing halves faced each other in ritual battle (see **Battles, Ritual**).

Given the local and ethnocentric character of Inca religion in Cuzco, the rulers of Tahuantinsuyu developed strategies for achieving religious legitimacy in conquered lands. One of these strategies consisted of creating doubles of Huanacauri in the sacred geography of conquered lands and in building Sun temples and ceremonial platforms, or **ushnus,** along the road system. They also incorporated all the leading conquered *apus*, or deities, into the imperial cult—for instance, **Catequil**, Coropuna, and Pariacaca. The pilgrimage center and oracle of **Pachacamac**, on the central coast of Peru, is a particularly noteworthy case. There, the Incas built a new temple dedicated to the Sun and to the "god who animated the earth," whose cult spread through the central and north coast of Peru. Pachacamac is the northwestern counterpart of the shrine on the **Island of the Sun** in Lake Titicaca. Both were situated at the extremes of the mythical route taken by Inti (the Sun); from his birthplace in the waters of the lake, to his setting in the ocean. At the center of this axis, traced through the night sky in the Milky Way, was the temple of Coricancha in Cuzco.

Further Reading

Bray, Tamara L., ed. *The Archaeology of Wak'as: Explorations of the Sacred in the Pre-Columbian Andes.* Boulder: University Press of Colorado, 2015.

Makowski, Krzysztof, ed. *Los dioses del antiguo Perú.* Vol. 1 and 2. Lima: Banco de Crédito del Perú, 2000, 2001.

Marzal, Manuel María, ed. *Religiones andinas.* Vol. 1. Madrid: Editorial Trotta, 2005.

McCormack, Sabine. *Religion in the Andes: Vision and Imagination in Early Colonial Peru.* Princeton, NJ: Princeton University Press, 1991.

■ KRZYSZTOF MAKOWSKI

ROADS

Heralded as one of the New World's greatest engineering feats, the Inca road and **bridge** network rivals that of the Romans in the Old World. The 40,000-kilometer (25,000-mile) network linked **Cuzco**, the imperial capital, to its far-flung domains, crisscrossing some of the world's most rugged and inhospitable environments. Although the Incas used or reengineered pre-Inca roads, the imperial roads and installations built along them were probably conceived as a whole, and together they display state planning on a scale never before seen in the Andes. On the eve of the Spanish invasion in 1532, the road system embraced parts of the modern nation states of Ecuador, Peru, Bolivia, Chile, and Argentina.

Two roads formed the backbone of the system: a highland road and a parallel coastal road. The highland road ran from a point just shy of the modern Ecuador-Colombia border, down through the Peruvian highlands, skirting Lake Titicaca and south into what is today northwestern Argentina. The coastal road, on the other hand, ran from Tumbes, in what is today northern Peru, through desert punctuated by the occasional lush river valley, down through one of the world's most arid deserts, the Atacama, and on to Santiago, Chile. A dozen or more lateral roads linked the two main north-south roads, while still others headed into the cloud forest flanking the eastern slopes of the Andes. Some roads, among the highest ever built, led to mountaintop sanctuaries, towering more than 5,000 meters (16,400 feet) above sea level (see **Capac Hucha**).

Llamas and trekkers on the Inca road at the Pampas de Huamanín in Huánuco, Peru; this road, in the Inca quarter of Chinchaysuyu, connected Cuzco to the northernmost reaches of the empire. Joe Castro/Guías del Caminante.

By all accounts, the most spectacular road of all linked Cuzco to Quito, passing along the backbone of the Andes through **Chinchaysuyu**, the northwestern quadrant of the empire. This is the road most early chroniclers traveled, and all described it in superlatives. "Oh," said **Pedro de Cieza de Leon**, writing in the 1540s, "Can anything comparable be said of Alexander, or of any of the mighty kings who ruled the world, that they built such a road . . ." (Cieza 1959 [1553]). Its importance and formal construction may reflect the focus in late Inca times on conquests in Ecuador. Indeed, the Inca ruler Huayna Capac is said to have rebuilt sections of the road, initially constructed by his father, Topa Inca Yupanqui. No other road featured more Inca centers, boasted longer stretches of formal construction or the greatest widths (at times the road is 16 meters [50 feet] wide), embellished with stone paving, culverts, drainage canals, and causeways that raised the road surface above swampy ground. Steep sections of road were negotiated with flights of steps, built of fieldstone. (Because Andean people did not have the wheel, roads did not need to accommodate wheeled vehicles, and steps were an easy solution to especially steep slopes).

The width of the road varied according to the importance of the road and the terrain it traversed. In the high jungle or cloud forest, the Incas built daring cobbled roads that clung to cliff sides, with steps and tunnels often carved into the living rock, such as the 20-meter-long (65-foot-long) tunnel cut through solid granite on the road between Puyu Pata Marca and Saya Marca, en route to **Machu Picchu**. There, the steep and rugged terrain forced engineers to design narrow roads 1–3 meters (3–10 feet) wide. On the desert coast, where it seldom rains, the road was rarely paved, and generally used a less formal construction than its highland counterpart. Some sections of coastal

ROSTWOROWSKI, MARÍA

Born in Lima in 1915, María Rostworowski is a self-taught Peruvian ethnohisto-
rian best known for her studies of late pre-Hispanic Peru, particularly of the Inca
Empire and coastal peoples. Her early writings focused on Inca kingship, specifically
on Inca succession. Rostworowski soon realized that the prevailing accounts of the
Incas were based almost exclusively on chronicles written by Spaniards during the
sixteenth to mid-seventeenth centuries. These essentially Cuzco-centric chronicles
said little about Andean groups other than the Incas, and almost nothing regarding
the coastal inhabitants. Based on administrative documentation, most of which had
hitherto remained unused, she refocused the study of the late pre-Hispanic Andes
to reconstruct the economy and society of the pre-Columbian coast. Whereas **John
V. Murra** claimed that the main Andean economic model was that of an autonomous, marketless, vertical economy that exploited the resources found at various
altitudes in different ecological tiers, Rostworowski posited instead that coastal societies followed a horizontal subsistence economy that comprised the coastal valleys
and included the use of markets, and therefore availed themselves of the resources
found in essentially the same altitudes. Rostworowski pioneered the combination
of archival research and fieldwork to develop a more precise reconstruction of the
pre-Hispanic landscape. In the 1980s she turned her attention once again to the
Incas, culminating with *History of the Inca Realm*.

Further Reading

Rostworowski de Diez Canseco, María. *Pachacútec Inca Yupanqui*. Lima: Imprenta Torres Aguirre,
    1953.
———. *Etnia y sociedad. Costa peruana prehispánica*. Lima: Instituto de Estudios Peruanos, 1977.
———. *History of the Inca Realm*. Translated by Harry B. Iceland. Cambridge: Cambridge Univer-
    sity Press, 1999 [1988].

■ JAVIER FLORES ESPINOZA

road, however, included flights of steps as the road made its way across low-lying hills.
Widths varied from 3 to 10 meters (10 feet to over 30 feet) and, as the road ran through
the desert, piles of stones or wooden posts served as markers. When the road reached
irrigated valleys, walls of adobe or *tapia* (tamped earth) prevented people and llama
caravans from trampling adjacent fields. Peoples living in areas traversed by the roads
and bridges were responsible for maintenance and repair and road building was also a
labor obligation (see **Labor Service**).

Travel along the roads was apparently restricted to those occupied in state business: the
Inca emperor, accompanied by his court, inspecting his distant domains; soldiers engaged
in conquest or quelling the frequent rebellions; great llama caravans carrying produce and
goods to stockpile the storehouses scattered throughout the realm; inspectors and *quipucamayoc* (**quipu** masters) on state missions; *mitmacuna* dispatched as colonists to far-flung
regions; or *chasquis*, the runners who carried messages from one end of the empire to the

other. Chasqui messengers running in relay covered 250 kilometers (155 miles) in a day, delivering messages from Cuzco to Quito, Ecuador, in a week, a distance of some 1,700 kilometers (over 1,000 miles) as the condor flies.

Installations along the road network ranged from large administrative centers (especially on the Chinchaysuyu road) such as Vilcashuaman, Hatun Jauja, Pumpu, Huamachuco, Huánuco Pampa, and **Cajamarca**, just to name a few, to medium and small-sized *tambos*, or way stations, and even smaller *chasquihuasi*, or *chasqui* houses for the *chasqui* messengers. *Tambos* often contained large halls for lodging travelers as well as communal kitchens, storehouses, and llama corrals.

The Inca road and bridge system did more than facilitate travel. It moved goods, people, and information and served as a physical and conceptual link between Cuzco and its hinterland. Sometimes the roads appear almost over-engineered and in this sense they are as much symbolic as practical—a visible reminder to subject peoples of Inca might and sovereignty, and a symbol of Tahuantinsuyu itself.

Further Reading

Cieza de León, Pedro de. *The Incas of Pedro de Cieza de León.* Translated by Harriet de Onis. Edited by Victor Wolfgang von Hagen. Norman: University of Oklahoma Press, 1959 [1553–1554].
Espinosa, Ricardo. *La Gran Ruta Inca: El Capac Ñan* [The Great Inca Route]. Lima: Petroperu, 2006.
Hyslop, John. *The Inka Road System.* New York: Academic Press, 1984.

■ ADRIANA VON HAGEN

RULE, IMPERIAL

In the mid-fourteenth century AD, the Incas began to expand their realm out of the Cuzco basin by dominating their immediate neighbors (see **Archaeology, Cuzco; Conquest; Expansion**). At the time, they presided over a regional polity in which social classes, and offices or institutions of leadership, may have just been taking form. Over the succeeding century or so, the Incas transformed their domain into a full-fledged empire, the largest polity ever seen in the indigenous Americas. *Empire* refers to a geographically extensive polity in which a core society imposes its control over a range of other societies. In most instances, the political formation at the heart of power is a highly stratified state, within which status and power are formalized in social classes and governing institutions.

To achieve their goal of grand-scale dominion, the Incas employed a mix of alliance, cooptation of compliant subject elites, diplomacy, threat, investiture or siege, and outright conquest. The empire ultimately took in an immense territory (about one million square kilometers) containing an estimated 10–12 million subjects, who spoke scores of mutually unintelligible languages. Its political core was a set of state institutions, based on a patrilineal monarchy and the Inca aristocracy. The social formation at the empire's heart elevated the Inca ethnic group above all other Andean peoples. The remainder of the empire was a patchwork of distinct societies with markedly diverse political forms, all brought under the rule of the state and an array of groups and individuals elevated to aristocratic status. The entire domain was organized into 80-odd provinces, based on a reconfiguration of existing ethnic groups and polities.

During the second half of the twentieth century, John Howland Rowe (1918–2004) came to be recognized as a preeminent scholar of Inca culture and society, as well as one of the pioneers of Peruvian archaeology. His perspective on the subject was through the lens of culture history and it reflected the influence of Alfred Kroeber and the Boasian anthropological tradition that characterized the University of California, Berkeley, during Rowe's four decades on the faculty there. His undergraduate training at Brown University in classical archaeology gave him an appreciation of the potential of the stylistic analysis of ceramics to construct relative chronologies, and these tools proved to be crucial for his seminal studies of culture change in the Andes during pre-Inca, Inca, and Colonial times.

Rowe became established as a leading authority on the Incas before he was thirty years old as the result of his 1944 Harvard monograph, *An Introduction to the Archaeology of Cuzco*. This volume offered the first rigorous description of the Incas as an archeological culture and provided an introduction to the pre-Inca cultures of the zone, such as the Chanapata culture. Rowe's reputation was enhanced by his masterly 1946 synthesis of Inca culture at the time of the Spanish conquest for the *Handbook of South American Indians*. In the decades that followed, Rowe focused on the archaeology and history of Peru, especially in Cuzco, and his work in the field on pre-imperial cultures, such as Killke, and his historical studies on the chronology and organization of Inca kingship and administration, have shaped our current understanding of these topics in Cuzco and Tahuantinsuyu. Rowe advocated an inductive approach coupled with meticulous historiography in the study of Inca and Andean culture history, and because he considered culture change as pervasive, he prioritized the need for chronological control. One important aspect in his investigations was the study of Inca resistance to the Spanish conquest and this was reflected in his analysis of Colonial wooden drinking vessels (**keros**), Colonial oil paintings of Inca royalty, and the nineteenth-century rebellion of Túpac Amaru II.

In addition to over 300 original publications, Rowe also influenced the field of Andean studies through the training of students in Berkeley and Cuzco. While at the University of California, Berkeley, he served as the primary advisor for over 20 PhD students, most specializing in the archaeology and/or history of the Central Andes. In 1960, Rowe, along with, Dorothy Menzel, founded the Institute for Andean Studies and its journal Ñawpa Pacha as a forum to discuss and publish research on Andean archaeology and ethnohistory.

Further Reading

Rowe, John Howland. *An Introduction to the Archaeology of Cuzco*. Expeditions to Southern Peru, Report 2. In *Papers of the Peabody Museum of American Archaeology and Ethnology, Harvard University* 27, no. 2, 1944.

———. "Inca Culture at the Time of the Spanish Conquest." In *Handbook of South American Indians*, edited by Julian H. Steward, vol. 2, *The Andean Civilizations*, 183–330. Washington, DC: Smithsonian Institution, Bureau of American Ethnology, 1946.

■ RICHARD L. BURGER

The Incas called their realm *Tahuantinsuyu*, the "four parts bound together." In their vision, the domain united the four parts (*suyus*) of the known world into a single entity, focused around the sacred political center of **Cuzco**. Running clockwise from the northwest, the four parts were called **Chinchaysuyu**, **Antisuyu**, **Collasuyu**, and **Cuntisuyu**. The descending rank of the four parts followed the same sociospatial order. Each was named after a people or distinguishing feature of the land: the coastal Chincha society, the warm eastern slopes (*Antis;* see **Andes, Central**), the Colla people of the Lake Titicaca basin, and the Cuntisuyu region southwest of the capital.

The borders between the *suyus* are imperfectly understood, but were apparently not arrayed by cardinal directions, even around Cuzco. Chinchaysuyu was the most populous, richest, and second-largest of the *suyus*. It took in most of the **royal estate** lands in the Urubamba valley north of the capital and extended broadly to encompass most of northern Peru, including the rival empire of the Chimú, as well as Ecuador. Collasuyu ultimately took in the greatest territory; but south of the rich *altiplano* it was sparsely populated. Antisuyu contained a few prestigious royal manors, and extended toward the warm forests. Cuntisuyu was the smallest and probably least populated of all the parts, although some peoples and places were held in high esteem, for example the Inca origin place at Pacariqtambo (see **Myths, Origin**). Owing to imperial resettlement programs, many people identified on **census** rolls as belonging to one *suyu* found themselves living or discharging their tax obligations in another (see **Labor Service**). The frontiers of imperial control, while sustained by cordons of forts (sometimes scores of kilometers removed), were often permeable zones, across which the Incas selectively encouraged economic and cultural relations (see **Fortifications**). Anything that was outside the empire was considered to be disordered and thus dangerous—for example, the peoples and lands of Amazonia and the plains east of the southern Andes.

Imperial development may be assessed in terms of strategy, governance, material presence, and cultural impact. In its grand strategy, the Inca approach varied contextually from a direct, high-cost, high-control strategy (territorial rule) to an indirect, low-cost, low-control strategy (hegemonic rule). The most intensive approach was applied along the spine of the Andes, from the southern *altiplano* to highland Ecuador. That region boasted the greatest imperial constructions and the most elaborate administrative presence. Each province had a governor (*tocricoc*), usually an ethnic Inca lord, who presided over 20,000–30,000 taxpaying households. The approach was less intensive toward the peripheries, along most of the coast, and in the vast territory of Chile and northwest Argentina. While those areas also contained provinces with governors, the Incas often ruled from an administrative distance, for example through resettled colonists or locally recognized elites who worked as state agents. The physical presence of imperial control, especially in the infrastructure of roads and support facilities, was also less visible there.

Imperial governance was based on standard principles, drawn from the Incas' evolving notions of sociopolitical hierarchy, applied to the societies brought under Cuzco's authority. The intent seems to have been to forge a nominally homogeneous polity, presided over by the divine king and his relatives. Despite their claims, however, the Incas never achieved uniform, ubiquitous control over their subjects. Instead, the imperial presence varied markedly over space and context. The archaeologist John Hyslop suggested that imperial rule actually consisted of an array of networks—military, political, economic, and ideological—that coincided at particular times and places.

Inca rule blended the personal and the institutional in the ***Sapa Inca***, the aristocracy and imperial institutions, such as the **temples** and service groups. Because the ruler personified the state, the imperial, the divine, and the royal were often treated as one and the same. The administration was conducted by imposed hierarchies of officials, local lords, and people drawn into special service, willingly or not. The practicalities of governance were complicated by the great variety of subject societies, which required accommodations to specific circumstances. While the structure and demands of imperial rule intruded heavily into the lives of the Incas' subjects, the contexts of interaction were limited and much of the cycle of community life continued as before for much of the year. A great deal of internal diversity was accepted or even enforced. Local languages, material culture or social customs were permitted so long as they did not interfere with imperial interests. Particular features were required, such as the distinctive headgear that identified subjects as members of one or another society, because they facilitated keeping tabs on things (see **Costume**). In imperial business, therefore, selective standardization was the order of the day.

The material stamp of imperial presence was manifested through facilities, insignia, and tools. The most important expression occurred in the Cuzco heartland, at the reconstructed capital and the royal estates that occupied most of the surrounding lands within 50–60 kilometers (30–37 miles) of the capital. Elsewhere, Inca power was most visible in the network of more than 2,000 administrative facilities, linked by the road system. Access to the largest provincial center (e.g., Huánuco Pampa), the smallest roadside ***tambo***, or way station, any **storage** facility, or the road itself was reserved for those on approved business. In the centers' design, the Incas applied their notions of the proper layout of space (e.g., **dualism** and quadripartition) and activities within it. The Incas' distinctive architectural style and art of stonecutting provided an unmistakable mark of imperial presence. Entry, movement, sight lines, and actions were accommodated to an imperial rhythm and hierarchical order. Subjects were permitted or required to be present within the facilities at specific times, either for labor duties or events within the Incas' politico-ceremonial cycle.

With respect to more portable things, distinctive styles were created for insignia, **textiles**, **metals**, **stonework**, and **ceramics** that immediately identified any object as having been made under imperial auspices. The ruler had an array of personal insignia, notably the fringed headgear that was equivalent to a crown, a painted standard, a wooden seat, and a feathered staff (see **Costume; Feathers**). More generally, the Incas' material culture marked its status, exclusivity, and power. The decoration of many manufactures (especially textiles and pottery) was geometric and highly standardized; it was therefore easily recognized and reproduced throughout the domain. Only a few representational objects were made, such as rulers' body doubles, or brother icons (*huauque*) or the human and camelid figurines that were interred in offerings. With a few exceptions like the *huauque*, however, they were generic representations. The presence of Inca textiles, pottery, or drinking vessels implied the extended persona of the ruler or his personal approbation (see **Keros**). The textiles denoted status, while the ceramics were used for the commensal hospitality in which imperial politics were played out and edicts were announced (see **Ceramics**; **Feasting, State-Sponsored**).

Numerous landscape modifications, such as **terrace** complexes and **irrigation** systems, also marked imperial authority. In a more subtle, but equally potent, manner, the Incas asserted a special relationship with the sacred places and beings of the landscape. Unusual rocks or outcrops were carved or enclosed throughout the realm, and, in the southern part of the empire, shrines were placed on over 50 high peaks. Those acts worked as part of the Inca imperial effort to revere or even civilize the many nonhuman actors of their world, or at least to insert themselves as the mediators between humanity and those powers (see **Capac Hucha**; **Huacas**; **Religion**).

In the less tangible realm, the use of **Quechua** as the imperial *lingua franca* structured communication at the highest levels of the domain. Similarly, standardized methods of accounting with *quipus* dictated the ways that people and things were classified and tabulated, within imperial contexts of activity. Finally, the cycles of ceremonial, productive, and political activities that Incas conducted imposed a broad imperial vision of the proper order of life within Tahuantinsuyu.

Further Reading

D'Altroy, Terence N. *The Incas*. 2nd ed. New York: John Wiley & Sons, 2014.

Dean, Carolyn. *A Culture of Stone: Inka Perspectives on Rock*. Durham, NC: Duke University Press, 2010.

Hyslop, John. *Inka Settlement Planning*. Austin: University of Texas Press, 1990.

Morris, Craig. "Symbols to Power: Styles and Media in the Inka State." In *Style, Society, and Person: Archaeological and Ethnological Perspectives*, edited by Christopher Carr and Jill E. Neitzel, 419–33. New York: Plenum Press, 1995.

■ TERENCE N. D'ALTROY

S

SACSAHUAMAN

On a hill overlooking Cuzco stands Sacsahuaman, the "temple-fortress." The Spaniards called this massive set of walls and buildings a fortress, which is how many modern observers refer to it as well (see **Fortifications**). There is no evidence, however, that the site ever functioned as a fortress except in 1536, three years after the Spaniards first entered Cuzco, when the puppet king Manco Inca laid siege to Cuzco, trying, unsuccessfully, to oust the invading Spaniards. The chronicler **Pedro de Cieza de León** called Sacsahuaman a "house of the Sun," which suggests it played a role in Inca Sun worship. Its military function may have been primarily symbolic, as its wide esplanade might have served as the setting for ritual battles or reenactments (see **Battles, Ritual**). **Pedro Pizarro** described such a ritual battle staged by king Topa Inca Yupanqui to commemorate his victories in the north of the empire.

Sacsahuaman's three zigzagging walls, overlooking Cuzco. The site served as a setting for ritual battles, included a sun temple, and housed a large storage depot. Adriana von Hagen.

Sacsahuaman is composed of three sectors. To the north lies a circular reservoir sur-rounded by the foundations of formal buildings. It may have been the spring of Calis-puquio (spring of good health), a shrine in the *ceque* system of Cuzco (see **Ceques**). A rock outcrop that features the so-called Throne of the Inca (another *ceque* shrine, carved into a series of steps), divided the reservoir area from the second sector—the plaza or esplanade, while the third sector includes the zigzag terrace walls and summit structures and at least two towers, which overlooked Cuzco.

Sacsahuaman's most notable feature is three tiers of zigzag-shaped retaining walls, commonly called "ramparts," which flank the plaza. These massive walls, which stretch along some 400 meters (1,300 feet), are regularly punctuated by around 50 zigzagging angles. The lowest wall contains the megalithic, perfectly fitted stones that so astounded fifteenth-century Spaniards and modern visitors alike: "And even those who have seen it and considered it with attention imagine, and even believe, that it was made by enchant-ment, the handiwork of demons, rather than of men," wrote the chronicler **Garcilaso de la Vega (**1966 [1609]), who played among the walls of Sacsahuaman as a young boy. The great boulders that form the ramparts are of limestone, quarried at the building site itself and from the many outcrops dotting the surrounding hills. Smaller, andesite blocks came from the quarry of Rumicollca (see **Quarrying and Stonecutting**). The Spaniards viewed the Inca constructions at Sacsahuaman as a convenient quarry, pilfering blocks to build their churches and residences in the city; only the sheer size of the megalithic blocks saved the ramparts from being completely dismantled in Colonial times.

The chronicler Cieza noted that the task of building Sacsahuaman was such an enormous undertaking that the Incas brought in 20,000 men from the provinces to quarry and cut the stones, haul them around the site with cables of leather and hemp, dig the ditches, lay the foundations, and cut the poles and beams for the timbers used in the construction. Cieza remarked that in his time, the workers' houses could still be seen near Sacsahuaman. The reliable Cieza has been borne out by archaeology: a 5-hectare (12-acre) settlement known as Muyu Cocha spread across a hill not far from Sacsahuaman may have housed the workers. Much of the pottery found on the surface was imported from the Lake Titicaca region, suggesting that Sacsahuaman's builders came from that area, famed for its stoneworkers. Cieza also observed that the scale of Sacsahuaman was so vast that it could not have been completed. Indeed, studies show signs of work in progress on the rampart walls; the construction project was perhaps cut short by the Spanish invasion.

Nearly all the chroniclers stress that Sacsahuaman served as an enormous storage center. Excavations on the summit unearthed a maze of small rooms, perhaps the remains of storerooms. According to one early eyewitness, there were so many store-rooms that "10,000 soldiers" could occupy them. No doubt this is an exaggeration, but nonetheless the array of stored goods claimed to have been kept there is astounding, including clubs, lances, bows, arrows, axes, shields, heavy jackets of quilted cotton, and other weapons; clothing; gold and silver, precious stones, sandals, feathers, skins of an-imals and birds, coca, and bags of wool. "Everything anyone had ever heard of," wrote Cieza, "was in it" (Cieza 1959 [1553]).

Further Reading

Bauer, Brian S. *Ancient Cusco: Heartland of the Inca.* Austin: University of Texas Press, 2004.

Cieza de León, Pedro de. *The Incas of Pedro de Cieza de León.* Translated by Harriet de Onís, edited by Victor Wolfgang von Hagen. Norman: University of Oklahoma Press, 1959 [1553–1554].

Garcilaso de la Vega, El Inca. *Royal Commentaries of the Incas and General History of Peru, Part One.* Translated by Harold V. Livermore. Austin: University of Texas Press, 1966 [1609].

Hyslop, John. *Inka Settlement Planning.* Austin: University of Texas Press, 1999.

■ ADRIANA VON HAGEN

SÁMANO ACCOUNT

The first encounter between Spaniards and Andean civilization took place not on land, but at sea. An undated document, signed by Juan de Sámano, a secretary of the Council of the Indies, and thus referred to as the Sámano account, chronicled the encounter. The meeting at sea took place in 1525, during Francisco Pizarro's second voyage of exploration along the coasts of what are today Panama, Colombia, and Ecuador. Just south of the Equator, Pizarro's pilot Bartolomé Ruíz captured a large balsa raft that was sailing north; the raft was rigged with cotton sails and manned by a crew of some 20 men. It carried a cargo of gold and silver objects, semiprecious stones, and fine garments "beautifully worked with elaborate craftsmanship." According to the Sámano account, the Native sailors planned to exchange their cargo "for some sea shells [probably Spondylus] of which they make beads of a reddish and white color." Several sailors jumped ship to avoid capture, but Ruíz seized three men, who subsequently learned Spanish and served as interpreters on Pizarro's third voyage and invasion of Tahuantinsuyu. Armed with the report of the balsa raft and its riches, Pizarro sailed to Spain where he convinced the Spanish sovereign to name him governor and captain-general of a follow-up expedition to the as yet-to-be-discovered Peru.

Sámano's account is one of the first reports of Spanish exploration along the west coast of South America. Although the authorship is disputed (it was originally attributed to Francisco de Xerez), the consensus among scholars today is that it was written by someone aboard Ruíz's ship. No matter who wrote the account, the narrative it contains is a testament to the skill of the Pre-Columbian navigators who sailed with Native craft technology off the west coast of South America, trading goods as far north as Mexico. The communities of coastal Ecuador that controlled the balsa raft trade may even have provided their seafaring expertise to the Incas, supplying the empire with the coveted Spondylus shell, harvested in the deep, warm waters off the coast of Ecuador (see **Seafaring**).

While the Native sailors encountered on Pizarro's second voyage were probably not Inca subjects, they were nonetheless aware of the existence of the Incas and the information they gave Pizarro fired his imagination, leading to further exploration and, ultimately, the conquest of Tahuantinsuyu.

Further Reading

Morlion, Magali. "Sámano Account (ca. 1527–1528)." In *Guide to Documentary Sources for Andean Studies, 1530–1900,* edited by Joanne Pillsbury, vol. 3, 627–29. Norman: University of Oklahoma Press, 2008.

■ ADRIANA VON HAGEN

SAPA INCA

Sapa Inca was an acclamation used to hail the Andean emperor, as he passed, carried high on the shoulders of his litter bearers. The phrase translates from the **Quechua** as *sole, unique,* or *only* Inca or Inca priest whose brilliant figure is visible to all. It was one of many names used to address the ruler of a vast jurisdictional empire made up of scores of ethnic groups who occupied the coastal plains, intermontane valleys, high plateaus, and eastern upper jungle reaches in what is today southern Colombia, Ecuador, Peru, Bolivia, Chile, and northwestern Argentina. Because the given personal names of rulers were considered too sacred to utter aloud, each Inca also had titles and praise names, the second of which often referred to one of his characteristics. The sobriquet *Huayna Capac,* for example, indicated that he was a young ruler.

A watercolor portrait of Manco Capac in Martín de Murúa's chronicle. Murúa, Martín de. *Códice Murúa—Historia y Genealogía de los Reyes Incas del Perú* (Códice Galvin). Madrid: Testimonio Compañía Editorial, S. A., 2004 [1590-1598].

Yupanqui is another designation used by many, often in a composite title (see table). The classic chroniclers defined it as *remembered, honored,* or *immortal.* A simple linguistic analysis of the **Quechua** root and its derivatives suggests the act of counting. The word *Yupanqui* itself can be glossed as accountant. *Yupa,* the root, means abundant or many, and it can be modified to signify multiples, innumerable, or infinite. Applied in context, then, the conquest and multiple alliances with ethnic groups characterized the person with this name as a counter of many people or ruler of innumerable nations. Expansion and the idea of control over huge numbers of people are implied, giving him the right to be worthy of honor, glory, respect, and praise. This analysis underscores the fact that the motivation for Inca imperialism was not, as others have postulated, the dominion over land or ground as a commodity, private property in the western sense, per se; nor, was it, as others have suggested, the control of trade routes. It was, instead, the control of labor that defined *rich* in the Native point of view (see **Labor Service; Wealth**).

This definition of the name Yupanqui corresponds well to the title of *El Cuzco* (the Cuzco) used to refer to the emperor at the time of the Spanish invasion as the one who dominated or supervised a hierarchy of decimally defined administrative positions (see

The Standard List of Inca Kings

Ruler's Praise Name	Translation	Given Name
Manco Capac	Creator or Original Omnipotent (King)	
Sinchi Roca	Warrior Roca	
Lloque Yupanqui	Left-Handed (Ruler) of Incalculable Peoples	
Mayta Capac	Omnipotent Mayta	
Capac Yupanqui	Omnipotent (Ruler) of Incalculable Peoples	
Inca Roca	King Roca	
Yawar Huacap	He Who Cries Blood	Inca Yupanqui, Mayta Yupanqui, Titu Cusi Hualpa
Viracocha Inca	Creator King	Hatun Topa Inca
Pachacuti Inca Yupanqui	Reforming King of Incalculable Peoples	Inca Yupanqui, Cusi Yupanqui
Topa Inca Yupanqui	Ruler of Allied Incalculable Peoples	
Huayna Capac	Young King	Titu Cusi Hualpa
Huascar Inca	King of the Golden Chain	Topa Cusi Hualpa
Atahualpa	Cock	

Administration, Decimal; Census). The political status of El Cuzco, like that of his subordinates, was measured by the number of his followers: the more followers, the higher the status. The rank of the emperor, like his subordinates, was symbolized to onlookers by the height of his seat or throne (the higher the throne, the higher the status); whether he was carried seated on a litter or prone in a hammock; and by the fineness of the weaving and decoration of his clothes.

Tied to the status and reputation of El Cuzco, as well as the hierarchy of imperial officials beneath him, was Andean society's definition of rich and poor. The rich leader had numerous followers whereas the poor man or person was an orphan, without kin or following. Such a conceptualization had wide-ranging ramifications—even to the desirability of a woman for marriage. The best match in the estimation of a leader was not the prettiest lady, or the strongest, or the one with the most material possessions, but the female who had the largest kin network, because after their union, the groom had the right to request help from the bride's kin—to open an irrigation ditch, plow and plant fields, or offer a feast for the ancestors.

The one exception was the Inca who, ideally (at least in late Inca times), took his biological sister as a principal wife to concentrate an essence that coursed through their veins, called *capac*. This substance made the Incas "very much more than kings" (Julien 2000), probably referring to their divinity. Theoretically, this incestuous pair became the progenitors of a new royal lineage or **panaca**, which evolved into an institution charged with caring for the sovereign's mummy and maintaining his memory by singing and re-counting his accomplishments (see **Mummies, Royal; Worship, Ancestor**).

The *Sapa* Inca, like his ancestors, claimed descent from a lineage that descended from the union of the Sun, their father, and the Moon, their mother. Therefore, the Inca ruler's proud claim to be the son of the Sun, their principal deity and ancestor, legitimized (in part) his rule. He served as the Sun's chief steward, offering the solar deity maize beer (*chicha*) from golden beakers (*aquillas*; *see* **Keros**). Simultaneously, he was the center of a large kinship network that, through his many secondary wives, tied his person and interests to those of subordinate ethnic groups throughout the empire.

The Spanish observers collected information on this lineage and admitted that the names and numbers and status of rulers that they heard recounted—especially in the city of Cuzco—were confused and confusing (see **King List**). The first to systematize the information in the mid-1550s was the chronicler **Juan de Betanzos** who was married to an Inca princess and became an official interpreter for the Spanish Crown. He qualified the accuracy of the information he accumulated in interviews, but put the data he considered the most reliable into a form that Spaniards could readily understand—a European-style dynasty of kings, starting with Manco Capac, the legendary founder (see **Myths, Origin**). This, with some variations from writer to writer, became the standard list of kings (see table). There may have been other rulers, because Andean informants stated that a do-nothing or discredited king did not found a *panaca*, was not memorialized, and dropped from collective memory. One mid-seventeenth-century chronicler lists over a hundred kings, naming five Manco Capacs and multiple Pachacutis. Ongoing research on naming practices suggests that this topic and the history of Andean memory require further research.

The Incas had no universally accepted law of succession. Therefore, transition from one ruler to the next could be fraught with rancorous negotiations, political intrigues, ousters, and assassinations. War became the ultimate solution when politics and diplomacy failed, because war was believed to test the strength of each contender and his favor with the gods. Images of the gods were carried into active combat zones as a source of strength and inspiration. In the civil war between Huascar and Atahualpa, victories on the battlefields were interpreted as indicating the Sun god's choice for the *Sapa* Inca (see **Wars, Dynastic**). The necessity of choosing sides and supporting one candidate or another and the inevitable reprisals that awaited those who backed the losing faction meant that the empire was inherently unstable and that each *Sapa* Inca had to negotiate and reestablish his relationships with ethnic groups in each generation or in the wake of each transition.

Further Reading

D'Altroy, Terence N. *The Incas*. 2nd ed. New York: John Wiley & Sons, 2014.

Julien, Catherine J. *Reading Inca History*. Iowa City: University of Iowa Press, 2000.

McEwan, Gordon F. *The Incas*. New York: W. W. Norton, 2006.

Pärssinen, Martti. *Tawantinsuyu: The Inca State and Its Political Organization*. Studia Historica 43. Helsinki: Finnish Historical Society, 1992.

Pease, Franklin. *Los últimos Incas del Cusco*. Madrid: Alianza América, 1991.

Ramírez, Susan Elizabeth. *To Feed and Be Fed: The Cosmological Bases of Authority and Identity in the Andes*. Stanford, CA: Stanford University Press, 2005.

———. "Bajo el nombre de los antepasados: La memoria viva en los Andes, siglos XVI-XVII." In *Un juego de engaños. Nombres, apellidos y movilidad en los siglos XV al XVIII*, edited by G. Salinero and I. Testón Núñez, 163–86. Madrid: Casa de Velázquez, 2010.

■ SUSAN ELIZABETH RAMÍREZ

SARMIENTO DE GAMBOA, PEDRO

One of the most adventurous of the Spanish chroniclers of Peru, Sarmiento was born in Alcalá de Henares, Spain, and traveled to Peru in the early 1560s, after spending several years in Mexico and Guatemala. He headed one expedition to search for the biblical land of Ophir, in the south Pacific, in the late 1560s, and a second expedition aimed at establishing Spanish settlements in the Straits of Magellan, in 1579. Between the two expeditions, Sarmiento lived in Peru and served in the administration of the fifth Viceroy of Peru, Francisco de Toledo (1569–1581). Toledo commissioned Sarmiento to write the first official Crown-sponsored history of the Inca Empire, the *Historia Indica* (1572).

In preparation for writing the *Historia Indica*, Sarmiento assembled some 100 highly knowledgeable members of the Inca nobility in Cuzco, most of whom were recognized as *quipucamayocs* (keepers of the knotted cords; see **Quipu**). Sarmiento and his scribe, Alvaro Ruíz de Navamuel, took depositions from the 100 witnesses about the lives of the Inca kings, as well as the basic institutions, policies, and procedures of Inca governance, and accounts of Inca rites, ceremonies, and myths. The information was synthesized into a history of the Inca Empire, which Sarmiento then read, apparently word for word (in Spanish), to 42 descendants of the noble lineages (**panacas**) of Cuzco, many of whom had served as witnesses. The names, ages, and *panaca* affiliations of the 42 witnesses are listed at the end of the *Historia Indica*. In reading his account to the descendants of the Inca nobility, Sarmiento sought to obtain their conformity as to the truth and accuracy of his history of the Incas.

It is important to note that Viceroy Toledo had a larger objective in commissioning Sarmiento to write his history: the justification of the Spanish conquest of the Incas, the killing of the last Inca king (Atahualpa), and the subsequent establishment of Colonial rule over the former territories of Tahuantinsuyu. The *Historia Indica* realized this objective by claiming that the Incas had gained power over their Andean subjects by illegitimate means and that, therefore, they ruled as tyrants, rather than as legitimate and just rulers. With the construction of this narrative line, which is repeated throughout the document, the Spanish justified (in their own eyes) the conquest of Peru and the legitimacy of their rule over the former Inca Empire.

Sarmiento's *Historia Indica* was probably never seen nor read, until modern times, beyond the confines of the Spanish Viceregal administration and the royal court in Spain. The document was sent back to Spain in 1572 and presented to Philip II. Its fate over the next couple of centuries is unknown. It was not seen again until 1893, when it was discovered in the library of the University of Göttingen, Germany.

Further Reading

Clissold, Stephen. *Conquistador: The Life of Don Pedro Sarmiento de Gamboa*. London: D. Verschoyle, 1954.

Pease, Franklin. "Sarmiento de Gamboa, Pedro (1535–1592?)." In *Guide to Documentary Sources for Andean Studies, 1530–1900*, edited by Joanne Pillsbury, vol. 3, 488–96. Norman: University of Oklahoma Press, 2008.

Sarmiento de Gamboa, Pedro. *History of the Incas*. Translated by Sir Clements Markham (1907). Cambridge, ON: In Parentheses Publications, 2000 [1572]. http://www.yorku.ca/inpar/ sarmiento_markham.pdf.

———. *The History of the Incas*. Translated and edited by Brian S. Bauer and Vania Smith. Austin: University of Texas Press, 2007 [1572].

Urton, Gary. *The History of a Myth: Pacariqtambo and the Origin of the Incas*. Austin: University of Texas Press, 1990.

■ GARY URTON

SEAFARING

Even in their mountain fastness the Incas were always aware of the ocean. Their intense interest in what we now call *hydrology* encompassed both the science of water management and irrigation, and the intuitive knowledge that all rivers would eventually flow to the sea. From their vantage atop the Andean watershed, the Incas observed that all streams in the Cuzco valley fed into the Vilcanota River. The river then turned eastward to join the waters plunging down the Apurimac gorge to the Amazonian lowlands and thence to the distant, unseen Atlantic beyond. On the other side of the continental divide, seasonal floods coursed westward in narrow ribbons crossing the coastal desert to reach the limitless expanse of the Pacific. It is no surprise then that Inca cosmology embraced the notion of an interconnected watery underworld and that the mythical birthplace of the Sun and the Moon was located on the sacred **Islands of the Sun and Moon** surrounded by the blue depths of Lake Titicaca (see **Myths, Origin**). Such was their ritual interest in the sea that Inca rulers ordered many tons of beach sand to be brought up from the coast and laid in a deep layer across their principal public plaza in **Cuzco**, so turning it into a symbolic "ocean" in microcosm.

The Incas' rapid expansion in the fourteenth and fifteenth centuries along the spine of the Andes was inextricably linked with the myth of an archetypal journey made by the creator god Viracocha from the southeastern reaches of the empire to his disappearance "across the waves" in the far northwest. There are varying versions of this myth that end with different points of departure on the Pacific coast, ranging from Acarí in southern Peru, to Manta on the coast of Ecuador. The variant accounts mirror the expanding frontier of the Inca Empire, bringing it into contact with coastal fishing communities that had honed their seafaring skills over many millennia. It is said that the Inca Topa Inca Yupanqui, in his conquests toward the coast of Ecuador, eventually reached Manta (Jocay), the principal town of the coastal polity of Jocay, and scaled a local mountain in order to "discover the sea" for the first time. The Inca king exercised his royal prerogative of discovery and worship of the Pacific Ocean by naming the ocean *Mamacocha* (mother

Totora reed boats on Lake Titicaca, southern Peru. Boats such as these have been used for millennia in the Andes. Sebastián Turpo. TAFOS Photographic Archive/ PUCP, Lima, Peru.

of the lakes) to emphasize the links between highland lakes and the ocean. Topa Inca Yupanqui is also said to have been accompanied by a "vast retinue" on a long sea voyage to the islands of Auchumbi and Ninachumbi and these journeys likely entailed visiting offshore island shrines.

A variety of small marine craft were instrumental in opening up the exploitation of inshore coastal resources. Some craft depended on inflated sea lion skins as flotation devices. The natural buoyancy of *totora* reeds was also used to advantage by tightly binding bundles together to fashion the famed reed boats depicted on Moche pottery vessels 1,500 years ago (see **Chronology, Pre-Inca**), and still used to this day for artisanal fishing at Huanchaco near Trujillo on Peru's north coast. The same technology was also used to build substantial *totora* reed rafts that the Incas would have commandeered to reach their sanctuaries on the islands of the Sun and Moon in Lake Titicaca. Similar journeys on balsa rafts were made to offshore shrines in the Pacific such as Macabí Island and Isla de la Plata. It is clear that the Incas, as highlanders, were dependent on the skills and knowledge of coastal and lacustrine dwellers to venture onto lakes and oceans.

Nowhere was this more apparent than on the far north coast of Peru where large oceangoing balsa sailing rafts brought in the most valued material of all, the precious red-rimmed thorny oyster *Spondylus princeps* (*mullu*), a marine shell extricated by specialist divers from the ocean depths that held immense symbolic value for the Incas. It is precisely this shell that is found in high-altitude **capac hucha** burials as offerings to the mountain deities that were a vital source of life-sustaining springs and flowing streams. In terms of Andean cosmology, the shell offerings affirmed the essential connection between mountains and sea. The Incas' political and economic ambitions were closely bound up with an ideological imperative to assert ritual control over the sources of life, including, ultimately, the "world ocean" at the limits of the known world. It was the effort to procure *mullu* in ever increasing quantities that must have been a prime motivating factor in their attempts to conquer and control the coast of what is today Ecuador.

In his northern campaigns, Topa Inca Yupanqui established the garrison town of Tumbes, lying on the southern shores of the Guayas estuary, as a vital port of trade for state-controlled production of valued marine shells. The waters north of Tumbes, including the Guayas estuary and the open seas beyond, were traversed with ease by coastal populations, but were an unfamiliar environment for the Inca highlanders. Smaller balsa rafts served for artisanal fishing, while larger craft served to maintain long-distance trading contacts involving the exchange of a range of exotic materials. While the rafts were the main means of pre-Columbian maritime transport and exchange, they were controlled by coastal seafaring populations and not directly by the Incas themselves. Initial attempts to cross the Guayas estuary met with disaster when a party of high-ranking noblemen borne on a balsa raft were set adrift and murdered at the hands of mariners from the island of Puna—an act of betrayal that is said to have incurred severe punishment.

Scholars have long agreed that an effective conquest and incorporation of the coastal polities into the Inca domain was problematic, even during the reign of Huayna Capac. An intriguing find of a high status Inca burial on Isla de la Plata made over 100 years ago, however, assumes special significance, lying as it does at the northern coastal extremity of the Inca Empire. We must surmise that the Incas would have had to negotiate their visits to the island on local craft with local sailors pressed into service. In 1891–1892, the North American investigator George Dorsey excavated two skeletons accompanied by a suite of miniature figurines and a set of paired miniature ceramic vessels. These elements identify the find as a *capac hucha* burial designed to mark the formal incorporation of the island, the surrounding sea, and the adjacent mainland into imperial sacred geography.

The first European contact with Andean cultures occurred when Pizarro ventured south from Panama in 1525 and made landfall near the San Juan River in Colombia. In the waters off Ecuador his navigator Bartolomé Ruíz described a vivid eyewitness encounter off the coast of Ecuador between the Spanish vessels and an oceangoing balsa sailing raft (see **Sámano Account**). This provides a compelling account of an advanced maritime capability and the list of goods "to barter with those with whom they were going to trade" encompasses a range of elite body ornaments and other accoutrements in gold, as well as finely woven garments, all used to signal the status of high-ranking lords among the populous trading polities of the Pacific coast. Fittingly, the account emphasizes that all these goods were traded for *mullu*.

Further Reading

Cabello Valboa, Miguel. *Miscelánea Antártica. Una historia del Perú antiguo*. Lima: Universidad Nacional Mayor de San Marcos, Facultad de Letras, Instituto de Etnología, 1951 [1586].

Garcilaso de la Vega, El Inca. *Royal Commentaries of the Incas and General History of Peru*. Translated by Harold V. Livermore. 2 vols. Austin: University of Texas Press, 1966 [1609, 1617].

Morlion, Magali. "Sámano Account (ca. 1527–1528)." In *Guide to Documentary Sources for Andean Studies, 1530–1900*. Edited by Joanne Pillsbury, vol. 3, 627–29. Norman: University of Oklahoma Press, 2008.

Sarmiento de Gamboa, Pedro. *The History of the Incas.* Translated and edited by Brian S. Bauer and Vania Smith. Austin: University of Texas Press, 2007 [1572].

■ COLIN MCEWAN

STORAGE

The dramatic reports of great cities, highways, and storehouses made by chroniclers of the early Conquest period have long framed our understanding of the Inca state economy. And yet, while descriptions by early chroniclers such as Miguel de Estete and **Pedro de Cieza de León** of the stockpiles of food, cloth, and weapons at highland centers such as **Cajamarca** and **Cuzco** provide a fascinating vision of a state able to mobilize and control vast quantities of agricultural and craft products, a detailed understanding of the social institutions that actually lay behind these state storage facilities has proved more elusive.

As scholars working within a political economy tradition have argued at great length, accounting for these institutional means of mobilizing and controlling surplus products is critical to understanding the emergence and persistence of sociopolitically complex formations such as Tahuantinsuyu, the Inca Empire (particularly within the environmental extremes of the Andean region). Over the past 50 years, archaeological survey, excavation, and the careful rereading of archival sources has pointed to both the importance and the variability of Inca state storage systems and pushed scholars to reconsider the nature of political control and economic organization in the late pre-Columbian Andes.

This growing body of research has revealed that storage facilities indeed formed a key part of the state-directed establishment of an integrated imperial landscape that included

Storerooms at the coastal settlement of Incahuasi in Peru's Cañete valley. Adriana von Hagen.

the construction of administrative sites, roadside way stations (*tambos*), the **road** network itself, and large agricultural **terracing** programs. Scholars have long noted several major spatial patterns in the distribution of state storage facilities, highlighting the massive concentration and scale of storage in the highland provinces, especially in comparison with the imperial core at Cuzco, the capital, and with the Pacific coastal zone. While research since 1995 has brought greater nuance to these dichotomies, the distinct provincial highland pattern of massive agricultural storage facilities remains one of the best-understood features of the Inca economic landscape.

This provincial highland pattern is best known from investigations at central highland administrative centers such as Huánuco Pampa, Pumpu, and Hatun Jauja. Adjacent to these sites are large installations of circular and square storehouses (*collcas*) arranged in long rows on nearby hillsides; in some cases, up to several thousand storehouses are associated with a single major administrative center. Constructed with fieldstone masonry, these modular constructions tend to consist of one or two rooms and often show carefully designed features to ensure optimal storage conditions. As archaeobotanical work has demonstrated, these *collcas* seem to have been used predominantly for the large-scale storage of agricultural products such as maize, Andean grains, and tubers. In some cases, excavations have recovered significant quantities of unprocessed, single-species plant remains. As such, these facilities drew on the long-standing highland traditions of staple food processing and storage developed over millennia of highland adaptation.

Patterns of state-level storage have long been central to interpretations of the nature of Inca imperial administration, often with an emphasis on those features that were unique to the Inca case. While a number of early commentators (from **Pedro de Cieza de León** in the sixteenth century through to Louis Baudin in the early twentieth century) saw large-scale accumulation as evidence for a benevolent state that emphasized the redistribution of staple goods to the general populace, the last fifty years of scholarship has moved firmly away from this position.

This alternative approach questioning the state's role in redistribution had some of its origins with **John V. Murra** and Craig Morris's seminal archaeological and ethnohistorical work in the central highlands, elaborated further in the 1980s and 1990s, particularly by a group of UCLA scholars. Explicitly drawing upon the economic anthropological focus on the role of specific cultural contexts, the emphasis was on the distinctive institutional characteristics of Tahuantinsuyu, rather than attempting to fit the Inca case into a reductive evolutionary framework. Moving away from previous assumptions of bureaucratic power, Morris argued for a political strategy of Inca state hospitality based on his investigations of the administrative center at Huánuco Pampa, with episodes of feasting and gift giving drawing upon the resources accumulated in centralized storage complexes.

The evidence from Huánuco Pampa—including the massive central plaza, locations for large-scale food preparation, and the monumental rows of *collcas* separated from local population centers—seemed to point toward such a strategy that emphasized political performance over larger interventions in the subsistence and crafting economies. Unlike a classic tributary state, the integration between the state and the local community was relatively loose given the focus on labor mobilization rather than tributary goods. Critically for the topic at hand, it was argued that the interregional movement of staples was minimal, with

A *quipucamayoc*, or *quipu* master, discusses storehouse inventory with the Inca ruler Topa Inca Yupanqui in this drawing by the Native chronicler Felipe Guaman Poma de Ayala. Guaman Poma de Ayala, Felipe. *El primer nueva corónica y buen gobierno*. Edited by John V. Murra and Rolena Adorno, 309/335. Mexico City: Siglo Veintiuno, 1980 [1615].

an emphasis on the long-distance movement of people instead; hence *collcas* at administrative centers acted as locally oriented storehouses rather than warehouses for large-scale transfers.

Subsequent work has modified this model of a storage-feasting-gifting complex, moving it in several new directions while maintaining the political economic focus on the broader mechanisms of Inca state power. Many scholars have commented on the ideological aspects of storage buildings as materialized expressions of state power, as well as the ways in which the spatial organization of *collcas* may have been a means of inscribing particular forms of state accounting into the landscape. Others have emphasized the key role that provincial storage facilities may have played specifically for the sustenance of Inca military and corvée labor, or rotating *mit'a*, forces (see **Labor Service**).

In addition to forming a basis for several important models of the overall structures of the Inca political economy, storage facilities have also been used as a key proxy for the *variable* presence of the Inca state. Research in southern Tahuantinsuyu is indicative of this approach; some have argued that the presence of substantial Inca-style *collcas* suggests fairly direct political hegemony over the northern Chilean highlands, while others propose that much smaller-scale storage components, which follow local templates, demonstrate a more limited Inca presence in northwestern Argentina.

While the highland model of state *collcas* outlined so far continues to be highly influential on discussions of the Inca imperial economy, several key questions remain to be fully explored. How easily can we draw a simple relationship between large *collca* installations and direct imperial control? What do we make of areas of apparently direct control

Restored *collcas*, or storehouses, above Cuzco's Urubamba valley. The Incas often placed storerooms on hillsides to enhance conditions for preservation of stored goods. Darryl Wilkinson.

without massive agricultural storage facilities (e.g., the Titicaca basin)? Did all large state storage facilities fulfill the same general goals (e.g., the Huánuco Pampa model), or were there multiple storage strategies engaged by the Inca state depending on regional conditions (as the facilities at Cochabamba in Bolivia, Incahuasi on Peru's central coast, and Farfán on Peru's north coast might suggest)?

It is also worth noting that synthetic analyses of storage in the Inca economy have tended to focus almost exclusively on major administrative centers. As a result, there are several important gaps in our knowledge about other scales of storage and resource flows. First, the articulation of large regional centers with other state storage facilities such as *tambos* and corrals remains an important unknown. Were these sites only supplied from local catchment areas or did they receive goods from regional storage facilities? Second, the storage of nonstaple goods (seemingly an important function even at sites such as **Sacsahuaman** overlooking Cuzco), has also tended to be ignored due to a lack of straightforward archaeological signatures. Third, the ways in which storage at the levels of the household and the community might have articulated with the state are also obscure. While ethnohistoric and ethnographic sources hint at architectural installations associated with the institution of *sapci* or community resources, it remains unclear how these relate to the *collcas* and other storage facilities found at smaller residential sites such as Aukimarka Baja in Huánuco, Peru, and Potrero-Chaquiago in Catamarca, Argentina.

We still also lack a clear understanding of the Andean precedents for Inca patterns of storage and resource flows. While the Late Intermediate Period that preceded the Inca florescence remains poorly understood in many respects, it is likely that the immediate origins of many Inca storage forms are to be found there. There are, for instance, substantial regional storage facilities in the Tarma region of Peru's central highlands that appear to predate the Inca presence. The pattern of imperial storage may date back even earlier to the Huari polity of the Middle Horizon, although some have questioned the importance of storage facilities in Huari administrative centers and their influence on later developments in the Andes (see **Chronology, Pre-Inca**).

In tackling these key problems concerning storage strategies in the Late Horizon, the interpretive balance in considering both the unifying forces and internal diversity of the complex political economy of Tahuantinsuyu is immediately apparent. Given the importance of the Inca state economy in understanding the global diversity of economic formations from a comparative standpoint, a better understanding of the multiple spatial scales and the long-term genesis of Inca systems of resource flow and accumulation remains a goal of considerable interest beyond the specific realm of Andean studies.

Further Reading

D'Altroy, Terence N. *Provincial Power in the Inka Empire*. Washington, DC: Smithsonian Institution Press, 1992.

Hyslop, John. *Inka Settlement Planning*. Austin: University of Texas Press, 1990.

LeVine, T., ed. *Inka Storage Systems*. Norman: University of Oklahoma Press, 1992.

Murra, John V. *The Economic Organization of the Inka State*. Greenwich, CT: JAI Press, 1980 [1956].

■ NOA CORCORAN-TADD

SUBSISTENCE

Subsistence practices in the Inca Empire varied widely due to the enormous variability in environments. By minimizing disruption to local food production, the Incas were able to generate the surpluses they needed to expand their empire and maintain it. Subsistence can be divided into three main activities: farming, herding, and fishing. Hunting of wild game such as guanaco, vicuña, and deer, was apparently restricted to the Inca elite, though commoners probably engaged in some small-scale hunting, such as trapping birds for their **feathers**.

Farming was the foundation of the Inca economy. It involved preparing the fields for planting, which often began with clearing new land. Farming implements were simple, consisting of a *chaquitaqlla* (foot plow), a hoe, and a clod buster. Modern *chaquitaqlla*s consist of a long wooden pole with a pointed end or metal tip, a handle, and a foot rest near the tip; drawings by the Native chronicler **Felipe Guaman Poma de Ayala** indicate that Inca-era ones were basically the same. The *chaquitaqlla* was used to dig up large chunks of earth that were then turned over. The clod buster was a rock attached to a handle that was used to break up the large clods of earth. A hoe consisted of a rock attached at an angle, much like a modern hoe. The hoe was used both for fieldwork and to clear irrigation canals.

Once the planting was done, which typically involved men and women, the field would be left until harvest, unless **irrigation** was practiced, in which case the field would periodically be watered from the local irrigation canal. When the field was ready to be harvested, all members of the family participated, and often *ayllu* members helped each other. The food was stored in each family's house. Today, and likely during Inca times, people celebrated the harvest, feasting, drinking, dancing and playing music, and making offerings of thanks to the gods. Harvest celebrations for different crops followed a **ritual calendar**.

Crops grown for the empire were transported to a regional administrative center where they could be stored for the empire's uses (see **Storage**). Thus, local people not only harvested and stored their own food, but harvested and transported the crops of the Incas as well.

In addition to local production, the Incas developed state farms in many regions of the empire and staffed them with permanent workers, either *mitmacuna* or *yanacuna* (see **Labor Service**). Crops grown on state farms were also transported to storage facilities, though often these farms were located close to such facilities.

Herding was a second major activity of Andean people. Llamas and alpacas were the two domesticated camelids; the former served principally as a pack animal, while the latter was largely exploited for its fine fiber (see **Animals, Domesticated**). Domesticated camelids also served as sacrificial animals, with hundreds used for this purpose yearly in **Cuzco** (see **Religion**). Finally, llamas and alpacas were a source of food. For local people, they were consumed when they were too old for other purposes, while for the Inca elite, they could be eaten at a younger, tenderer age.

It is likely that most highland households herded llamas and alpacas, though the numbers of animals varied widely. Unlike fields, which were considered the property of an individual's *ayllu* and not the individual, animals were owned by households. Many chroniclers observed that individuals also owned herds, and certainly local lords maintained herds, some of considerable size.

Llamas and alpacas were essential to the operation of households. Llamas were needed for transporting goods from fields to home. Alpaca fiber was used for clothing, although llama fiber could also be used. There were no tools specific to herding, as the animals were simply driven to pasture or fields until they returned home. This was work of older children and adolescents. Pasture land was likely owned by *ayllus* and used jointly by its members.

The Incas also developed large herds of camelids for state purposes. While fields could be divided for state and local uses, herds could not. Chroniclers and legal documents from the Colonial period note the taking of local herds by the Incas. As large herds of camelids thrived on the *altiplano* in pre-Inca times, it is no surprise that this region was a target of early Inca **conquests**.

The Incas needed large herds of llamas for transporting food to warehouses and also to provision the armies as they conducted their campaigns. A male llama can carry about 30 kilograms (65 pounds) of weight for 20 kilometers (12 miles) a day, though every third day it must be relieved of its burden. Thus, the armies had to use a third more llamas than were needed for transport in order to supply their food demands. In the highlands, llamas can forage for their own food, so they do not need additional supplies for their use. This was not the case on the coast.

The other major use of domesticated camelids was for their fiber. Every year, each household was required to make one garment for the state; the fiber for that garment was provided by the empire. The finer fiber of alpacas may have been reserved for the upper echelons of Inca society, and the even finer fiber of the wild vicuña was reserved for royal uses. Both were likely spun and woven by the ***acllacuna*** at state facilities. In contrast to local herds, *yanacuna* herded state flocks.

Fishing constituted the third major subsistence activity of the Incas, but it was largely restricted to the coastal zones and the shores of Lake Titicaca. Along the coast, marine resources were extremely important and had been since early prehistory. Fish, shellfish, marine mammals, birds, and seaweed were all consumed by communities. It is uncertain whether such resources were transported into the highlands during Inca times, but it is said that if the ***Sapa* Inca** (the sole, unique Inca ruler) desired fish, it took three days for *chasquis* running in relay to carry it to Cuzco (see **Roads**). Fish and seaweed could be dried and stored for periods of time, much like the freeze-dried food of the highlands.

Tools for exploiting the bounty of the sea included cotton nets with bottle gourd floats; hook and line fishing, with hooks made of cactus spines or shell; and boats. Along the shores of Lake Titicaca, fishing was conducted in reed boats similar to those found along the coast. While we do not have examples of the kinds of boats used, boat images on Moche pottery, dating to the Early Intermediate Period, indicate two kinds were used—a small individual boat of reeds lashed together, which the fishermen straddled, and a larger raft of logs. The latter often had sails, and one such raft was encountered by members of Francisco Pizarro's expedition on one of his early voyages down the Ecuadorian coast (see **Invasion, Spanish; Sámano Account; Seafaring**). Sea lions were clubbed, and birds were caught with nets or perhaps killed with slings.

Guinea pigs offered another source of protein besides camelid meat and plants such as maize or quinoa. Although guinea pigs provided only a small amount of meat per animal, they reproduce rapidly. They eat a wide variety of food, and even today people keep guinea pigs in their kitchens where they eat table scraps. There is no evidence that the Inca exploited them at the empire level; they were more likely a staple of local people, including the Inca nobility in Cuzco.

Exploiting different ecozones (see **Farming**), local communities maintained a nutritious diet, and surpluses were created and used by the Inca Empire. It is worth noting that when a community could not provide enough food for its members because of environmental problems, the Incas provided them food from their storehouses, which the people then repaid when conditions improved. Thus, the Incas were able to smooth out natural swings in productivity, although it was also a way to maintain control over their subjects.

Further Reading

D'Altroy, Terence N. *The Incas.* 2nd ed. New York: John Wiley & Sons, 2014.

Guaman Poma de Ayala, Felipe. *The First New Chronicle and Good Government: On the History of the World and the Incas up to 1615.* Translated by Roland Hamilton. Austin: University of Texas Press, 2009 [1615].

■ MICHAEL A. MALPASS

TAMBOS

The Incas maintained at least 1,000 and perhaps as many as 2,000 *tambos* (roadside lodgings) along their **road** system. In general, travelers encountered these accommodations every 15–25 kilometers (10–15 miles), roughly a day's journey (which varied, of course, according to the terrain). *Tambos* survived the fall of Tahuantinsuyu and many were maintained well into Spanish Colonial times and a few remain even today.

The *mit'a* labor (see **Labor Service**) of nearby communities maintained the *tambos* for travelers engaged in state business, feeding them in communal kitchens provisioned by foodstuffs and firewood from storage facilities provided by the state. These also warehoused fodder for llama caravans, which sometimes rested overnight in adjacent corrals.

Tambos ranged in size from simple, one-room roadside structures to more elaborate, multiroom compounds with adjacent storage facilities and corrals. Some *tambos* were part of larger administrative centers, while the majority stood alone, along long stretches of

The *tambo* of Pariachuco near Conchucos, Ancash, Peru, is a classic example of an Inca roadside installation. Ricardo Espinosa/Guías del Caminante.

road. Some medium-size *tambos*, especially in **Collasuyu**, may even have played a role in local administration, while others had a variety of functions beyond providing food and shelter for travelers, such as pottery production, road control, mining, military support, and *chasqui* duty (messengers who ran in relay; see **Roads**).

Classic Inca *tambos* are usually found in isolated areas, alongside a road, and included facilities for lodging and storage. The architecture is Inca in style—often a *cancha* or walled compound, made up of several rectangular or square, one-room structures surrounding a central patio (see **Architecture**). They were built of fieldstone or adobe, although the occasional *tambo* does boast fancy stonework. In the highlands, *tambos* were thatched with bunch grass. Some *tambos* on especially busy sections of Inca road—especially between Cuzco and Quito—contained *callancas*, long rectangular structures with several doorways opening onto a plaza (see **Architecture**) that could accommodate large groups of travelers, especially during inclement weather.

Further Reading

Espinosa, Ricardo. *La Gran Ruta Inca: El Capac Ñan* [The Great Inca Route]. Lima: Petroperu, 2006.
Hyslop, John. *The Inka Road System*. New York: Academic Press, 1984.

■ ADRIANA VON HAGEN

TEMPLES

Unlike other ancient civilizations, there is no architectural template for Inca places of worship that distinguishes them from secular public buildings, or even from those related to religious activities such as the *acllahuasi*, or house of the chosen women (see **Acllacuna**).

First of all, devotion was not necessarily directed at images and sacred objects that could be placed within a room. Instead, it focused on places scattered across a sacred landscape, usually far removed from settlements: snow-covered peaks, lagoons, springs, rock outcrops, and distinctively shaped boulders. The Sun, the Moon, and other leading celestial deities were worshipped as they moved across the sky. As celestial bodies made their ways across the heavens, or the sun projected shadows, architecture provided the frame for these celestial observations. Moreover, according to the myths recorded after the conquest, terrestrial deities, founding or mythical ancestors, and noble lineages were transformed into stone. Many of the rocks that commemorated these transformations were carved and provided with an architectural setting.

In the same manner, an elaborate architectural landscape and carved stones surrounded the springs and waterways. These sacred places included areas where officiants met, such as open or roofed courtyards and structures, or groups of structures known as *canchas* and *callancas*, respectively (see **Architecture**; **Settlement Planning**). Even though images and mummy bundles of prominent ancestors were kept in specially made structures, these were not monumental. In fact, in many cases these structures were not even part of the ceremonial complex and they often played a secondary role in the architectural layout.

Second, ceremonies (see **Religion**) implied periodic movement of participants, as members of ritual pilgrimages (see **Capac Hucha**) or as squadrons of runners who participated in races beyond the city limits. The itineraries of these movements were

TELLO, JULIO C.

During his life, Julio C. Tello achieved international recognition and dominated the archaeology of Peru, both intellectually and institutionally. He was a charismatic figure, known for his unflagging energy and determination, even in the most difficult of field conditions. In 1880, the year of Tello's birth in the highland village of Huarochirí, archaeology in Peru consisted of descriptive accounts of ruins by foreign travelers. Tello was the first Peruvian trained as a professional archaeologist. His style of anthropological archaeology emphasized fieldwork, but combined it with a knowledge of ethnology, bioarchaeology, and ethnohistory. Tello attended Lima's San Marcos University, where he completed his medical degree. He was then awarded a fellowship to attend Harvard University, where he earned a Master's degree in Anthropology. His fellowship was extended, so that he could travel to Europe to take archaeology and anthropology classes in London, Berlin, and Paris, before returning to Peru.

A brilliant career followed his return. Over the following four decades, and until his death in 1947, Tello established a pair of archaeology museums and shaped the archaeology programs at Lima's two leading universities. He founded several anthropology journals, and carried out a series of major surveys and excavations along the coast and in the highlands. He also was elected to the Peruvian congress and introduced laws to protect the nation's archaeological heritage, as well as measures to improve the health and education of Peru's indigenous population.

Most of Tello's research was devoted to the study of pre-Inca cultures, particularly Chavín (see **Chronology, Pre-Inca**), but he directed investigations in Cuzco, where he discovered Wiñay Wayna, near **Machu Picchu**, and at **Pachacamac**, near Lima, where he excavated and reconstructed the residence of the **acllacuna**, the chosen women. In his writings, Tello emphasized that the Incas' remarkable accomplishments were made possible by the legacy of the preceding Andean civilizations. He also argued forcefully that the Incas could only be understood by combining historical research with archaeological fieldwork.

Further Reading

Burger, Richard L., ed. *The Life and Writings of Julio C. Tello: America's First Indigenous Archaeologist.* Iowa City: University of Iowa Press, 2009.

■ RICHARD L. BURGER

determined by clusters of sacred places (see **Huacas**), defined by the Spanish chroniclers as temples or shrines. Thanks to descriptions by the chroniclers **Bernabé Cobo** and **Juan Polo Ondegardo** of some 328 (or 350) of these sacred places as part of Cuzco's *ceque* system, and the astounding progress made in locating them, we can now assert that they were linked—both physically and conceptually—by bodies of water (see **Religion**). These included lakes, springs, creeks, or tributaries all originating in Cuzco's Huatanay

River basin and its canal system, born of the *tincuy,* or meeting, of two rivers below the temple of **Coricancha**. The sources compiled by Cobo indicate that each group of shrine-*huacas* located on the same *ceque* was worshipped by the same kin group—*ayllus* or *panacas*. This worship took place on specific days of the ceremonial calendar. As a consequence, the river basin surrounding Cuzco's urban core and even areas beyond the horizon were transformed into a ritual stage and place of devotion.

Third, given the divine nature of the *Sapa* **Inca** (unique, sole Inca ruler) and his lineage (see **Kingship, Divine**), the places where he, his incarnations or body doubles, and representatives manifested themselves before the public were also considered sacred. This is illustrated by the plazas, which contained *ushnus* or libation shrines. *Ushnus* could be located in the middle or to the side of a plaza, or commonly at the top of a platform or a stepped pyramid. In provincial administrative centers such as Huánuco Pampa or Pumpu, these plazas formed the core of the complex. The palaces and royal estates identified by the chroniclers included plazas and religious buildings, as is the case of **Machu Picchu**, said to have been a royal estate of the Inca Pachacuti.

Thus, the spaces devoted to worship and the types of architecture are so varied that they defy classification into rigid formal types. Moreover, non-Inca deities and their places of worship were incorporated into the official imperial religion. This implies the adoption of architectural forms and techniques that differ from those of the Inca, particularly on the central and north coast.

The architecture of residential or administrative buildings is remarkably similar to that of religious structures. Just to cite one example, the **Coricancha**, Cuzco's Sun temple, was considered the symbolic center of Cuzco, and therefore of the empire. It was not only regarded as the principal Sun temple, but the rulers' ancestors were venerated there as well as the empire's leading deities. Its singular role, however, was not reflected in its architectural layout, which is formally indistinguishable from the other *cancha* enclosures (see **Architecture**; **Cuzco**; **Planning, Settlement**) that formed part of the capital's urban core. Most chroniclers described these *cancha* compounds as royal palaces, yet they also served other purposes, such as meeting places for the *panacas*. Nevertheless, the Coricancha was clearly different from, and more elaborate and formal than, other *canchas*, with its fine stonework, double-jambed doorways, finely finished interior niches, and as the chroniclers recorded, gold plaques decorating some of its walls. It also had a unique curved retaining wall and a garden filled with life-sized plants made of precious metals.

The two solar temples that follow it in importance, **Pachacamac** on Peru's central coast and the shrine on the **Island of the Sun** in Lake Titicaca, are nothing like the Coricancha in design. In both cases, a gateway opened onto a long road that connected plazas and ceremonial spaces with features that recalled the sacred landscape. At Pachacamac the Incas transformed a hill into a stepped pyramid overlooking the Pacific Ocean and a lagoon, while on the Island of the Sun the Incas carved imposing rocks along the shores of Lake Titicaca. Architecture related to other great religious shrines and pilgrimage sites such as the mountain peaks of **Catequil**, Pariacaca, or Coropuna seems rather modest by comparison. Nevertheless, they provided a suitable setting for ritual activities on their slopes and along the routes to their summits.

Further Reading

Bauer, Brian S. *The Sacred Landscape of the Inca: The Cuzco Ceque System*. Austin: University of Texas Press, 1998.

———. *Ancient Cuzco. Heartland of the Inca*. Austin: University of Texas Press, 2004.

Stanish, Charles, and Brian S. Bauer. *Archaeological Research on the Islands of the Sun and Moon. Lake Titicaca, Bolivia: Final Results from the Proyecto Tiksi Kjarka*. Cotsen Institute of Archaeology at UCLA, Monograph 52. Santa Fe, NM: Leyba Associates, 2004.

■ KRZYSZTOF MAKOWSKI

TERRACING

Terracing greatly increases the amount of arable land by providing flat areas for planting. This is especially advantageous in a region with sloping terrain. While the remains of extensive terrace systems still sculpt the Andes, even more land was terraced during Inca times. Of the roughly two and one-half million acres of terraced land in this region, however, only about 40 percent are currently in use. While it is not certain whether the remaining 60 percent was built or used during Inca times, it is clear that the Incas often developed and expanded agricultural land when they conquered a given region, targeting specific areas for extensive terracing and **irrigation** schemes.

Several kinds of terraces can be identified in the Andes, and they all share common construction features. First, a retaining wall of rock was built to hold the terrace soil. Generally, the wall has larger rocks at the bottom and smaller ones near the top, which provides stability. Usually, the wall is slightly sloped in an uphill direction. Soil was then brought in from elsewhere to fill in the terrace; excavations have revealed that some ter-

Peg steps on a terrace at the royal estate of Tipón south of Cuzco provided easy access for movement between terraces. Adriana von Hagen.

races have pebbles and sand at the bottom, aiding in drainage. The surface of the terrace may be designed to slope from the back to the front, or it may be level.

Among the several terrace types known from the Andes, bench terraces and valley-bottom, walled terraces are perhaps the most common. Bench terraces follow the contours of a hillside. Sometimes called stair-step terraces, these often have higher walls to make a wider surface for planting. Some of the elegant terraces near Pisac in the Urubamba valley near Cuzco are six feet high but not much wider. Such terraces sometimes have projecting stones that functioned as steps laid into the retaining wall. Valley-bottom, walled terraces are constructed where the natural slope is gentle. A retaining wall is only necessary at wide intervals. Such terraces are usually found along valley bottoms and often contain rich alluvial soils.

Some terraces were designed to receive irrigation water while others relied on rainfall. Canal systems brought water from the upper terraces to the lower ones, and distributed the water along the surface of the terrace.

In many regions of the Andes, a main canal brings water from a stream flowing from permanent snowfields above the valley down to the terrace system. From there it flows horizontally above a series of terraces; vertical drop canals bring it down to a set of terraces. Canals along the back of each terrace have an input off this vertical canal that can be blocked with a stone. Water is distributed across the surface of the terrace from that canal.

Terraces do more than just provide additional planting surfaces. Terracing deepens soils, reduces erosion, and controls moisture. It creates a microenvironment that often mitigates frost damage because the contour terraces cause turbulence in the cold air moving down slope. Terraces provide a deeper soil bed for better root development than an unmodified slope. In areas where rainfall is scarce, they also allow for **irrigation**. All of these factors increase agricultural productivity.

Stone-faced terraces at Choquequirao in the Inca province of Vilcabamba, west of Cuzco, not only prevented erosion, but also provided land for planting crops. Adriana von Hagen.

A son of the Inca ruler Manco Inca and grandson of Huayna Capac, the last un-disputed king of Tahuantinsuyu, Titu Cusi, as he is usually referred to, was born in Cuzco, probably around 1533, if not a little later. His history of the Spanish invasion, *Historia de los yngas*, "History of the Incas" (or *Instrucción* as it is commonly known), is one of the few accounts of the Incas authored by a Native Andean and the only one written by a member of the Inca nobility. Titu Cusi, in fact, was the penulti-mate ruler of **Vilcabamba**, the neo-Inca state founded in the forested fastness of Vilcabamba by Manco Inca, in the wake of his failed uprising against the Spanish invaders in Cuzco, in 1536.

In 1561, Titu Cusi succeeded his brother Sayri Túpac as ruler of Vilcabamba. Ongoing negotiations between the Spaniards and the Vilcabamba Incas—in which the Spaniards sought to lure the Incas away from Vilcabamba with promises of rich estates in Cuzco's Urubamba valley—had reached a stalemate by the time Titu Cusi began to narrate his history to a scribe. When Titu Cusi died in 1571, succeeded by his brother Túpac Amaru I, the destiny of the Vilcabamba Incas had been sealed by the 1569 arrival of Viceroy Francisco de Toledo, who had resolved to end Inca rule in Vilcabamba.

Titu Cusi's account, dated 1570, is addressed to Philip II, king of Spain, and consists of four parts. The first is instructions to the Licentiate (lawyer) Lope García de Castro who was to represent Titu Cusi in the courts of Spain. Titu Cusi sought, first, to restore the Incas to "good favor" in the eyes of the Spanish king, and, second, to impress on the courts the suffering he had endured in the "wilderness" because, noted Titu Cusi, "His Majesty [Philip II] and his vassals have taken possession of the land" (2006 [1570]) that belonged to his ancestors. The second part of Titu Cusi's chronicle, which is couched in a narrative style that quotes direct speech, appears to reflect Inca oral tradition, much of which was no doubt current in Vilcabamba at the time. It contains a history of the Spanish invasion from the arrival of Francisco Pizarro on the shores of northern Peru, to the capture and execution of Atahualpa in Cajamarca, and culminates with the murder by Spanish renegades of Titu Cusi's fa-ther, Manco Inca, at Vitcos. The third part deals with Titu Cusi's rule of Vilcabamba. The final document is a power of attorney, made to García de Castro.

Further Reading

Regalado de Hurtado, Liliana. "Titu Cusi Yupanqui, Diego de Castro (ca. 1535–1571)." In *Guide to Documentary Sources for Andean Studies, 1530–1900*, edited by Joanne Pillsbury, vol. 3: 662–64. Norman: University of Oklahoma Press, 2008.

Titu Cusi Yupanqui, Diego de Castro. *Instrucción al licenciado don Lope García de Castro (1570)*. Edited by Liliana Regalado de Hurtado. Colección Clásicos Peruanos, no. 9. Lima: Pontificia Universidad Católica del Perú, Fondo Editorial, 1992 [1570].

———. *History of How the Spaniards Arrived in Peru*. Translated by Catherine Julien. Indianapolis: Hackett, 2006 [1570].

■ ADRIANA VON HAGEN

Terracing technology long preceded Inca expansion, both in the Cuzco region and elsewhere, but the Incas probably were responsible for a vast increase in terracing. The Incas divided conquered peoples' lands into three parts: those of the ***Sapa* Inca**, the Inca religion, and the local community. Using *mit'a* labor, they constructed new irrigated terrace systems that allowed for the production of surpluses. In some regions, unirrigated terraces were augmented by the construction of irrigated terraces below them.

Inca-constructed communities, such as the **royal estates**, are especially famed for the terraces that formed part of their overall design. **Machu Picchu**, the most renowned of these, includes two sets of contour terraces constructed to support the crops of its occupants. Nevertheless, Machu Picchu's terraces were insufficient to feed its estimated 300 permanent residents, and food was probably brought in from elsewhere.

Inca agricultural specialists developed an understanding of the best locations and construction techniques to use in different regions. They used *mit'a* labor to build the terrace systems, grow the crops, and create surpluses for the empire. The success of Inca agricultural policies is reflected in the rapid expansion of the empire and in the fact that many of their terracing systems are still in use today.

Further Reading

Denevan, William. "Terrace Abandonment in the Colca Valley, Peru." In *Pre-Hispanic Agricultural Fields in the Andean Region*. Part I, edited by William Denevan, Kent Mathewson, and Gregory Knapp, 1–44. B.A.R. International Series 359(i). Oxford: B.A.R., 1987.

Wright, Kenneth, and Alfredo Valencia Zegarra. *Machu Picchu, A Civil Engineering Marvel*. Reston, VA: ASCE Press, 2000.

■ MICHAEL A. MALPASS

USHNU

While perhaps best interpreted as "sacred platforms for ritual performance," numerous definitions of the term *ushnu* can be found in the historical chronicles and the archaeological literature. Although physical descriptions of *ushnu*s can be divided into two or three main categories, the multiplicity of interpretations has created significant confusion regarding the definition of an *ushnu*.

There are two primary descriptions of *ushnu*s. The first of these is a masonry construction in the form of a platform or a truncated, stepped platform. Usually found in the center of or flanking plazas, these platforms are ascended by stairs or ramps. Persons standing atop these platforms are generally visible throughout the plaza. Prototypical forms of these *ushnus* are found in northern highland **Chinchaysuyu** (the northwestern quadrant of the empire) at sites such as Pumpu, Huánuco Pampa, Vilcashuaman,

The *ushnu* of Vilcashuaman in Ayacucho, Peru, is regarded as a prototypical ceremonial platform, found at many important Inca settlements in Chinchaysuyu, the northwestern quadrant of the empire. Joe Castro/Guias del Caminante.

Recognized as the "father of archaeology" in some of the South American countries where he worked and lived for more than four decades (1892–1933), Uhle was born in Dresden in 1856, and died in Loben, now Poland, in 1944. He was the first to introduce the idea of an Andean chronology, and his chronological proposals still retain much of their merit. The linchpin of his chronology is that the presence of Inca material remains is a historical fact. Uhle was well acquainted with Inca material as early as 1887 when an important collection from Cuzco arrived at the Royal Ethnological Museum at Berlin, where he worked.

In 1892 Uhle began a project in Argentina to study the southeastern extension of the Inca Empire, where he visited and worked at many Inca sites, as well as in neighboring Bolivia. Inca archaeology and history still remained important topics in Peru, Chile, and Ecuador. Of special importance are his excavations at Tomebamba, an important Inca administrative center in Ecuador.

His critical approach to Inca history was characterized by confronting data in early Colonial written sources with evidence from excavations. In 1905, he excavated in several places at and near Cuzco and identified the numerous sculptured rocks dotting the hills around Sacsahuaman as burial places of ancestors, related to kin groups (see **Panacas**), as well as Sun altars, providing a fairly complex and modern description of *huacas* (see **Religion**). He did not consider so-called *intihuatanas* (upright, carved stones) to be astronomical devices. Uhle was very interested in Inca social organization and its role in the *ceque* system. When applied to Inca "origins," his chronological scheme proved the Incas' modest origins (i.e., local Killke-style pottery; see **Chronology, Inca**) and their use of the **Aymara** language before adopting **Quechua**. At the time, many Peruvian historians criticized his ideas, but modern scholarship has shown many of them to be correct.

Further Reading

Kaulicke, Peter, ed. *Max Uhle y el Perú Antiguo*. Lima: Fondo Editorial Pontificia Universidad Católica del Perú, 1998.

Kaulicke, Peter, Manuela Fischer, Peter Masson, and Gregor Wolff, eds. *Max Uhle (1856–1944). Evaluaciones de sus Investigaciones y Obras*. Lima: Fondo Editorial Pontificia Universidad Católica del Perú, 2010.

Protzen, Jean-Pierre, and David Harris, eds. "Explorations in the Pisco Valley: Max Uhle's Reports to Phoebe Hearst, August 1901 to January 1902." *Contributions of the University of California Archaeological Research Faculty*, 63. Berkeley: Archaeological Research Faculty, University of California, 2005.

Rowe, John H. "Max Uhle, 1856–1944. A Memoir of the Father of Peruvian Archaeology." *University of California Publications in American Archaeology and Ethnology* 46, no. 1, 1954.

Shimada, Izumi. "Pachacamac Archaeology: Retrospect and Prospect." In Max Uhle, *Pachacamac: A Reprint of the 1903 Edition*. University Museum Monograph 62. Philadelphia: University Museum of Archaeology and Anthropology, University of Pennsylvania, 1991.

Uhle, Max. *Pachacamac. Report of the William Pepper, M.D., LL.D., Peruvian Expedition of 1896*. Philadelphia: Department of Archaeology of the University of Pennsylvania, 1903.

———. *Pachacamac: A reprint of the 1903 edition*. University Museum Monograph 62. Philadelphia: University Museum of Archaeology and Anthropology, 1991.

Valencia, Alfredo. *Colección Arqueológica Cusco de Max Uhle*. Cuzco: Instituto Nacional de Cultura, 1979.

■ PETER KAULICKE

and likely **Cajamarca**, all in Peru. A few others are reported in highland Argentina and Chile at sites such as Shincal.

While most chroniclers and scholars place *ushnu*s in plazas, the chronicler and Church inquisitor **Cristóbal de Albornoz** located them both in plazas and on royal roads. Not surprisingly, his description of *ushnu*s matches the stepped platforms described above, as he spent much of his time in Peru's Chinchaysuyu region. Relying primarily on Albornoz, modern researchers working near Ayacucho, Peru, have identified a series of stepped platform structures located outside of plazas that they describe as *ushnu*s.

The second form of *ushnu* is a low basin or font with a large stone placed upon it. The chroniclers **Juan de Betanzos** and **Pedro Pizarro** describe the *ushnu* in Cuzco's central Aucaypata plaza in this manner; a similar structure graces the main upper plaza in Incallacta, Bolivia. Finally, the term *ushnu* is frequently applied to any platform flanking or in the center of a plaza at an Inca site, regardless of form or function.

While these descriptions are the two most commonly used by archaeologists, **R. Tom Zuidema** has argued that the term originally referred to an opening or a duct into the ground through which liquids could be poured. According to Zuidema, only later did the term refer to the structures described above, and only if these were associated with an opening or duct, he argues, is the *ushnu* appellation correct.

Neither the term *ushnu* nor any of its variations is mentioned by any of the earliest western visitors to the Inca Empire. Betanzos and Pedro Pizarro do not employ the word in describing the platform, upright stone, and basin complex found in Cuzco's central plaza. Nor does **Pedro de Cieza de León** use the term to describe the largest of what is now considered the prototypical *ushnu*, the stepped structure at Vilcashuaman. The word's earliest use is found in Domingo de Santo Tomás's **Quechua** dictionary published in 1560, almost a decade later than Betanzos and Cieza, in which he defines it as "altar" without further elaboration. Only in the 1570s do other chroniclers such as **Cristóbal de Albornoz** and **Cristóbal de Molina** begin to employ this term in connection with Cuzco's Aucaypata plaza.

Colonial chroniclers and modern scholars have interpreted *ushnu*s as sanctified central spaces, openings into which libations and other offerings were made, stages from which the Inca king and lords could preside over festivals and ceremonial events, seats of the Sun, and places from where astronomical observations were made. Determining which or how many of these functions occurred at a particular *ushnu* is often problematic, reflecting the paucity of detailed historical descriptions (most of which are focused on Cuzco) and the lack of modern excavations and published reports. Only the Anonymous Chronicler, writing in the late sixteenth or early seventeenth century, for example, associates an *ushnu* (that of Aucaypata, Cuzco) with astronomical observations related to the agricultural calendar, while modern scholars have suggested that the site of Huánuco Pampa was organized and constructed around a series of astronomical alignments emanating from its *ushnu*.

Nevertheless, almost all chroniclers and scholars agree that *ushnu*s were places reserved for rituals, spectacles, and religious and political performances, though the same performances may not have been performed at each such stage or platform. Both Cieza and Molina describe the Inca ruler and lesser lords presiding over ceremonies from the tops of *ushnu* platforms such as the one found in Vilcashuaman. Betanzos describes the *ushnu* as a place where common people could pray and make offerings, and where libations were poured. Molina, describing the *Citua* ritual, notes that the *ushnu* was the gathering point for squadrons of soldiers running in the direction of the empire's four *suyus*, and where the ***ayllus*** and ***panacas*** (descent groups) of Cuzco's Incas gathered in the Aucaypata along with the ancestral mummies and mummies of former Inca rulers and their attendants.

Ushnus were certainly important stages for Inca ritual performance. Whether every *ushnu* had a similar cultural role remains to be proven.

Further Reading

Albornoz, C. de. "La Instrucción para descubrir todas las guacas del Pirú y sus camayos y haziendas." In P. Duviols, "Albornóz y el espacio ritual andino prehispánico." *Revista Andina* 2, no. 1: 169–222, 1984 [1570–1584].

Anónimo. *Relación de las Costumbres Antiguas de los Naturales del Peru*. In *Biblioteca de Autores Españoles*. Vol. 209, *Crónicas Peruanas de Interés Indigena*. Madrid: Atlas, 1968 [1580–1621].

Betanzos, Juan de. *Narrative of the Incas*. Translated and edited by Roland Hamilton and Dana Buchanan. Austin: University of Texas Press, 1996 [1551–1557].

Cieza de Leon, Pedro de. *The Travels of Pedro de Cieza de León, A.D. 1532–50, Contained in the First Part of His Chronicle of Peru*. Translated and edited by Clements R. Markham. Works Issued by the Hakluyt Society, no. 33. London: Printed for the Hakluyt Society, 1864. Reissued, New York: Burt Franklin, 1964 [1553].

———. *The Second Part of the Chronicle of Peru*. Translated and edited by Clements R. Markham. Oxford: Hakluyt Society, 1883 [1554].

Coben, L. "Other Cuzcos: Replicated Theaters of Inka Power." In *Archaeology of Performance: Theater, Power and Community*, edited by T. Inomata and L. Coben. Lanham, MD: AltaMira Press, 2006.

———. "Theaters of Power: Inca Imperial Performance." PhD diss., University of Pennsylvania, 2012.

———. "If All the World's a Stage Then What's an Ushnu?" In *Inca Sacred Space: Landscape, Site and Symbol in the Andes*, edited by F. Meddens, K. Willis, C. McEwan, and N. Branch. London: Archetype Publications, 2014.

Cobo, Bernabé. *History of the Inca Empire: An Account of the Indian's Customs and Their Origin, Together with a Treatise on Inca Legends, History, and Social Institutions*. Translated and edited by Roland Hamilton. Austin: University of Texas Press, 1979 [1653].

———. *Inca Religion and Customs*. Translated and edited by Roland Hamilton. Austin: University of Texas Press. 1990 [1653].

Garcilaso de la Vega, El Inca. *Royal Commentaries of the Incas and General History of Peru*. Translated by Harold V. Livermore. Austin: University of Texas Press, 1987 [1609].

Hyslop, John. *Inka Settlement Planning*. Austin: University of Texas Press, 1990.

Meddens, F. "Function and Meaning of the Usnu in Late Horizon Peru." *Tawantinsuyu* 3:1–14, 1997.

Meddens, F., N. Branch, C. Vivanco Pomacanchari, N. Riddiford, and R. Kemp. "High Altitude *Ushnu* Platforms in the Department of Ayacucho Peru, Structure, Ancestors and Animating Essence." In *Pre-Columbian Landscapes of Creation and Origin*, edited by John E. Staller, 315–55. New York: Springer, 2010.

Pizarro, Pedro. *Relación del descubrimiento y conquista del Perú*. Lima: Pontificia Universidad Católica del Peru, 1978 [1571].

Santo Tomás, Domingo de. *Lexicón o vocabulario de la Lengua General del Perú*. Edición Facsimilar con un prólogo de Raúl Porras Barrenechea. Lima: Edición del Instituto de Historia, 1951 [1560].

Sarmiento de Gamboa, Pedro. *The History of the Incas*. Translated and edited by Brian S. Bauer and Vania Smith. Austin: University of Texas Press, 2007 [1572].

Staller, J. E. "Dimensions of Place: The Significance of Centers to the Development of Andean Civili-
    zation: An Exploration of the *Ushnu* Concept." In *Pre-Columbian Landscapes of Creation and Origin*,
    edited by John E. Staller, 269–312. New York: Springer, 2010.
Zuidema, R. T. "El Ushnu." In *Reyes y Guerreros: Ensayos de cultura andina:* 402–54. Lima: Grandes Es-
    tudios Andinos, Fomciencias, 1989.

■ LAWRENCE S. COBEN

V

VILCA

Vilca is a hallucinogen whose source is a small leguminous tree, *Anadenanthera colubrina*, which grows wild in warm, dry valleys below 2,100 meters (6,890 feet) from northern Peru to northwestern Argentina. Vilca is botanically related to a quite similar species called *yopo*, *Anandenanthera peregrina*, found in the Orinoco savannas. The leguminous pods of the *vilca* tree contain 5–20 round, flat reddish-brown seeds. When pulverized, *vilca* has been used as a snuff, smoked, ingested, and as an enema. The psychoactive ingredients are two tryptamines, DMT (N, N-dimethyltryptamine) and bufotenine. Effects of these alkaloids on the human organism were not fully studied until the 1960s. A three-phased sequence, most clearly described when taken as a snuff, starts with an almost immediate and sometimes violent stimulating rush, followed by a period of hallucinations and, lastly, a phase of lucidity that initiates reflective conversation.

Vilca was engrained in Andean culture history as a shamanic vehicle to an altered state of consciousness. So far, however, archaeologists have retrieved only a small portion of its long prehistory of use. Evidence of its application is found in inhalers, pipes, clysters, and elaborately carved wooden or stone mortars. Two millennia before the Incas, *vilca* was an important hallucinogen at Chavín de Huántar. The Huari civilization, which arose around Ayacucho, and its contemporary, the Tiahuanaco (see **Chronology, Pre-Inca**), incorporated *vilca* into public performance and private use. The Incas used *vilca* less frequently because shamanic performance conflicted with the codification of Inca state religion. At a local level, however, and at shaman-directed oracular sites, notably Chuquipalta (also known as Yurac Rumi; see **Vilcabamba**), Vilcanota, and Vilcacunga, hallucinogens were used to dispense answers to questions while under the influence. To facilitate access to seeds and the fine wood elaborately carved to make mortars (*vilcanas*), *vilca* may have been cultivated in ecologically suitable places where it did not occur naturally. The word *vilca* also signifies "sacred" in Quechua, raising the question of whether the tree gave rise to the value of the sacred emotion or the reverse.

After the Spanish conquest, the psychoactive use of *vilca* underwent sustained attack from the Catholic clergy. Shamanic behavior and the performances that hallucinogens triggered were viewed as intolerable competition with Christian belief in transubstantiation. A campaign led by the Jesuits, equating *vilca* use with devil worship, succeeded in marginalizing and then suppressing *vilca* use. As a result, public knowledge of the halluci-

Born in 1544 in Levanto, Chachapoyas, northern Peru, of a Spanish father, Luis Valera, who served with Francisco Pizarro, and a Native woman, whose baptismal name was Francisca Pérez, Valera studied in Trujillo, Peru, and joined the Jesuit order in Lima in 1568. He worked in the Jesuit missions of Huarochirí, in the highlands east of Lima, and in Cuzco, as well as Julí and Potosí. In 1583 Valera translated a catechism from Spanish into **Quechua** and **Aymara** for the Third Lima Provincial Council. That same year, however, Valera was imprisoned for unspecified charges, apparently because his Jesuit superiors disapproved of his writings, which were critical of the Spanish Colonial administration. After several years of imprisonment and house arrest, he was exiled to Spain, where many of his papers were burned in 1596 in an English pirate attack on the Spanish port city of Cádiz. **Garcilaso de la Vega** subsequently came into possession of the surviving papers. Valera died the following year in Alcalá de Henares, Spain, from injuries incurred during the sack of Cádiz.

With the exception of one document, not one of the accounts attributed to Valera has survived in their original form; they only endure in the chronicles of others—especially in the *Royal Commentaries of the Incas and General History of Peru* by fellow *mestizo* author Garcilaso, who had access to Valera's manuscript, *Historia Occidentalis* (found among the papers rescued from the pillage of Cádiz). Garcilaso noted that Valera wrote about the Incas in "elegant Latin," idealizing the rulers of Tahuantinsuyu and their achievements. Valera also collected myths and legends and interviewed Native informants about their history and religion. Garcilaso cites long passages from Valera, whom he credits in particular for information about the northern part of Tahuantinsuyu, about which Garcilaso himself had little knowledge, and for details of events in Peru that occurred after Garcilaso had left for Spain in 1560.

Blas Valera's name is intimately linked to a set of documents that make extraordinary claims about his role following his supposed survival of the sack of Cádiz. For example, the Italian priest **Giovanni Anello Oliva**, author of an account of the Incas, claimed that Valera did not die after the pirate attack but that he secretly returned to Peru, where he wrote the *Nueva Corónica y Buen Gobierno*, widely acknowledged to have been authored by **Felipe Guaman Poma de Ayala**. This claim is not generally accepted by historians of Colonial Peru.

Further Reading

Hyland, Sabine. *The Jesuit and the Incas: The Extraordinary Life of Padre Blas Valera, S.J.* Ann Arbor: University of Michigan Press, 2003.
———. "Valera, Blas (1544–1597)." In *Guide to Documentary Sources for Andean Studies, 1530–1900*, edited by Joanne Pillsbury, vol. 3, 694–96. Norman: University of Oklahoma Press, 2008.

■ ADRIANA VON HAGEN

nogenic use of *vilca* was largely lost in the Andes before the end of the Colonial period. Some medical use of the seed, which in low dosage acts as a purgative, continued into the twentieth century.

Further Reading

Knobloch, Patricia J. "Wari Ritual Power at Conchopata: An Interpretation of *Anadenanthera Colubrina* Iconography." *Latin American Antiquity* 11, no. 4: 387–402, 2000.
Torres, Constantino Manuel, and David B. Repke. *Anadenanthera: Visionary Plant of Ancient South America.* New York: The Haworth Herbal Press, 2006.

■ DANIEL W. GADE

VILCABAMBA

Vilcabamba is both a province northwest of Cuzco and the name of two towns, one established by the Spaniards and the other, Vilcabamba "La Vieja" or "the old," founded by Manco Inca, Huayna Capac's son, in the aftermath of the Incas' unsuccessful attempt to oust the Spaniards from Tahuantinsuyu, the Inca Empire, in 1536–1537. After the failed siege of Cuzco, Manco Inca and his followers fled into the province of Vilcabamba, initially settling in Vitcos, said to have been founded by Manco's great-grandfather, Pachacuti, a century or so earlier. Vitcos, however, was vulnerable to Spanish attack, and so in early 1539, with the Spaniards in pursuit, Manco and his followers fled into deepest Vilcabamba, a two-day march from Vitcos.

Vitcos probably functioned as a royal estate (see **Estates, Royal**) decades before it became Manco's de facto capital in the wake of the Spanish invasion. The oldest sector is built of white granite, and boasts some of the finest stonework in the region, with a wall studded by double-jambed doorways, probably the remains of a royal compound, opening onto a small plaza. The central sector, constructed of fieldstone set in mud mortar, may have served as Manco's residence. The southern sector is the site of a famous carved stone, shrine, and oracle known as Yurac Rumi (white rock). Spanish clergy had the shrine complex destroyed in 1570, tearing down the buildings, scattering the stones, and setting fire to the thick thatch roofs.

Manco's Vilcabamba, on the other hand, is quite distinct from Vitcos. While typically Inca in layout, and featuring many of the hallmarks of Inca **architecture** and town planning—a *callanca* (a long, rectangular building), an uncarved boulder fronting a plaza, fountains and plazas—its setting in lush, lowland rainforest is unusual. Especially curious are the Spanish-style roofing tiles scattered among the ruins, attesting to the postconquest date of Vilcabamba's construction.

From the top of Vilcabamba's ceremonial entryway a long, narrow staircase descended into the city, "Half a league wide . . . and a huge distance in length," according to Spanish eyewitnesses who saw it in 1572. They noted 400 houses as well as fields planted with coca, sugarcane (an introduced crop), manioc, sweet potatoes, and cotton. The houses were roofed in thatch, while the ruler's residence was covered in roof tiles. "The town had a square large enough to hold many people, where they used to run horses and rejoice in merriments" (Múrua 2001 [1590–1598]).

Túpac Amaru I, the last ruler of Vilcabamba, beheaded in the plaza of Cuzco in 1572. Guaman Poma de Ayala, Felipe. *El primer nueva corónica y buen gobierno*. Edited by John V. Murra and Rolena Adorno, 418/451. Mexico City: Siglo Veintiuno, 1980 [1615].

Yurac Rumi, the sacred rock at Vitcos in the Inca province of Vilcabamba. Adriana von Hagen.

A long avenue crossing small streams led into the center of Vilcabamba. There, a 5-meter-high (16.5-foot-high) granite boulder flanks a large plaza, surrounded by a *callanca*, a possible **ushnu**, and what may have been an *acllahuasi*, which housed the so-called chosen women. In this setting, the Incas had "nearly the luxuries, greatness and splendor of Cuzco in that distant, or rather, exiled land—and they enjoyed life there" (Múrua 2001 [1590–1598]).

For thirty-five years Vilcabamba served as a bastion of resistance to Spanish rule. Manco and his descendants, Sayri Túpac, **Titu Cusi**, and Túpac Amaru, harassed the Spaniards, raiding caravans on the road between Lima and Cuzco. The arrival of Viceroy Francisco de Toledo in 1569 clinched the fate of the Vilcabamba Incas. In 1572, the Viceroy, determined to quash the neo-Inca ruler and his city, dispatched 250 Spanish soldiers and 1,500 Native auxiliaries to Vilcabamba. They captured Túpac Amaru, marched him to Cuzco in chains, and had him beheaded in the city's main plaza. The execution of Túpac Amaru and the fall of Vilcabamba signaled the end of Inca resistance to Spanish rule and the fall of Tahuantinsuyu.

The jungle covered the ruins and Vilcabamba's name faded from memory. The American explorer **Hiram Bingham**, who stumbled upon **Machu Picchu** in 1911, at first thought Machu Picchu was Vilcabamba. Although that same year Bingham ventured as far as Vilcabamba "La Vieja" (called Espíritu Pampa, "plain of the spirits," by his local guides), he dismissed it as the site of the lost city because of its lowland jungle setting and the lack of fancy stonework. Moreover, jungle overgrowth made it impossible at that time to discern the site's original size, "half a league wide . . . and a huge distance in length" (Múrua 2001 [1590–1598]). If Bingham had available a key passage in the chronicle of Martín de Múrua (unpublished at the time), which described how some of the buildings had been roofed with Spanish-style tiles, he might have realized that he had indeed discovered the legendary, lost neo-Inca capital.

Further Reading

Hemming, John. *The Conquest of the Incas*. New York: Harcourt Brace Jovanovich, 1970.

Lee, Vincent. *Forgotten Vilcabamba: Final Stronghold of the Incas*. Wilson, WY: Sixpac Manco Publications, 2000.

Múrua, Martín de. *Historia General del Perú*. Madrid: Dastín, 2001 [1590–1598].

Titu Cusi Yupanqui, Diego de Castro. *History of How the Spaniards Arrived in Peru*. Translated by Catherine Julien. Indianapolis: Hackett, 2006 [1570].

■ ADRIANA VON HAGEN

VILLAGE LIFE

Reconstructing the daily lives of villagers during Inca times is challenging because few of the Spanish chroniclers were interested in such mundane details of life. Yet, the chronicles of Native Andeans, such as those of **Garcilaso de la Vega** and **Felipe Guaman Poma de Ayala**, did include details of daily life. Archaeology has begun to fill in some of the missing information, and also evaluate what the chroniclers said. Thus, the combination of ethnohistory and archaeology provides a more complete picture of the daily lives of both the conquered and the conquerors.

Village life in the empire revolved around activities associated largely with age and gender distinctions (see **Women**), along with the activities required of households by the Incas. We do not have much information about conquered peoples from the Spanish sources, but we do know some basic activities of Inca village life, and at least some of these activities were likely similar in other communities as well.

Until puberty, male and female children basically learned the tasks that would be required of them in adulthood. Boys helped in the fields and herded animals, while girls assisted in the many tasks of the household: cleaning, spinning, preparing meals, and watching over younger children. Until marriage, young adults lived with their parents. After marriage, depending on the social norms of the group, they might have set up a new household in a "trial marriage" arrangement, or lived with the parents of the bride or the groom.

Both Inca and non-Inca men were eligible for military service, and many served in that capacity, both as part of their *mit'a* service and as more permanent assignments (see **Labor Service**; **Warfare**). Males of conquered groups were expected to serve in the military or corvée labor gangs, as needed, and married men would often bring their wives and families with them. Younger, unmarried men served as messengers and cargo bearers, while older men were the actual warriors.

For Inca boys, a major part of their puberty rituals involved mock battles and having their legs whipped that served to make them worthy of battle. An elite corps of a few thousand noble males was trained from adulthood for this task, and they formed the shock troops of the empire. In addition, the ruler, or *Sapa* **Inca**, also had a personal guard comprised of loyal troops, which could also include non-Incas. Indeed, late Inca kings had among their retinues warriors from conquered groups, including the most feared: the Cañari of Ecuador, the Chachapoya of northern Peru, and the Caracara of Bolivia.

When conquered people were not serving their *mit'a* duties, they remained in their home villages. Most were farmers and herders and made their own tools. It is not clear whether occupational specialization was widespread at the village level, although potters, metalworkers, and other craft specialists existed. Hence, we may assume these were pre-Inca occupations as well. For the Chimú of the north coast, craft specialization was marked, especially metalworking, and many of the best metalsmiths were taken to Cuzco and other leading Inca settlements to make fine goods for the Incas. How this labor was incorporated into the fabric of life in Cuzco is not known.

Women's basic activities involved child-rearing, food preparation, spinning and weaving, as well as helping in the fields, both in preparing the fields and harvesting. Women picked to serve as chosen women, or *aclla,* fulfilled specific activities for the empire (see **acllacuna**). These women spun and wove cloth for the state; they entertained and served food and *chicha*; they acted in religious roles as attendants in the temples; and they could be given as wives to administrators. *Mamacuna,* adult women who oversaw the work of the younger *acllas,* were the most important members of the *aclla* class and made the finest garments for the Inca nobles and upper administrative personnel. Some noble Inca women served as priestesses in the temples that worshipped female deities such as *Quilla*, the Moon (see **Deities**). The principal wife and mother of the *Sapa* Inca wielded considerable power and influence.

For both conquered people and the Incas, other aspects of village life revolved around the particular social group to which they belonged. As most Andean people were organized into *ayllus*, individuals had responsibilities to their respective *ayllus*. These duties included assisting with canal and reservoir cleaning, preparing food for festivals, and conducting rituals in honor of the ancestors and deities (see **Religion**). In addition, *ayllu* members were expected to fulfill their labor obligation to the Incas. Thus, if a family had to serve in the army, other members were required to work their fields while they were gone.

Mit'a labor involved tasks in which a person was skilled, but depended on what and where the Incas needed a specific task carried out. As mentioned, many men served in the army. Other jobs included bringing products from the villages to the Inca centers. Craftspeople may have been required to work at regional centers making their particular crafts. Building **roads** and **bridges** was a major labor requirement. The rotation period lasted weeks or months and disrupted the normal lives of conquered villagers (see **Labor Service**).

For the Incas of Cuzco, different social groups were in charge of rituals at the shrines of the *ceque* system. Most of these shrines were in the vicinity of Cuzco. Worship involved collecting the sacrificial objects, going to the shrines, conducting the proper rituals, and returning home. As a social group could be responsible for more than one shrine, this added to the yearly work of the residents. The magistrate **Juan Polo Ondegardo** wrote that many villages had similar networks of shrines, suggesting such networks were pan-Andean.

In summary, village life varied with the seasons. For conquered villagers, daily work involved farming, herding, or making crafts as well as cleaning canals or conducting rituals to common ancestors. When villagers were dispatched as *mit'a* laborers they were often accompanied by their families. If the person did not return, as many did not, due to mortality in the Inca conflicts, this would have added a burden to the family. Preparing and working the fields of the Inca and the deities would have further added to the labor burden of local people during the year. Goods used by conquered people would have been locally produced and made primarily of locally available materials, such as stone, wood, or ceramic. Village leaders, however, as symbols of their affiliation with the empire, might have had access to goods produced by the Incas at their administrative centers.

No doubt, the lives of Cuzco's nonroyal social groups were similar to those of conquered people, though without the *mit'a* obligation. Certainly, royal lineages were somewhat better off, enjoying the labor of *mit'a* workers or *yanacuna* awarded to them. Finally, the material culture of the Cuzco Incas included goods produced by craft specialists and, if they were produced for members of the nobility, were commonly made of bronze, gold, or silver.

Further Reading

Bauer, Brian S. *The Sacred Landscape of the Incas: The Cusco Ceque System.* Austin: University of Texas Press, 1998.

D'Altroy, Terence. *The Incas.* 2nd ed. New York: John Wiley & Sons, 2014.

■ MICHAEL A. MALPASS

VISITAS

This term, which translates as "visit," was used in the Colonial Andes for a range of different kinds of administrative as well as ecclesiastical investigations, or inquests, carried out by officials designated as *visitadores* (visitors). The vast majority of *visita*-based documentation in archives today pertains to the collection of data on censuses and tributes from Colonial indigenous communities, as well as inquests by state officials into issues that ranged from how those communities were organized and taxed under the Incas, to inquiries concerning the effects of earthquakes, floods, and other catastrophic events. Religious *visitadores* investigated matters that concerned the Church, such as the accuracy of parish registries and the scrutiny of the conversion and religious instruction of Native parishioners. To the degree that such early Colonial inquiries concerned the organization of communities under the Incas in the past, or the views of contemporary Natives on the Incas and their institutions and practices of local governance, such documents are of inestimable value for helping researchers today to construct accounts of the Inca world.

The tradition of sending out *visitadores* to investigate matters in the countryside began almost as soon as the Spaniards imprisoned Atahualpa in Cajamarca in 1534. That year, Francisco Pizarro ordered a *visita* to be carried out relating to the awarding of Native peoples to two Spaniards in grants known as *encomienda* (the grant of oversight of a group of Native peoples to a Spaniard who had the responsibility for their welfare and religious conversion in exchange for the right to collect tribute from them). Major programs of administrative *visitas* took place in 1540 and 1543, and a large-scale visitation and tribute assessment was carried out by Pedro de la Gasca in 1549–1550. Few of the documents produced by these inquests have been found in archives to date. From the earliest *visitas*, Colonial officials worked closely with local record keepers, the *quipucamayocs* (see **Quipu**) to compare Inca population counts and tribute levels, reckoning these data to the Colonial circumstances. Both Inca and Colonial inspectors ensured that all people who were subject to inspection were counted in the census procedure. Hiding from **census** takers was a crime under the Incas, and it was the cause of strong censure of local headmen, the *curacas*, in Spanish Colonial times.

Two of the most complete *visitas*, which have been used by modern scholars to great advantage in investigating Inca provincial organization, were those carried out in 1562 by Iñigo Ortiz de Zúñiga, in Huánuco, in the central Peruvian highlands, and another undertaken in 1567 by Garci Diez de San Miguel, in Chucuito, on the southwestern shore of Lake Titicaca. The *visitadores* who led these investigations collected a wide range of information including the name, age, sex, position, and economic status of tribute payers and the members of their households. These data have proved extremely useful for historical demographers in their attempts to reconstruct population figures, age pyramids, and life cycle trends for early Colonial and late-Inca populations.

Upon assuming office, the fifth viceroy of Peru, Francisco de Toledo (1569–1581), carried out one of the most comprehensive fact-finding missions, which he referred to as a general inspection (*visita general*). While the Crown had instructed Toledo only to undertake a tribute register (*libro de tasa*) of the Native population, the viceroy used the process to collect more wide-ranging information, including testimony on whether tribute assessment had risen or declined in communities since the time of the Incas, as well as questions concerning the history and fate of Native inhabitants under Spanish rule.

Toledo used the information from the *visita general* to effect profound changes from Inca traditions in the organization of the rural population. Most notably, it provided him with the blueprint for resettling the population from scattered settlements into agglutinated towns laid out in a standardized grid pattern. Only a portion of Toledo's *visita general* survives today. It was published by Noble David Cook in 1975, and has been mined by scholars to great benefit in efforts to understand the culture, history, and economic organization of the Inca Empire.

Further Reading

Cook, Noble David. *Tasa de la visita general de Francisco de Toledo*. Lima: Universidad Nacional de San Marcos, Dirección Universitaria de Biblioteca y Publicaciones, 1975.

———. "Visitas, Censuses, and Other Sources of Population Information." In *Guide to Documentary Sources for Andean Studies, 1530–1900*, edited by Joanne Pillsbury, vol. 1, 129–43. Norman: University of Oklahoma Press, 2008.

Diez de San Miguel, Garci. *Visita hecha a la provincia de Chucuito por Garci Diez de San Miguel en el año 1567*. Edited by Waldemar Espinoza Soriano. Documentos Regionales para la Etnología y Etnohistoria Andinas, no. 1. Lima: Casa de la Cultura del Perú, 1964.

Guevara-Gil, Armando, and Frank Salomon. "A 'Personal Visit': Colonial Political Ritual and the Making of Indians in the Andes." *Colonial Latin American Review* 3, no. 1–2: 3–36, 1994.

Ortiz de Zuñiga, Iñigo. *Visita de la provincia de León de Huánuco en 1562*. Edited by John V. Murra. 2 vols. Documentos para la Historia y Etnología de Huánuco y la Selva Central, no. 1–2. Huánuco, Peru: Universidad Nacional Hermilio Valdizán, Facultad de Letras y Educación, 1967–1972.

■ GARY URTON

W

WARFARE

The Incas were engaged in wars almost continuously, from the initial conquests to the suppression of rebellions, as well as conflict on the frontier and the civil war in the empire's final years (see **Wars, Dynastic**). Militarism was also prominently celebrated in Inca culture. Conquistadors, chroniclers, and Native authors were keenly interested in the topic. To their accounts can be added archaeological studies of forts, skeletal remains, and destruction episodes.

The Inca ruler Huayna Capac goes to battle carried in a litter, wielding a shield and whirling a sling. Guaman Poma de Ayala, Felipe. *El primer nueva corónica y buen gobierno.* Edited by John V. Murra and Rolena Adorno, 307/333. Mexico City: Siglo Veintiuno, 1980 [1615].

Scale and logistics were the great military strengths of the Incas—not technology, tactics, or battlefield organization. Conscripts fought with the same weapons their ancestors had used. In the highlands, the primary projectile weapon was the sling, with smooth round or egg-shaped slingstones, followed by the *bola* (*ayllu*), two or three stones linked by a cord, thrown against the legs of enemy fighters or Spanish horses. Coastal conscripts used spear-throwers and spears with fire-hardened points, metal tips, or fish spines; bows and arrows were used in many regions, especially the forested eastern lowlands. Hand-to-hand weapons included clubs of hard palm wood, maces with stone or bronze heads shaped like rings or stars (*champi*), small hafted axes of metal or stone, thrusting spears with fire-hardened points or metal tips, and *macanas*, hardwood broadswords said to cut like steel. Soldiers had helmets of thick wool, cane, or wood, and sometimes wore padded cotton armor; at the back, they might bear a protective shield of leather or palm-wood slats. They carried small shields of hard palm wood, decorated with bright cloth and **feathers**.

Perhaps as important were the components of ritually effective defense: shining discs of precious metal strung at the chest and back, painted standards for each squadron, musical instruments, and effigies of royal ancestors carried into battle "because," noted the chronicler **Bernabé Cobo**, "they thought that this was a great help to them in their victories and it made the enemies fearful" (Cobo 1990 [1653]).

As an Inca army approached, we are told, first the slingers fired, then the archers, and then the lancers. Finally the soldiers fought hand-to-hand with maces and small hatchets tied to the wrist, "and with these they did great damage and chopped heads as with a sword" (Cobo 1990 [1653]). Skeletal remains in the Cuzco area have more lethal cranial injuries in Inca times than before, demonstrating elevated hand-to-hand combat as the empire emerged (see **Health and Illness**).

Inca conscripts were male subjects aged 25–50 performing their **labor service**, who had little specialized military training. Although the Incas came to prefer certain ethnic groups for garrisons or for the emperor's guard, such as the Cañari and Chachapoya, they never developed a professional army, relying instead on forces that could be quickly mustered and disbanded. At the emperor's call to arms from the *ushnu* in **Cuzco's** main plaza—chronicler **Pedro de Cieza de León** called it the "stone of war"—the word passed down through the provincial governors and Native lords to call up men through the decimal hierarchy. By the contact period, Inca armies numbered in the tens to hundreds of thousands. Atahualpa reportedly had 40,000–80,000 soldiers at Cajamarca. In 1533, 35,000 troops were stationed in the provincial center of Hatun Jauja, according to accounts of *quipucamayocs* (see **Quipus**). Manco Inca mustered at least 100,000 troops with 80,000 auxiliaries at the siege of Cuzco. Such numbers speak to the unprecedented scale and efficiency of Inca administration.

An Inca army on the march was a splendid sight. Foot soldiers marched in decimal squadrons, bearing their regional headdress and arms, following their Native officers. *Orejones*, Inca nobles who wore earspools, formed a distinctly higher level of command; they also composed the vanguard and were given particularly crucial tasks. The army was commanded by the ruling Inca or a close male relative. The Inca ruler traveled on a litter with an escort of armed guards, wives, and servants. There were porters and thousands of pack llamas with their drovers, carrying food and coca leaf; soldiers' wives; guides;

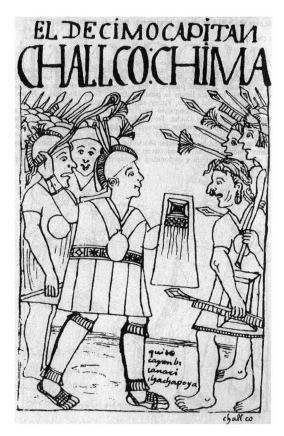

Inca troops skirmish with Chachapoya and Cañari warriors, among other recalcitrant northern peoples, who resisted Inca rule and faced harsh reprisals. Guaman Poma de Ayala, Felipe. *El primer nueva corónica y buen gobierno*. Edited by John V. Murra and Rolena Adorno, 140/161. Mexico City: Siglo Veintiuno, 1980 [1615].

shell-trumpeters; ancestor effigies; and the bearers of the royal standard. Large armies move slowly, and the spacing of **tambos** (way stations) every 15–25 kilometers (9–15 miles) suggests relatively short stages compared with other ancient armies.

Moving and feeding such armies was a critical challenge for the empire, answered by the remarkable armature of the Inca **road** network and its support settlements. Large forces could be stationed long-term at major provincial centers, consistently located on travel corridors and in open plains where an army could camp. Hundreds of *collcas* (storehouses) pepper major centers on the Inca road to the hostile northern frontier; such *collcas* stored food, and, according to Cieza, also furnished the army with clothes, shoes, tents, and arms. As the empire grew, the supply system—storehouses, pack llamas and porters, and supplies requisitioned at need—became critical, enabling the Incas to concentrate overwhelming forces at a single point and set prolonged sieges where necessary. These were fundamental military advantages.

Most campaigns were against chiefdom-level societies at various degrees of complexity, and some victories were achieved merely by the show of force. The Incas also manipulated Native groups by allying with one against the other. Military campaigns doubled as propaganda campaigns; groups who surrendered were treated leniently, their leaders given enhanced authority, while those who resisted could be massacred or deported. Archaeological evidence points to destruction episodes at several sites where enemies offered stiff resistance or rebelled. Elsewhere, prominent Native buildings were razed and replaced with new Inca architecture.

Over time, imperial goals shifted from active conquest to stronger control of the provinces and the defense of the frontier against unconquered people. Settlement patterns confirm a *pax Inca* in most provinces with Inca forts on some frontiers (see **Fortifications**). But the ideal of conquest was never abandoned, for it was underpinned by aims and incentives both economic and ideological. For the ruler, conquests yielded booty and new tributaries to support the royal lifestyle and the broader regime. For those of Inca caste and the Native nobility, war was a route to gifts, land grants, and sumptuary privileges. Common soldiers stood to gain captured women, special clothing, precious ornaments, and, for exceptional service, a hereditary position in the administrative hierarchy.

Warfare was also celebrated in less tangible ways. The drumbeat of conquest in the chronicles reflects Inca military values: Cieza states that the histories of the *quipucamayocs* honored the valiant, victorious kings, while of those who were "remiss, cowardly, given to vice and a life of ease without expanding the realm of the empire, it was ordered that little or nothing be remembered" (Cieza 2010 [1553]). *Orejones* trained for war from boyhood, internalizing core values of honor and martial prowess. In triumphal processions and staged battles in Cuzco, captives, soldiers, and Incas dramatized imperial victory. Human trophies fashioned from the bones, skulls, and skin of prominent enemies were conserved and displayed in battle. On a cosmological level, triumph in war was linked to agricultural fertility, a concept that was probably far older than the Incas. Victory, then, signaled not just military superiority, but also divine favor and the promise of good fortune.

Further Reading

Andrushko, V. A., and E. C. Torres. "Skeletal Evidence for Inca Warfare from the Cuzco Region of Peru." *American Journal of Physical Anthropology* 146:361–72, 2011.

Bram, J. *An Analysis of Inca Militarism.* New York: J. J. Augustin, 1941.

Cieza de León, Pedro de. *The Second Part of the Chronicle of Peru.* Translated and edited by Clements R. Markham. Cambridge: Cambridge University Press, 2010 [1553].

Cobo, B. *Inca Religion and Customs.* Translated and edited by Roland Hamilton. Austin: University of Texas Press, 1990 [1653].

D'Altroy, Terence N. *Provincial Power in the Inka Empire,* Washington, DC: Smithsonian Institution Press, 1992.

———. *The Incas.* 2nd ed. New York: John Wiley & Sons, 2014.

Hemming, John. *The Conquest of the Incas.* New York: Harcourt Brace Jovanovich, 1970.

Murra, J. V. "The Expansion of the Inka state: Armies, War, and Rebellions." In *Anthropological History of Andean Polities,* edited by John V. Murra, Nathan Wachtel, and Jacques Revel, 49–58. Cambridge: Cambridge University Press, 1986.

Nielsen, A. "Ancestors at War: Meaningful Conflict and Social Process in the South Andes." In *Warfare in Cultural Context: Practice, Agency, and the Archaeology of Violence,* edited by A. Nielsen and W. Walker, 218–43. Tucson: University of Arizona Press, 2009.

Rowe, John H. "Inca Culture at the Time of the Spanish Conquest." In *Handbook of South American Indians,* edited by Julian Steward, vol. 2, *The Andean Civilizations,* 183–330. Washington, DC: Smithsonian Institution, Bureau of American Ethnology, 1946.

Topic, J. R., and T. L. Topic. "Hacia una comprensión conceptual de la guerra andina." In *Arqueología, Anthropología e Historia en los Andes: Homenaje a María Rostworowski*, edited by R. Varón Gabai and J. Flores Espinoza, 567–90. Lima: Instituto de Estudios Peruanos, 1997.

Urteaga, H. H. "El ejercito incaico." *Boletin de la Sociedad Geografica de Lima* 35–36:283–331, 1919.

■ ELIZABETH ARKUSH

WARS, DYNASTIC

The Inca Empire was a collection of ethnic groups united through religion and kinship, reinforced by reciprocity and redistribution, and guaranteed by force. Access to tribute labor allowed the Incas to build their network of **roads** and **bridges**, monumental **architecture**, highly engineered agricultural **terraces**, well-provisioned *tambos*, and state storehouses. Nevertheless, there was no recognized and practiced law of succession and thus the end of each reign proved a dangerous time for the empire. Because primogeniture was not the rule, sons did not necessarily succeed fathers, brothers sometimes followed brothers, and nephews could rule after uncles. Political intrigue, power struggles, coups, assassinations, or battle marked these transitions. These followed from one ruler to another, when the last ruler named a successor; or when one would-be ruler took power after showing unusual merit and/or the blessing of the gods; or even when competition, confrontation, or war settled the question. Each candidate, ideally, had been tested and judged to be apt and each was subject to positive auguries (see **Divination**). War had acquired a religious dimension, demonstrated as early as the Chanca war (see **Myths, Origin**). Troops carried idols of their gods onto the battlefields, because their supernatural powers, the Natives believed, aided and even determined the outcome. Once a new ruler emerged, he reestablished ethnic alliances by visiting subject peoples' provinces and renegotiating the relations set up by his predecessor.

Huayna Capac, who was known among his contemporaries as "el Cuzco," the last emperor of a united kingdom, had been returning from a mission near Pasto and Popayán (in the far southwest of modern Colombia) when he fell ill from an unknown disease, probably smallpox, a few years before the Spaniards invaded in 1532 (see **Diseases, Foreign**). On his deathbed, Huayna Capac named a son, Ninan Cuyuchi, as his successor, but his augury was negative and he died soon thereafter. Early observers left several versions of what happened next. In one scenario, Huayna Capac then named another son, Huascar, as his heir, but his prognostication likewise proved unfavorable. When attendants approached Huayna Capac for a third name, they found him dead. Other accounts claim that Huayna Capac intended to split his jurisdiction between Huascar, who would govern the peoples of the south, and Atahualpa, his half brother, who would hold sway over the populations of the north.

Regardless of which is accurate, Huascar, by most accounts, assumed the mantle of heir apparent, marrying his sister (Chuqui Guapay), despite the objections of their mother. Atahualpa acted as a provincial governor in the north and took control of his father's seasoned army led by the generals Chalcochima, Quizquiz, and Rumiñawi. But, jealousies, insecurities, and suspicions of treason poisoned the half brothers' relations, which quickly deteriorated. Huascar and Atahualpa would battle for the title of "el Cuzco" and their father's vacant throne. In this scenario, the confrontations on the battlefield would allow the Sun, their legendary forefather and origin of their lineage, to determine who was most apt. Both Huascar and Atahualpa made sacrifices to their gods, imploring their help, and visited famous **oracles** for predictions on the outcome of the contest. Both faced infamy and death should they lose the god's favor and show weakness or incompetence in the field. Defeated leaders were labeled *atisqa* (defeated, weak) and their followers—and their labor—were claimed by the victor.

Memories of the civil war differ. One version recounts how Huascar's forces, which included aggressive Cañari troops from what is today Ecuador, won the first matches. At one point, they captured Atahualpa and held him prisoner in Tomebamba, a leading Inca settlement; he escaped, according to accounts, by transforming himself into a snake. Others report how southern and northern armies met at Riobamba or Mochacaxa, where Atahualpa's forces won, killing one of Huascar's commanders. Subsequent battles were fought outside of Tomebamba, where the outcome changed overnight. At this encounter, Huascar's forces triumphed on one day only to be ultimately overtaken by Atahualpa's forces the next. They retreated to Cusipampa, in the northern highlands between Tomebamba and **Cajamarca**, where they were again routed. Atahualpa's experienced troops maintained their advantage pushing them south to Cajamarca in the northern highlands of Peru, where they regrouped and recruited thousands of fresh men, 10,000 of whom were formidable Chachapoya. In the next battle, Atahualpa's general wisely focused on breaking the Chachapoya line. This success demoralized Huascar's forces, some of whom must have thought that Atahualpa's victories demonstrated the Sun's favor. Atahualpa's general, Quizquiz, continued to dominate at Pumpu, a center in the central high plains. Additional victories followed in the Yanamarca Valley (north of Hatun Jauja), at Angoyaco, and at Quipaypán (between Apurímac and Cuzco).

As the confrontations turned against him, an oracle told Huascar that he must appear at the front of his troops to reverse the outcomes of these confrontations. Huascar followed the oracle's counsel. Though versions differ on how Huascar was captured, a particularly vivid story recounts how Huascar donned a headdress and other fineries adorned with gold and, on his litter, entered the field of battle. The Sun made his figure shine so that his image "wounded the eyes" of onlookers, making it easy for Atahualpa's generals to seize him.

Atahualpa, too, consulted oracles. He stopped while in the north at the well-known shrine of **Catequil** in Huamachuco, where he asked about the outcome of the war. The oracle replied that there had been too much bloodshed already. An outraged Atahualpa beheaded the attendant and knocked the top off the oracle's image. Then he decided to dismantle the constructions and flatten the site. As his forces leveled Catequil's sanctuary, Atahualpa learned of the arrival of Pizarro and his men. He decided to meet them in Cajamarca, a nearby ceremonial center (see **Invasion, Spanish**). Meanwhile, Huascar also had been informed. Both he and his brother independently remarked that the tall, bearded strangers must be the gods or their messengers who had answered his prayers and supplications and come to aid him in his struggles.

But, their initial interpretations proved faulty. Huascar was already a captive by the time that Atahualpa had met Pizarro in the plaza of Cajamarca and been imprisoned himself.

During the next few months, Atahualpa tried to buy his freedom, promising Pizarro a rich ransom of gold and silver. Atahualpa also ordered the murder of Huascar after learning that he had offered Pizarro twice his ransom. Atahualpa himself was garroted when rumors circulated that he had ordered his troops to amass and wipe out the Spanish invaders.

Pizarro named two successors before arriving in the southern ceremonial center of "the Cuzco," the capital of the realm. Eventually, one fled and established a rump government in the jungles of **Vilcabamba**. But, the days of the *Sapa* **Inca**, the unique, unquestioned, and omnipotent Inca, son of the Sun god, had been eclipsed.

Further Reading

D'Altroy, Terence N. *The Incas*. 2nd ed. New York: John Wiley & Sons, 2014.

Pease, Franklin. *Los últimos Incas del Cusco*. Madrid: Alianza América, 1991.

Ramírez, Susan Elizabeth. *To Feed and Be Fed: The Cosmological Bases of Authority and Identity in the Andes*. Stanford, CA: Stanford University Press, 2005.

■ SUSAN ELIZABETH RAMÍREZ

WEALTH

The Incas did not recognize wealth in the form of general-purpose money or traffic in commodities such as precious metals or spices. Even so, certain things conferred wealth on the owner or had a special value. They included having access to a large labor force, owning large camelid herds or other productive resources, and possessing coveted material goods. Because individual or familial ownership contrasted with the more typical group sharing of productive resources, the wealthy were distinguished as much by the privilege of their socioeconomic stature as by the quantity of their wealth.

Wealth can be analyzed in two contexts in Tahuantinsuyu, the Inca Empire: in state economic policy and among the aristocracy. Because the Inca economy relied upon **labor service**, rather than specie, for its tax base, much of what the state mobilized was heavy staples, such as food. The Inca transport system also lacked waterborne and wheeled transport, so that much state production had to be replicated regionally. The state's conferral of high-status goods, especially finely woven cloth (*qompi*) (see **Costume**; **Weaving and Textiles**); gold, silver, and ceramic tumblers (see **Keros; Metallurgy**); fine ceramic brewing and service vessels (see **Ceramics**); and stools provided rank and privilege to the honored individuals. Those items, while not convertible, were accompanied by perquisites, such as labor service and estate lands, which did constitute a main form of wealth in the realm (see **Estates, Royal**). By manufacturing and distributing such items, the Incas found an efficient way to reduce the costs of compliance among the ethnic lords and their subjects.

Much of the socioeconomic life and politics of Andean society was mediated through ritualized exchanges of labor. At the local level, a lord (*curaca*) could command a portion of the labor of his followers, so that a lord with many subjects could be considered wealthy (see *Sapa* **Inca**). The Incas used that principle to legitimize their extraction of labor service as tax. Andean politics took place in a context of commensal hospitality, in which lords' generosity marked their stature (see **Feasts, State-Sponsored**). The products of the available labor force, especially fine cloth and maize beer, *chicha*, were dispensed to lubricate decision making and underwrite power relations. The Incas applied this notion to their own goals, using the production of their taxpayers to host annual feasts at provincial centers, where several days of feasting were followed by announcements of the following years' labor obligations (see **Labor Service**).

While the empire's resources were institutional wealth, it also makes sense to speak of the wealth of the aristocracy. State resources were used for governmental interests, such as military activity and maintaining social order. In contrast, the elite's resources were used to maintain a privileged lifestyle and to compete for status in the volatile atmosphere of Inca politics. Certain productive resources were especially desirable, because of the products that they yielded and the history invested in the land. The estate lands in the Urubamba valley (e.g., Pisac, Ollantaytambo, and **Machu Picchu**) were particularly well developed and staffed, and were thus coveted by royal families (see **Estates, Royal**). Individual estates boasted up to 6,000 families who worked at farming, herding, providing household service, and fabricating the material goods used to maintain an elegant existence. Based on significant land and water modifications, the manors provided an opulent lifestyle for the rulers' descendant families. **Coca** leaf estates in the lowlands, and gold and silver mines, were also highly valued.

Vast flocks of llamas and alpacas constituted a form of wealth on the hoof, for their fiber, meat, transport, and ritual values (see **Animals, Domesticated**). A tunic of fine tapestry weave, theoretically awarded only by the order of the **Sapa Inca** (sole or unique ruler), was a mark of particular status. When the Incas began to expand their domain, they focused early efforts on the *altiplano*, where camelid herds formed the basis of wealth for the local populace. The scale of herds was impressive, as individual lords could own tens of thousands of animals, while the Incas' Sun temple network was said to own over a million animals, a number probably significantly surpassed by the state's flocks.

In comparative context, discussions of primitive valuables, circuits of exchange of status goods (e.g., in the Melanesian *kula* ring), and special-purpose moneys (e.g., cowries; iron bars, raffia cloth) have considerable depth in economic anthropology. Many of those objects are consumable currencies (e.g., tobacco, opium, salt, spices, sugar, rum, cloth, cotton, and coca leaf). Those items generally carry some, but not all, of the features of money: medium of exchange, standard of value, repository of value, and unit of accounting. They are also imbued with cultural weight that extends beyond simple accounting functionality. In this context, coca leaf may have been the closest thing to a consumable or political currency that existed in the Inca economy. It was widely exchanged, but it seems to have been sought mostly for use, ritual exchanges, and offerings, so its role was more properly social and ceremonial than monetary.

A number of the societies drawn under Inca rule possessed items that come closer to a conventional, western economic view of wealth. Among the most prominent were the beads called *chaquira*, of bone, shell, and gold, that circulated among the peoples of the northern part of the empire, serving as media of exchange and standards of value. They were employed by a class of traders (*mindaláes*), who worked both independently and as the agents of regional lords. They circulated through market networks, which did not form a part of the Inca imperial economic system.

A second form of wealth, found along the far north coast of Peru and into Ecuador, were copper-alloy *hachas,* axe-shaped objects found in north coast tombs. They were organized into decimal series by weight, and seem to have served as media of exchange. Like the beads, they were not employed directly by the Incas, but their use was also not impeded.

Further Reading

D'Altroy, Terence N., and Timothy K. Earle. "Staple Finance, Wealth Finance, and Storage in the Inka Political Economy (with Comment and Reply)." *Current Anthropology* 25:187–206, 1985.

Hosler, Diane, Heather Lechtman, and Olaf Holm. *Axe-Monies and Their Relatives.* Studies in Pre-Columbian Art and Archaeology, no. 30. Washington, DC: Dumbarton Oaks, 1980.

Murra, John V. *The Economic Organization of the Inka State.* Greenwich, CT: JAI Press, 1980 [1956].

Salomon, Frank L. "A North Andean Status Trader Complex under Inca Rule." *Ethnohistory* 34, no. 1: 63–77, 1987.

■ TERENCE N. D'ALTROY

WEAVING AND TEXTILES

The Incas and their subjects inherited a long and varied weaving tradition that went back to Andean societies that flourished millennia before the time of the Inca Empire. Given that virtually all clothing (see **Costume**) in the empire took the form of woven textiles, it is best to talk about spinning and weaving and textile structures as a single, unified tradition of skills, practices, and preferences. A handful of excellent Colonial sources shed light on the technology of weaving and the qualities, classification, and uses of different types of textiles. These include the *mestizo* (mixed Spanish/native ancestry) chronicler **Garcilaso de la Vega** who, growing up in immediate postconquest Cuzco, was familiar with weaving techniques in the capital; **Felipe Guaman Poma de Ayala**, a Native chronicler from the Lucanas region of Peru who wrote about and produced drawings of spinners and weavers, as well as numerous illustrations of both elite and commoner clothing; and the mid-seventeenth-century chronicler **Bernabé Cobo**, who lived in Cuzco more than a century after the conquest but who observed weavers and clothing and who may have had access to the work of Garcilaso and other chroniclers. Accounts from these knowledgeable chroniclers, as well as preserved fabrics from coastal burials and a handful of highland sites give us a remarkably clear picture of the art of weaving and the clothing and headdress styles of the Inca Empire.

Inca weavings were produced with two principal materials: camelid fibers and cotton. The preferred materials for the highland-dwelling Inca peoples were fibers of the four native camelids—the domesticated llama and alpaca and the wild vicuña and guanaco (see **Animals, domesticated**). Fibers of domesticated camelids were most common in highland weavings, although few examples survive, due to poor preservation in the rainy highland environment. Textiles made of cotton, or a combination of cotton and camelid fibers, were common on the coast, where preservation is good.

Inca weavers produced cloth in two major categories in terms of quality. The finest, most expertly produced weavings were known as *cumbi.* These fabrics, woven by male

A weaver at a horizontal loom in Yanaoca, province of Canas, Cuzco, Peru. Camilo Alata. TAFOS Photographic Archive/PUCP, Lima, Peru.

Weavers with horizontal looms in the province of Canas, Cuzco, Peru. Gregorio Condori. TAFOS Photographic Archive/PUCP, Lima, Peru.

or female specialists called *cumbicamayoc*, were restricted to the Incas and those who were given *cumbi* as gifts. The **acllacuna**, who lived in state-run production facilities, also produced fine textiles. They were overseen by senior women who no doubt were master weavers themselves. Textiles made of *cumbi* cloth were stored in great quantities in state storehouses from where they were dispensed by the Inca or his agents for strategic political purposes.

The other type of cloth, not as fine as *cumbi*, was known as *ahuasca*. Garments made of *ahuasca* cloth were produced by commoners in their households, where the tasks of cloth production—for example, the shearing of the camelids or harvest and ginning of cotton, the spinning and plying of fibers, and the weaving of textiles on looms—went on as part of daily family activities. In addition, households were required to produce textiles with fiber from state storehouses as part of their annual labor obligation.

A woman using a drop spindle spins camelid fiber in Yanaoca, province of Canas, Cuzco, Peru. Mariano Chilihuani. TAFOS Photographic Archive/ PUCP, Lima, Peru.

In the highlands around Cuzco, raw camelid and cotton fibers were spun by hand, using a drop spindle (*phusca*). This device was composed of an approximately 30.5-centimeter-long (1-foot-long) wooden or cane shaft to the lower end of which was affixed a spindle whorl (*piruru*) commonly made of stone, ceramic, or wood. The raw fibers were held in the free hand and stretched and fed out to the hand holding the drop spindle. The spindle was dropped while spun rapidly and the raw fibers formed a thinly spun thread.

Spun and plied threads are commonly described as either S or Z. These notations are used to indicate whether the spindle is dropped and spun to the right (clockwise) to produce fibers within the thread body that run obliquely from upper left to lower right, like the slant of an S, or if the spindle is dropped and spun counterclockwise, producing threads with oblique axes running upper right to lower left, like the slant of a Z. Inca thread of the south highlands and coast was generally spun in the Z direction. Two or three Z-spun threads would be twisted together, using the drop spindle, in the S-direction to produce Z-spun/S-plied threads for weaving. North coast Chimú weavers, contemporary with the Incas, commonly prepared threads S-spun/Z-plied. Spun and plied camelid threads (but only infrequently those made of cotton) would often be dyed before warping began.

Two weavers set up the warps on their loom in Ayaviri, Puno, southern Peru. Anonymous. TAFOS Photographic Archive/PUCP, Lima, Peru.

Warping is the process of extending a continuous warp thread back and forth across a frame often composed of a pair of stakes embedded upright in the ground, or across a horizontal frame, to provide the fixed, lengthwise threads through which the weft threads pass in the act of weaving. The warped threads of a textile contain a thread crossing (often called *sonqo*, heart) at the center of the warping. It is this crossing that, in plain weave textiles, will be worked up and down by the heddles to alternately raise and lower groups of warp threads through which the weft is passed producing the fabric surface (warp + weft). Inca textiles are woven so finely and tightly that it is often extremely difficult to tell which group of threads constitute the warp component and which the weft. The Andean textile specialist Ann Rowe has provided a detailed discussion of the determination of warp vs. weft in a variety of Inca textiles.

Inca weavers produced cloth on one of three different types of looms: back-strap, vertical/upright, or horizontal. The first two types are illustrated in chronicler Guaman Poma de Ayala's work which depicts Native weavers at work, under the abusive hands of Colonial officials.

Back-strap looms are composed of distal and proximal header sticks to which the warp threads are attached. The distal header stick is attached to an elevated structure (tree, post, etc.), while the header stick nearest to the weaver carries a strap that is passed around the back of the weaver and attached to both ends of the header. The weaver leans forward or backward to apply the appropriate amount of pressure on the warp threads as he/she passes the weft thread through the warps. This type of loom is common even today in the Cuzco region, where weavers produce what are termed *complementary warp weavings*. In such weavings, warp threads of different colors are alternately raised or lowered in an operation called *pallay* (to pick [up]) with successive passes of the weft. The emergent designs produced by this technique are colored opposite (e.g., color vs. white, or one color vs. another color) on the top and bottom sides of the finished fabric.

One of two types of fixed-tension looms, the upright loom was most commonly used in the production of tapestry weave textiles. The weaver would work in different runs of weft threads of one or another color, generally interlocking the threads of one color with those of another color where the two runs met to produce different designs across the surface of the completed textile. Another type of fixed tension loom, the horizontal loom, was probably used as well—primarily for the production of tapestry weaves.

With the various materials, devices, and techniques described above, Inca weavers fashioned some of the finest textiles produced by hand anywhere in the world. Cloth was a highly valued object in the Inca world. The Incas and their administrators used their finest textiles to seek favors and compliance with state plans—including conquests, and to show utmost respect to other peoples with whom they came into contact. They even offered fine cloth in sacrifice to the gods and shrines.

Further Reading

Cobo, Bernabé. *Inca Religion and Customs*. Translated and edited by Roland Hamilton. Austin: University of Texas Press, 1990 [1653].

Garcilaso de la Vega, El Inca. *Royal Commentaries of the Incas and General History of Peru*. Translated by Harold V. Livermore. 2 vols. Austin: University of Texas Press, 1966 [1609, 1617].

Guaman Poma de Ayala, Felipe. *Nueva corónica y buen gobierno*. Edited by John V. Murra and Rolena Adorno. Translated by Jorge L. Urioste. Mexico: Siglo Veintiuno, 1980.

Murra, John V. "Cloth and Its Function in the Inca State." *American Anthropologist* 64, no. 4: 710–28, 1962.

Rowe, Ann Pollard. "Inca Weaving and Costume." *Textile Museum Journal* 34–35: 4–53, 1995–1996.

Stone-Miller, Rebecca, ed. *To Weave for the Sun: Andean Textiles in the Museum of Fine Arts, Boston*. Boston: Museum of Fine Arts, Boston, 1992.

■ GARY URTON

WOMEN

Institutions with a distinctive Andean character shaped what it meant to be a woman or man in Inca times. Norms of gender parallelism—a model in which women were conceptualized as descending from a line of women and men, in like fashion, as descending from a line of men—governed much of community and imperial life. While not the sole gender system (see *Acllacuna*), it contributed significantly to female and male identities, interlocked with the gendered division of labor, governed the transmission of rights to land and resources, shaped religious structures, and gave form to the power relations tying Inca rulers with conquered polities.

Andean women experienced their lives in gender specific, yet interrelated, worlds. This dynamic—of autonomy and interdependence—was supported by Andean traditions of parallel transmission of rights to community resources. Although parallel transmission was not the only means through which these rights were acquired in the Andean *ayllu*, it was a preeminent channel for procuring them. Women, through their mothers, enjoyed access to community land, water, herds, and other resources that sustained life. We cannot estimate what portion of *ayllu* resources were in the hands of women, but parallel transmission rights ensured that women, independently of kinsmen or husbands, could obtain their society's means of subsistence.

The gendered division of labor in the Andes meshed with traditions of parallel descent: cultural norms defined appropriate activities for women and men while embedding them in a wider conception of complementarity. Andean practices of living were daily expressions of the dynamics of gender parallelism and gender interdependence. Women's contributions to production were manifold. Cooking, brewing *chicha* (maize beer), preparing fields for cultivation, planting seeds, harvesting, weeding, herding, and carrying water filled a woman's day. Women's work in the *ayllu*—from weaving, cooking, and sowing, to child care—was never considered a private service for husbands. Their labor, complemented by the work of men, grounded the continuance of household, kin, and community. The Incas retained this conception of interdependent male and female work as fundamental to their system of tribute (see **Labor Service**).

Although men wove for their households and some, the *cumbicamayoc*, were specialists who created textiles prized by the elite, women were the weavers of the Andes. They were inseparable from the spindles carried on their journeys. In addition to weaving cloth for the entire household, women under Inca rule were responsible for tribute in textiles owed the state. Women of the Inca nobility were also renowned weavers. They played critical roles during imperial ceremonies by making prized textiles; they also produced highly desirable "gifts" in cloth distributed by the Inca to political underlings (see **Costume; Labor Service; Weaving and Textiles**).

Textiles enjoyed special stature in Inca society. The acquisition of cloth, along with its distribution by the Inca elite, reinforced and catalyzed the empire's political institutions. Weavings also communicated Andean histories. The designs woven in belts, tunics, and shawls not only represented incidents in household life, but they also recorded political status and duties, provided descriptions of a year's critical events, and chronicled significant episodes of community and imperial pasts. Noblewomen and commoners inscribed perspectives on history as they wove garments for household and empire.

Women were also actively engaged in agriculture. They classified seeds, tubers, and grains, and then selected which to set aside for immediate consumption and which to plant. The affinity between women and agrarian labor was expressed in the gendered alignment of the cosmos: a sacred bond joined women with the divine forces of fertility— Pachamama (Mother Earth) and her daughters, Maize, Potatoes, and other Andean crops. Women prayed and sang to Pachamama when they first planted seeds in the earth; at harvest time, women ceremonially lauded the "mothers" of crops for their powers to create foods in abundance.

Sacred practices, framed in the language of gender parallelism, heightened the experience of living in gender-specific, but mutually enhancing, worlds. Community-wide, religious institutions, devoted to like-gendered divinities, anchored parallelism in the heavens and in the earth. In some *ayllus*, women's organizations were dedicated to "corn mothers," here designated the "sisters" of male deities; other religious groups paid homage to the moon or to bodies of water, also female in character and structure. Mothers passed down ritual clothing and instruments of worship to their daughters. In addition, some deities were venerated by women from neighboring communities, building alliances that spanned *ayllu* borders.

Sexual parallelism, which ordered relations both within and among communities, also grounded imperial political/religious structures. The Inca cosmos was one of parallel hierarchies, with Inca divinities—Sun and Moon—standing above representatives of lower social orders. Like Inca kings, Inca queens (*Coyas*), as "daughters "of the Moon, were imbued with holiness; like Inca kings, Inca queens remained the objects of religious devotion after death. Under the queen's dominion, women's religious groups were transformed into institutions of an imperial state. The *Coya*, with independent rights to land and tribute, could bind other women to her debt in a web of political obligation and authority. The *Coya* stood at the apex of a political structure composed of women, stretching from Cuzco into the hinterlands.

According to Inca tradition, a Queen-divinity introduced the cultivation of maize, the empire's most cherished crop, into the Cuzco valley. Veneration of Mama Huaco—one of the founding, mythical Incas (see **Myths, Origin**)—was in the hands of the *Coyas* who, mirroring women's work in the *ayllu*, were noted for their concern for the quality of crops. Much has been written about Inca mastery of **irrigation** and **terracing**—male pursuits; much less about the role of women in agronomy. Women's agricultural tasks included the selection of seeds, and full-time specialists, with the knowledge, training, and resources needed for agricultural experiments, would, by Andean measures, be women from the Inca elite. Very probably, Inca queens supervised special fields used as agricultural laboratories for refining strains of cultigens. Most likely, Cuzco noblewomen, in the course of imperial rituals tying Cuzco to the provinces, transmitted this knowledge to others.

But gender parallelism existed with other gender configurations and the consolidation of Inca rule heightened paradoxes inherent in gender parallelism and between it and another gendered structure of power. The "conquest hierarchy," contrary to parallelism, expressly used gender symbols to represent political subjugation. Here, "the conquerors," portrayed as male, were of a higher rank than "the conquered," conceived of as female. Throughout the Andes, *ayllus* linked maleness to the thunder/mountain gods who, in myth, claimed superiority over local, "female" shrines (see **Acllacuna**; **Deities**, **Religion**).

The association of men with warfare is tellingly expressed in the Andean division of labor. If weaving and planting were considered exemplars of women's labor, plowing and combat were the iconic tasks of manhood. Of course, men did much more than that: they weeded, helped in the harvest, carried firewood, and herded llamas; men wove in their communities and *cumbicamayoc* wove textiles that were esteemed throughout the empire. Nonetheless, the division of labor was expressed figuratively in the association of women with textile manufacture and men with implements of force: women were buried with their spindle whorls, men with their weapons. Even though there was very little that either gender would not do, pairings of women with textiles and men with weaponry grounded figures of Andean collective understandings and ideologies of personhood.

Before Inca expansion, the primary function of the conquest hierarchy was to rank kin groups within the *ayllu*. At this scale, the "conquest hierarchy" was principally a classificatory structure, suggesting prestige, but not dominion. In *ayllu* political organization, the symbolic "conquerors" (kin groups, figured as male) had no prerogatives over the resources of "the conquered" (kin groups, figured as female). "Conquerors" carried no political weight; nor did "the conquerors" have rights to women.

Nonetheless, this framework harbored suggestions of inequalities, giving men prerogatives in realms of power. Yes, women's institutions, framed through gender parallelism, were important arenas of imperial reach; yes, the gender-linked attributes of weaving and arms were conceived as a complementary unity of societal reproduction. But as the Incas consolidated their control over the Andes, the ideological structure of the conquest hierarchy became a design for imperial dominion—with gendered consequences.

The "conquest hierarchy," transformed to meet the needs of empire, became the framework for a political—not prestige—hierarchy. Men, not women, filled the growing number of offices in the imperial bureaucracy: men were **census** takers, the controllers of state storehouses, the judges, the political overseers and middlemen. Another consequence was that "male conquerors," embodied by the Sapa Inca, now the titular husband of all "conquered" women, could claim rights to all women under his rule. Converted to an institution of imperial rule, the "conquest hierarchy" spawned the creation of the most renowned class of women in the empire—the *aclla,* the Inca's "chosen women" (see *Acllacuna*). This transformation bore profound consequences for gender relations and for the meanings and possibilities afforded Andean women.

Further Reading

Silverblatt, Irene. *Moon, Sun, and Witches: Gender Ideologies and Class in Inca and Colonial Peru.* Princeton, NJ: Princeton University Press, 1987.

■IRENE SILVERBLATT

WORSHIP, ANCESTOR

The relationship with ancestors was a fundamental feature of Inca culture and society. By *ancestors* we refer not only to historically remembered progenitors, but also to mythical community founders who were said to have brought **ayllu**s (kin-based communities) into existence in the very distant past. Most *ayllu*s were composed of lineages defined by descent from specific ancestors and joined as a collectivity through common descent from a distant founder.

The term *ancestor worship* refers here to ritualized performances through which living *ayllu* members expressed their ongoing relationship with community forebears. Because these rites served to display group membership and differentiate groups from each other, they had important political dimensions. The descendant-ancestor bond was often as much a matter of affiliation as it was of literal descent; outsiders could adopt ancestors as their own by participating in their worship, thus defining themselves as members of the descendant community. Exact genealogical reckoning held importance mainly for *ayllu* chiefs (*curacas*) and Inca royalty; common folk simply considered themselves members of an extended kin group originating with a distant founder. In any case, whether reckoned by affiliation or literal descent, ancestors played an active role in the life of the *ayllu*s.

Founding ancestors were said to have emerged from underground or, less frequently, to have fallen from the sky. Origin narratives collected by early Spanish chroniclers tell us that the first human beings journeyed north from Lake Titicaca via underground waterways. Some emerged into daylight from springs, while others came forth from lakes, caves, hilltops, and even the roots of trees. Wherever they emerged, they founded *ayllu*s. The places of emergence were venerated as *pacarinas* (dawning places); *ayllu* mummies

An Inca mummy is carried on a litter during the feast of the dead. Guaman Poma de Ayala, Felipe. *El primer nueva corónica y buen gobierno*. Edited by John V. Murra and Rolena Adorno, 230/256. Mexico City: Siglo Veintiuno, 1980 [1615].

were often interred there as well, thus returning in death to their kindred's place of origin (see **Myths, Origin**).

Ayllu origin narratives typically end with founding ancestors turning to stone. According to the chronicler **Pedro Sarmiento de Gamboa**, the ancestors of the Inca kings, five brothers and five sisters, emerged from a cave in Pacariqtambo and set out in search of a place to settle. Eventually they crossed a hill called Huanacauri overlooking the Cuzco valley, site of their future city. On that hilltop one of the brothers, Ayar Uchu, turned to stone and became a very powerful and sacred *huaca* (shrine). On reaching the site itself, another brother, Ayar Auca, turned into a *huanca* (large boulder indicating possession of an agricultural locale). The senior brother, Ayar Manco, became the first paramount ruler (Manco Capac); after death his body became a rock and was venerated as the oldest of the royal mummies.

Rural *ayllus* also had their ancestral *huacas* and *huancas*. The *Huarochirí Manuscript* (see **Avila, Francisco de**) tells how primordial lovers, Anchi Cara from Allauca and Huallama from Surco, turned to stone while making love in a mountain spring that gave rise to their respective irrigation systems. They were worshipped during canal-cleaning festivals with panpipe **music** and offerings of **coca** leaves. In the central highlands many *ayllus* were composed of two groups consisting of original inhabitants called *huari* and newcomers called *llacuaz*. The agriculturally oriented *huaris* directed their veneration mainly at immovable *huancas*, while the pastoral *llacuazes* were more focused on portable ancestral stones that accompanied them when they entered the territory.

Far from being inert chunks of matter, ancestral stones powerfully condensed the life force of *ayllu* founders and ensured their permanence. To generalize, Andeans did not think in terms of Western body/soul dualism; all matter had the potential for active life (though not all matter realized this potential). Bodies of the deceased, when properly mummified, condensed a life force similar to that of the petrified founding ancestors. These *ayllu* mummies were called *mallqui*, a term also meaning "a tree complete with its roots" (perhaps alluding to the subterranean sustenance roots that provide for the visible branching tree above ground). Typically, flexed bodies of the dead were wrapped in layers of cloth and placed in caves, burial towers, or shaft tombs.

The most important mummies had their own shrines. In 1614, for example, the priest Avendaño located and destroyed Libiac Concharco, the mummified founding ancestor of the Checras region of Chancay, in the highlands of Lima. The mummy was ensconced in a curtained shrine, wrapped in six layers of embroidered cloth and bedecked with feathers and golden ornaments. People of the region attributed their prosperity to Libiac Concharco, and often carried him from place to place to receive offerings.

Mallquis were felt to be essential for the well-being of their *ayllus*, responsible for seasonal rains and the health and fecundity of people, crops, and herds. Their relationship with the living was a reciprocal one. Like living people, mummies got hungry and thirsty and needed sustenance and care. Fields and pastures were set aside to provide for them. Most *ayllus* had one or more priests who changed the mummies' clothing regularly and made sure they received offerings of meat, blood, toasted maize, coca leaves, and maize beer, **chicha**. Llamas, guinea pigs and, in extreme cases, children, were sacrificed to them. The priests also served as mediums who could communicate with the *mallquis*, ask for their counsel in times of crisis, and relay their advice to the *ayllu* (see **Oracles**).

People approached *huacas* and *mallquis* as they did chiefs and Inca nobility, with a gesture of obeisance (*mocha*) that entailed extending the right hand, placing the left hand on the forehead, and making a kissing sound with the lips. Collective worship took place before harvest and sowing when *ayllu* members gathered at their *pacarinas*, or places or origin. The priest took confessions, one-by-one or collectively, after which the people made offerings, danced, and sang traditional ballads recounting their *ayllu's* origin story. Probably these festivals provided a context in which origin myths might be revised and reinterpreted in light of then-current political realities and other changing circumstances.

In 1574, the priest and chronicler **Cristóbal de Molina** observed a purification festival (*Citua*) that took place in Cuzco at the beginning of the rainy season (August/September). Richly adorned mummies of deceased Cuzco nobility were placed on golden stools in the plaza in order of seniority. They were joined by the city's populace, who also sat in rank order. The Inca ruler, together with a high priest, drank **chicha** (maize beer) from a large golden beaker and poured libations for the Creator, the Sun, and Thunder (see **Deities**; **Religion**). Then there came a procession of priests bearing yet more mummified nobility from Upper and Lower Cuzco. They too were seated in rank order, after which everyone set to sharing food and drink, singing and dancing together. The Inca shared *chicha* with the noble mummies, who consumed it through the persons of their appointed retainer-priests; the mummies in turn sent beakers of *chicha* to the Inca ruler. This pattern repeated among the rest of the participants; thus the living and dead celebrated together (see **Mummies, Royal**).

Molina and other observers saw these festivals as excess and debauchery, not understanding the profound significance of commensality for Andean people (see **Feasts, State-Sponsored**). Food sharing was the fundamental expression of kinship; to eat and drink together was to partake of the same substance. It was important to include deceased relatives—*mallquis*—in *ayllu* commensality; the retainer-priest's body provided a conduit through which the animating force of food and beverage passed to the mummified ancestor. The intoxication and intense conviviality that shocked Spanish missionaries occurred in this ritual framework and had the purpose of joining the living and the dead in prosperous, harmonious community.

The Spanish conquest was profoundly traumatic for the Andean populace in many respects, not the least of which was the destruction of *huacas* and *mallquis*, along with the requirement that the dead receive Christian burial within churches and cemeteries. People grieved for their forebears, bereft of offerings and suffering from hunger and thirst. They found unbearable the idea that their recently dead kinsmen were weighted down by earth or enclosed in cramped niches, and went so far as to surreptitiously remove these beloved cadavers to traditional burial places, and to continue their traditional services behind the missionaries' backs. Indeed, some of our best information about pre-Spanish burial practices and ancestral rites comes from missionaries who zealously tracked down the would-be *mallquis* and carried them back for Christian burial.

Severing the bond between living Andean peoples and their ancestors dealt a decisive blow to the Inca way of life. Ancestor worship forged connections among the living and the dead that were fundamental to Inca society and culture. Bonds between the living and their dead were physical and communicative, forged through close proximity and commensality. In these collective acts of communication with the dead, the *ayllu* constituted itself as a moral and political entity at every level—from small rural settlements to the royal lineages of Cuzco.

Further Reading

Cobo, Bernabé. *Inca Religion and Customs.* Translated and edited by Roland Hamilton. Austin: University of Texas Press, 1990.

Dillehay, Tom D., ed. *Tombs for the Living: Andean Mortuary Practices.* Washington, DC: Dumbarton Oaks Research Library and Collection, 1995.

Gose, Peter. *Invaders as Ancestors: On the Making and Unmaking of Spanish Colonialism in the Andes.* Toronto: University of Toronto Press, 2008.

MacCormick, Sabine. *Religion in the Andes: Vision and Imagination in Early Colonial Peru.* Princeton, NJ: Princeton University Press, 1991.

Ramírez, Susan Elizabeth. *To Feed and Be Fed: The Cosmological Basis of Authority and Identity in the Andes.* Stanford, CA: Stanford University Press, 2005.

Rostworowski de Diez Canseco, María. *History of the Inca Realm.* Translated by Harry B. Iceland. Cambridge: Cambridge University Press, 1999.

Salomon, Frank, and George L. Urioste, trans. and eds. *The Huarochirí Manuscript: A Testament of Ancient and Colonial Andean Religion.* Austin: University of Texas Press, 1991.

■ CATHERINE J. ALLEN

Z

ZUIDEMA, R. TOM

Zuidema (1927–) began his anthropological training with studies of Southeast Asian societies at Leiden University, the Netherlands, in the 1950s. He was a student of two prominent Dutch structural anthropologists of the 1940s and 1950s, J. P. B. de Josselin de Jong and P. E. de Josselin de Jong. Zuidema switched his focus of research to the Andes following Indonesian independence, in 1949. He subsequently moved from Leiden to Madrid, in the early 1950s, to deepen his studies of Spanish sources on the Incas. Zuidema earned his first PhD at the University of Madrid in 1953 with a dissertation titled *La organización social y política Incaica según las Fuentes Españoles* (The Social and Political Organization of the Incas According to the Spanish Sources). His second PhD was awarded at Leiden University in 1964, with a dissertation titled *The Ceque System of Cuzco: The Social Organization of the Capital of the Inca.*

Upon completion of his Leiden dissertation, Zuidema took up his first teaching post at the University of Huamanga, in Ayacucho, Peru, from 1964 to 1967. He then taught at the Department of Anthropology at the University of Illinois at Urbana-Champaign in 1967, a position from which he retired in 1994. Zuidema's research and publications over the years have been heavily influenced by his close reading of the Spanish chronicles, as well as by his ethnographic experiences in the Ayacucho region of Peru. He trained numerous graduate students who earned PhDs at Illinois with their research in Andean archaeology, ethnohistory, and ethnography.

Zuidema's early studies focused on the social and political organization of the Inca capital by way of the *ceque* (line, orientation) system within the city and valley of Cuzco. Zuidema showed that the basic structures of the *ceque* system included dual (moiety) and quadripartite (*suyu*) divisions, which were subdivided into 41 *ceque* lines along which were organized some 328 sacred sites, or *huacas*. These structures provided the framework for political, social, and ritual relations and activities among 10 groups of descendants of the Inca kings (*panacas*), and 10 groups of descendants of non-noble, but privileged, status residents (*ayllus*) who collectively oversaw state ceremonies and religious celebrations within the capital city. In his early studies, Zuidema was concerned primarily with the structural properties of the *ceque* system, particularly as they related to Andean forms and principles of social and kinship organization, as well as certain presumed marriage patterns, which, he thought, were crucial for the reproduction of political relations among the *panacas* and *ayllus* over time. His attention increasingly turned to questions concerning the historicity of the *ceque* system, the place of mythology in rationalizing the structures of the system, and the temporalities of the system as they were realized in what he termed the "*ceque* calendar."

Further Reading

Salomon, Frank. "The Historical Development of Andean Ethnology." *Mountain Research and Development* 5, no. 1: 79–98, 1985.

Urton, Gary. "R. Tom Zuidema, Dutch Structuralism, and the Application of the 'Leiden Orientation' to Andean Studies." In *Structure, Knowledge, and Representation in the Andes: Studies Presented to Reiner Tom Zuidema on the Occasion of his 70th Birthday. Journal of the Steward Anthropological Society* 24, no. 1–2: 1–36, 1996.

Zuidema, R. Tom. *The Ceque System of Cuzco: The Social Organization of the Capital of the Incas.* Leiden, Netherlands: E. J. Brill, 1964.

———. *El calendario inca: Tiempo y espacio en la organización ritual del Cuzco: La idea del pasado.* Lima: Fondo Editorial del Congreso del Perú and Fondo Editorial de la Pontificia Universidad Católica del Perú, 2010.

■ GARY URTON

INDEX

Note: Page numbers in italic type indicate illustrations.

ABOUT THE EDITORS AND CONTRIBUTORS

THE EDITORS

Gary Urton is the Dumbarton Oaks Professor of Pre-Columbian Studies and Chairman of the Department of Anthropology at Harvard University. His research focuses on a variety of topics in pre-Columbian and early Colonial Andean intellectual history, and draws on materials and methods in archaeology, ethnohistory, and ethnology. He is the author of many articles and author/editor of several volumes on Andean/Quechua cultures and Inca civilization. His books include: *At the Crossroads of the Earth and the Sky* (1981), *The History of a Myth* (1990), *The Social Life of Numbers* (1997), *Inca Myths* (1999), and *Signs of the Inka Khipu* (2003). A MacArthur Fellow (2001–2005), Urton is the founder/director of the Harvard Khipu Database Project.

Adriana von Hagen is an independent scholar and writer who specializes in the archaeology of Peru. Her books (with Craig Morris) include *The Incas: Lords of the Four Quarters* and *Cities of the Ancient Andes*, among others.

THE CONTRIBUTORS

Juan Ossio Acuña is a full professor in the Department of Social Sciences, Pontificia Universidad Católica del Perú, Lima.

Catherine J. Allen is Professor Emerita of Anthropology at The George Washington University, Washington, D.C.

Elizabeth Arkush is Associate Professor of Anthropology at the University of Pittsburgh in Pennsylvania.

Tamara L. Bray is Professor of Anthropology at Wayne State University, Detroit, Michigan.

Richard L. Burger is Professor of Anthropology and Archaeological Studies at Yale University, New Haven, Connecticut.

Rodolfo Cerrón-Palomino is full Professor of Linguistics at Pontificia Universidad Católica del Perú, Lima.

Lawrence S. Coben is Executive Director of the Sustainable Preservation Initiative and a Consulting Scholar at the University of Pennsylvania Museum of Archaeology and Anthropology in Philadelphia.

Noble David Cook is Professor of History at Florida International University, Miami.

Noa Corcoran-Tadd is a PhD candidate in Anthropology at Harvard University, Cambridge, Massachusetts.

R. Alan Covey is Associate Professor of Anthropology at the University of Texas, Austin.

Tom B. F. Cummins is the Dumbarton Oaks Professor of the History of Pre-Columbian and Colonial Art at Harvard University, Cambridge, Massachusetts.

Marco Curatola Petrocchi is Professor of History at Pontificia Universidad Católica del Perú, Lima.

Terence N. D'Altroy is the Loubat Professor of American Archaeology in the Department of Anthropology at Columbia University, New York.

Javier Flores Espinoza is a translator and Adjunct Professor of Contemporary Economic History at the Universidad del Pacifico in Lima, Peru.

Daniel W. Gade is Professor Emeritus of Geography at The University of Vermont, Burlington.

Christine A. Hastorf is Professor of Anthropology at the University of California, Berkeley.

Peter Kaulicke is Professor of Archaeology at Pontificia Universidad Católica del Perú, Lima.

Steve Kosiba is Assistant Professor of Anthropology at the University of Alabama, Tuscaloosa.

Heather Lechtman is Professor of Archaeology and Ancient Technology and Director of the Center for Materials Research in Archaeology and Ethnology at the Massachusetts Institute of Technology, Cambridge.

Krzysztof Makowski is Professor of Archaeology at Pontificia Universidad Católica del Perú, Lima.

Michael A. Malpass is the Charles A. Dana Chair in the Social Sciences and Professor of Anthropology at Ithaca College, Ithaca, New York.

Colin McEwan is Director of Pre-Columbian Studies at Dumbarton Oaks Research Library and Collections, Washington, D.C.

Gordon F. McEwan is Professor of Anthropology at Wagner College, Staten Island, New York.

Melissa S. Murphy is Associate Professor of Anthropology at the University of Wyoming, Laramie.

Stella Nair is Associate Professor of Art of the Americas at the University of California, Los Angeles.

Jean-Pierre Protzen is Professor Emeritus of the Department of Architecture at the University of California, Berkeley.

Kylie E. Quave is Visiting Assistant Professor of Anthropology at Beloit College, Beloit, Wisconsin.

Susan Elizabeth Ramírez is Neville G. Penrose Chair of History and Latin American Studies at Texas Christian University, Fort Worth.

Irene Silverblatt is Professor of Cultural Anthropology and History at Duke University, Durham, North Carolina.

Peter W. Stahl is Professor of Anthropology at the University of Victoria, British Columbia, Canada.

Mary Van Buren is Associate Professor of Anthropology at Colorado State University, Fort Collins.

Holly Wissler is an Applied Ethnomusicologist in Cuzco, Peru.

R. Tom Zuidema is Professor Emeritus of Anthropology at the University of Illinois at Urbana-Champaign.